The Good Food Compendium

The Good Food Compendium

An indispensable guide to sensible nutrition
and eating pleasures
for those who care about
fine fare and wholesome living.

JO GIESE BROWN

Illustrated by Dave Falcon

DOLPHIN BOOKS
Doubleday & Company, Inc.   Garden City, New York
1981

Jacques Pépin's Cold Zucchini Soup, © 1975 by The New York Times Company.
Reprinted by permission.
Lyrics from "Anticipation" by Carly Simon © 1971 Quackenbush Music, Ltd.
Used by permission—All rights reserved.

DESIGNED BY MARILYN SCHULMAN

A Dolphin Book

Library of Congress Cataloging in Publication Data

Brown, Jo Giese.
The good food compendium.

Includes index.
1. Food, Natural.   2. Cookery (Natural foods).
3. Nutrition.   I. Title.
TX369.B76   641.3'02
ISBN: 0-385-13523-8
Library of Congress Catalog Card Number 78–22306

Copyright © 1981 by Jo Giese Brown
Copyright disclaimed on any U. S. Government material throughout this work

Acknowledgments

A special thanks to people whose friendship, encouragement, and help, both professional and personal, has been especially beneficial: Dr. Stephen Rittenberg, Julie Sack, Gladys and Jim Giese, Judi Barrett, Virginia and George Elbert, Denise McCluggage, Dr. James McPherson, Jimmy and Libby Giese, Duffy Bart, Mattie Pearl Walker, Elda and Dan Unger, David and Lucy Levine, Evan Kress, Hilda Brown; the copy editor—Estelle Laurence; the researchers—Joyce Baron, Linda Greenlee, and Jo Anne Saito; the typist—Cheryl Balin; the illustrator—Dave Falcon, whose thoughtful and humorous drawings add an important dimension; the editors—Karen Van Westering, without whose help and superb organizational sense this book wouldn't be nearly as readable as it is; Lindy Hess, for her creative ideas; and their enthusiastic assistant, Eleanor Funk; the people at WNBC who gave me my own weekly news spot on food, which was the starting point for the book; the news director, Earl Ubell, and co-ordinating producer, Molly Sidi. And finally, to my husband, Barry, whose support and love made it possible.

Dedicated to
Josie
and
Gladys
and
Wendy

Contents

INTRODUCTION

Food has always had a powerful attraction for me. I vividly remember as a child arriving home from school to the smell of bread fresh out of the oven, or getting up early on Sunday to eat grandmother's cinnamon rolls while they were still hot and sticky. Some people remember places and cities by historical monuments and buildings; I remember them by the foods I tasted there.

I hold my grandmother Josephine responsible for kindling my interest in food. That interest had a fertile spawning ground since I grew up in the Pacific Northwest, an area lush with gorgeous produce and fresh fish. No matter the size of our back yard, my family always had an orchard that produced at least cherries, plums, apricots, peaches, apples, grapes, and raspberries. Just outside our kitchen window was a fecund purple plum tree. I remember, when I was five, sitting with my dolls under the shade of that tree, mesmerized for hours by its purple colors, the shape of its heavy fruit-laden branches, and its special preharvest fragrance. At the other side of the yard, behind my doll house, were the peach trees. The harvest was so bountiful that often by summer's end many of our overripe peaches had fallen to the ground. My brother and I, and the rest of the spunky neighborhood kids, would stage battles with the leftover bruised peaches; if you've never been splattered with an overripe peach, it's a sure sign you didn't grow up in *my* neighborhood.

Although we weren't really a family of fishermen, as kids we liked to haul in the bounty from the lakes and the Sound surrounding Seattle. Holding a simple string with a hook attached, I would hunch over little streams where watercress grew and snag trout as they swam by. In fact, today, my parents live on an island surrounded by a lake full of trout, which they catch from their front porch. My brother and I also caught salmon in the waters off Astoria, and the whole family dug for clams on Puget Sound.

Living in Seattle was a superb introduction to healthy, natural food at its best. From these early experiences, I learned the simple pleasure and warmth that comes from selecting, preparing, and cooking food for family and friends.

I think it's worth noting that my early indoctrination in food was also nonsexist. I never thought cooking was women's work since I saw my grandfather preparing foods, too. In fact, for years he was a famed entree chef on the Great Northern Pacific Railroad. Passengers, as the family legend goes, would wait to take the train with the dining car he was working because of his juicy roast beef.

Later, as a journalist, I carried those childhood food memories with me. As I traveled around the country writing and producing television documentaries, I never lost my interest in food. No matter what my destination, I was never at a loss to find something remarkable to eat: in Arizona, perhaps Indian-style pan-fried bread; in Miami, stone crabs and key lime pie; or in Texas, Hot Shot's Bar-B-Que. But as cities and dreary motel rooms faded together, I began to wonder why I was wandering around the country like a nomad. What did I really like best and why couldn't I do *that* professionally? Wafting back to me came the smells from grandmother's kitchen.

Why not spend my professional time reporting about my favorite subject? Food. After years in television concentrating primarily on the science-health field, I saw the possibility of mixing my acquired expertise with my natural love. I became WNBC Television's first Food Editor and Consumer Food Reporter.

Nutrition is a relatively new science and much of the credible research and information doesn't leak from the professionals out to the public. But, somehow, the quacky food fads manage to propel themselves across the land. As a food reporter, I feel my job is to sift through the quackery, pry loose the credible data and translate it into usable information for the general public. I seek out stories that will expose consumers to ideas they can actually incorporate into their everyday lives—practical ideas that might begin to change basic food habits. My aim as I wrote this book was the same: to create a book chock full of practical ideas that could change everyday eating habits *today*.

My approach is *not* filled with admonitions. Food writers who rely on scare tactics such as "Don't eat *that!*" or "Avoid *this* at all costs" seem to me counterproductive. In most cases, the result of those admonitions is consumers who say, "If there's nothing safe to eat in our food supply, what does it matter what I eat?" I prefer a positive approach. I concentrate on the world of food items that are *good* for you to eat. I never suggest that a food item be avoided unless I can also recommend substitutions. I feel it doesn't help to yell "No!" unless in its place I can say "Yes" to something else *more* desirable.

I take the subject of food and health seriously, but I have fun with it, and you should, too. Food is the best game around; children instinctively know this, but sometimes adults lose sight of it. With this book as a guide, readers can truly play the best game in town: they can feed themselves, their families, and their friends well, *and* at the same time enjoy the process more.

Carly Simon recorded a hit song, "Anticipation," in which the last line goes, "These are the good old days." Consciously or unconsciously, I've striven to make that my life philosophy and it certainly carries into food as well. Many people wait for some nebulous tomorrow instead of embracing today, *today*. Why wait to change your food habits until you are overweight, or until you finally do

have that feared heart attack? Why wait one more day to begin an exercise program? Make the changes *now* and these days truly can be the "good old days" for you.

I think it's also appropriate here to say a word about the real and unfortunate chasm that exists between nutritionists and gourmets. If you ask your favorite gourmets what they have in common with someone like Roslyn Alfin-Slater, a well-known nutritionist at U.C.L.A., they probably wouldn't think they share much common ground. The gourmets are often hell bent on concocting glorious, expensive, and beautiful creations while ignorant of the nutritional consequences. On the other hand, the nutritionists are often too engrossed in their tables and charts to embrace the potential fun, beauty, and sensual pleasure of food. Unfortunately, there's little opportunity for the two groups to come together. When was the last time the Nutrition Department at Columbia University invited James Beard to speak? Or vice versa?

My concern is to bring gourmet cooking and nutrition together for the ultimate pleasure in eating. The ultimate pleasure is twofold: it must embrace the pleasure of eating food (the gourmet's philosophy), and the more lasting pleasure of keeping our bodies properly nourished and healthy (the nutritionist's philosophy).

Food should taste delicious and be gorgeous to look at, and I'm all for presentations bordering on the theatrical, but it should also go one important step further; the food has to be good enough—for your body—to eat. It must contribute to, not jeopardize, your health.

FRESH VEGETABLES:
Mother Nature Knows Best

There's a lot of talk these days about eating more fresh vegetables. Food writers from the New York *Times* to the Los Angeles *Times* keep busy heralding a revolution in fresh vegetable consumption. You'd think we were on the brink of rediscovering the carrot. But so far, the revolution in vegetable consumption in this country remains "a case of talking about it might make it so." The most recent figures from the Department of Agriculture show the consumption of vegetables to be up slightly, but still lagging far behind other countries. According to the United Fresh Fruit and Vegetable Association in 1950, the average American consumed 160 pounds of vegetables a year; twenty-five years later, including the period in which Americans have supposedly rediscovered the vegetable, we were consuming 164 pounds; compare that to European annual consumption of 200 pounds.

How many fruits and vegetables should you eat every day? Here's a simple way to figure quantities which takes into account both fruits and vegetables. Each day, you should have at least 4½ half-cup (4-ounce) servings.

At least 1 serving should be of a fruit or vegetable that's a good source of vitamin C: cabbage, green peppers, rutabagas, or a piece of citrus fruit. Another serving should be of dark green or deep yellow vegetables or fruits high in vitamin A: broccoli, kale, spinach, yellow squash, carrots, or apricots.

 Why Vegetables?

Contrary to what children who have been forced to eat too many rutabagas or beets may think, the reasons one should eat fresh vegetables are not debatable. From the chart below, you can see that vegetables, combined with fruits, provide nearly all the vitamin C obtained from food, almost half the vitamin A, and considerable amounts of iron, thiamin, niacin, phosphorus, riboflavin, even some protein, as well as many other trace minerals.

Vitamin A is necessary for good night vision, growth, reproduction, and the health of skin and respiratory tract. A deficiency of vitamin C in the diet can cause such problems as wounds that fail to heal, weakened and poorly formed bones and teeth, and iron deficiency resulting from poor iron absorption.

Although clinical evidence of vitamin A deficiency in the United States is minimal, it has become a problem nutrient for some sectors of the population, especially Spanish Americans, who have the lowest consumption of fresh vegetables in this country. I saw this firsthand one day when I gave some salad greens to my new housekeeper from San Salvador. Much to my chagrin and surprise, I found Carmen scrubbing the lettuce leaves with a steel wool pad. Fresh salad greens were foreign territory to her. Soon after this incident, Carmen, feeling ill, went to a clinic and the doctor revised her diet, insisting that she begin eating more fresh vegetables in addition to her customary diet of beans and tortillas.

Another reason for eating fresh vegetables

Percentage of Nutrients Contributed to Diet by Fruits and Vegetables*

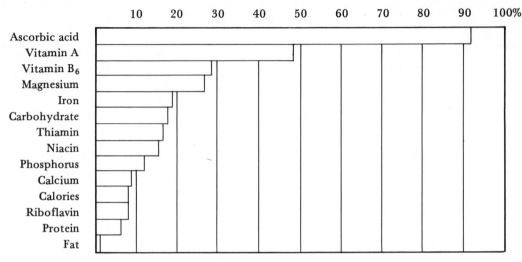

| | 10 | 20 | 30 | 40 | 50 | 60 | 70 | 80 | 90 | 100% |

Ascorbic acid
Vitamin A
Vitamin B$_6$
Magnesium
Iron
Carbohydrate
Thiamin
Niacin
Phosphorus
Calcium
Calories
Riboflavin
Protein
Fat

SOURCE: *The National Food Situation* (NFS-158), November 1976, U.S. Department of Agriculture.

*Fresh and processed.

is they are low in calories and virtually fat free. We're a nation of compulsive overeaters and dieters—47 per cent of Americans think they are overweight. I know dieters so extreme they have worn painter's gauzy masks to stop themselves from putting any food in their mouths, and other who have used chopsticks to prevent themselves from eating too much; these dieters would probably be better off with less gimmicks and more reliance on fresh vegetables. Without sugar, starch, or fat added, fresh vegetables can be eaten in large amounts, even on a reducing diet. For all practical purposes, you can't overeat them. They fill you, but with very few calories and lots of natural fiber.

Better over-all health is also connected with eating fresh vegetables. Six out of ten major diseases in this country have been directly linked with diets heavy in fats and salt and sugar. In 1977, the Senate Select Committee, in mapping out the Dietary Goals for the United States, advised an increase in the consumption of carbohydrates to account for 55–60 per cent of one's calories. Translated, that means consumption of more fruits, whole grains, and *vegetables*.

Nathan Pritikin, a maverick inventor turned self-trained nutritionist, is taking this carbohydrate idea even further. He treats advanced heart disease patients with a diet of 80 per cent complex carbohydrates. Although his diet was designed originally for very sick people who are highly motivated to change their dietary habits to save their lives,

his patients have had some startlingly Cinderella-like improvements. And what are his patients eating mostly? *Vegetables.*

I'm not advocating switching to an all-vegetable diet, but I am pointing up the importance of eating *some* vegetables along with other foods. A recent study revealed that, given a choice, people eat more than the USDA suggested amount of meat, but 71 per cent eat less than the suggested amounts of vegetables and fruits.

Taking nutritional, health, and personal preferences into consideration, you're ready to get on the vegetable bandwagon. But, on a practical level, what do you do? What do these doctors, nutritionists, and politicians mean when they say we should be eating more vegetables? Is a vegetable, a vegetable, a vegetable? Does it make a significant difference if you take yours canned, fresh, or frozen? Is it important whether you stir-fry, steam, or boil? Are processed vegetables inferior? Are fresh or processed vegetables wasted the most and why? Which form uses the least of our nation's energy?

I sought answers to such questions and even though I do investigative reporting in the food field, I didn't find any easy answers. I wanted to make my buying and cooking decisions based on *fact,* not misinformation and popular whimsy. As all of us, I had acquired food habits over the years and wondered if my solutions were really the best in terms of nurtrition, labor, convenience, and price. I wanted to know, for example, what nutrients were left when string beans were brought home fresh or frozen—especially since they look pretty good both ways—and what happens to those nutrients in the cooking processes?

Whether you consider yourself a fast-order

Nutrients depart the cooked bean

convenience cook or an extravagant gourmet, this chapter and the one that follows will provide the necessary information to make meaningful decisions about vegetables you use every day based on nutrition as well as aesthetics and price. Those people using fresh vegetables will gain insight into the selection, preparation, and techniques that preserve their nutrients. Chapter 2 is for those readers who routinely use processed vegetables. They may discover the advantages of some forms of processed vegetables that are more nutritious than others. With some thought, you won't be like the customer I saw at the check-out counter over the Fourth of July buying frozen ears of corn and frozen green beans when both were in plentiful supply and cheaper at the fresh produce counter. You'll be armed with sufficient information to make the right decision.

Fresh Vegetables

The word fresh implies something wonderful and bright . . . something sunny and young and unspoiled. So it seems to me an unnecessary redundancy to say that the natural way to buy produce is to buy it fresh. But, since statistics show a decline in the consumption of vegetables in their fresh form, this is not such an unnecessary repetition. For example, in 1950, 60 per cent of the vegetables consumed in this country were fresh, 36 per cent canned, and 3 per cent frozen. Today, fresh is down to 45 per cent, tying with canned at 45 per cent, and the use of frozen vegetables has increased threefold to 9 per cent of the market.

It seems like a contradiction that even though the official charts show fresh consumption is down, there's a growing (literally) interest among gardeners who are eating their own fresh produce, in many instances for the first time. Some of this public interest is fired by the trendmakers who in recent years have decreed that "fresh is in." This message will slowly make its way to the entire population and I predict we'll see figures for fresh consumption start to climb if prices don't escalate too drastically and availability remains good.

To my mind, fresh is what vegetables are and anything else is something else and shouldn't even be honored by being called by the same name. With a few exceptions, which I'll discuss as I go along, I always reach for the fresh. I'm admittedly prejudiced in favor of the quality, taste, and fragrance of the fresh, and I'm pleased that in most instances good nutrition backs up my choice.

The same vegetable in a different form is often as different as a basketball is from a football. Think back on the string beans you've had in your life. A fresh string bean can be a wonderful thing to eat raw or cooked. It has a great crunchy texture, wonderful vibrant color, and in the middle of summer, it is the essence of summer itself.

But what about those gray-green beans served in steam tables on cafeteria lines? Those pale, processed imitations don't deserve to be classified with the same name as the fresh, but we haven't created an appropriate culinary vocabulary that labels them for what they are: impostors.

Part of the problem is that people have acquired a taste for processed foods. Even when the fresh are readily available, some people don't have a taste for them. Originally, the idea behind processing foods was to preserve certain foods for later use when they were not available fresh. What has happened is that many people have become accustomed to the processed foods and opt for them even when the fresh is cheaper, tastier, and higher in nutritional quality.

My grandmother, after whom I'm named, was part of the generation that had vegetable patches in their back yards. They didn't make a big deal out of it, or advertise how "organic" it was. That was just the way things were done. Then along came my mother's generation, freed from the "drudg-

Processed vegetables are imposters.

ery" of vegetable gardening by the miracle of freezing and the increased use of canned goods. My mother and her generation were sold on the processed forms, because even today when she has a choice between fresh, canned or frozen, I notice that it takes an adjustment for her to buy the fresh.

On the other hand, there is a tendency among some people to regard any fresh food as representing perfection in terms of nutritional value and to regard all processed foods as nutritionally inferior. But this belief may not be accurate since there is often a world of difference between produce that's garden fresh and market fresh.

In selecting fresh produce, nutritional quality is related to several factors: desirable color, lack of decay, lack of bruising, the stage of maturity the produce reached before it was picked, and good genetic characteristics. Some of these factors, especially genetics, consumers can't do a thing about. We have no control over the fact that the tomatoes available for purchase on a given Wednesday in May weren't part of the batch bred for increased vitamin C. So, instead, let's concentrate on areas we do control—selection, preparation, and cooking.

SELECTION TIPS

* Avoid packages of already prepared vegetables in combinations for stews, soups, etc. All that chopping in advance is a questionable procedure.

* Avoid vegetables in colored plastic bags. For example, when you buy carrots in orange-colored cellophane, it's impossible to see if they're actually healthy-looking carrots or not.

* Root crops like beets and carrots should be purchased without their tops attached. They lose moisture through these tops.

* When you can find them, buy tomatoes with the stem scar still attached. It helps retain moisture.

* Some vegetables lose their moisture faster than others and should be refrigerated immediately: sweet corn, squash, lima beans, broccoli, spinach, asparagus. The cold temperature holds down moisture loss and you have better vegetables longer.

* When buying from a roadside stand on a hot, sunny day, be careful not to buy already wilted vegetables. If the vegetables have been harvested without being immediately chilled, they'll be droopy and will never revive, even in cold water at home.

* You get less vitamins when you buy bruised, wilted, damaged produce. How a fresh vegetable looks is an index of retention/loss of vitamins. The reason for selecting fresh, crisp vegetables is more than eye and crunch appeal; you're getting the best nutrition when you select vegetables at the height of their appearance. Sort of the Bo Dereks of their kind.

Buying and Storage Guide to Fresh Vegetables

Vegetable	Peak Availability	Handling Notes and Storage Methods	What to Look For
ARTICHOKES	April-May, November-February: bronze-tipped outer leaves caused by light frost	Refrigerate.	Check base end for signs of worm injury. Good green coloring. Recipes available Artichoke Advisory Board, P.O. Box 287, Santa Cruz, CA 95061 Don't buy when petals are open or spreading; they are over-mature and are often tough.
ASPARAGUS, Green	General: May-June California: February-June	Refrigerate at grocery store and at home.	Closed, compact tips. Tender asparagus tips should be brittle to the touch. Did you ever wonder when you see asparagus standing upright in water in the grocery stores what's happening to the vitamins? What happens is a trade-off. Because asparagus is a relatively fragile fresh produce, you have your choice of either buying it dried out and thus losing its vitamins through deterioration or buying it looking fresh (à la the water bath), and losing some of its vitamins through the water.
BEANS Green Snap Wax Yellow	April-June	Moist refrigeration. Place dry beans in plastic bag in refrigerator.	Wash beans before refrigeration. Helps retain moisture content. Avoid those with scars.
BEAN SPROUTS	Year round	Refrigerate.	Buy only crisp-looking, white sprouts; brown color shows the beginning of deterioration.
BEETS	June-October	Moist refrigeration to prevent wilting.	Remove tops and use and store separately; the greens when not discolored, yellowed, or ragged are excellent. Avoid shriveled, flabby-bodied beets. In judging beets, the condition of the tops or leaves alone does not indicate quality of the beets.
BROCCOLI	Year round Peak: January-March	Refrigerate. Has one of the highest respiration rates.	Firm, compact, small flower buds. Avoid yellowish-green in color —they are overmature.
BRUSSELS SPROUTS	Year round except June and July	Cool, moist refrigeration. At temperatures of 50° F. and higher outer leaves begin to lose their green coloring.	Firm, compact sprout.
CABBAGE	Year round	Cool refrigeration. Don't let it dry out.	Solid, hard, heavy heads. Old cabbage or poor storage conditions

Vegetable	Availability	Storage	Buying notes
		Keep it wrapped and in compartment where humidity is high.	may be indicated by separation of leaves at the base. In winter, when other vegetables are often higher priced, cabbage is a good buy.
CARROTS	Year round	Keep moist in plastic bags.	Avoid carrots with tops still attached (withdraws moisture from roots), and large green areas at top. Misshapen carrots can cause extra waste in preparation. Unknown to most consumers, there are two types of carrots: those that immediately head for fresh market and those that the growers put into storage. Fresh market carrots are usually smaller, more tender, and brighter in external color than carrots harvested for storage. Better for fresh carrot sticks. The larger storage carrots are better for shredding and cooking.
CAULIFLOWER	Year round. Peak: October-November	Refrigerate. Keep wrapped.	Buy small head with flowerets tightly together. Large (as large as 12″) or small heads are equally desirable. It is usually pre-packaged at the shipping point in film. This film cuts shipping costs by eliminating the need to retain the heavy-ribbed, largely inedible, outer leaves. If you're buying by the pound, buy with smallest amount of leaves attached to the base. They are inedible, so why pay for them?
CELERY	Year round	Refrigerate.	The celery stem should be smooth; if it is rough the celery is likely to be pithy. For best taste, select light green stalks; dark green stalks may be too strong.
CORN	Once a summer crop only, now available year round. Peak: July-September	Refrigerate.	Never buy corn from a grocery or roadside stand, especially, unless there is evidence it has been precooled or refrigerated. The sugar turns to starch in less than 8 hours and you no longer have sweet-tasting corn. Avoid ears with dried husks or dried-out stem ends. The determining factor in moisture retention seems to be the longer the shank (the stubby barklike end), the more moisture loss. Don't buy corn stacked in a high pile. The interior of the pile is getting warm and the sugar is turning to starch.
CUCUMBERS	Year round	Must be refrigerated, between 45° and 50° F. If below 45° F., cucumbers get chilled and develop water-soaked spots.	Smaller cucumbers have smaller seeds and are more desirable.
EGGPLANT	Year round	Refrigerate. At room temperature, become soft and wrinkled.	A wilted, soft, shriveled eggplant will usually be bitter or otherwise poor in flavor.

Buying and Storage Guide to Fresh Vegetables (continued)

Vegetable	Peak Availability	Handling Notes and Methods	What to Look For
CURLY ENDIVE and ESCAROLE	Year round	Refrigerate.	These are often confused—endive grows in bunchy head with ragged-edge leaves that curl. Center has yellowish leaves. Escarole has deep green leaves. Like all salad greens, look for crispness.
GREENS Collard Greens	Year round. Peak: December-April	Refrigerate.	They should be crisp, never wilted or flabby, and clean.
Dandelion Greens	Year round	Refrigerate.	Leaves still attached to roots are best; when separated, they wilt rapidly.
Kale	Year round. Peak: December-February	Refrigerate.	Leaves should always be crisp, green, and clean.
Mustard Greens	Year round. Peak: December-February	Refrigerate.	Range in color from dark to light green; some show a slight bronze tint, which is normal.
Parsley	Year round. Peak: December-February	Refrigerate.	Curly-leafed parsley is most common in market, but look for the flat-leaf Italian type—I think it's tastier.
Spinach	Year round. Peak: December-February	Refrigerate.	Should not be long-stemmed or scraggly. It's sold by the bag and by the bunch. The bunch is usually half the price of the bagged.
Swiss Chard	April-November	Refrigerate.	In general, avoid greens that have yellowing showing.
For watercress, arugula, and various lettuces, see Chapter 5, Salads.			
MUSHROOMS	Grown in artificially controlled atmosphere year round	Refrigerate.	I prefer buying loose (in bulk) as I can check the underside and see that the mushroom is compact. An underside that reveals an umbrellalike network of ribbing means the mushroom is aged.
ONIONS Yellow White Red Bermuda	Year round	Dry storage.	Avoid onions with green sunburn spots. The best onions will be hard and firm. Don't store onions and potatoes together for very long periods. Scientists say the onions will draw moisture from potatoes, which may result in decay.
Green Onions (Scallions)		Refrigerate.	

Vegetable	Availability	Storage	Notes
PEAS, Green, immature	Summer	Refrigerate.	Formerly was a major fresh vegetable in terms of volume, but now is down considerably so choice is usually limited and price high.
PEPPERS Red Green	June-October	Refrigeration will suffer chill damage with low temperatures.	Must be firm; may yield to slight pressure, but should not be soft.
POTATOES	Year round	Dry storage.	Should show no green from fluorescent-light burn; and no bruises or cuts.
PUMPKINS	October-November	Room temperature	For cooking, select heavy, solid pumpkins. For carving, choose hollow pumpkins.
SQUASH Acorn Spaghetti Summer Winter Hubbard Zucchini	August-March August-March Year round August-March August-March	Refrigerate. Refrigerate. Regrigerate. Refrigerate. Refrigerate.	Avoid squash with pits or any kind of physical injury.
SWEET POTATOES (Yams)	Supplies sparse, June and July	Do not chill. Keep at 55°-60° F.	Two types to choose from: firm flesh and soft flesh.
TOMATOES	Year round. Peak: July-September	Refrigerate, after ripened.	Stems attached, no bruises. If the tomato you've purchased is not yet fully ripened (and most supermarkets now do not sell fully ripened tomatoes), it will never ripen if put in refrigerator. Keep it in a place with temperature between 65° and 75°F., until ripened. Then place in refrigerator.
TUBERS and ROOTS Parsnips Rutabagas, yellow flesh Sunchokes Turnips, white flesh	Year round, winter increased availability	Dry storage, short period; or refrigeration, long period.	All of these, especially the rutabaga, have good nutrition and at a very reasonable price, in comparison with other vegetables.

Preparation: Yours or Theirs?

There's a circular argument going on today over preparation losses from processed versus fresh foods with consumers and processors pushing the blame back and forth. One one hand, it is popular for consumers to blame the big food companies for processing all the goodness out of foods. But on the other hand, the big food companies strike back by blaming careless home preparation and cooking practices for destroying more vitamins and minerals than are lost in their commercial processing. Arguments about preparation losses are especially relevant to fresh produce because it is so vulnerable to improper handling at all the stages from preparation to cooking.

An in-house report by the Institute of Food Technologists assumes that the housewife is basically a blooming idiot, incapable of learning how to prepare foods in a nutritious manner. Their argument, obviously in favor of their processed foods, is that since such large nutritional losses routinely occur in the home, the actual vitamin content of food served at the table frequently ends up the same regardless of the type of food processing.

An ad taken by the food processors might go like this:

Dear Consumer:

We suggest you buy our processed vegetables because we know by the time you finish preparing and cooking once perfectly good fresh vegetables, your clumsy practices will have reduced them to the nutritional levels of their processed counterpart.

Love,
The Food Processors

Although the food processors might privately feel this way, they'd never dare take out such an ad. But I don't buy their conclusion. I believe that if given an awareness of what losses occur at various stages of preparation and cooking, the home cook would choose to minimize these losses.

PREPARATION LOSSES

Preparation losses

Inevitably, nutrients are lost the moment a vegetable is plucked from the vine, and when you lose part of a vegetable, you lose the nutrients that part would have supplied. The amount of nutrient loss during preparation varies according to cultural practices, habits, and individual preferences. The following list shows typical weight losses when vegetables are prepared for cooking. Although the losses are high, these are actually rather conservative estimates. The useful point of this list is not the fact that there is usually 31 per cent waste from carrots (that's interesting too), but to see in general what high losses exist.

Fresh Vegetable Losses*

Asparagus	25%	Kohlrabi	46%
Lima Bean	60%	Lettuce	31%
Snap Bean	10%	Mustard Greens	27%
Beet	47%	Okra	12%
Beet Greens	25%	Parsnip	22%
Broccoli	39%	Pea	55%
Brussels Sprouts	23%	Pepper	16%
Cabbage	27%	Potato	16%
Carrot	37%	Radish	51%
Cauliflower	55%	Spinach	18%
Celery	37%	Squash	
Chard	14%	(Summer)	3%
Collards	55%	Squash	
Sweet Corn	62%	(Winter)	26%
Cress	37%	Sweet Potato	14%
Cucumber	30%	Tomato	12%
Eggplant	13%	Turnip	34%
Kale	36%		

Some of the losses are inedible, such as the woody stem on a head of cauliflower or the cob from corn on the cob, but other losses represent real possibilities for saving. These losses often occur because of cultural habits, and not necessity. On a trip to the produce markets in Venice near the Rialto Bridge, I was dismayed to see huge garbage cans next to each produce stall filled with the outer leaves of dark salad greens. There seemed to be a custom, perhaps passed down through centuries, that as the people hawked their produce at this ancient site, they tore off the outer leaves, probably to make their product look more presentable. I saw enough discarded greens to serve salad to all of Venice that afternoon. In contemporary times, with the availability of sanitary water for washing and with nutritional insight, the continuation of such a practice makes little sense.

Eliminating unnecessary waste involves a conscious appreciation of the multiple steps necessary to get a product to you. Next time, before you casually discard a piece of produce, mentally retrace its steps:

* Waste expressed as percentage of purchased weight

A scientist bred the seed.

A farmer prepared the soil.

Laborers planted, fertilized, irrigated, and harvested.

It was packaged, transported, and retailed.

If at the end of the line, through habit or thoughtlessness, you unnecessarily throw out 30 per cent of a head of cabbage, or trim away 20 per cent of green beans, that hurts.

THREE COMMON MALPRACTICES

Common malpractices

The following common practices are symptomatic of poor fresh vegetable preparation that leads to nutrient losses.

Carrots: To prepare carrots for cooking, you religiously peel away the skin and give the carrot that real clean look it never had before, right? Peeled vegetables generally lose 14–26 per cent of their nutrition in the peeling. In addition, peeled carrots lose 22 per cent of their iron when cooked, whereas unpeeled carrots lose very little. Since the carrot peel is also rich in thiamin, niacin, and riboflavin, you might want to rethink this step and do one of two things:

1.   Use a scrub brush instead of a peeler and scrub the carrots as clean as you can. Don't try for that totally antiseptic look.

2.   If your sense of aesthetics is not pleased by suggestion ⚜ 1, and you don't like the hint of bitterness in the carrot skin, at least use a light touch when you peel, and take off as little as possible. You might want to try an electric peeler, which takes very little pressure.

Broccoli: To prepare, you yank off those little leaves that cluster near the buds and cut off the stalk, leaving behind only the pretty little buds, right? One reason we eat broccoli is for the vitamin A and the little ripped-off leaves have twenty times as much vitamin A as the stalk and several times as much as the flower bud. So, get into the habit of cooking the leaves right along with the flower bud. I do this and I've never seen anyone, when served broccoli with leaves, pick them off. Don't throw away the stalk either. Cut it into broccoli sticks, to be eaten raw or slightly cooked like carrot sticks. Sometimes I purée the stalks, and cook them briefly mixed with spices, lemon, and a bit of buttermilk. I then have a lovely broccoli sauce that's served on top of the broccoli.

Lettuce: You know that old saying, "Two heads are better than one"? Well, that barely applies to head lettuce (the tight bunch of light green lettuce), which has so few nutrients, it hardly makes a difference if you have one or two heads. Let's say you know the difference, and you've been buying lettuce with dark leaves. But in cleaning and preparation, you throw away the outer leaves. Maybe they have a tatter here or there. Those dark outer leaves that you and the merchants of Venice routinely throw out have as much as thirty times more vitamin A value than the inner leaves. Consequently, 75 per cent of the vitamin A is being thrown out with those leaves. What should you do with those leaves? What I do now is to give them the once over, once again. Upon closer scrutiny, there's usually part of the leaf that is usable. (See Salad Soup, page 140.)

TIPS FOR VEGETABLE PREPARATION

Washing: Washing before cooking permits the extraction of water-soluble vitamins, but these losses are generally slight if the process doesn't take long.

Less means more here: less washing means the greater the likelihood of more vitamins left at the end.

Soaking: When preparing fresh carrots, celery, peppers, soaking them in ice water makes them crispy, but some of the vitamin C is lost, too. Instead, sprinkle vegetables with ice water, wrap them in a damp cloth

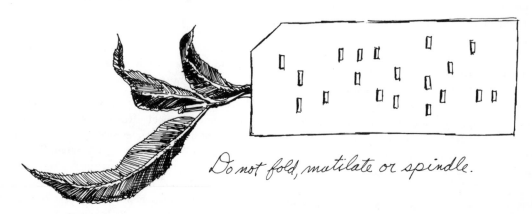

Do not fold, mutilate or spindle.

or kitchen towel, and store them in the refrigerator.

Peeling: Some vegetables, like potatoes, have skin that is a strong barrier to nutrient loss, but when you peel the potato's skin off it looses 13 per cent of its nutrients immediately. With all vegetables, peel with a gentle touch.

Cutting: This can seem like *Catch-22*. Small pieces cook faster (reducing nutrient loss), but they expose more surface area (increasing nutrient loss). The solution? Compromise. Settle on medium-size pieces. And when it comes to fancy cutting, like elegant strips of french-style green beans, you can count on retaining only 28 per cent of the original vitamin C.

The chart on the following pages shows what vegetables in popular use have to offer nutritionally, and hopefully, while thumbing through them, you may put to rest some nutritional myths. I'm thinking in particular of one friend sitting at his desk in the newsroom munching on a pile of parsley carefully wrapped in damp paper towels. Since most people don't have a fondness for such quantities of parsley, I asked him what he was doing. He said his girl friend had told him parsley was high in iron, so he was increasing his iron intake, naturally, without using pills. I showed him how much parsley he'd have to eat to get anything approaching the amount of iron he thought he was getting. (It was bushels.) The parsley made his breath sweet, but that wasn't his problem.

The seven categories (Calories, Protein, Carbohydrate, Iron, Sodium, Vitamin A and C) are areas about which most people have some previous knowledge so that they can begin to translate what it means nutritionally if a vegetable is high in one of these categories.
Briefly:

Calories are something everyone, rightly or wrongly, is concerned about. I could have omitted this category since fresh produce is uniformly low in calories, but I thought it would be reaffirming to see the consistently low calories.

Protein was included to erode the notion that protein is available only in animal foods like meats and fish. Although the figures are low, you can see vegetables do make a contribution to our over-all protein intake.

Carbohydrate was included because, for most people, it is advisable to increase carbohydrate intake while lowering fat intake.

Iron is an important mineral in which children under the age of six and menstruating women are often deficient. It's interesting to note from the chart that a vegetable like lima beans is high in iron.

Sodium takes into account the high sodium content of some natural foods, which will be of special interest to people on sodium-restricted diets. These calculations are based on cooking with no salt.

Vitamin A, in its different forms, is found in dark green, leafy vegetables, and in some orange vegetables and fruits. It's long been associated with good eyesight.

Vitamin C is an important nutrient found almost solely in vegetables and fruits.

Using myself as a guide, I've tried to list the food quantity in terms the reader can relate to. I relate poorly to 100 gm of carrots, but tell me about a carrot 5″ long and I instantly know what you're talking about. So I've simplified these units, wherever possible.

I've also made the charts as useful as possible. Since potatoes are rarely, if ever, eaten raw, I've given their information in terms of the ways they are cooked. Remember, when looking at the comparative values of the same vegetable raw and cooked, a cooked vegetable usually has less bulk and more vegetable, so sometimes the nutritional figures for cooked vegetables will be higher, even though it seems they should be less because cooking cooks out some of the nutrients.

Nutritional Guide to Fresh Vegetables

Vegetable	Amount	Calories	Protein (gm)	Carbo-hydrate (gm)	Iron (mg)	Sodium (mg)	Vit. A (I.U.)	Vit. C (mg)
ARTICHOKES	1 large bud cooked (including edible and refuse parts)	varies from 8 to 44						
ASPARAGUS	1 cup cooked	20	2.2	3.6	0.6	1	900	26
Provides almost 1/2 of day's recommended allowance of vitamin C, 1/3 of vitamin A, approximately 1/10 of iron for an adult. Ideal for low-sodium diets.								
BEANS								
Fresh Green Snap	1 cup cooked small amount of water	31	2.0	68	.8	5.	680	15
Fresh Yellow Wax							290	
Limas	1 cup cooked	189	12.9	33.7	4.3	2	480	29
The cellulose content of snap beans is valuable in contributing bulk in the intestine.								
BEAN SPROUTS								
Alfalfa	100 gm raw	41	5.1	—	1.4	—	—	16
Soybean		105	12.0	—	0.4	—	—	12
Mung bean		35	3.8	—	1.3	—	—	19
Sprouts add an interesting texture when used raw or barely warmed, but nutritionally they are no miracle food as they are sometimes touted.								
BEETS	1 cup cooked, diced or sliced	54	1.9	12.2	.9	73	30	10
	1 cup cooked beet greens	93.6	2.5	4.8	2.8	110	7,400	22
Beet greens are more remarkable nutritionally than beets. A cupful provides more than the Daily Recommended Allowance of vitamin A and a third of the iron, as well as being an excellent source of calcium. Prepare them as you would spinach.								
BROCCOLI	1 lb. raw	145	16.3	26.8	5.0	68	11,340	513
	1 cup cooked	40	4.8	7.0	1.2	16	3,880	140
One cup provides 68 per cent of Recommended Daily Allowance of vitamin A for adult, more than twice the daily allowance of vitamin C. There need be no waste with broccoli, as the stalk is completely edible. Cut it in 1/4" horizontal disk-like slices and use along with floweret or separately. But use.								

BRUSSELS SPROUTS	1 cup (7-8 sprouts) cooked	56	6.5	9.9	1.7	16	810	135	One cup provides more than twice the recommended allowance of vitamin C. Don't cut stem ends too close before cooking; outer leaves will fall off. Provides an alkaline reaction in the body.
CABBAGE	1 cup raw domestic, shredded finely	2.2	1.2	4.9	.4	18	120	42	
	Cooked	29	1.6	6.2	.4	20	190	48	
	1 cup raw red, shredded finely	28	1.8	6.2	.7	23	40	55	
	1 cup raw savoy, crinkled leaves, shredded finely	17	1.7	3.2	.6	15	140	39	
CARROTS	1 whole raw carrot, approximately 7½″ long, 1⅛″ diameter	30	.8	7.0	.5	34	7,930	6	Three quarters of a cup of raw carrots can supply more than twice the adult Daily Recommended Allowance of vitamin A. Carrots retain nutrients well in storage, and vitamin A actually increases.
	1 cup cooked, diced	45	1.3	10.3	1.3	48	15,230	9	
CAULIFLOWER	1 cup raw flowerets	27	2.7	5.2	1.1	13	60	78	One cup of cooked cauliflower provides more than the Daily Recommended Allowance of vitamin C. Cauliflower can pick up a yellowish cast if cooked in hard water. Squeeze a teaspoonful of fresh lemon juice over the cauliflower, or add to the cooking water.
	1 cup cooked	28	2.9	5.1	.9	11	80	69	
CELERY	1 outer stalk, 8″ long	7	.4	1.6	.1	50	110	4	The best thing to be said of celery is that it has few calories, a good munch food.
CORN	1 ear, 5″ long, 1¾″ diameter	70	2.5	16.2	.5	Trace	310	7	
CUCUMBERS	1 cup raw, sliced	16	.9	3.6	1.2	6	260	12	Try cooking cucumbers instead of eating them raw. Sliced thinly, lightly sautéed in oil, with chopped parsley sprinkled on top, they make a wonderful accompaniment for fish.

Nutritional Guide to Fresh Vegetables (continued)

Vegetable	Amount	Calories	Protein (gm)	Carbo-hydrate (gm)	Iron (mg)	Sodium (mg)	Vit. A (I.U.)	Vit. C (mg)
EGGPLANT	1 cup boiled	38	2.0	8.2	1.2	2	20	6.
	Can be used as an accompaniment to or a substitute for meat in many dishes.							
CURLY ENDIVE and ESCAROLE	1 cup raw	10	.9	2.1	.9	7	1,650	5
	Good sources of vitamin A. Make tasty additions to salad, or eaten by themselves.							
GREENS								
Collard greens	1 cup cooked leaves	63	6.8	9.7	1.5	—	14,820	144
Dandelion Greens	4 oz. raw	51	3.05	10.4	3.5	86	15,877	39
Kale	1 cup cooked	43	(5.0)	6.7	1.8	47	9,130	102
Mustard Greens	1 cup cooked	32	3.1	5.6	2.5	25	8,120	67
Parsley	1 tbsp. raw	2	.1	.3	.2	2	300	6
Spinach	1 cup raw	14	1.8	2.4	1.7	39	4,460	28
	1 cup cooked	41	5.4	6.5	4.0	90	14,580	50
Swiss Chard	1 cup cooked leaves	32	3.2	5.8	3.2	151	9,450	28
Turnip Greens	1 cup cooked	29	3.2	5.2	1.6	—	9,140	100

Collard Greens: Excellent source of calcium and vitamin A.
Dandelion Greens: Delicious raw in a salad.
Kale: Best when cooked. Cut leaves from thick stalks and discard stalks, which are generally too tough for good eating. Good source of calcium.
Spinach: High in calcium, but body is unable to absorb all of it.

Vegetable	Amount	Calories	Protein (gm)	Carbo-hydrate (gm)	Iron (mg)	Sodium (mg)	Vit. A (I.U.)	Vit. C (mg)
MUSHROOMS	1 cup raw, sliced	20	1.9	3.1	.6	11	Trace	2
ONIONS	Mature, 1 cup cooked	61	2.5	13.7	.8	15	80	15
PEAS, Green	1 cup raw	122	9.1	20.9	2.8	3	930	39
	1 cup cooked	114	8.6	19.4	2.9	2	860	32

PEPPERS								
Green	1 medium, raw	36	2.0	7.9	1.1	21	690	210
Red	1 medium, raw	51	2.3	11.6	1.0	—	7,300	335
POTATOES	1 4¾" long, baked in skin	145	4.0	32.8	1.1	6	Trace	31
	1 same size, boiled	173	4.8	38.9	1.4	7	Trace	36
	10 medium strips, french-fried	137	2.2	18.0	.7	3	Trace	11
PUMPKIN	1 cup canned	81	2.5	19.4	1.0	5	15,560	12
	A good source of vitamin A, like most squash.							
SQUASH								
Acorn	1 cup cooked, mashed	113	3.9	28.7	2.3	2	2,870	27
Summer	1 cup cooked, sliced	25	1.6	5.6	.7	2	700	18
Winter, Hubbard	1 cup cooked, sliced mashed	129	3.7	31.6	1.6	2	8,610	27
Zucchini	1 cup cooked, sliced	22	1.8	4.5	.7	2	540	16
SWEET POTATOES	1 5" long potato, baked in skin	161	2.4	37.0	1.0	14	9,230	25
	The deep yellow meat of sweet potato is an especially good source of vitamin A.							
TOMATOES	1 medium raw	19	1.0	4.1	.4	3	790	20
TUBERS and ROOTS								
Parsnips	1 cup cooked, diced	102	2.3	23.1	.9	12	50	16
Rutabagas	1 cup cooked, diced	60	1.5	13.9	.5	44	940	44
Turnips	1 cup cooked, cubed	36	1.8	11.3	.6	53	Trace	34

All these are often heavily coated with wax. Prepare them in ways so that you're not eating the wax. Try these cooked in place of potatoes, rice, carrots; as additions to stews; sliced raw in salads; or as crudités. In a potato salad, use half rutabagas and half potatoes.

SOURCE: Compiled from *Nutritive Value of American Foods*, Handbook #456, U.S. Department of Agriculture.

Ways To Cook Them

Vegetables can be cooked almost any way and unfortunately they often are. The widespread ignorance of how to cook fresh produce to retain its maximum nutrition came home to me when I was invited to dinner with friends at the beach in Malibu, California. It's the sort of dinner invitation one looks forward to with pleasure: a beautiful place and wonderful friends who have taken special care in arranging for a lovely evening.

These friends are sitting practically on top of the nation's vegetable garden. Anything and everything fresh is available to them. So, what do these lucky people do? On the night under discussion, they started with the best fresh produce, but by the time it was served at the table, it had practically nothing left nutritionally.

There's a play called *Little Murderers*, and I half-jokingly refer to these friends and people like them as little murderers! Smart people who commit murder daily on innocent vegetables, and do it in the name of cooking a wonderful meal for themselves and their families.

The crime my friends were guilty of was drowning a big beautiful cauliflower in boiling water. Any vegetable can be a victim, but at this dinner my friends held that cauliflower under water for what must have

seemed like an eternity to the cauliflower, but was probably more like forty-five minutes. When the rest of the meal was cooked, and the cauliflower, with that familiar gray tinge, was limp and squishy to the touch, it was served.

A bit dramatic perhaps, but it does serve to point up the all too common and unnecessary practice of overcooking vegetables. To add to their crime, my friends covered the cauliflower with a sauce that became a convenient shroud. (Restaurants do this a lot.) In fact, there are often more nutrients left in the water than in the vegetable after such harsh cooking. Vitamin C and certain B vitamins, which are what we eat vegetables for, are easily dissolved in water. Southern blacks have a traditional way of recovering this valuable water. They call it their pot licker, or liquor, depending on your preference, and they dunk their bread in it. Pot licker tastes good and can be used in soups and sauces, or for poaching poultry and fish. It should be used in a few days or you won't have many vitamins left. It can also be frozen for later use, but since there's usually such a small quantity, I think it makes more sense to use it fresh.

The manner in which vegetables are cooked is not just a question of aesthetics, such as preferring your carrots bright orange instead of dull orange. Looking at the Steamed versus Boiling chart on page 24, you can quickly see it's a serious question of nutrients lost or retained.

The cooking methods vary from steaming, boiling, baking, frying, to stir-frying, pressure cooking, and microwaving. Aside from eating vegetables raw, the next best way to prepare them is whatever method takes the least time, requires the least heat, and uses the least water.

All vegetables should still be slightly crisp when cooked. Most people like the texture of crunchy foods—it gives the jaws a distinct

Expired asparagus.

satisfaction. When it comes to vegetables, home cooks often rob themselves of this crunch pleasure by overcooking. I think one reason many kids don't like vegetables is they've been given overcooked ones that end up slimy and stringy in their mouth. My theory, which I've practiced on my nephews, is that most kids will eat vegetables just fine; they are just waiting for them to be cooked properly.

The chart below makes it easy to understand what happens to vitamins A and C during different cooking processes. It emphasizes the point that the process used in cooking vegetables truly does make a difference in how nutritiously we eat. With the correct cooking procedure, it is possible to retain a high degree of the original nutrients.

What Happens to Vitamin A and Vitamin C When Vegetables Are Cooked in Varying Amounts of Water

| Vegetable | PERCENTAGE OF VITAMIN C AND VITAMIN A RETAINED | | | | | | | |
| | Pressure-Cooked | | Water to Cover | | 1/2 Cup Water | | Waterless* | |
	Vit. C	Vit. A	Vit. C	Vit. A	Vit. C	Vit. A	Vit. C	Vit. A
Asparagus	67.6	78.5	45.2	64.6	66.4	92.3	69:4	101.5
Beans, Green	76.1	94.4	58.3	85.6	64.0	90.3	74.8	96.3
Beets	93.8	81.4	74.0	72.4	87.3	82.8	81.1	96.2
Broccoli	68.0	88.6	50.6	76.0	68.7	84.3	70.2	97.7
Cabbage	75.5	96.8	44.3	73.3	57.4	89.7	68.4	95.6
Carrots	79.1	88.4	63.1	84.5	75.1	86.3	72.5	98.9
Cauliflower	75.5	89.8	47.3	80.7	54.0	83.7	70.7	97.4
Corn	74.9	88.2	60.2	86.4	65.1	87.3	69.6	93.1
Peas	73.7	89.7	51.3	83.2	70.0	89.4	78.8	91.2
Potatoes	57.3	86.3	41.0	78.9	48.4	80.5	79.4	85.8
Spinach	61.7	74.8	49.1	80.7	51.7	87.2	70.0	91.3
Squash	65.3	92.3	50.5	82.4	66.5	84.2	74.8	91.9

SOURCE: *Commercial Vegetable Processing*, By B. Luh and J. Woodroof, Avi Publishing Company, 250 Post Road East, Westport, Connecticut.

*Waterless means cooking with the least amount of liquid possible.

STEAMING

An alternative for my friends back at the beach could have been: Using exactly the same pot in which they killed the cauliflower in the first go round, they place a collapsible steamer basket in the bottom. (These sell for about four dollars, but I've seen them for as little as a dollar. Steamers also come in fancy pottery pots, but they are unnecessarily expensive and bulky.) The steamer only needs a few inches of water in the pot. The cooks then add the cauliflower when the water is steaming, making sure that it rests on the

Steaming

basket with no water touching it. Think of it this way: When the water touches a vegetable, it acts as a direct funnel for the water-soluble vitamins to escape. Don't make an escape funnel—keep water away from vegetables. With the lid on and the heat high, the cauliflower should be done in 5–10 minutes. And there is still some pot licker to be saved and used in other ways.

If you're serving a dinner for family or friends, whether fancy or casual, with multiple courses, don't start steaming the vegetables until the first course is served. Arrange the vegetables in their steaming baskets and then minutes before you're ready to serve them, turn on the fire.

The re-emergence of the kitchen room is a good sign because the preparation of food can be ongoing while guests, or family, are present, and often participating. Previously, the well-organized cook prepared food in advance, and at the desired time, concoctions were magically brought forth from the kitchen. Now our less formal entertaining style, which doesn't try to hide the cooking processes, offers the opportunity for better nutrition by encouraging more on-the-spot last-minute cooking, a perfect technique for vegetables.

Properly steamed vegetables served to people who are unfamiliar with anything but the overcooked variety produce the sensation of a whole new kind of cooked vegetable. For one Easter picnic, I barely steamed some skinny little asparagus and my brother marveled at their bright color and crisp texture, just as if he'd never eaten asparagus before.

My experience is that one reason people prefer processed vegetables is because they feel they don't have time to prepare the fresh. But a steamer basket turns fresh vegetables into convenience foods in just a matter of minutes. This steaming technique works with everything from artichokes to zucchini and as you see, the charts show that this is the most nutritious way to cook vegetables.

I like to steam vegetables that are usually cooked other ways. Try steaming new potatoes in their skins for just six minutes. They are terrific. The skin of the potato left on is such an effective barrier that boiled or steamed whole potatoes show little loss of vitamin C—the story is different after they are peeled.

Sometimes after steaming vegetables like asparagus and broccoli, I like to prepare them vinaigrette. After the vegetable is steamed and is still hot, pour on an ample amount of vinaigrette salad dressing. (See Salad Dressings.) The vegetable should be covered. If it is to be eaten hot, serve immediately. If served chilled, refrigerate. One of my favorites prepared this way is asparagus. I arrange the asparagus circularly on a large, round, bright blue Spanish platter with the tips pointing out around a stack of cherry tomatoes; it makes a wonderful color combination.

Or, try a similar idea with steamed broccoli and a vinaigrette dressing. Cut the broccoli stalks so they are thin and long with only a small part of the flower bud attached to each stalk. Since these aren't as large as the asparagus, I like to arrange them on a smaller plate with the flowerets on the outside edge of the dish. At the center of the plate where the stalk ends come together, leave a hole; pile two or three slices of cucumber, ½″ thick and cut into star shapes.

Both these dishes can either be served warm or chilled, as finger food for appetizers or as the salad or vegetable course for a dinner.

Steaming: Length of Time

All the advantages of steaming will be lost if you do it too long. Everyone knows that time is a critical factor in cooking. This is obvious with clearly visible physical characteristics like color and texture. But cooking time is also critical for the invisible nutrients like vitamin C. For example, in a test situation where vegetables were boiled for 2, 5½, and 11 minutes, the vegetables lost 25, 32, and 33 per cent of their vitamin C into the cooking water.

How much time does it take to steam vegetables? The least amount necessary to create what your family considers a delicious product . . . this time obviously varies from vegetable to vegetable, and from family to family. If you try cooking your vegetables less than formerly, but no one in your family will eat them, keep trying. They may come around.

The following guidelines for steaming show the way I like some of my vegetables. You might compare it with what you've been doing:

Carrots: 1 pound fat carrots cut into 1-inch pieces — 7 minutes

String Beans: 1 pound — 7 minutes

Broccoli: 1 pound flowerets and cut stalk — 5 minutes

Cauliflower: 12 ounces, separated into individual flowerets — 2 minutes

Having a little pocket timer in the kitchen is absolutely essential. As I'm cooking, I keep several going at once, one in my pocket as I move from room to room. Because 3 minutes, which is all that is needed for some vegetables, goes by so quickly, the second you put those vegetables on the heat, set your timer. You may forget when 3 minutes is up, but the timer won't.

BOILING

The following chart dramatically shows the advantages of steaming over boiling. This information is so readily available that it makes

Boiling

me furious when food mavens with big followings suggest that it's great to cook vegetables in huge pails of boiling water. The difference in nutrient losses is significant (other studies show that you lose 75 per cent of the vitamin C with this technique). The attitude of some well-known food writers that it's fine to plop green beans in water and boil them is irresponsible. After all this evidence, if you decide you still want to continue boiling your vegetables, at least start them in boiling water. Started in cold water, they lose nutrients even before the water begins to boil.

MICROWAVE

Although the microwave people would like you to believe their technique provides a substantial nutritional edge, so far practical demonstrations haven't shown this to be true. In tests comparing microwaved vegetables with vegetables cooked in a small amount of water there were no significant differences in vitamin retention. And it appears from other studies that vitamin C retention is no better with microwaving than it is with other types of minimum-water cooking.

But microwaving can have two advantages over steaming: you don't have to keep check-

Vegetables: Steamed Versus Boiling

Vegetable	Cooking Method	Loss of Dry Matter (%)	Loss of Protein (%)	Loss of Calcium (%)	Loss of Magnesium (%)	Loss of Phosphorus (%)	Loss of Iron (%)
Asparagus	Boiled	14.0	20.0	16.5	8.8	25.8	34.4
	Steamed	7.9	13.3	15.3	1.4	10.4	20.0
Beans, String	Boiled	24.6	29.1	29.3	31.4	27.6	38.1
	Steamed	14.2	16.6	16.3	21.4	18.8	24.5
Cabbage	Boiled	60.7	61.5	72.3	76.1	59.9	66.6
	Steamed	26.4	31.5	40.2	43.4	22.0	34.6
Carrots	Boiled	20.1	26.4	8.9	22.8	19.0	34.1
	Steamed	5.1	14.5	5.1	5.6	1.1	20.7
Cauliflower	Boiled	37.6	44.4	24.6	25.0	49.8	36.2
	Steamed	2.1	7.6	3.1	1.7	19.2	8.3
Potatoes	Boiled	9.4	—	16.8	18.8	18.3	—
	Steamed	4.0	—	9.6	14.0	11.7	—
Spinach	Boiled	33.9	29.0	5.5	59.1	48.8	57.1
	Steamed	8.4	5.6	0.0	17.8	10.2	25.7
Average for all vegetables	Boiled	39.4	43.0	31.9	44.7	46.4	48.0
	Steamed	14.0	16.0	10.7	18.6	16.7	21.3

SOURCE: *Commercial Vegetable Processing*, by B. Luh and J. Woodroof, Avi Publishing Company, 250 Post Road East, Westport, Connecticut.

ing to see if the water has boiled out of the steaming pot, and for those people who judge the success of a cooking procedure by the amount of dishes that don't get dirty, you can cook the vegetables in the same dish you serve them in.

Microwaving isn't any faster than steaming; the cooking times are about the same. When you add the standing time necessary afterward for the microwave to continue cooking, in many instances, the reportedly super-fast microwave proves to take longer.

If you already have one, fine. But it seems a silly investment to rush out and buy a five-hundred-dollar microwave to cook vegetables in a way that a four-dollar steaming basket can match.

If you do have a microwave, here are some general suggestions for how best to use it in preparing vegetables.

1. Set vegetables in serving dish or casserole dish.

2. Most vegetables will need a few tablespoons of moisture added to the dish. This can either be water, or a cooking broth like chicken, or butter.

3. Cover tightly with a lid or seal with plastic wrap and cook at high heat.

This Microwave Vegetable Cooking chart gives you specific information on cooking procedures and times for individual vegetables. Those of you just beginning to cook with a microwave oven may find them useful.

Microwave Vegetable Cooking

Vegetable	Amount	Cooking Procedure	Time	Setting	Standing Time
ARTICHOKES	1 medium	1 tbsp. water in 8"x8" covered dish	4-6 min.	High	3 min., covered
	2 medium	1/4 cup water in covered cake dish	5-7 min.	High	3 min., covered
	3 medium	1/2 cup water in round covered cake dish	7-9 min.	High	3 min., covered
ASPARAGUS	15 (4") pieces	1/4 cup water in 1½-qt. covered casserole	5-7 min.	High	3 min., covered
BEANS, Butter	1 lb. (2 cups shelled)	1/2 cup water in 1-qt. covered casserole. Stir.	6-8 min.	High	3 min., covered
	2 lbs. (4 cups shelled)	1/2 cup water in 1½-qt. covered casserole. Stir.	9-11 min.	High	3 min., covered
Green or Wax	1 lb., snapped or french cut	1/4 cup water in 1½-qt. covered casserole	7-9 min.	High	3 min., covered
BEANS, Lima	1 lb. (2 cups shelled)	1/2 cup water in 1-qt. covered casserole. Stir.	6-8 min.	High	3 min., covered
	2 lbs. (4 cups shelled)	1/2 cup water in 1½-qt. covered casserole. Stir.	9-11 min.	High	3 min., covered
Pinto	2 cups (1 lb.)	Soak overnight; 3 cups water in 2-qt. covered casserole. Stir.	20-25 min.	High	3-5 min., covered
BEETS	4 medium, whole	Barely covered with water in 2-qt. covered casserole	15-17 min.	High	3 min., covered
	4 medium, sliced	1/2 cup water in 1-qt. covered casserole	12 min.	High	3 min., covered
BROCCOLI	1 small bunch (1½ lbs.)	Cut away tough part of stalk, split tender ends; 1/2 cup water in 1½-qt. covered casserole.	7-9 min.	High	3 min., covered
BRUSSELS SPROUTS	1/2 lb. (2 cups)	2 tbsp. water in 1-qt. covered casserole	4-6 min.	High	3 min., covered
	1 lb. (4 cups)	3 tbsp. water in 1½-qt. covered casserole	5-7 min.	High	3 min., covered

Microwave Vegetable Cooking (continued)

Vegetable	Amount	Cooking Procedure	Time	Setting	Standing Time
CABBAGE	1 small head, chopped	2 tbsp. water in 1½-qt. covered casserole	10-12 min.	High	3 min., covered
	1 medium head, whole	2 tbsp. water in 2-qt. covered casserole	12-15 min.	High	3 min., covered
CARROTS	4 medium, sliced	2 tbsp. water in 1-qt. covered casserole	4-6 min.	High	3 min., covered
	6 medium, sliced	2 tbsp. water in 1½-qt. covered casserole	6-8 min.	High	3 min., covered
CAULIFLOWER	1 small head	1/2 cup water in 1½-qt. covered casserole	5-7 min.	High	3 min., covered
	1 medium head	1/2 cup water in 2-qt. covered casserole	9-11 min.	High	3 min., covered
CELERY	4 cups coarsely chopped	1/4 cup water in 1½-qt. covered casserole	6-8 min.	High	3 min., covered
	6 cups coarsely chopped	1/4 cup water in 2-qt. covered casserole	10-12 min.	High	3 min., covered
CORN, cut off the cob	1½ cups	1/4 cup water in 1-qt. covered casserole	3-5 min.	High	3 min., covered
on the cob	2 ears	Put ears in open glass dish. Pour melted butter over corn. Turn ears 2 or 3 times during cooking.	4-6 min.	High	3 min., covered
	4 ears	Same as above	8-10 min.	High	3 min., covered
EGGPLANT	1 medium (4 cups cubed)	Peel and dice; 2 tbsp. water in covered casserole	4-6 min.	High	3 min., covered
ONIONS	2 large, cut in quarters or eighths	1/2 cup water in 1-qt. covered casserole	5-7 min.	High	3 min., covered
	4 large, cut in quarters or eighths	1/2 cup water in 2-qt. covered casserole	7-9 min.	High	3 min., covered

	Amount	Directions	Time	Power	Standing
PARSNIPS	2 medium	2 tbsp. water in 1-qt. covered casserole	5-7 min.	High	3 min., covered
	4 medium	1/4 cup water in 2-qt. covered casserole	7-9 min.	High	3 min., covered
PEAS, Green	2 cups shelled	2 tbsp. water in 1-qt. covered casserole	4-6 min.	High	3 min., covered
	3 cups shelled	2 tbsp. water in 1-qt. covered casserole	5-7 min.	High	3 min., covered
POTATOES, baked (Irish) Idaho	1 medium	Scrub potatoes and dry. Spread paper towel on oven shelf. Put potatoes on paper towel about 1" apart. Times are approximate and vary with size and variety. When baking more than 4, rearrange after half the cooking time has expired.	5-6 min.	High	Wrap in foil, let stand 5-10 min.
	2 medium		7-9 min.	High	
	3 medium		10-12 min.	High	
	4 medium		14-16 min.	High	
boiled	6 medium, cut in half, peeled	1/4 cup water in 2-qt. glass casserole; stir once after 6 min.	12-16 min.	High	3-5 min., covered
buttered (Irish)	4 medium, sliced	2 tbsp. butter in 1½-qt. glass casserole	12-14 min.	High	5 min., covered
	6 medium, sliced	2 tbsp. butter in 2-qt. glass casserole. Stir after 5 min.	17-19 min.	High	5 min., covered
RUTABAGA	1 (1 lb.)	Wash, peel, and cube rutabaga; 1/2 cup water, 3 tbsp. butter, in 1-qt. covered casserole.	7-9 min.	High	3 min., covered
SPINACH	4 cups (1 lb.)	Wash. Cook in water that clings to the leaves in 2-qt. covered casserole.	3-5 min.	High	3 min., covered
SQUASH, Acorn or Butternut	1 (1 lb.)	Cook whole. Pierce skin with sharp knife in several places. Cook on paper towel.	4-6 min.	High	5 min., covered
SWEET POTATOES	4 medium, cut in half lengthwise, peeled	1/2 cup water in 1½-qt. covered casserole	8-10 min.	High	3 min., covered
	6 medium, cut in half lengthwise, peeled	1/4 cup water in 2-qt. covered casserole. Stir after 5 min.	12-14 min.	High	3 min., covered

Microwave Vegetable Cooking (continued)

Vegetable	Amount	Cooking Procedure	Time	Setting	Standing Time
SWEET POTATOES (continued)					
baked whole	1 medium	Scrub and dry potatoes. Cover oven shelf with paper towel, put potatoes on towel about 1″ apart.	5-7 min.	High	Wrap in foil after cooking, let stand 5-10 min.
	2 medium		7-9 min.	High	
	3 medium		14-16 min.	High	
	4 medium				
TOMATOES	4 large (2½-3″ diameter) (1 lb.)	Clean, peel, and halve tomatoes, 2 tbsp. water in 1½-qt. covered casserole.	4-6 min.	High	3 min., covered Add 1/2 tsp. salt
TURNIPS	2 or 3 medium (1 lb.)	Peel and cube; 3 tbsp. water in 1½-qt. casserole.	7-9 min.	High	3 min., covered
ZUCCHINI	1 (1 lb.)	Wash, remove stems; cut into thin slices; 1/4 cup water in 1-qt. covered casserole.	5-5½ min.	High	3 min., covered

SOURCE: Extrapolated from *The Magic of Microwave Cookbook*, courtesy of Magic Chef.

STIR-FRYING

Almost all vegetables can be stir-fried to their benefit and yours. This super-fast cooking technique is a good one nutritionally because it involves a minimum amount of cooking time, a minimum amount of liquid, and a maximum amount of heat quickly applied.

The only disadvantage to stir-frying is that it's an active participation food preparation. No absent chef here.

The combinations of vegetables for stir-frying are limited only by your imagination:

Bean sprouts, green pepper strips, shredded lettuce, and zucchini.

Bean sprouts, mushrooms, Swiss chard, and scallions.

Often one tends to think of stir-fried vegetables in terms of greens and browns (green leaves of lettuces, other green vegetables, the brown of mushrooms and sprouts), but for extra color add the red from cherry tomatoes or tomato slices (be careful not to bruise them), or red bell peppers.

Things to remember:

1. A wok isn't a necessity. Although to be authentic you would want to use a wok, you can get nice results using a frying pan.

Don't ignore this method because you don't have a wok. No excuse.

2. All vegetables should be cut into like-size pieces so they cook at approximately the same rate.

3. Especially hard vegetables (carrots, broccoli stalks, cauliflower, string beans, turnips) should be steamed first over high heat for a moment to soften them and then stir-fried.

4. A soft vegetable, like lettuce, should be added last so it doesn't get wilted and limp. It should be barely heated through.

5. Assemble all ingredients in advance so stir-frying can proceed as quickly as possible.

BASIC STIR-FRIED VEGETABLES

Ingredients:

2 tablespoons oil

3 slices fresh ginger root minced. (Skip the dried. It doesn't even come close.)

1 pound cut-up vegetables (1 vegetable or several mixed)

¼ cup chicken stock (fresh or made from bouillon cube)

SAUCE

4 tablespoons soy sauce

1 teaspoon cornstarch

Serves 4

1. Heat the oil in the pan until very hot. Add ginger root. Add vegetables and coat with the oil. Add stock.

2. Mix soy sauce and cornstarch and stir in very quickly.

3. Simmer with lid on until vegetables are done (depends on vegetable—perhaps 3–5 minutes).

A variation I like is to add ½ cup of thinly sliced chicken. Add the chicken—raw—at the same time as the vegetables. I also like to add a few sliced fresh water chestnuts near the end of the cooking process. The zippy fresh water chestnuts taste nothing like their pale canned counterparts and they add their own special sweet crunchiness.

BAKING

Since baking usually involves cooking for long periods of time at high temperatures, it's not the greatest method nutritionally for preparing vegetables. The exception to this is when a vegetable, like a potato, is being baked in its own skin and is keeping its nutrients to itself.

I have a southern friend who doesn't consider a vegetable properly cooked until it's gone through at least two or three cooking processes and it always ends up *baked*. With summer squash, she first boils the sliced squash in water until it's tender. Next, the squash is sautéed in butter with sliced onions. Finally, what's left of the squash from these two other processes is mashed into a purée and baked bubbling hot for at least an hour. It smells delicious, it tastes good, but nutritionally, it's zilch. And I thought my friends with the cauliflower were overdoing it!

The following is a favorite family recipe for baked eggplant that tastes divine. From the nutritional point of view, this leaves something to be desired, but then that's true of baked vegetables in general.

BAKED EGGPLANT
FRANCES WELCH

Ingredients:

3 pounds eggplant

1 large onion, diced

Oil, small amount

3 eggs

2 cups skim milk

Bread crumbs

Serves 6–8

1. Preheat oven to 350° F.
2. Peel eggplant, cut in large cubes, and simmer with diced onion in small amount of oil in covered skillet until tender, about 10 minutes.
3. Mix eggs with milk.

4. Combine eggplant mixture with milk mixture and place in casserole.
5. Cover top of casserole with bread crumbs and bake in preheated oven about an hour.

When cooked, this has a light consistency that places it somewhere between a soufflé and a delicate dressing. My mother-in-law serves it with broiled fish dinners, but it goes nicely with poultry as well.

PRESSURE COOKING

When university food departments test cooking methods for nutrient retention, this method works so well (right up there with steaming), it should be worth dusting off that old pressure cooker you, or your mother, have around.

The problem is the pressure cooker's bad reputation from years past. Not many people my age are eager to rush out and buy a gadget that they've heard exploded in their mother's face. Perhaps their mothers didn't follow the directions carefully, but still the stories linger. The high price also makes one think twice. However, if you follow the manufacturer's instructions carefully, pressure cookers are perfectly safe to use and offer both nutrients and speed.

Pressure Cooking Vegetables

When cooking fresh vegetables, place required amount (at least ½ cup) of water in the cooker. Then place the cooking rack over the water and set the vegetables on the rack. Seasoning may be added before or after cooking. Cook for length of time given in time table. Cool cooker under a faucet of running water or in a pan of cold water until the pressure is completely reduced. More than one vegetable may be cooked at the same time in the cooker.

DO NOT FILL COOKER OVER TWO-THIRDS FULL!

Vegetable	How to Prepare	Required Amount of Water for Cooking		Cooking Time in Minutes
		4-qt. Cookers	6-qt. Cookers	
Artichokes	Wash, trim, and score hearts.	½ cup	1 cup	10
Asparagus (Tips)	Wash and snap off tough parts. Large ends may be used in soup.	½ cup	1 cup	1-2
Beans, Green Lima	Shell and wash.	½ cup	1 cup	2-3
Beans, Green or Wax	Wash. Remove ends and strings. Cut in 1" pieces.	½ cup	1 cup	3-4
Beets (whole)	Wash thoroughly. Remove all but 3" of top and leave roots on. After cooking, slip skins off.	½ cup	1 cup	10-18
Broccoli	Wash, score stems, remove leaves and tough stalk parts.	½ cup	1 cup	2-3
Brussels Sprouts	Wash. Remove wilted leaves. Leave whole.	½ cup	1 cup	3
Cabbage (quartered)	Remove wilted outside leaves. Wash and cut in quarters.	½ cup	1 cup	3-4
Carrots	Wash, brush, and scrape or peel. Slice or leave whole.	½ cup ½ cup	1 cup 1 cup	(sliced) 3 (whole) 4-8
Cauliflower	Wash and hollow out core or separate flowerets.	½ cup ½ cup	1 cup 1 cup	(whole) 5 (flowerets) 2
Celery	Separate stalks. Remove tough, stringy fibers. Scrub and wash well. Cut in ½" pieces.	½ cup	1 cup	2-3
Corn (on the cob)	Remove husk and silk. Wash.	1 cup	1½ cups	3-5
Greens (mild-flavored) Beet Greens Spinach Swiss Chard	Select young, tender greens. Remove wilted leaves. Wash thoroughly several times and lift from water after each washing.	½ cup ½ cup ½ cup	1 cup 1 cup 1 cup	3 1-3 2
Kohlrabi	Wash, peel, and cut into cubes or slices.	½ cup	1 cup	5-6
Onions (whole)	Wash and peel medium white or bermuda onions.	½ cup	1 cup	5-7
Parsnips	Wash, peel, or scrape. Leave whole or cut in halves.	½ cup ½ cup	1 cup 1 cup	(halves) 7 (whole) 10

Pressure Cooking Vegetables (continued)

| Vegetable | How to Prepare | Required Amount of Water for Cooking | | Cooking Time in Minutes |
		4-qt. Cookers	6-qt. Cookers	
Peas, Green	Wash and shell.	½ cup ½ cup	1 cup 1 cup	(small) 1 (large) 2
Potatoes (in jackets) (baking size)	Wash and scrub thoroughly.	1 cup	1½ cups	15
Potatoes (for mashing)	Wash and peel. Leave small potatoes whole and cut large potatoes in half.	1 cup	1½ cups	10
Potatoes (small)	Wash and scrub new potatoes	1 cup	1½ cups	10
Pumpkin	Wash, peel, and cut into small pieces.	½ cup	1½ cups	10-12
Rutabagas	Wash, peel, and dice.	½ cup	1 cup	3-5
Squash, Hubbard	Wash, peel, and cut into small pieces.	½ cup	1 cup	10-12
Sweet Potatoes (whole)	Wash, and scrub thoroughly. Do not peel.	½ cup	1 cup	10
Turnips	Wash, peel, and dice.	½ cup	1 cup	3-5

SOURCE: Courtesy of National Presto Industries, Inc.

CROCK POTS

This pot cooks vegetables over a very long period of time at a low temperature and keeps all the juices in the same pot. You do lose some additional vitamin C by this long cooking. It's really a process that's more beneficial for meats that need long simmering rather than for vegetables, which are best cooked briskly.

 Adapting Recipes

Using the information in this chapter and later ones about preparation and cooking techniques, one can quickly learn to adapt recipes to obtain their maximum nutritional value. You'll catch on to what steps to avoid and how to make substitutions. Once you get in the habit, you'll naturally start changing all recipes to healthier proportions and ingredients.

"But," you say, "this is a famous chef's recipe." It doesn't matter. Perhaps he or she hasn't thought these things through from a health point of view and you have.

The essence of adapting a recipe is to read it through once and then, using what you know about nutrition, amend it *before* you begin. With vegetables shorten cooking times when appropriate. Don't follow by rote, but rely on your own knowledge of what's healthy. If it says boil and you know steaming is better nutritionally and if it will give a similar result, steam instead. If it says to fry in oil and you're concerned about cholesterol, sauté in broth instead. You'll probably find as I have that ingredients like heavy cream, salt, oils, and sugar grow even less appealing as you become more aware of their often unnecessary presence.

There are examples everywhere of recipes that can be reinterpreted for a healthier end result. To illustrate how easy it is to adapt recipes, I'm using a recipe that appeared in the New York *Times*. A friend prepared it according to the *Times*'s instructions. It was delicious. I prepared it my way. It was equally delicious, but much more healthful.

Here's the *Times*'s recipe for Jacques Pépin's cold zucchini soup.

COLD ZUCCHINI SOUP

Ingredients:

5 or 6 small to medium-size zucchini

1 large onion, peeled, and thinly sliced,
    about 1 cup

1 ½ teaspoons curry powder

3 cups chicken broth

1 cup heavy cream

½ cup milk

Salt and freshly ground pepper

Finely chopped chives for garnish

Serves 6–8

1. Rinse the zucchini and pat dry. Trim off the ends. Cut one zucchini in two and thinly slice one half. Stack the slices and cut them into very thin matchlike strips. There should be about 1 cup. Place in a saucepan and add cold water to cover. Boil 3–4 minutes and drain. Set aside.

2. Cut the remaining one-half zucchini and the other zucchini into 1″ lengths. Cut each length into quarters.

3. Place the pieces of quartered zucchini in a kettle or saucepan and add the onion slices. Sprinkle with curry powder and stir to coat the pieces. Add the chicken broth and bring to the boil. Cover and simmer about 45 minutes.

4. Spoon and scrape the mixture into a blender or food processor and blend to a fine purée. There should be about 4 cups. Add the cream, milk, and salt and pepper to taste. Add the reserved zucchini strips. Chill thoroughly. Serve sprinkled with chopped chives.

1. Let's start with Step 1.

You're instructed to place the sliced zucchini in a saucepan with cold water and then boil. Then drain the liquid.

Ooch. That hurts. You know that if you put vegetables in a pan with cold water, they will start to lose nutrients even before they begin to cook. Then, with most of the nutrients lolling about in the water, you're instructed to throw the water out.

We should pause here a moment to consider the two ways to think about a soup made from zucchini. Zucchini has a delicate, light flavor, but it's not worth doing nutritional handstands over. So you can either think: "It's got so little in it, what does it matter what I do to it?" or "Because it has so little, I should guard what's there." I prefer the latter reasoning.

Step 1 Revised.

Steam zucchini over as little water as possible for 2–3 minutes. Instead of throwing this water out (and there shouldn't be much, perhaps only ¼ to ½ cup), add it to the chicken stock and use that much less chicken stock.

Step 2. As is.

Step 3. Can be shortened. This step is for the flavor to seep in from the curry and the broth and the 45 minutes can be shortened to 25 minutes.

Step 4. Making a creamy soup doesn't necessarily mean adding heavy cream. If you stop and look at those vegetables when they come out of the blender or food processor, they will be naturally creamy in texture. All they need from you is a little skim milk added to enhance their natural texture and make them less thick. Skip the cream.

I served this creamy soup my way to a friend on a rigid diet and she felt tickled that she was able to eat something she would not ordinarily consider "dietetic." But cream and creamy aren't necessarily the same thing.

Specialty Vegetables

What determines a "specialty vegetable" lies in the heart of the receiver. What's a special treat to someone may be common fare to others. Fresh black-eyed peas are everyday fare to Southerners, while fresh bamboo shoots are practically unheard of.

My reason for including specialties is that often one shops by habit, not "seeing" the wide range of produce that's available. By habit, you select the staples you need and you and your cart are on your way, often by-passing the opportunity to sample whole bins of interesting-looking vegetables. Why, for example, would one pass up Chinese long beans when they are in season? If your kids object to regular green beans, maybe this variety, which is from 12"–24" long, slender and tender, will seem less like eating serious beans and more like fun. Not only does experimentation spark up things for the family, it also keeps the cook from getting bored.

To introduce friends to specialty vegetables I've given them as gifts: a plump spaghetti squash with a bright bow tied around it and cooking instructions attached; tiny french carrots arranged in their own straw basket; and Chinese long beans wrapped in colorful tissue paper with long streamers. If you've found an offbeat vegetable you like, don't keep it to yourself, gift it to a friend.

Food gifts

If you're confused by the array of vegetables available and don't know what some of them are, ask. Sometimes people don't ask because they don't want to appear dumb. I know, I've been there myself. The first time I did a television segment on "Greens," I went to my neighborhood store and put one type of green from kohlrabi to kale each in its own plastic bag and then I asked the produce man to identify the ones I wasn't familiar with and into each bag went a written name tag. My dumbness was showing, but I learned a lot. Even though the produce departments in many grocery stores have gotten as impersonal as the stores themselves, I've found most department managers are very willing to take a moment to answer a question.

The fun of eating, vegetables included, is trying things outside your culture. Many years ago in the restaurant at Washington National Airport in D.C., I was dawdling over a sandwich while waiting for a flight. It was an ordinary restaurant serving the standard airport fare, but the luncheon crowd had left and the owner of the restaurant and his large Italian family seated themselves at the table next to mine and started eating lunch. They had plates with mounds of greens on them.

My curiosity wouldn't allow me to see food and not know what it was, so I asked for a taste. I was given a heaping plateful and it was delicious—dandelion greens—much better than standard airport fare. Then the story unfolded. They were newly here from the old country and often the mother and grandmother went out to the green patches next to the freeways to gather dandelions. I'm sure those two ladies dressed in black made a wonderful sight as they pruned the freeways from the airport into the nation's capital. On return trips to Washington I never drive those freeways without thinking of that family. I wish I had requested their recipe, or even taken their names, but since I didn't, here's my adaptation:

Interesting looking Vegetables

WILTED DANDELION GREENS

Ingredients:

2 pounds dandelion greens,[1] washed and
  trimmed of stems

½ cup olive oil, or less

4 cloves garlic, mashed

Serves 6–8

1. Briefly steam dandelion greens until
wilted and tender.

2. Heat oil in skillet. Drain greens of excess water and transfer to skillet. Add garlic.
Heat until greens are well coated with oil
and serve warm.

The list of specialty vegetables which follows is compiled with the help of *The
Packer,*[2] an availability guide published for
the produce industry, so it concentrates on
items that are truly available. I've chosen not
to include specialties that are available only
in ethnic stores. When I'm introduced to
something new, whether it be chayote squash
or nopales, I want to be able to find it—I
think you do, too. But keep a few points in

mind: Some stores won't carry these all the
time, and others won't carry them at all.
There are also stores that specialize in handling offbeat items. And watch the seasons.

In the past, a peeve of mine has been the
way that specialty produce is introduced.
Maybe this season it's white radishes or
celeriac. Their texture, flavor, and color are
touted like the pedigree of a prize Hereford
at the summer fair, but rarely, if ever, does
one see mention of their nutritional value.
Why? Is it because they suspect that
consumers aren't concerned that food writers
extol spaghetti squash in terms of its
wonderful spaghetti-like strands rather than
its vitamin content?

My research has revealed that some of the
time this nutrient information is not available. Frank Hepburn, at the U. S. Department of Agriculture, studies the nutrient content in food. He says part of the problem is
one of priority. His Nutrient Data Group has
very limited testing facilities so vegetables
that aren't eaten in significant quantity don't
warrant being tested.

On the following list, if there's no accompanying nutritional information, that's because it has not been gathered. Since the tests
are lengthy and costly, if you see a specialty
item on my list that the U. S. Department of
Agriculture has no nutrient information on
touted somewhere else as being high in a par-

---

[1] In addition to being picked fresh, dandelion
greens can be purchased as specialty produce.

[2] Published by Vance Publishing Corp., 300 West
Adams Street, Chicago, Illinois 60608.

ticular nutrient, it's a good bet the people blowing the horn are making up nutritional information data to serve their own pecuniary interest.

Increasingly, fresh herbs are sold right along with the fresh produce. In California, year round, I grow my own herbs in an indispensable garden next to the kitchen. Herbs go wonderfully with everything from fresh pasta to fish, but contrasted with the delicacy of fresh vegetables, just a little basil here or a few fresh chives there make a wonderful accent. Herbs are a healthier way to season foods rather than always relying on salt to bring out flavors. Even though I grow my own, I'm glad that stores have started stocking fresh herbs, too. Now on occasion when I need an herb in large quantity, I supplement mine with theirs.

Speaking of herbs, there's a new mild garlic that deserves some attention. It's a Texas-size garlic that's grown in California by Frank La Salle. Depending on the clove, it's three to ten times larger in size than regular garlic. In recipes, Frank suggests using these new garlics in a 1:3 ratio. For example, if a recipe calls for three cloves of a standard garlic, use one of Frank's. One of their biggest advantages is how easy they are to work with; no more wrestling with those tiny garlics to get the skin off. Frank suggests storing any leftover garlic in plastic wrap in the refrigerator; I suggest dropping it in a wide-mouth jar of olive oil. Although they are available at some grocery stores, the best way to buy the giant garlic is by mail. Write Mama La Salle's Gardens, Box 33, Cuyama, California 93214.

(NOTE: The nutritional information for specialty vegetables is given for 1 cup raw amounts unless otherwise indicated.)

Anise, Sweet Also called fennel, this vegetable has a delightful licorice flavor. Recently, I served it raw, as is, to some fennel first-timers and they wanted me to confess what *I* had done to it. Nothing. Nature had done it already. Terrific in salads (see Chapter 5,

Salads), or served as you would raw celery sticks. Select those with firm stalks and vibrant green color.

Apio This celery-type vegetable has a new name that's a mouthful. Would you believe Arracacia Zanthorhiza? It's from the same family as carrots and celery and is available mostly around New York. The root resembles a parsnip and is eaten as a vegetable in stews and soup. Apio must be peeled before cooking because the skin may be stringy. As with other root vegetables, select those that are firm to the touch and not wilted.

Bamboo Shoots Once it was possible to buy only the canned; now it is sold fresh, usually grouped with other produce used in oriental cooking like snow peas, bean sprouts, and fresh water chestnuts.

Nutritional Value:

Calories	Protein	Carbohydrate	Iron
40	4.0 gm	7.8 gm	.43 mg

Sodium	Vitamin A	Vitamin C
—	30 I.U.	6 mg

Bean, Chinese Long Something not to be missed. These are thinner than green beans, much longer (at least 12″ and sometimes as long as 24″) and very tender. Select them firm, not limp. Chinese long beans can be cooked exactly the same way you cook green beans, and they can be stir-fried. Their availability varies. One delicious idea to do with any leftover steamed beans is to purée them in a food processor (or blender) with a dash of soy sauce. The puréeing brings out the unusual nutty taste of the pods.

Bok Choy Sometimes called "white cabbage," or Chinese chard, this is a form of Chinese cabbage. It is an inexpensive year-round staple that is good pan-fried or boiled in soups. Should be selected as one would choose fresh, crisp lettuce.

Nutritional Value:

Calories	Protein	Carbohydrate	Iron
11	.9 gm	2.3 gm	.5 mg

Sodium	Vitamin A	Vitamin C
17 mg	110 I.U.	19 mg

Breadfruit   Used as a starchy vegetable by millions of Polynesians and South Americans, it has only recently become available here on a limited basis. Can be used in place of potatoes, rice, and pasta, and, like its counterparts, must be cooked. It's a good source of calories, iron, and vitamin C.

Nutritional Value:

Calories	Protein	Carbohydrate	Iron
360	5.9 gm	91.5 gm	4.2 mg

Sodium	Vitamin A	Vitamin C
52 mg	150 I.U.	101 mg

Calaba (Calabaza)   Specialty squash also known as West Indian pumpkin. It's a Latin American favorite. Usually 6″–8″ in diameter. Use and select as you would a large squash. Available in winter.

Nutritional Value:

Calories	Protein	Carbohydrate	Iron
40	1.2 gm	9.8 gm	0.07 mg

Sodium	Vitamin A	Vitamin C
—	1,055 I.U.	42 mg

Cardoon (Cardoni)   Related to the artichoke, outwardly this vegetable resembles a celery with thistles. To eat, peel the leaves and eat the mid-rib. Must be cooked; makes an interesting and easy addition to salads. The same availability as artichokes.

Nutritional Value:

Calories	Protein	Carbohydrate	Iron
18	.5 gm	4.1 gm	1.5 mg

Sodium	Vitamin A	Vitamin C
—	trace	1 mg

Carrot, French   Sometimes called cocktail carrots, these 2″–3″ midgets are attractive to use when you don't need the bulk of a regular-size carrot. They are perfect raw for cocktails, and cooked in stews. (Nutritional information same as for traditional-size carrots. See chart, page 17.)

Cassava   Large, fleshy, tuberous tropical root. Tastes vaguely like a potato. These are eaten only after being cooked and skinned.

Nutritional Value:

Calories	Protein	Carbohydrate	Iron
60	6.9 gm	9.2 gm	2.8 mg

Sodium	Vitamin A	Vitamin C
4 mg	—	82 mg

Chayote Squash   Sometimes called vegetable pear, this beautiful icy green vegetable looks like a squash that's been squished. It's delicious cut into pieces and steamed, or try scooping out the top and stuffing it, using one of the recipes for stuffed vegetables. Its season parallels that of summer squash—from May to December.

Nutritional Value:

Calories	Protein	Carbohydrate	Iron
28	0.6 gm	7.1 gm	0.5 mg

Sodium	Vitamin A	Vitamin C
5 mg	20 I.U.	19 mg

Cucumber   There's a wide variety of cucumbers available now. Try the lemon cucumber (available from July to November), which is light in color and has a sweet taste. Or the skinless cucumber, which really isn't skinless, but does have a thinner, edible skin. Or the burpless cucumber, a hothouse cuke that does not cause gas. (Nutritional information, same as for cucumbers; see chart, page 17.)

Daikon   The daikon, a Japanese radish, used to be seen only in food stores specializing in Japanese delicacies, but now I've seen it even in large American grocery store chains. From 4″–12″ long, these can be eaten raw (usually thinly grated), or they can be used in soups like a potato. When cooked, they become less pungent and, of course, lose some of their characteristic crunchiness.

Nutritional Value:

Calories	Protein	Carbohydrate	Iron
19	.9 gm	4.2 gm	0.6 mg

Sodium	Vitamin A	Vitamin C
—	10 I.U.	32 mg

Dandelion Greens Considered a weed by fastidious gardeners, I've already revealed my fondness for these wild somewhat bitter-tasting greens. The young leaves are the most tender. The greens can either be eaten raw in salads or cooked in a recipe as suggested on page 35. Dandelions are usually available in the spring months and are an excellent source of vitamin A. (For nutritional information, see chart, page 18.)

Endive, French Botanically, this vegetable is known more correctly as witlof and chicory, but is more often called French or Belgium endive. It has elegant 5″ long, slender white leaves with yellow tips and has an interesting, somewhat bitter taste. Raw endive makes an interesting salad either alone or with other delicate greens that don't overpower it. Unfortunately, it is usually expensive.

Nutritional Value:

Calories	Protein	Carbohydrate	Iron
20	1.7 gm	4.1 gm	1.7 mg

Sodium	Vitamin A	Vitamin C
14 mg	3,300 I.U.	10 mg

Jicama Widely used in Mexico, this is called the Mexican potato. It is a recent addition to markets in California and is sometimes available in other parts of the country as well. Jicama has a thick inedible skin that has to be peeled. It's terrific sliced and served raw as you would carrot sticks. Cooking brings out an extraordinary, unexpected, sweet flavor.

Nutritional Value:
(100 gm raw)

Calories	Protein	Carbohydrate	Iron
55	1.4 gm	12.8 gm	.6 mg

Sodium	Vitamin A	Vitamin C
—	trace	20 mg

Leeks Resemble an onion with an overgrown thick stalk. Often called for in French recipes, I find little to recommend it; after cooking, leeks end up stringy and slightly slimy.

Nutritional Value:
(100 gm raw)

Calories	Protein	Carbohydrate	Iron
52	2.2 gm	11.2 gm	1.1 mg

Sodium	Vitamin A	Vitamin C
5 mg	40 I.U.	17 mg

Okra Available May through September (and sometimes longer), this special vegetable is a must for southern seafood gumbos. Check the ribs for firmness when purchasing.

Nutritional Value:

Calories	Protein	Carbohydrate	Iron
46	3.2 gm	9.6 gm	.8 mg

Sodium	Vitamin A	Vitamin C
3 mg	780 I.U.	32 mg

Rhubarb Traditionally a home-grown vegetable, it is now hothouse-produced and available year round. The leaves of the rhubarb are poisonous (high concentration of oxalic acid) and the plant is never eaten raw. Although I grew up with it as a child and remember liking fresh-baked rhubarb pies from my aunt's garden, I now find little use for it because it needs the addition of so much sugar to make it edible.

Nutritional Value:
(1 cup cooked with sugar added)

Calories	Protein	Carbohydrate	Iron
381	1.4 gm	97.2 gm	1.6 mg

Sodium	Vitamin A	Vitamin C
5 mg	220 I.U.	16 mg

Spaghetti Squash The spaghetti squash is one of my favorite finds and it's a terrific example of food being a continuously interesting adventure. The spaghetti squash looks like just a big yellow squash, so usually the grower puts a little decal on its side or the grocer hangs a sign over the bin labeling it. Until recently, the spaghetti squash was a backyard crop, but the last few years, commercial sales have been booming. It's a seasonal crop, picked in September and held in storage throughout the winter. It's also very reasonably priced, along with other squashes on the produce shelves. During fall and winter, you should be able to find it; if you can't, ask your produce man to order it for you. If the demand increases, which I think it will, you'll be seeing this more routinely in your produce departments.

Probably the easiest way to prepare spaghetti squash is to bake it in a 350° F. oven for 1 hour, until slightly soft to the touch. The time depends on how large a squash you selected. Before baking, pierce a few steam holes in it with a fork, so it doesn't burst while cooking. When it is cooked, cut it in half lengthwise and scoop out the seeds. For someone who has never done it before, the next step is lots of fun. With a fork, lift away the meat of the squash from the outside shell. *Voilà!* You'll see that the squash is not in solid pieces, but in strands. Spaghetti from squash.

You'll be surprised at its slightly sweet taste, its lovely texture. Another good thing about spaghetti squash is that 1 cup of regular cooked spaghetti noodles has about 200 calories while this has only 50.

I've been told that some big eaters pour their favorite sauce[3] right into the cooked

squash and eat it. That's one way to do it. I prefer using the squash itself as the serving dish.

Sunchoke—or Jerusalem Artichoke The Jerusalem artichoke is neither from Jerusalem nor an artichoke, and so the sunbelt growers have wisely renamed it sunchoke, after the sunbelt area in which it is grown.

These light brown, nutty-flavored, gnarled tubers, about the size of big walnuts, are sold prepackaged, 6–8 per bag. They can be eaten peeled, raw by themselves, as a crunchy addition to salads, added at the last minute to Chinese stir-fried vegetables, or cooked. (For a salad idea, see Salad chapter.)

Nutritional Value:
(4 small tubers raw)

Calories[4]	Protein	Carbohydrate	Iron
	2.3 gm	16.7 gm	3.4 mg

Sodium	Vitamin A	Vitamin C
—	—	4 mg

Taro-Dasheen In Hawaii, this tuberous vegetable is known as the taro, while in the southern United States it is called dasheen. It looks somewhat like a medium-size white potato, requires less cooking time than potatoes of equal size, and is used in the same way. Once cooked, the taro should be mealy and have a delicate, nutty flavor.

Nutritional Value:
(¾ cup cooked)

Calories	Protein	Carbohydrate	Iron
98	1.9 gm	23.7 gm	1.0 mg

Sodium	Vitamin A	Vitamin C
7 mg	820 I.U.	4 mg

[3] Any sauce that you would serve with noodles is fine: tomato sauce, pesto, vegetable sauce.

[4] Varies from 7 freshly harvested to 75 after long storage.

Recipes

The recipes and suggestions that follow will hopefully entice you into practicing the ideas of food preparation, handling, and nutrition that I've been talking about. The recipes vary from suggestions on what to do with a newly introduced vegetable, to enlarging the scope of what can be served as a raw vegetable, to a variety of suggestions for using vegetables as a main course dish.

PRESENTATION

An important part of any dish is the presentation. The care you've taken in selecting, preparing, and cooking the vegetables properly should be further reflected in the care with which they are presented. If it seems incongruous that someone who is concerned about nutrition should also be so concerned about beauty, it isn't. The most nutritious food is unpalatable and unacceptable when it's served in a careless or unattractive way.

This "pretty enough to eat" feeling is nowhere more in evidence than in Japan, where it's carried to an art form. One evening, my husband and I were having our first ceremonial meal in Kyoto. (The ceremonial dinner is a formal multi-course, drawn-out affair, revered especially in the crowded island of Japan because each customer has his own spacious room and garden for viewing.) The appetizer course was the prettiest arrangement of food I've ever seen. Inside a small handwoven basket, no larger than 3″×4″, were artfully placed, beautifully prepared seafoods and vegetables. After we had eaten the food and marveled at the beauty of it all, our hostess motioned for us to eat the *basket*, too. With some reluctance, since I had been brought up as a nonbasket eater, I sank my teeth into a side of that lovely basket. It was delicious and crunchy, woven out of

seaweed and truly almost too pretty to eat.

You may not want to go to the extent the Japanese do, but it's worth while to spend an extra moment selecting the proper colored plates that complement green beans or a well-shaped platter that does justice to your eggplant caviar. This isn't frivolous. It's personal at-home advertising that sells the food you've taken the time to prepare.

These recipes introduce you to my favorite ways of preparing vegetables and I hope they will act as a springboard to help you rethink some of your favorite dishes.

Colors to complement your palate

RAW VEGETABLE CRUDITÉS

After reading this far, you know that the best way to eat vegetables is as close to their raw state as possible. Americans accomplish this with the relish tray. In my childhood, it was a flat, longish, narrow glass dish filled with sticks of fresh vegetables, which were sometimes stuffed with cream cheese. With a little imagination in combining colors and in cutting pretty shapes, you can enhance the appeal of vegetables far beyond the relish dish.

One way to enhance *crudités* (French

word pronounced CRU-DA-TAY, meaning crisp, usually raw vegetables, eaten as an appetizer) is by artful *cutting*. I do not mean cutting radishes into rose petals. I believe a radish, even a cut one, should still look like a radish. Here are some suggestions:

Cucumbers With the tines of a fork, serrate the skin of a cucumber lengthwise. When you cut into rounds, each round will now have a fully curlicued, dainty outer edge.

Broccoli Stalk The stalk of broccoli is often thrown out. Instead, cut into very narrow and short pieces, or slice it horizontally across the stalk into natural star shapes.

Parsnips, Turnips, Jicama Since these lend themselves to be cut into strips, vary the strips by cutting some thick, some thin, and using a zigzag cutting gadget on others.

In restaurants, sometimes the French make artistic still life-like arrangements of fresh vegetables—with the vegetables poking out every which way. They serve this with a knife. You cut off what you want for yourself. This is a nice idea to do at home as well.

I saw another idea for unusual crudités on my first trip to Paris. I was invited to a restaurant along the Seine where the centerpieces were mammoth 2′ high arrangements of fresh vegetables. Little dishes of sauces were served in which to dip the vegetables.

I have since duplicated this Parisian wonder at home and it works equally well on a large scale for 50 people or just for 4. It makes either a great first course placed in the middle of the table as the edible centerpiece, or as an hors d'oeuvre.

Another beautiful presentation is to gather any small baskets you have around the house, line them with white linen, and serve each vegetable in its own basket. The color combinations of the vegetables and the natural woven straws are lovely.

Suggested Raw Vegetables:
Carrots, small cocktail size whole, or large carrots cut into thin strips
Mushrooms, whole or in thin slices
Fennel, strips or whole
Jicama, strips (See list of Specialty Vegetables)
Sunchoke, slices (See list of Specialty Vegetables)
Turnips, strips
Cauliflowerets
Red or Green Bell Peppers, chunks or strips
Cucumber, slices or rounds
Radishes, whole
Asparagus, whole
Cherry Tomatoes, whole
Zucchini, round slices
Parsnips, strips
Broccoli Flowerets, whole
Broccoli Stalks, thin, long strips (stalk is better if steamed first) or horizontal, natural star shapes

Develop good eating habits

FOR SMALL GATHERINGS

Use a large purple cabbage for the base. Gently flatten the outer leaves to make a well. Be careful not to crack off the leaves from the base. Place the fresh vegetables you've selected into the graceful crevices the cabbage naturally makes. Need more space? Pry the cabbage open more to obtain additional openings.

Small gatherings

This is a little like flower arranging, only better because you don't need any skills. If you feel all thumbs, remember that vegetables are so gorgeous, they practically arrange themselves with only a little nudging from you. Keep a few whole for decoration. Place a whole red pepper here, or a few whole mushrooms scattered there.

A restaurant in Rome accomplished somewhat the same effect using large round wine goblets filled with stalks of fresh vegetables that initially served as centerpieces and then as the appetizer while you ordered. The room was gray and white and the colorful vegetables made a wonderful fresh impression instead of the more expected rose in its vase. At home, it's a good way to save money on fresh flowers.

LARGE PARTIES OVER 14 PEOPLE:

Because this needs to be a bigger vegetable arrangement, one vegetable (the cabbage) as a base won't suffice. Instead, make your own "vegetable" base out of styrofoam covered with lettuce.

Use a rectangle of 2″ thick styrofoam as large as you think you might need for the number of people you're inviting; for 30 people, 16″×20″ is about right. Place the styrofoam base on a serving tray or piece of wood (this won't show) the same size as the styrofoam. With glue attach a hemispherical-shaped piece of styrofoam to the center of the rectangular base. This gives your base a height, which makes the vegetable arrangement look prettier—it's going to have peaks and valleys.

Using toothpicks, cover all visible styrofoam surfaces with pliable lettuce leaves. They should mold themselves to the form.

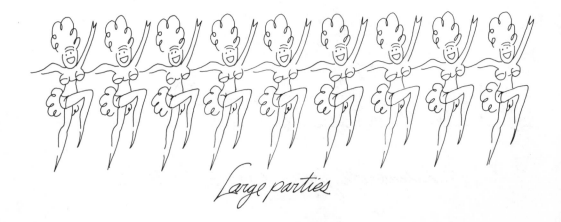

Large parties

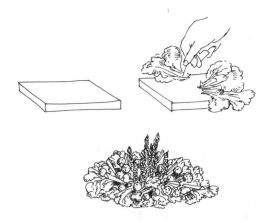

When the lettuce is attached all around and no styrofoam is peeking through, you're ready to start adding the vegetables. Some stalks, such as celery and carrots, may be actually pressed into holes in the styrofoam, and allowed to stick up to give additional height. Lay other vegetables around gracefully. It's fun, it doesn't take long, and the end result is beautiful as well as healthy and much nicer than more traditional hors d'oeuvres like sausages wrapped in crumbling pastry. Do the arranging as close as possible to the party, then refrigerate with a damp towel draped on top. Serve with a few ice cubes scattered about the base to keep the vegetables chilled.

DIPS

Ah . . . here's where the feeling of lightness can be ruined. People often serve rich cream dips (frequently sour cream, which is 88 per cent fat, is the base), and you fall into the trap of eating mostly dip surrounded by a little vegetable.

The essence of a healthful dip for fresh vegetables is one that's spicy and piquant enough so that you don't need too much.

ZANY PEANUT BUTTER DIP

Since everyone likes peanut butter, this dip is a sure winner. My friend Richard Kletter's thirtieth birthday party inspired it; for the first time, he was feeling older and, ironically,

the dip he created was genuine grown-up kid stuff. It's so delicious I guarantee you'll never see vegetables disappear as quickly as when people have this to dip them into.

Ingredients:

1 cup smooth old-fashioned peanut butter[5]

⅓ cup sesame oil

4 tablespoons soy sauce

2 tablespoons Worcestershire sauce

1⅓ cups orange juice (preferably from fresh oranges, but can be made from frozen concentrate)

6 tablespoons red wine vinegar

Juice 1 lemon (optional)

Makes 2 cups

1. Blend all ingredients in blender or food processor. If it doesn't taste quite tart enough, add some lemon juice. The dip should have a slightly runny consistency so that the dip almost, but not quite, runs off the vegetables.

2. Serve at room temperature. Refrigerated, this keeps for weeks.

LIGHT TARAMA DIP

Tarama, primarily a Greek or Turkish product, is an orange-colored paste made from the roes of mullet, carp, mackerel, or codfish.[6] Small 4-ounce jars of the already prepared paste can be purchased in delicatessens and specialty stores for about sixty cents, which gives a powerful wallop of flavor for very little money.

Throughout Greece, tarama is traditionally used to make taramasalata, a dip that literally swims in olive oil. I prefer this

---

[5] Using the old-fashioned peanut butter, where the oil separates, you can scrape off some of the excess oil from the top of the peanut butter before you begin.

[6] Although fish roe is fairly high in fat, it has a good proportion of unsaturated fats and fortunately, a little bit goes a long way.

lighter, healthier version that I devised with some Greek friends. You still have the distinctive tarama flavor, but without the traditional oily heaviness.

Ingredients:

  1 pint uncreamed, low-fat cottage cheese

  ½ cup buttermilk

  1 (4-ounce) jar tarama

  Juice 1 lemon

  1 tablespoon minced onion

Makes 2 cups

1. In blender or food processor, blend cottage cheese with buttermilk. Blend in 2 ounces tarama and see how this taste pleases you. (For some palates, 4 ounces tarama may be too strong.)

2. Add lemon juice, onions, and serve chilled. Keeps in refrigerator for a week.

HUMMUS

Hummus is a Middle Eastern dip that is often served with pita bread, but is great with raw vegetables as well. It can be made very simply by blending chick-peas with garlic. *Voilà!* You've got simple hummus. Or you can add other ingredients that give it more zest and color. Both ways are nice.

Ingredients:

  ½ cup sesame seed paste (tahini)[7]

  ⅓ cup water

  ¼ cup olive oil

  6 tablespoons lemon juice

  4 cloves garlic, mashed

  2 (15-ounce) cans chick-peas, drained,
    about 3½ cups

  ½ teaspoon cumin

  1 teaspoon ground coriander seeds

  5 scallions, chopped

  Paprika

Makes 5 cups

[7] Available in health food stores and increasingly in grocery stores.

1. In a processor or blender, blend first five ingredients.

2. Add next four ingredients and enough paprika to give the dip a slightly red color.

3. Serve at room temperature. Keeps in refrigerator for weeks.

SINGLE VEGETABLES AS APPETIZERS

One vegetable interestingly prepared makes a nice appetizer by itself.

Radish Take the radish. Nutritionally it offers very little (see Salad Score Sheet, page 133), but it's packed with a peppery flavor, so why not serve it instead of potato chips, which nobody needs? The Germans take big white radishes and with a vegetable spiraler, they cut them into a long series of connecting spirals. It's refreshing, pretty, and very inexpensive. The spiraler is now widely available for about $1.00 in gadget stores.

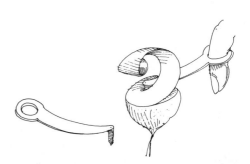

Fennel Another sort of offbeat vegetable I like to serve as is is fennel. It looks like hairy celery. Unfortunately it offers about as much nutrition as celery, but it makes up for that with very few calories and a surprising licorice-like flavor.

Cherry Tomatoes Little cherry tomatoes are fun to stuff. I think they are better stuffed and served raw; cooked, their frail skins tend to collapse. Cut off the tops. With the smallest melon ball scooper, remove the pulp and reserve. Fill the tomatoes with your favorite dip and chill. I fill mine with my mother's clam dip, which I've amended so it doesn't need cream cheese.

GLADYS' CLAM DIP

My mother has been making this as long as I can remember, and no family reunion is complete unless Gladys brings her clam dip. Mom has always used cream cheese and would perhaps think it heresy to make it any other way, but hoop cheese[8] works too, although the texture is different. With cream cheese you get a stiffer dip that goes well with crackers or celery; with hoop cheese it ends up with a softer consistency.

Ingredients:

  16 ounces hoop cheese or farmer cheese
  or
  16 ounces cream cheese
  1 (12-ounce) can minced clams, drained
  Worcestershire sauce
  Tabasco
  Paprika

Makes 2 cups

  1. Place the cheese of your choice in the blender or food processor. Add the drained minced clams and blend until smooth. If you need liquid, add some of the clam juice.
  2. When well blended, spike with as much Worcestershire and Tabasco sauce as you like.
  3. Refrigerate overnight so the flavors have a chance to penetrate. When the dip is room temperature and soft, fill tomatoes and sprinkle paprika on top.

MR. CHOW'S SPECIAL SEAWEED

Mr. Chow's is a wonderfully elegant Chinese restaurant located in Beverly Hills, London,

and New York City. One of its unique specialties is local greens that masquerade as "seaweed." It is served as an appetizer. I prefer serving it at home as a finger-food hors d'oeuvre, with a glass of white wine. As opposed to other snacks like crackers, this makes an excellent low calorie, preservative-free snack. Its unusual flavor and texture is sure to bring comment and people will invariably guess they're eating "seaweed." It's up to you to decide if you want to spill the beans.

Ingredients:

  Safflower oil, about 1 quart
  1 pound romaine
  or
  1 pound collard greens
  or
  2 pounds bok choy
  Salt and sugar (optional)

Makes 2–3 cups

  1. Heat safflower oil in wok or frying pan using enough oil to cover bottom with 3 to 4 inches. A wok is better for this because its slanted sides let you use less oil to achieve this depth.
  2. Take whichever greens you are using,[9] and starting at the lengthwise edge of the leaf, roll the whole leaf tightly into a firm little sausage roll. The tighter it's rolled, the easier it is to cut.
  3. With a sharp knife cut the rolled leaf into the thinnest horizontal strips possible. These should be thin, shred-like pieces.
  4. When the hot oil has a haze forming over it, drop in the greens. Stand back because initially the oil may spatter. Stir over high heat until the greens turn crisp; it is a somewhat delicate matter to get them crisp yet not burned. Remove crisp greens with slotted spoon and drain well on paper towels.

---

[8] Hoop cheese is a term used on the West Coast for what is called farmer cheese on the East Coast. It is essentially a cottage cheese made with less than 1 per cent fat.

[9] I prefer the collard greens because they have a stiffness that works well. I've found that bok choy isn't as suitable because it has more stalk than leaf.

5. While they are still warm, you could season them with a dash of salt and perhaps the smallest sprinkle of sugar.

At the restaurant, the "seaweed" is prepared in advance and then reheated to fill the orders. When I give parties, I cook it right before the guests arrive and then just pop it back into a preheated 350° F. oven for a moment's reheating.

Nutritionally, a minute amount of the greens' high vitamin A content is dissolved into the cooking oil, but no substantial losses are occurring during the cooking process because it is done so quickly. Afterward, however, the vitamin A can be destroyed by prolonged exposure to air, heat, and drying so, nutritionally speaking, this is not a great recipe to prepare in the morning for an evening party.

NEW YEAR'S "CAVIAR"

New Year's is a special time to celebrate and some do it with the traditional champagne served with caviar. Oh, those agonies of deciding whether to buy the pressed Russian beluga at $400 a pound or the fresh domestic at $200 a pound, if you can find it. (I feel those prices rising as quickly as I type this.)

If you feel like something special, but you aren't up to the steep prices of fresh caviar made from fish roe, I've got an alternative: "caviar" you make yourself from eggplant. Sometimes it is called poor man's caviar, but since nobody wants to be poor, I prefer thinking of it as vegetarian caviar. It's called "caviar" because it vaguely resembles caviar, but don't get your hopes up too high; this resembles the real thing in color only, a nice shade of gray-black. (And this is one of those instances where, lectures from seventh-grade home economists aside, food that is gray in color *can* be okay). The texture is as different from caviar as the flavor, but calling this eggplant purée caviar has been giving it extra glamour for years.

Ingredients:

2 (1-pound) eggplants, firm, shiny, and unblemished

⅓ cup oil

1 clove garlic, mashed

1 large onion, chopped

4 tomatoes, chopped and drained

2 tablespoons vinegar

Allspice, ginger, tomato paste (optional)

Salt and pepper to taste

Makes 3–4 cups

1. Peel eggplants and cut into chunks. Sauté in oil with garlic and onion until barely cooked.

2. Add tomatoes, vinegar and continue cooking for 15 minutes.

3. At this stage, some recipes call for a dash of allspice or ginger; that's purely a personal decision. But if you add these spices, you can use less salt. You could also add a few tablespoons of tomato paste, tasting as you go, so it doesn't get too "tomatoey."

What you end up with is a reasonably priced, totally vegetarian caviar. And you didn't sacrifice any fish to make their roe into caviar. As an added bonus, it keeps in the refrigerator for a week. I serve it on rye crackers.

DIANE'S ARTICHOKE PETALS

My friend Diane Galfas prepared this for a poolside party one spring. It was one of those bring-your-own-best-dish occasions in which four friends combined their talents. Everything from the grilled fish (over fennel), wild rice salad, and raspberry mousse was delicious, but the artichoke petals vegetable platter was certainly the most unusual.

Ingredients:

Leaves from 4 medium artichokes

2 cups vinaigrette dressing (see page 142)

Cherry tomatoes

Oil-cured black olives

¼ pound cooked shrimp, diced (optional)

Serves 4

1.   Prepare the artichokes by bluntly clipping the pointed petal edges with scissors. Place the artichokes in a steamer and cook for 30–35 minutes.

2.   While the artichokes are still hot, pour the 2 cups of vinaigrette dressing over them. At this stage, the artichokes can either be chilled and served cold later, or they can be held at room temperature and served warm.

3.   When cool enough to handle, pull petals from artichoke bottom and arrange on a serving platter.[10] For a spectacular effect, arrange the petals circularly on a large platter with the whole arrangement resembling one large petal. In the center, place cherry tomatoes, olives, and artichoke hearts. You could also arrange ingredients individually on small serving plates. Of course, you eat only the soft innermost end of the artichoke leaves.

OPTION: Boil a small amount of shrimp, dice them into small pieces, and marinate in the same vinaigrette dressing, but with some spicy mustard added for extra spike. Sprinkle the shrimp over the petals after they are arranged on the plate. The shrimp aren't a necessity, but add an interesting flavor.

I've included this recipe not for any nutritional brilliance of the artichoke (see Nutritional Guide to Fresh Vegetables, page 16), but because it is a spectacular deviation from the conventional way of dealing with the artichoke. Traditionally, the French have concentrated on the meaty hearts and have discarded the leaves (horrors!), or have stuffed the artichoke whole. This recipe represents a delicious way to save what in some cookbooks is described as waste.

Another option is to depetal a cooked artichoke and arrange the petals artfully around a dip, to be used as "scoopers" instead of crackers.

---

[10] When arranging the petals, expect to have leftover vinaigrette from bowl in which petals were marinated. Save it for another use.

SUMMER PASTA
(Made with a garden bouquet of vegetables)

One of the most delightful things to do with garden-fresh vegetables is to make a sauce for pasta. It's easy and delicious. You can use almost any combination of vegetables, or only one vegetable by itself; just keep in mind you want them to be slightly crunchy and if you're combining several you want to end up with a pleasing combination of colors. The suggested combination of zucchini, broccoli, beans, peas, tomatoes, and basil is Italian in inspiration.

I made this for the first time when a friend of mine, Judy Angelo, shared extra vegetables from her garden in New Jersey. It seemed a shame to do anything heavy and complicated to them . . . so, I took my favorite pasta and crowned it with the vegetables.

Ingredients:

4 cups total:

Shelled peas

Zucchini

Broccoli, flowerets and stalks

Carrots

Green beans

½ cup cherry tomatoes

½ cup olive oil

¼ cup minced onions

¼ cup chopped scallions

4 cloves garlic, pressed

½ pound prosciutto, diced finely (optional)

½ cup each chopped parsley and basil

Pepper to taste

1 pound pasta, cooked

1 cup grated Parmesan cheese or Romano

Serves 4 as main course or 6–8 as first course

1.   Dice the hard crunchy vegetables you are using (carrots, zucchini, broccoli) into small pieces. Dice enough so you have 4 cups

vegetables. (This figures out to be 1 cup of vegetable per person.) This task must be done by hand. No matter how much I like to use my food processor for everything, it doesn't do this well. The vegetables will be too small or too irregular and the sauce won't look as pretty as it should. Cut cherry tomatoes in half.

2. Heat olive oil in large skillet. Sauté onion, scallions, and garlic until wilted. At this stage you can add the prosciutto, but it is offered as an option.

3. Steam the diced vegetables, except cherry tomatoes, for about 3 minutes in steamer until cooked.

4. Add all vegetables to olive oil mixture. Add the cherry tomatoes last with parsley and basil. Season with pepper to taste. The aim here is just to reheat the vegetables as little as possible so they retain their color, texture, and vitamins. I've read innumerable variations on this recipe that all call for heavy cream at this last step. I can't fathom why anyone would want to encumber this ethereally light sauce with cream.

5. Toss cooked vegetables over 1 pound cooked pasta. I find this looks pretty if you combine 8 ounces spinach pasta and 8 ounces regular egg noodles.[11] Sprinkle with 1 cup grated well-aged Parmesan cheese, or use Romano if no well-aged Parmesan is available.

VEGETABLES STUFFED

Here's my alternative to the all too American habit of sitting down to a big piece of meat as an entree. I think one of the healthiest and also most satisfying alternatives is a wonderful vegetable, stuffed. People think of a green pepper stuffed, or a tomato, but I've added some unexpected vegetables, like cauliflower and eggplant. If you think for a

[11] Speaking of pretty color combinations with pasta, at Christmas I make this sauce using only broccoli and cherry tomatoes and toss it over spinach and tomato pasta. It looks beautiful and very festive.

Stuffed Vegetables

moment that your family or friends would feel cheated if you served "just a stuffed vegetable," look at what's in the stuffing. And this can be used with any stuffable vegetable.

Possible Candidates:

Green Bell Peppers	Cauliflower
Red Bell Peppers	Eggplant
Zucchini	Tomatoes

STANDARD STUFFING

2 medium onions, chopped fine

⅛ cup safflower oil

1 pound mushrooms, chopped (I make this an all-vegetarian dish. If you think that wouldn't have enough appeal for your family, you can use 1 pound ground beef or lamb instead.)

1 cup uncooked brown rice

1 tablespoon tomato paste, mixed with 1 cup water or chicken broth

3 tablespoons wheat germ

Pepper

Dash cinnamon

2 tablespoons chopped parsley

Pine nuts or walnuts (optional)

Makes enough stuffing for 4 peppers and 3 tomatoes

1. In a large skillet, sauté onions in oil until soft. Add mushrooms or meat and cook until soft (mushrooms) or brown (meat).

2. Add rice and tomato paste mixed with liquid. If you are stuffing tomatoes or zucchini, and will add their pulp to the stuffing, add 1/4–1/2 cup liquid here. Add wheat germ for extra crunchiness and for its vitamin E and B value. Season with pepper and a dash of cinnamon. That's the spice that makes the different taste.

3. Cook for 25 minutes, or until rice is almost done. (The rice will be cooked again in the vegetables.)

4. Add parsley. Here you could also add coarsely chopped pine nuts or walnuts for extra texture. Set aside.

VEGETABLES

It's important to choose handsome vegetables with good color and regular shapes. For example, a skinny, misshapen green pepper will look ugly, and will be a hard, if not impossible, shape to stuff. The preparation varies with the vegetable.

Handsome Vegetables

Tomatoes, Eggplant, and Zucchini need to have their pulp removed to make a shell for the stuffing. For the tomato, cut a little hat off the top and scrape out the inside with a spoon. Save the hat to be put back on after it's stuffed. For the zucchini and eggplant, cut in half lengthwise and scrape out pulp, making a shallow boat. Don't throw the pulp out. The pulp is mixed in with the cooked stuffing.

Stuff[12] the *uncooked* shells and bake in a greased dish for 20 minutes at 350° F. Some recipes may call for the baking to take longer . . . it isn't necessary. The rice stuffing is already almost cooked. You're just baking the vegetable. Keep the hat off the tomato during the baking. It cooks faster that way. Place it back on for the presentation.

Bell Peppers—Red and Green should have their tops cut off about 1″ down from the top. Save the tops to be placed back on later. Remove the seeds and small bit of pulp from the insides and discard. Steam the pepper tops and bottoms until just tender, about 3–5 minutes. Stuff the *cooked* shells, place in greased dish, and bake in 350° F. oven for 20 minutes.

Cauliflower has a very special look when you see it stuffed for the first time. It makes a glorious centerpiece.

This is the vegetable that requires a little extra dexterity to accomplish the stuffing. Cut off bottom to make a flat, steady base. Steam cauliflower whole in steamer till just tender, but still compact and firm—about 10 minutes. Let it cool.

To stuff, gently pull individual flowerets apart and, using a teaspoon filled with the stuffing, very gently tuck stuffing in between each floweret and down into the base of the cauliflower. This must be done with care or you'll end up holding a part of the cauliflower in your hand and there'll be a gaping hole left in the vegetable. Continue filling spaces in between all the flowerets until the entire head is stuffed. Any leftover stuffing can be put around the base.

If it looks slightly red-tinged and messy at this stage from the tomato paste, pour milk over it to clean it up and restore the white color.

Bake for 20 minutes in a 350° F. oven in casserole dish and serve on round platter.

---

[12] To stuff does not mean to jam down without breathing space. You'll end up with a soggy filling. Fill stuffing in gently with breathing space around.

Don't serve just one vegetable stuffed. Make a varied platter of assorted vegetables. It's no more work and is more interesting. A platter of these vegetables accompanied by a glass of wine and some crusty bread and I dare anyone to ask, "Where's the meat?"

CHRISTIANE'S VEGETABLE TORTILLAS

For weeks I tested vegetable recipes for this chapter. I peeled, steamed, and stuffed vegetables in every imaginable way with a Chilean friend as helper and witness to the madness. Then one night when I thought I was finished, she volunteered to make some vegetable tortillas.

Christiane's vegetable tortillas were so special they had to be included here. If you've lived close to Mexico, the name tortilla comes to mean a round, very thin, crepe-like, flat piece of ground meal, usually cornmeal. But in Spain, a tortilla is a thick, round, omelet-like pie.[13]

Christiane's Chilean grandmother, who originated this recipe, had taken the Spanish idea of a tortilla and refined it to something lighter and even better. These tortillas can be served as one would normally serve a quiche, as an appetizer or main course, but they are healthier in that they use no heavy cream, have no calorie-laden crust, and are easy enough for even a beginning cook to put together. In fact, Christiane learned how to make these when she was nine years old.

The tortillas are more distinctive if you use only one vegetable per tortilla. Cut the vegetables, except the potatoes, coarsely. If you purée them, you get a smoother, less interesting texture. The amounts called for should give you big mounds of vegetables. Don't panic, it's okay. They are the main ingredient of the tortilla.

Ingredients:

    1 medium onion, finely chopped

    1 clove garlic, chopped (or more if you like)

[13] In Italy this is called a frittata.

Olive oil (as little as possible)

4 eggs, room temperature

2 pounds carrots, cut coarsely

    or

1 (16-ounce) bunch spinach, coarsely chopped

    or

½ head lettuce, coarsely chopped in big pieces

    or

1½ pounds potatoes, cooked and cut into thin slices

⅓ cup olive oil

> *Makes 1 tortilla*
> *Serves 6 as main course*
> *or 10 as appetizer*

1. Sauté onions and garlic in as little oil as possible until wilted.

2. Separate eggs. Beat whites until stiff; gently fold in yolks. (Cholesterol-conscious cooks can omit three of the yolks.)

3. In a bowl, mix together the onions and prepared vegetables. Christiane says some of her Chilean friends cook the vegetables at this point, but the refreshing thing about her tortillas is the crunchiness, color, and flavor of the fresh, raw vegetables. (Potatoes, the exception, must be cooked.) The vegetables get warmed when they are added to the egg mixture later, but to cook them beforehand would be to create an entirely different sort of tortilla.

4. Pour vegetable mixture into eggs. This step is especially critical. Christiane says lots of people make tortillas, but never so soft or big as her grandmother's. The secret is mixing the vegetables and beating the eggs separately, and then mixing the two together lightly.

5. Using a 10″ frying pan, heat ⅓ cup olive oil till very hot and a haze forms over the oil.

6. Add the vegetable-egg mixture to the pan. It should fill the pan and be about 1½″ thick. With a rubber spatula, keep loosening the sides of the tortilla. Continuously shake the pan as you would in making an omelet or

crepe so the bottom of the tortilla doesn't stick.

7. When the bottom is nicely browned, the tortilla needs to be turned. This can be accomplished in one of two ways:

* Slip the tortilla onto a plate, hold the pan over the plate, and turn the plate upside down so that the tortilla goes back into the pan with the cooked side up.

* If the pan has a flat lid, holding the lid in place, turn the pan upside down and slip the tortilla from the lid back onto the pan.

This part can be tricky. Sometimes during the turning it breaks, but that's okay. Just turn it again and it will go back together as it's cooked more. Cook the other side until nicely browned—3–4 minutes.

8. It should be served hot and cut into wedges with a pie cutter.

The variations that Christiane's family have devised are practically endless. With potatoes, they combine parsley and grated cheese. Although I prefer a garden-type tortilla with just vegetables, her family often adds slices of ham to tortillas with green vegetables.

In Chile the tortilla is served as part of a meal, with meat or rice accompanying it, but my favorite is to serve a variety of different tortillas. One night Christiane made three separate tortillas (carrot, spinach, and lettuce) and it was truly a wonderful and healthy feast.

JO'S ADAPTATION OF POIRET'S EGGPLANT SOUP

I'm always receptive to suggestions about what would make an interesting segment for the television spots I do. A few years back in the middle of the kind of hot, sweltering summer that only New York City can provide (it was so hot your shoes stuck to the asphalt), I was stumped for an idea for that week's show. I wanted, preferably, to do something dark and cool and underground.

Poiret's eggplant soup.

My mother-in-law, Shirley Goodman Brown, who is the director of the Fashion Institute of Technology in New York City, came up with that week's inspiration. The Institute was currently hosting a costume exhibit of the French fashion designer Poiret. Shirley suggested that some of his recipes from the early 1900s might be interesting adapted for today, filmed with his extravagant sequined and laced creations in the background. The gallery was also well air-conditioned. I'm blessed with a mother-in-law who is usually right on target.

In the early 1900s, Poiret's sleek fashions caused a revolution. His fluid styling freed women from the corset and the bustle, but of necessity, also changed the eating style of the day as well. Diet and exercise came into vogue with his dresses, which revealed the body line, not unlike today's fashions.

I adapted a recipe of his for cream of eggplant soup, but by doing away with the thickeners he used, potatoes and heavy cream, hopefully I've kept women readers thin enough so that they could slip into his creations today.

Eggplants are available year round, but the best supply is in August and September, and since that often coincides with the last heat wave of the summer, that's a perfect time to experiment with Poiret's eggplant soup. Nutritionally, eggplant (see page 18) contains only a smattering of many of the major nutrients.

Ingredients:

    ½ cup minced onion

    ¼ cup minced celery

    2 tablespoons safflower oil, butter, or
        margarine

    2 small eggplants or 1 large (the larger
        ones are less tender and more bitter)

    Curry powder to taste

    1 tablespoon minced fresh basil

    1 tablespoon minced fresh thyme

    Pepper to taste

    3 cups chicken stock, fresh or canned

    ½ cup skim milk

                                Serves 5

1. In a large pan sauté minced onions and celery in oil until soft.

2. Skin eggplant, saving large pieces of the skin for garnish. Dice eggplant and add to onion and celery mixture. Simmer covered for 5–10 minutes until eggplant is tender.

3. Add dash of curry to taste. Using pestle, crush basil and thyme in a mortar to release their fragrance, add to pot. Pepper to taste. Add chicken stock and simmer for 15–30 minutes until the flavors are full and robust.

4. The next step can be done in several ways, depending on the equipment you have available. Using either a food mill or a colander, push the eggplant through till you end up with only liquid. Or easier yet, put into blender or food processor and purée until smooth. The trick at this stage is to get a creamy consistency naturally. If you've puréed it too much, you'll have to add potatoes for body and cream for creaminess. But if you watch the pot carefully as you're puréeing, you can capitalize on the natural creaminess of the vegetables and end up with a thick purée.

5. Add the skim milk. Transfer to a soup tureen and chill.

6. Cut eggplant skins into pretty shapes —squares, trapezoids—and float them on top of each soup bowl when serving.

One of the best things about this summer soup is that it takes just one eggplant (large)

or two (small) to serve 5 people. And each serving is under 75 calories. If Paul Poiret were alive today, I think he would approve.

CABBAGE

Remember the old walrus who said: "The time has come . . . to talk of many things: Of shoes—and ships—and sealing wax—of cabbages—and kings"? In connecting cabbages with kings, the walrus knew what he was talking about. Although the cabbage is often taken for granted, in terms of nutrition it ranks royally indeed. A cup of raw cabbage provides about 82 per cent of the Recommended Daily Allowance of vitamin C. For instance, 1 cup chopped raw cabbage contains:

	Vitamin C
Danish, Domestic	42 mg
Red, Domestic	55 mg
Savoy, Domestic	39 mg

Of the four popularly available varieties the best in terms of vitamin C is the red cabbage. It's also my favorite to eat raw, in salads or sliced and eaten as one would carrot sticks. Also, it's nice to cook the cabbage and use in dishes traditionally calling for white cabbage. When cooked, the red turns blue!

Common cabbage (that's its name, or Savoy) has crinkled leaves. I have a friend who is an artist and works with silk flowers she imports from France. She often uses "common" cabbage as a centerpiece and rightfully so. It's gorgeous. When buying cabbage, the outer leaves tell a lot. They should be of good color . . . red or green. If they are already wilted and yellowing, forget it. They should fit somewhat loosely on the head, but if there are too many loose outer leaves, avoid it; there will be too much waste. These leaves also tend to be tougher, but if you can use them, perhaps by cooking a bit longer to tenderize them, that's to your advantage, since they have the highest concentration of vitamins. We eat cabbage raw for good natural roughage and high vitamin C content. But vitamin C is a delicate vitamin. Sometimes you can cook it straight out of foods. You have a choice: You can either eat it raw, perhaps in coleslaw, or cooked as sauerkraut. Cooked, you actually tend to eat more because it's not so bulky. Here's one example where you probably end up with the same amount of vitamin C whether you eat a little bit raw or lots cooked.

I like to slice cabbage very thin—about the width of regular spaghetti and add it at the last minute to the broth of poached chicken. Cooked for just a few minutes, it retains its crunchy texture. The spaghetti-like character, but cabbage flavor, adds an interesting twist.

My favorite traditional way with cabbage comes from a Polish friend.

IRENE'S KAPUSTA

There's no doubt Irene's family is Polish. Whenever I phone, I am greeted by an incomprehensible barrage of Polish by her Polish mother and aunt. With three Polish cooks in the house, this is what they make for large gatherings; it is easy to prepare, delicious, and authentically Polish.

Ingredients:

2 pounds pork (any kind, loin or chop),
1 (1-pound) can pickled sauerkraut
2 pounds fresh white cabbage, shredded
    cubed
2 onions, sliced
4 tablespoons salt
1 teaspoon pepper

Serves 8 as main course

1. In a large, heavy-bottomed pot, mix ingredients with 1 cup water. Cook over low temperature for 2 hours.
2. When the kapusta is almost ready, make *smashka* (pronounced zazmaska). The smashka is a little like a French roux, but more flavorful because of the addition of the small quantities of bacon.

SMASHKA

5 slices bacon (use non-nitrite preserved
    bacon)
2 tablespoons flour

1. Fry the bacon and remove from pan and cut into cubes.
2. Add flour to bacon drippings until flour is well blended.
3. Add bacon cubes.
4. Add smashka to pot of cabbage. The smashka should thicken it to a nice consistency. Cook until warmed throughout. Now the kapusta is done and it's delicious, just like something from the old country.

Served with a good dark bread and a glass of red wine, this makes a hearty winter's meal.

POTATOES

The choice is between fresh, frozen, and dried flakes. Recently potatoes have been so maligned that I feel compelled to put the record straight . . . especially in view of the startlingly high statistics for the use of processed potatoes.

Just looking at potatoes, all speckled and spotted, they don't look like great beauties. But unprocessed, they are one of the most well-rounded vegetables. We usually think of citrus fruits in terms of supplying vitamin C, but the potato provides 20 per cent of the vitamin C in the U.S. food supply. One 4-ounce (that's small; most potatoes are 7–8 ounces) baked potato provides almost half the vitamin C an adult needs daily.

And then there's that myth that potatoes are fattening. One medium-sized baked potato has only 90 calories . . . or about the same as a pear or banana.

BAKED

If you want to bake a potato, don't use foil. That foil gets you a *steamed* potato. If you get your potatoes from a vegetable market where they think they are doing you a favor by wrapping them in foil, take it off. The foil ruins the texture. Just scrub the potato clean, put in a couple of steam vents on top, and bake in a 450° F. oven for 45 minutes.

MASHED

People love mashed potatoes, but think they have too many calories. One cup of fresh potato mashed with milk has only 137 calories, but it does lose some nutrients since the skin is removed.

STORAGE

When you bring home that bag of fresh potatoes, buy only what you'll be able to use in 10 days' time and show proper respect by storing them in a cool, dark, dry place, but not in the refrigerator—that's too moist.

PROCESSED

So far, I've been talking about fresh potatoes. The picture gets much trickier when the potatoes get processed. I was stunned to learn that by the 1980s, some people in the potato industry feel that processed potatoes will account for more than *75 per cent* of the total U.S. consumption. I think that's bad news for a variety of very serious nutritional reasons.

Frozen french fries are the most popular form of processed potatoes. This is what's served in most fast-food restaurants. They're fattening, averaging about 260 calories per 4-ounce serving. They never taste like homemade and they often don't taste like potatoes, just the oil they were fried in.

Instant potatoes in the form of flakes or granules are also very popular. And it turns out that you actually pay very little extra for all that convenience in terms of money. The cost of processing vs. fresh is about the same: an average of five cents per serving. But processed potatoes cost you in two very important ways. First, they rarely taste anything like the real thing. Second, and more disturbing, they usually have lost too much vitamin C in the processing.

A study done by the University of Idaho (appropriately) showed that reconstituted potato flakes contain approximately one quarter to *one twentieth* of the vitamin C which was originally in the raw potatoes from which they were produced. And in talking with the FDA, they told me they have no plans to demand that processors restore the vitamin C lost during processing.

I wonder at what point the processed product differs so dramatically in nutritional configuration from the fresh that it should no longer be called by the same name. It seems to me that when a processed product has less than one twentieth of an important vitamin inherent in the natural product, then the new product should not be able to call itself, in this instance, a potato, not even a *processed* potato, and not even an *imitation* potato. Unless the vitamins and minerals are put back, the new product is not even imitating the natural. Maybe we should invent a new word for products that are processed beyond nutritional recognition, so that consumers wouldn't be misled into thinking they are buying a real food product. How about phony food?

I remember a pathetic incident in my neighborhood grocery store one winter's morning. There was a senior citizen in badly worn clothes buying herself a box of processed potato flakes. I'm sure what she wanted was the warmth and comfort of some mashed potatoes on a cold winter's day, but what she was getting was the equivalent of white paste. As nicely as I could, I asked her why she was buying the box of artificial goo.

To reply, she opened her mouth and revealed no teeth. In a tired voice, she said she just wanted something soft and warm to eat and easy to fix. When I explained to her the nutritional problem in buying a phony food replacement, she just shrugged her shoulders. She was clearly too tired to think about such things. (For more on the elderly, see Chapter 11.)

I recommend that all of us, including that senior citizen, rely more on fresh potatoes. The convenience people in the potato racket get a leg up because they say that their product is so easy to use. What, I ask, could be easier or more convenient, than steaming some new potatoes in their skins for a few minutes? That's even a shorter time than required for the potato flakes that turn into potato pablum after cooking. It's also shorter than the time required to stick frozen fries into the oven. So steam some new potatoes, roll them in chopped parsley, and you have a delicious, pretty, and nutritional accompaniment to a meal. Or use the new conveniences in the kitchen to give you better nutrition as well. Use your microwave to bake a potato in 5–6 minutes.

As a matter of speaking, people sometimes use the phrase, "Oh, it's just small potatoes," to refer to something of no consequence. Don't be misled: potatoes are a food of real consequence.

POTATO TIP

* There's a new potato variety called "Butte" that's available to consumers now. It's 50 per cent higher in vitamin C and almost 20 per cent higher in protein than the famous Russet Burbank potato.

HEAVEN AND EARTH

This is a perfect dish to make in the first brisk days of autumn. The traditional German dish named Heaven and Earth is a baked casserole of apples and potatoes, but I call potato pancakes topped with fresh applesauce Heaven and Earth because it was a favorite my German grandmother made for me when I was little.

This is not the preferred way to deal with vegetables—shredding them up and then frying them—but we can keep the vitamin loss to a minimum by preparing this right at the time it's going to be eaten. The potatoes should not be prepared in advance and then held until dinnertime to be cooked.

POTATO PANCAKES

Ingredients:

1 pound potatoes
Vinegar
1 egg, beaten
1 tablespoon caraway seeds
2 teaspoons chopped shallots
Oil

Makes 6–8 pancakes
Serves 3–4

1. Peel and grate potatoes. This grating can be done with a food processor or by hand. Add a drop of vinegar to keep them white.

2. Add the egg, caraway seeds, and shallots. The cooking is the tricky part because you should fry them fast in a pan with very hot oil. If the oil is hot enough, it will start to sear the outside of the pancake instantly and not let the oil inside. Drop just enough batter on the pan to make a small, flat pancake. Keep flattening them out and turning them over until they are golden brown.

APPLESAUCE

While the pancakes are browning, make the applesauce. This is so simple I can't understand why anyone buys canned applesauce.

5 apples (McIntosh), peeled and cored
   and cut into pieces
Lemon juice
1/4 cup white wine, dry or sweet
Dash cinnamon
1/8 cup honey (optional)

Makes 2 cups

1. I prefer an apple with a slightly tart taste. It gives the applesauce more bite. After you've prepared the apples, squeeze a little lemon juice over them to keep them from turning dark.

2. Put apples in a heavy saucepan with white wine and a dash of cinnamon. The Germans also use ¼ cup sugar. If the apples you're using have a sweet taste naturally (which most do), don't use any sugar. If you demand a sweeter taste, use the honey.

3. Cook until apples are tender, about 5 minutes.

4. Have your grandmother serve you this warm with potato pancakes.

CORN ON THE COB IN SUMMERTIME

Each summer in August, the corn grows as high as an elephant's eye and the roadside stands abound with fresh corn. I love the whole idea of rushing home with a big supply to put on the stove. But aside from the yummy taste and the fun of eating it harmonica-style, what are we really getting? Basically, we're buying corn because it tastes good, adds variety, but not because of any special nutrients.

Several colleagues around NBC told me I disillusioned them when I did a TV segment on corn because they always felt they were doing something really healthy when they were eating it. Although corn does have some vitamin A, its real value is its contribution to the caloric intake in the form of corn tortilla or corn bread. Most people on American diets already have enough calories. One ear without dripping butter has 70 calories.

Since it has so few nutrients, you shouldn't worry about how to cook it, just relax and enjoy the taste. Probably the best way to cook corn is to drop the ears in a large pot of boiling water. When the water returns to a boil, the corn is cooked. Remember, this does not take long, because all you are cooking is the edible part of the corn, which is ¼″ thick at most.

Corn is one of those vegetables, really a grain, that gets nervous if it's not immediately eaten or chilled because it starts to turn to starch within an hour of picking. This process is slowed down a bit by refrigeration.

I have some friends who remember sweet corn right from the field from their childhood, and now they cheat by adding a little sugar to the boiling water. That doesn't interest me. Don't add salt either—it tends to toughen the kernels.

If you are feeling energetic and want to freeze some, remember it takes 4–6 ears just to yield 1 pint of frozen corn and with all the labor involved, the only way freezing makes any sense is if you have extra in your garden or you get it free from friends.

What vegetable is it that you throw away the outside, cook the inside, eat the outside, and throw away the inside?*

Corn on the cob.

* SOURCE: Action for Children's Television.

JIMMY CARTER'S WHITE HOUSE VEGETARIAN DINNER

The best vegetarian dinner I have ever eaten was the Food Day Dinner at the White House in the spring of 1977. The dinner was the highlight of a week of Food Day activities around the nation focusing attention on food-related issues ranging from questions of personal nutrition to controversies over global hunger.

The dinner for about thirty of the nation's food experts and activists was served in the Roosevelt Room, just a few steps from the Oval Office, and was a far cry from past years when issues about food and vegetarianism were often considered either not important enough or too controversial for politicians to touch. The dinner was not without controversy. Carter was scolded by the Cattlemen's Association for hosting the meatless meal, which the cattlemen considered "bizarre." They wanted equal time. An all-meat meal?

Taxpayers might be pleased to know that an invitation to the White House is not necessarily a free ride. If the President of the United States eats with you, then, for security reasons, the White House chef prepares the food and the White House usually picks up the tab. But if it's an honorary dinner, where the President is not eating, but may be coming for a drink during dinner (he sent his apple cider down ahead), then the group being honored often brings their own food and pays for it too.

This dinner was catered by Healthfood Caterers, Linda and Mitch Berliner of Maryland. The glamour and excitement of being in the White House rubbed off on the food. It was delicious and the table looked like a Thanksgiving cornucopia spread of fresh fruits, vegetables, and breads.

MENU

Black Bean Soup
Crunchy Broccoli Nut Casserole
Whole Wheat Muffins
Hummus
Guacamole
Vegetable Crudités
Fresh Fruits
Apple Cider

Most formal state dinner menus say something horrible about our nation's nutritional habits. They place far too much emphasis on red meat, heavy creams, and sugar.

This informal buffet dinner was an important step in a new direction. In an Estab-

lishment setting (under Roosevelt's portrait, no less), a totally vegetarian menu reigned supreme that previously might have been considered more typical of an "alternative" lifestyle. The vegetarian menu was a beautiful and practical demonstration that it is possible to eat healthfully using only vegetables, fruits, and grains. The very *existence* of a vegetarian menu in the White House questioned our national emphasis on animal sources of protein.

CRUNCHY BROCCOLI NUT CASSEROLE

Ingredients:

1½ cups uncooked brown rice
3 cups water
1–3 tablespoons oil
1 large onion, chopped
2 cloves garlic, minced
½ teaspoon dill weed
1 teaspoon thyme
1 teaspoon oregano
½ bunch parsley, minced
½ pound mushrooms, sliced
1 green pepper, seeded and sliced
1 bunch broccoli (about 2 pounds), with
    stalks trimmed into ½-inch slivers
½ cup cashews or other nuts (walnuts,
    pecans)
½ pound Swiss Gruyère cheese

1. In a heavy pan with tight-fitting lid, combine rice with water. Bring to a boil, reduce heat to a simmer, and cook covered until all water is absorbed, about 45 minutes.

2. In a large frying pan, heat oil. Combine onions, garlic, dill, thyme, and oregano in pan. When onions start to wilt, add parsley, mushrooms, green pepper, and broccoli. Stir often.

3. As soon as broccoli has changed to dark green color (it should be tender, but crisp), toss in nuts and remove from heat.

4. Preheat oven to 350° F. Spread cooked rice on bottom of a 12″×7″ oiled

casserole. Cover with vegetable-nut mixture. Grate cheese on top.

5. Bake about 15 minutes or less, until cheese is melted and bubbly.

TIPS

* When preparing a stew, instead of just placing the vegetables at random in the pot, try individual vegetable bundles. Cut the vegetables lengthwise in 4–5″ long pieces, arrange in lengthwise bundles, and secure with a string tied around them. When the stew is served, each person gets his or her own vegetable bundle. (These "bundles" don't need the added protection of cheese-cloth. The string holds them together just fine.)

* If you have leftover steamed vegetables that are beginning to fade, instead of throwing them out, throw them into a food processor or blender and make a vegetable purée.

It's the simplest:
Reheat the leftover vegetables and immediately before serving, purée them.

An unexpected side effect is that vegetables without their characteristic shape or texture often become unidentifiable. Recently, a friend served a puréed green vegetable that everyone guessed was green peppers; it was green beans.

* Since the outer leaves of romaine are apt to be bitter, some people don't enjoy eating them raw. A viewer suggested they be cut, cooked with a little water, and eaten as a vegetable with butter, or added to soups or stews. In Europe, where she grew up, she ate romaine only as a cooked vegetable, one head to a person, she said.

PROCESSED VEGETABLES: Yes, No, Maybe?

When buying vegetables, if you were confronted with vegetables only in their fresh form, selection would be a natural one. You'd buy fresh. But the presence of vegetables in their processed forms, canned and frozen, makes the choice more complicated. In order to answer questions about which vegetables really have the most to offer, it's necessary to take a close look at these processed forms.

 Frozen Vegetables

In the last 10 years, the sales of frozen potato products have increased 822 per cent and frozen peas have virtually replaced the fresh. If this trend continues, kids won't know what a real spud looks like and fresh peas in the pod will be considered exotics from the good old days.

Frozen Vegetables

A preference for frozen vegetables is developing because consumers want more convenience, and frozen foods fill this need. In an extensive consumer poll conducted by General Mills, women ranked ease and convenience as slightly more important to them than either nutrition or price. With this in mind, it seems logical that the use of fresh produce is creeping up only slightly, while frozen vegetables are making significant gains.

There are so many misconceptions about the use, reuse, storage, and handling of frozen vegetables, I thought it would be beneficial to explore some of the most common myths.

SEVEN COMMON MYTHS ABOUT FROZEN FOOD AND VEGETABLES

Myth 1: If the Product Feels Hard, It Is Frozen. Sounds reasonable, doesn't it? But it doesn't work that way. Temperature is actually a better indicator of when a product is really frozen than hardness. Water freezes at 32° F., but that's not the freezing temperature for other foodstuffs. Use a storage temperature of 0° F. as the indicator that the freezer is at the correct temperature. You can accomplish this simply by using a four-dollar freezer thermometer. Keep it in a highly visible place in the freezer compartment so you can check to be sure that the freezer is working as it should be. If it reads above 0° F., most vegetables won't be frozen, although they probably will feel hard to the touch.

Myth 2: Frozen Foods Can Be Held in Storage Almost Indefinitely. Most products can be held for 6 months and some for 1 year —provided temperature stays at 0° F. (See chart, page 66.) Unnecessarily long storage results in loss of nutrients, color, and texture.

Myth 3: Frozen Vegetables Should be Thawed Before Cooking. Nope. This just provides those nutrients with another chance for escape. If in doubt, follow the directions on the package and you won't thaw first.

Myth 4: Cooking is the Same for Frozen Vegetables as for Fresh. Frozen vegetables are commercially blanched prior to freezing. If you prepare them as you would raw vegetables, you'll get overcooked, discolored, soggy, less nutritious, tasteless vegetables.

Myth 5: Follow the Manufacturer's Advice on Cooking. They Know Best. In talking with a spokesman from the frozen food industry, it became readily apparent to me that they write those directions on the package by habit, not insight. For best results, cut their recommended cooking time at least in half. Steam the vegetables in a steamer or cook them in the smallest amount of water possible.

Myth 6: Frozen Vegetables Can't Be Refrozen. People are expected for dinner and they cancel at the last minute, or you live in New York City and the power goes out—what to do with those vegetables? If the vegetables are totally thawed, they should be cooked first and then refrozen. If they are partially thawed, but still have ice crystals, they may be refrozen without cooking, but should be used as soon as possible.

Myth 7: There Are No Additives in Frozen Vegetables. The freezing process does provide the preservation, but additives are still found in some instances. For example, vegetables like potatoes darken when exposed to air so antioxidants are used to prevent this enzymatic browning. Often this is ascorbic acid (vitamin C), sometimes it is BHT, which is under investigation. Unless the vegetables come with a sauce, the additives are usually not listed.

I admit to being a newcomer to and light user of frozen produce. The most I use are a few packages of frozen peas and soybeans. (Soybeans, which are rarely available fresh, are available frozen year round in stores selling oriental grocery items. To cook, steam them briefly, about 4 minutes, in their shells until they begin to soften. Serve at room temperature in their shells as a cocktail snack instead of peanuts or other nuts. Everyone shells his own.) But for most people who don't live right smack in the middle of Southern California's garden basket as I do, I've found after much investigation that frozen vegetables are the best alternative to the real thing; they retain their nutrients, color, and texture much better than vegetables processed in other ways.

So, it's somewhat distressing that although recent gains are up threefold from the fifties, frozen vegetables still have only 9 per cent of the market compared with 45 per cent for canned vegetables. This resistance to frozen foods comes mainly from the older generation, which grew up on canned goods and for whom frozen foods still seem "glamorous" and not for everyday consumption. But I predict that the next generation of consumers will be using frozen vegetables as the preferred processed form and will view canned vegetables as something of an antiquated processing form whose period of mass usefulness passed with the advent of home freezing space.

If people are beginning to use more frozen vegetables, a primary concern becomes whether they are increasing or decreasing their potential for better nutrition. The answers look very favorable.

The antiquated process

NUTRITION

As might be expected, both canned and frozen vegetables contain substantially less vitamins than comparably well handled, properly stored and cooked fresh produce. Frozen foods are higher in quality than canned goods because they don't undergo the high heat treatment necessary in the current canning processes. Nonetheless, when vegetables are frozen and then cooked, their contents of common vitamins almost invariably will be significantly lower than in comparably cooked fresh produce. This is contrary to what some frozen food manufacturers would have us believe (their slogan: "Frozen is just as good as fresh."). The combination of quick blanching (boiling) and prolonged storage causes frozen vegetables to lose on the average about 26 per cent of their vitamin C. It is also interesting that the nutritional loss in frozen foods occurs at a slower rate than in fresh produce. Here's a way to look at it: During storage in a typical

Vitamin Losses from Canning and Freezing

| Vegetables | Method of Preservation | Loss of Vitamins as Compared to Values of Fresh Vegetables | | | | |
		A (%)	B₁ (%)	B₂ (%)	Niacin (%)	C (%)
Asparagus, lima beans, brussels sprouts, cauliflower, green beans, broccoli, whole-kernel corn, green peas, potatoes (frozen, mashed, heated), leaf spinach	Frozen, boiled, and drained	Mean 12	20	24	24	26
Same as above, except broccoli, brussels sprouts, and cauliflower not included	Canned, drained solids	Mean 10	67	42	49	51

SOURCE: Owen Fennema, "Effects of Freeze-Preservation on Nutrients."

home refrigerator, fresh green beans can lose 50 per cent of their vitamin C in just 2 days, while frozen beans stored at 0° F. take 1 year for a similar loss.

Like their fresh counterparts, frozen vegetables contain more nutrients whole, uncut. In most cases, destruction of vitamin C is less than 10 per cent, but with the cut snap beans, corn, and chopped spinach, the loss ranges from 27–48 per cent. If you have a choice, it's wisest to buy frozen vegetables whole, not cut or fancy prepared.

When judging basic characteristics like taste and color in addition to nutritive properties, freezing, while not perfect, is superior to canning. The major disadvantage occurs at that moment when you bite into a frozen green bean and you get something less than a crunch and more like a mush. This unfortunate change in texture is caused when the cell walls are ruptured by ice crystals and is something that for now one has to accept as part of the freezing process. Even as much as I like frozen vegetables for what they are,

there is a time for all things and sometimes it's not the time for frozen vegetables or any other form of processed vegetable. For example, in the middle of a sweltering summer, *Vogue* magazine featured frozen vegetables in a big color spread. Their idea was how jazzy it is to plop frozen vegetables into a food processor and in a few moments have a cool summer soup. Aside from the fact that their suggested soup tasted bad, it was also poor timing to suggest that in the middle of summer their readers rush out and buy frozen foods when fresh produce is at the height of its growing season. How much more sense it would have made had the editors featured frozen vegetables when it was freezing outside and fresh crops weren't being harvested.

STORAGE

Often people buy frozen foods, shove them into their frozen food compartment, and

Storage

never check to see if they are really kept frozen. I talked about storage temperature in Myth 1, and it is important because a rise in storage temperature can cause the rate of vitamin degradation to accelerate. How well vegetables retain their nutrients and also their other positive aesthetic qualities is determined by storage temperature.

As a general rule, when the temperature increases, the life of the frozen food decreases.

If you have a freezer, but are resisting buying a freezer thermometer, there's another way of estimating your freezer temperature. From Cornell University we get the Ice Cream Test. Put a container of ice cream in the freezer. After a few hours, take it out and try spooning the ice cream from the container. If the ice cream is easy to spoon, the temperature in your freezer is probably between 21° and 30° F. If it is difficult to spoon, the temperature range is likely to be between 10° and 20° F. If the ice cream is hard and brick-like, and the spoon literally bounces off, the freezer temperature is where it should be at 0° F. If the temperature continues to be much warmer than 0° F., even when you set the dial colder, your freezer probably needs repair.

Storage is also one of the obvious disadvantages of frozen vegetables—once frozen they require a continuous expenditure of energy to remain frozen. But if you have freezer space you might as well take advantage of it. It uses less energy when it's kept relatively full and the proximity of the frozen packages tend to insulate each other.[1]

There's a variety of storage choices available for frozen foods depending on the kind of facility you have at home. The amount of time (days, months, years) I've listed after each type of facility may be a new way for

some of you to think about the lifespan of frozen foods. Don't get this confused with whether the food is still safe for human consumption or not. As long as frozen vegetables remain frozen, they are still safe, but they are losing quality. There's the story about Admiral Byrd, who is said to have frozen food at Antarctica and found it still safe some 30 years later. Safe, yes, but I'll bet there weren't any nutrients left.

Admiral Byrd

The storage guidelines I've put together are suggestions to use in determining the length of time frozen foods maintain maximum *nutrition* under the given conditions. If vegetables are stored longer than suggested at the same temperature, they will still be safe to eat, but they will have much less vitamin content and will be losing color and texture.

Your storage choices are:

Ice-cube Section of One-door Refrigerator— Days Use a freezer thermometer and you'll see that your reading is somewhere near 15°–20° F. That's too high to hold frozen foods for more than a *few days*. At this temperature, you don't really have a freezer situation. I have a friend in an old New York City rent-controlled apartment who has one of those tiny refrigerator contraptions that her landlord probably put in 50 years ago and forgot about. With her type of freezer space, she can't keep ice cream from melting, and although it's not as obvious, she can't keep vegetables frozen either.

[1] Speaking of energy, if you want to keep your bills down, buy a manual defrosting unit, not one of the snazzier automatic defrost refrigerator-freezers. The automatic defrosters use 60 per cent more energy than the ones you defrost yourself. Also, choose a refrigerator with the freezer on top. They use 50 per cent less energy than the bottom freezers.

Frozen Food Compartment of Conventional One-door Refrigerator—Weeks The temperature will probably be about 10°–15° F. You should use and replace these foods within *several weeks* at the most.

Freezer Compartment of a Two-door Combination Refrigerator Freezer—Months Temperature should and can be 0° F. or lower. If it's higher, adjust temperature control to colder reading, or call for service repair. At 0° F., many foods can be kept for a year (see chart). If for some reason (most likely having to do with an aged appliance) you can't keep it at zero, and it reads as high as 8° F., the vegetables should be used within several months at the most.

Separate Household Freezer—Months to 1 Year Temperature should maintain 0° F. or lower. Frozen foods can be maintained for up to 1 year (see chart).

Maximum Storage Time 0° F.

Vegetables	Months
Asparagus	6–8
Beans, green or wax	8–12
Beans, lima	12
Broccoli	12
Brussels sprouts	12
Carrots	12
Cauliflower	12
Corn, whole kernel	16
Eggplant	8–12
Greens	12
Mixed vegetables	8–12
Mushrooms	6–8
Okra	12
Peas, black-eyed, or green	12
Peppers	8–12
Potatoes, french-fried	2–3
Pumpkin, mashed	16
Squash, summer	8–12
Squash, winter	12
Sweet potatoes	12

This chart tends to be on the conservative side. That way you stand a better chance of using the food while it's still at its peak. You'll also notice various vegetables differ in storage stability. That's due to their chemical composition, rate of heat penetration, and enzyme inactivation.

By now you know that the best temperature for freezing is at least 0° F., or lower, and in a home situation you can keep most frozen vegetables for 6 months to 1 year at that temperature. I came across some information that shows how crucial temperature is from a commercial point of view. Commercial freezers maintained at −5° F. can keep cauliflower, green beans, peas, and spinach for *5 years* without measurable change in color, flavor, and chemical and physical characteristics, with most nutrients still present. Although you're not going to get those results at home, or even want to, a watchful eye on the temperature does ensure better results.

WASTE

Since frozen vegetables are ready to use with no waste involved, I was surprised when I read a study conducted by the University of Arizona which showed frozen vegetables had a very high rate of consumer waste. The investigating team found that many consumers lacked the knowledge necessary to make full use of frozen vegetables. It appears that whenever there was a question in the user's mind as to whether the once-frozen vegetables could be safely refrozen, or refrigerated, the easy solution was to throw the suspicious vegetables in the garbage. So if you're in doubt as to their use, or reuse, refer back to the list of myths again.

QUESTIONS ABOUT FUTURE USE

Concerned people question whether frozen foods and vegetables have a rosy future because the cost of keeping these products continually frozen escalates with the increasing cost of energy. Nutritionally speaking, the rosiest thing about frozen vegetables in the future is the anticipated increased use of the boil-in-the-bag pouches. This is the preferred packaging from a nutritional point of view because the vegetables never touch the water. Unfortunately, at this time it's still often slightly more expensive, but perhaps, as the volume of sales increases in this area, prices will become more competitive.

SHOPPING TIPS

* Check available freezer space before leaving home.

* When shopping, make your selection from the freezer last.

* Have all frozen foods packed together. They keep each other colder.

* Rattling a box of frozen vegetables tells you nothing. Some vegetables are processed loose. Others are already in a compact mass.

HOME FREEZING

My experiences with home freezing have been very successful. (See Buying Wholesale, page 122, Tomato Sauce.) In contrast to home canning, freezing needs little special equipment, and even less special knowledge. If you're considering processing vegetables and wonder which is the preferred method on the home front, canning and freezing nutritionally even out about the same. Decisions as to whether to freeze or can a particular vegetable depend on the vegetable itself, rather than nutritional considerations. Broccoli freezes well, while corn, at home, by cus-

tom more than anything else, is usually canned.

The slow freezing process done in home refrigerators or freezers can't begin to compare with the flash freezing done by commercial processors. The super-quick commercial flash-freezing process contributes to better nutrient retention because the rapidity of the process helps preserve the natural color, flavor, and texture and holds down oxidation of nutrients, especially vitamin C. On the home front, you don't have this advantage of speed and you lose nutrients by having to freeze the vegetables without the liquid in which they were blanched (frozen *with* this liquid, they would be mushy).

I thought I could short-cut the nutrient losses that occur with blanching by perhaps doing away with it. But it turns out blanching is a "must." It stops the enzymatic reaction, and if not checked, the enzymes continue working to change the color, the texture, and the odor and nutrient loss continues unabated. There is one positive thing you *can* do. Since you are freezing vegetables, in many instances, practically already cooked by the blanching process, do not cook them again when you defrost them; just warm them quickly.

For the novice, freezing is practically a foolproof method. Almost anyone can wrap something in plastic and plop it in the freezer. One of the worst problems is freezer burn, which happens when the package is not airtight.

You know how the experts tell you to get the air out of the bag before freezing? You can push and shove, but it's hard to be sure it's all gone. It becomes a mystery game . . . is it gone, or is it there? One trick I like (and your kids would probably enjoy helping out) is to put the item to be frozen into a bag, then, starting to close the bag, insert a straw, and suck the air out; fasten with a twist tie. Try it. It works.

Tips for Preparing Vegetables for Freezing

Vegetable	Preparation	Blanching For 1 Gallon Water	Blanching Minutes
ASPARAGUS Stalks, brittle and well colored; tight, compact tips	Cut or break off tender portions. Remove scales and wash thoroughly. Sort spears according to thickness. Leave whole or cut into 2" lengths.	30-40 medium spears	3
BEANS, GREEN, SNAP Deep color; tender fleshy pods; minimum of fiber; pod snaps when broken; beans in pod, not yet formed	Sort, wash, and snip stem ends; leave whole or cut into uniform lengths.	1 qt.	2
BEANS, LIMA Pods green, beans tender, mature but not overripe. Either large or small varieties	Shell, discard immature, old, or split beans.	3 cups	2
BEETS Young, tender; fast growing; first of the season	Remove tops, wash, and cook until tender. Remove skins and slice or dice.	No additional heating necessary	
BROCCOLI Compact, dark green heads; tender stalks free from woodiness	Wash and trim; peel large stems. Cut if desired.	3 cups, about 12 stalks	3 (small heads) 4 (large heads)
BRUSSELS SPROUTS Dark green, compact heads	Remove coarse outer leaves; wash and sort into small, medium, and large sizes.	3 cups	3 (small heads) 4 (medium heads) 5 (large heads)
CARROTS Young, tender, and small	Wash and peel; leave whole, slice, or dice.	3 cups or 6-8 small whole carrots	3
CAULIFLOWER Solid, well-formed heads; snow white except for purple variety	Trim, break into flowerets of uniform size, about 1" across; wash carefully and drain.	3 cups	3-4, depending on size of flowerets
CORN, SWEET Ears well developed, but kernels milky when tested with the thumbnail	Husk and remove silk; scald on the cob; after scalding, chill well. Package on the cob, or cut from cob (preferred).	2-4 ears depending on size	5 (small ears) 8 (medium ears) 10 (large ears)

Vegetable	Preparation	Amount	Yield
EGGPLANT Medium size; tender; seeds not prominent	Peel and cut into slices 1/3″ thick; to preserve natural color, soak for 5 min. in solution of 1/2 tsp. ascorbic acid and 1 qt. water.	1 medium	4
MIXED VEGETABLES	Combine previously prepared, tray-pack vegetables such as lima beans, peas, carrots, and sweet corn.		
MUSHROOMS White, tight caps, medium and small in size	Wash, trim, and sort according to size. Leave whole or slice. Soak for 5 min. in a solution of 1 tsp. lemon juice and 1 pt. water; drain and heat 2 cups mushrooms in 1 tbsp. fat in uncovered frying pan for about 3 min. Cool.	1 qt.	3 (slices) 3½ (quarters) 5 (whole, 1″ diameter)
ONIONS Top quality, full mature	Peel, wash, and chop.	No heat treatment	
PEAS Slightly immature, young, and sweet; bright green in color	Shell and wash.	2½ cups	
PEPPERS, GREEN Well formed, crisp, no soft spots	Use cooked: Wash, remove seeds; halve and slice or dice. For raw use: Wash, remove seeds, and chop.	3 medium No heat treatment	2
PUMPKIN Full-colored, mature, fine texture	Wash, cut in halves, and scoop out seeds. Place cut side down on baking sheet and bake, 350°-400° F. until tender. Scoop out pulp, mash, and cool.	No additional heating necessary Leave 1″ headspace	
RUTABAGAS Young, tender	Wash, peel, and cut into 1/2″ cubes.	3 cups	2
SPINACH, CHARD, OTHER GREENS Small, tender leaves	Remove thick stems and wash carefully.	1 qt. Leave 1″ headspace	2½
SQUASH Summer: tender rind, small size	Wash, cut in 1/4″-1/2″ slices or 1″ cubes	3 cups	3-4
SQUASH Winter: fully mature with hard rind	Wash, cut in halves, and scoop out seeds. Place cut side down on baking sheet and bake at 350°-400° F. until tender. Scoop out pulp, mash, and cool.	No additional heating necessary Leave 1″ headspace	

Tips for Preparing Vegetables for Freezing (continued)

| Vegetable | Preparation | Blanching | |
		For 1 Gallon Water	Minutes
TOMATOES, STEWED Ripe, free of blemish	Tomatoes for slicing and salads are unsatisfactory frozen under home freezing conditions.		
	Wash and cut into pieces and freeze, or simmer until table ready.	No additional heating necessary	3
Tomato juice	Wash, core, cut into pieces. Heat to boiling and strain.	No additional heating necessary. Leave 1" headspace	
TURNIPS Young, tender	Wash, peel, and slice or dice.	3 cups	

ADDITIONAL READING

There are a variety of printed pamphlets available on the subject of home freezing that can undoubtedly make your life easier.

1. There is, of course, the *Blue Book,* published by the Ball Corporation. Edition 30 of the *Blue Book* is $2.50, available from the Ball Corporation, Box 3300, Muncie, Indiana 47302. The *Blue Book* is devoted primarily to canning, but has an excellent fourteen-page section on freezing. There is also a Spanish edition.

2. From Cornell University, there's the *Handbook for Freezing Foods,* a straightforward blue and white sixty-page pamphlet which gives step-by-step procedures not only for vegetables but for fruit, meat, game, poultry, fish, and shellfish as well. It also includes numerous tips. For example: "Not more than 20 pounds of food should be frozen at one time in a 10-cubic-foot freezer that will hold 300 pounds of food." For a copy of *Handbook for Freezing Foods,* write Mailing Room A, 7 Research Park, Cornell University, Ithaca, New York 14853.

3. The U. S. Department of Agriculture has a forty-eight-page black and white pamphlet, *Home Freezing of Fruits and Vegetables.* It's available from the Superintendent of Documents, U. S. Government Printing Office, Washington, D.C. 20402. Ask for Home and Garden Bulletin No. 10.

Canned Vegetables

There are two things to be said for canned foods in general: They require no refrigeration and have an extended shelf life. But that's about it for the good side. Their primary drawback, besides the loss of color, texture, and fragrance, is the destruction of nutrients. The chart (on page 63) shows in a very clear way that water-soluble vitamins (C, B_1, B_2, and niacin, some of the main reasons we eat vegetables), are retained much better in freezing than in canning. This makes sense because in canning these water-soluble vitamins are leeched out of the vegetable into the water. When the can is opened, the vegetable is drained of its juice and there go the leeched nutrients. Although the comparative nutrient losses wouldn't be so dramatic if the juice from the canned vegetables were used, you could still expect the figures to show additional losses for the canned because of the heat treatment they are subjected to as part of the canning process. Also, this chart doesn't take into account the nutrient losses that routinely occur with the recooking most people do after opening a can of vegetables. The cooking preparation prior to canning often destroys up to 30 per cent of the vitamin C. With recooking, as is often the case in a casserole that calls for baking vegetables, the loss of vitamin C may be as high as 75 per cent.

Canned vegetables, to their detriment and yours, also often have salt and sugar added, both of which are usually inadequately labeled. So, you ask, where is the canned vegetable's right place in our everyday meals? I tally it up this way:

Canned Vegetables

Aesthetic losses
Nutritional losses
Additions of salt and sugar

Looking at it from this perspective, I figure their place in one's meals is a small place, indeed, if at all.

Canned Vegetables

Significant losses also occur during the storage process and since there's not much you can do about the loss of nutrients during the canning process, I'm concentrating on what you can do about your storage conditions.

STORAGE

Nobody talks too much about this, especially the manufacturers, who want to make canned goods seem so carefree you can push them into any handy cupboard. But properly stored you get a much better product.

Where should canned goods be stored?

Although the manufacturers say almost any place, they then hedge a bit by adding that a cool, dry cellar is most suitable. When was the last time you saw a cool, dry cellar?

Since the best place for storage is probably not available, the second best thing is to know where canned goods should *not* be stored: avoid overheated garages in the summer, and radiators, hot water pipes, ovens, and other heat-producing devices. Avoid storage over 75° F. The best temperature is between 50° and 60° F.

How long will they keep?

Although the manufacturers say indefinitely (if nothing happens to the container), it is best to have a regular turnover at least once a year.

Does outside damage indicate inside damage?

As long as the can does not leak, outside damage does not affect the insides. Don't fool around with any container that is leaking or bulging; it could contain toxins that cause botulism, a food poisoning that is often fatal. Throw the can and all its contents away.

Help! My canned goods were stored in a cold place and they froze. Now they've thawed. Can I still use them?

Yes, although you can expect that vegetables in a creamy sauce might curdle or separate and you can also expect a slight further breakdown of texture.

Is it safe to leave the unused portion of canned goods in the can after it's opened?

Although it's safe, I wouldn't recommend it because the tinny flavor of the can continues to permeate the vegetables.

Is it safe to cook right in the can?

I asked a spokesman from the Canner's Association this question and in an unsolicited, enthusiastic testimonial about canned goods in general, he also revealed that his wife usually cooked their dinner this way! In the cans, on the stove! Attractive it isn't, but it turns out to be safe. As long as the can is open, you can cook in it on top of the stove or in the oven.

The canners are in somewhat of a bind because even when they *are* able to make improvements in their product, their clientele expects a canned vegetable to taste a distinctive way. There was a story several years ago about an advancement in processing techniques that allowed canners to take the peas from the vine and process them within the hour, obviously increasing the nutrition and the freshness of their product. The problem, according to the story, was that the freshly canned peas were downgraded by government inspectors and not accepted by consumers. The old double bind. Inspectors and consumers said they had an off-flavor they weren't accustomed to—the off-flavor, one suspects, of a fresh pea. So, ironically, to upgrade the product, the processors let the peas sit in the open air for an additional few hours till they assumed more of the distinctive, and I think peculiar, flavor consumers were accustomed to, and also lost some of their nutrition as well.

The only bright point I see on the horizon for canned vegetables is that they may not be in cans much longer. The metal can we are used to may soon be replaced by a thin-skinned plastic container that is now under development. The new containers have the advantage of requiring less intense heat than their metal counterparts to cook the vegetables. The potential advantage to the consumer is that fewer nutrients will be destroyed. Because the plastic weighs much less, there eventually should be a transportation savings, but so far the packages themselves are so expensive to produce, there aren't any savings for anyone.

The only canned vegetables I use with any regularity are beets, and it turns out that I'm not unusual, since 90 per cent of the beets sold in this country are canned. Because beets are so colorful, you don't lose color by opting for them canned, and they are tasty and easy to use. Nutritionally, as with most canned vegetables, you get less vitamin C, more salt, and a little increase in iron from the canning process. Beets, in general, are not an item high in nutrients, so their loss in the processing is not a major concern. All that "Eat your beets, dear. They're good for you," would be better saved for vegetables higher in nutrients.

BORSCH

I use canned beets to make a quick borsch that my Russian husband loves. I make this in the summer and it packs well in a thermos for picnics.

Ingredients:

  1 quart buttermilk (made from skim milk)
  1 (8-ounce) can beets, with liquid

GARNISH

  1 cucumber, sliced
  1 hard-boiled egg, chopped
  Fresh chives, chopped
  Fresh dill, chopped
  Yoghurt

Serves 4

Combine buttermilk and beets in food processor or blender until beet mixture is smooth and creamy and the consistency you like your soup. Chill. When ready to serve, accompany this with little saucers of the garnish. I've found that yoghurt dabbled on the top tastes just as good as the more traditional sour cream.

HOME CANNING

A few years back, with some extra time in the middle of summer, I decided I wanted to put some food by for the winter, even though I was living in New York City with two grocery stores right around the corner.

It was my grandmother's genes in me speaking up, for as a child I remember spending many days in our large all-white tile kitchen, watching Grandmother doing her canning. Raspberry preserves were her specialty, and to this day, I love raspberries with a fierceness that speaks of something other than raspberries. So, on that day, I was remembering back to Grandmother and I envisioned a whole row of little jars filled with foods of wonderful colors.

Well, to say the event was a misadventure is an understatement. Aside from some obvious drawbacks, such as not having my own garden, which would have made more economical sense, I compounded the trouble by buying large canning jars that wouldn't fit inside the largest pot I had for boiling water. That was also the year the stores sold out of lids. I found that it takes more than genes to

Home Canning

do home canning. It's an art form and not many city-bred people my age know the first thing about it or how to proceed safely.

For anyone interested, I recommend three booklets.

1. The *Blue Book,* published by the Ball Corporation, which manufactures jars and lids, is without doubt the authority on the subject. It covers all the basics in detail, including one section on diet foods. One of the special sections I like best gives instructions on how to plan a garden for a family of 6; it tells how much your yield will be and how much you'll have to can. For gardening families, this garden guide alone is worth the $2.50 price of the book. To order a copy, write to Ball Corporation, Box 3300, Muncie, Indiana 47302.

2. I'm sneaking in a comment here about the canning of fruits because this is the only area in which the *Blue Book* seems weak. In the making of jams and jellies, sugar, as the booklet points out, does help in the gel formation, contributes to flavor, and serves as a preserving agent. But the ratio given in the *Blue Book* is usually 4 cups fruit juice to 3 cups sugar. If you're interested in making jams and jellies from your own home-grown fruits and want to use less sugar, request a free copy of leaflet ✗2992, *Making Jams and Jellies with Little and No Sugar,* from the University of California Cooperative Extension Service, 155 West Washington Boulevard, Los Angeles, California 90015.

3. The U. S. Department of Agriculture puts out *Home Canning of Fruits and Vegetables,* one of those basic, old-fashioned-looking pamphlets that's less inspiring than the Ball *Blue Book,* but supplies the basic how, what, and why of canning. Send twenty cents to the Superintendent of Documents, U. S. Government Printing Office, Washington, D.C. 20402. The stock number is 0100-1595.

 Comparing Prices

Wouldn't it be great if there was some clear-cut price break so one would always know which vegetables were the best buy? No such luck. Although frozen vegetables have the reputation of being more expensive, that's not necessarily the case. Neither canned nor frozen vegetables offer any consistent price advantage. In a casual survey, I found that cost per serving was more related to brand and package size than to the processing technique.

At the time I compared spinach, I found frozen spinach was the best buy at eleven cents a serving, followed by canned at thirteen cents and fresh at nearly twenty-five cents. That's the price story, but taste-wise, I'm not at all surprised if little kids hate spinach when given anything but the fresh. Although the frozen was the price bargain, to me it tasted as much like spinach as green cardboard, and the canned isn't even worth mentioning. Maybe that's why the USDA palms the canned stuff off on the kids at school lunch? So, don't always go for the best price. If price must be the main criterion, in some instances you'd do better to select another vegetable.

Certain frozen vegetables, such as peas, do cost much less than their fresh counterpart. To compute the real price of a pound of fresh peas, you must figure in the 15 minutes shelling time and the fact that, after discarding the shells, you end up with less than ½ pound of peas. So you're actually paying at least double the marked price for the fresh peas, plus your labor.

If you love the process and find shelling peas a joyful reminiscence of summers past, well, that's fine and it counts for something. For me it counts for quite a lot since peas in the pod always remind me of my brother, whose favorite things include having his back rubbed, eating sunflower seeds, and snacking on fresh peas. But if you don't have such sentimental attachment to shelling peas, and since peas of good color and excellent taste can be purchased cheaper frozen, with no labor and no waste, here's clearly a good way to save time and money. (Of course, frozen peas suffer the same nutrient loss as other vegetables.)

You can also pay as much as *100 per cent* extra for frozen vegetables that come with sauces. In my local supermarket, I noticed recently that broccoli au gratin (that's melted cheese on top) sold for double the price of broccoli. Yeeks! A 100 per cent price increase for a teaspoon of cheese. Or how about frozen carrots that cost almost 80 per cent more with a brown sugar glaze?

If you are tempted to buy a package of already combined frozen vegetables, remember you can often get twice as many for the same money when you do the combining yourself. And when the manufacturer calls the combination by a fancy name like Broccoli Florentine (mixed broccoli, carrots, and onions) or Vegetables Monterey (broccoli, cauliflower, red pepper), watch out. Be prepared to pay 20 per cent more for the fancy name.

If you're trying to compare cost of frozen to canned, there's a simple rule: there are approximately the same number of servings in the standard 9- or 10-ounce frozen package as there are in the 16-ounce can of the same vegetable.

One thing I've found helpful in comparing price and quality are dry runs. They work great with vegetables, or anything in the store. Here's how to do it: go to your usual grocery store, but armed only with pad and pencil and maybe the Vegetable Cost Chart (page 76), but no money. Without being bothered by pushing a cart and without having to make selections for that evening's meal, you can relax and compare prices and nutritional information. Once I have the time to read labels instead of just grabbing, I find it's a real eye opener. I don't usually do this in any systematic way, but the Vegetable Cost Chart would be helpful on a vegetable comparison pricing dry run.

SUPERMARKETING: CHOOSING VEGETABLES ON THE BASIS OF COST

The Vegetable Cost Chart is designed to help you figure quickly and accurately the cost per serving. For a specific vegetable at given prices, you can determine which is the best buy—fresh, canned, frozen, or dried—and at what price different forms of the same vegetable will be the best buy. This is not something you'd want to do with every shopping trip, but done once or twice, it's helpful.

Servings per unit are based on ½ cup for all cooked vegetables other than cooked dried beans, for which the serving per unit is ¾ cup. (The servings per unit of fresh vegetables are based on high quality produce. If the quality is poor, more will be discarded, resulting in fewer servings per pound.)

Vegetable Cost

Vegetable	Unit	Servings Per Unit	Cost Per Unit	Cost Per Serving
ASPARAGUS				
fresh	1 lb.	3	————	————
canned	14-15 oz.	3-4	————	————
frozen	10 oz.	3	————	————
BEANS, LIMA				
fresh, in pod	1 lb.	2	————	————
fresh, shelled	1 lb.	4-5	————	————
canned	16-17 oz.	4	————	————
frozen	10 oz.	3	————	————
BEANS, NAVY, KIDNEY, AND LIMA				
canned	15-16 oz.	3	————	————
dried	1 lb.	8-9	————	————
BEANS, SNAP				
fresh	1 lb.	4-5	————	————
canned	15-16 oz.	4	————	————
frozen	9-10 oz.	3	————	————
BEETS				
fresh	1 lb.	4	————	————
fresh	bunch	3	————	————
canned	16-17 oz.	4	————	————
BROCCOLI				
fresh	1 lb.	3	————	————
frozen	10 oz.	3	————	————
BRUSSELS SPROUTS				
fresh	1 lb.	5	————	————
frozen	10 oz.	3	————	————
CABBAGE				
fresh	1 lb. cooked	4	————	————
	1 lb. raw	8	————	————
CARROTS				
fresh	1 lb.	4	————	————
fresh	bunch	3	————	————
canned	16-17 oz.	4	————	————
CAULIFLOWER				
fresh	1 lb.	4-5	————	————
frozen	10 oz.	3	————	————
CORN, SWEET				
fresh	1/2 doz.	6	————	————
canned, cream-style	16-17 oz.	4	————	————
canned, whole kernel	16-17 oz.	3	————	————
frozen	10 oz.	3	————	————
KALE				
fresh, trimmed	10 oz.	3	————	————

Vegetable Cost (continued)

Vegetable	Unit	Servings Per Unit	Cost Per Unit	Cost Per Serving
PEAS				
fresh	1 lb.	2	_____	_____
canned	16-17 oz.	4	_____	_____
frozen	10 oz.	3	_____	_____
POTATOES				
fresh	1 lb.	3	_____	_____
canned	16-17 oz.	4	_____	_____
SPINACH				
fresh	1 lb. bulk or 10 oz. package	3	_____	_____
canned	15 oz.	4	_____	_____
frozen	12 oz.	4	_____	_____
SQUASH				
fresh, summer	1 lb.	4	_____	_____
fresh, winter	1 lb.	2	_____	_____
frozen	1 lb.	4	_____	_____
SWEET POTATOES				
fresh	1 lb.	3	_____	_____
canned	18 oz. vacuum	4-5	_____	_____
TOMATOES				
fresh	1 lb.	3-4	_____	_____
canned, juice	46 oz.	12	_____	_____
canned, whole	16-17 oz.	4	_____	_____

SOURCE: *Choosing Vegetables on the Basis of Cost*, Cooperative Extension, Division of Agricultural Sciences, University of California at Berkeley.

3
FRUITS:
Naturally Sweet

I'm a pushover for fresh fruits. Just mentioning their names can cause me to salivate . . . papayas, mangoes, kiwis, tangerines, watermelons. I like everything about them: their colors; the taste; the wonderful memories of eating them in the past, and the pleasure of looking forward to them in the future.

Although I can't understand it, people in this country seem to be losing their taste for fresh fruits. Curiously, this is occurring just at a time when consumers also are very interested in convenient, healthful foods. Fruits, already conveniently packaged for travel in their own skins, in most instances require no cooking and are delicious to eat out of hand.

It's somewhat ironic that in the years since 1950 consumption of every major fresh fruit has declined, and declined dramatically in some instances. I was surprised when I came across this information. I thought that, with friendly encouragement from the Sunkist people and the Washington apple growers, we were doing our share of eating our nation's fruits. In fact, our consumption of fresh fruits is one fourth that of Europeans, for whom a slice of fresh fruit is considered a wonderful and ample dessert. West Germany, Italy, Spain, and Switzerland all have a rate of consumption in excess of 200 pounds per person per year; East Germany, 265; France, 167; yet in the United States, each of us consumes only 86 pounds.

One of the peculiarities of fresh fruit consumption in this country is that other countries consume their local production in large numbers and we don't. For example, I never thought of the Japanese in terms of oranges, but, after us, they are the world's second-largest citrus producer. The average Japanese eats over 60 pounds of fresh citrus a year, compared to our 30 pounds. The best indication of the value the Japanese place on oranges is that at their temples the huge centuries-old Buddhas usually have offerings of

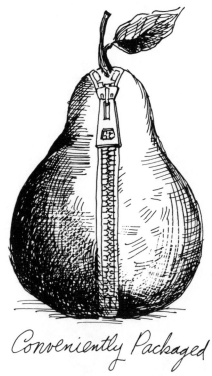

Conveniently Packaged

fresh oranges placed in their laps. The United States is the world's largest producer of oranges and we claim they're one of our most popular fruits, but we eat less than half the Japanese consumption and would hardly think of offering them in reverence to a spiritual god.

When it comes to apples, Hungary is the world's second-largest apple producer and Hungarians each eat 130 pounds of apples a year. West Germans are the third-largest producers and they consume 65 pounds of fresh apples per person. Yet in the United States, the world's largest producer, the consumption of apples, which ironically, are also one of our most popular fruits, is a mere 19 pounds.

The decline of fruit consumption is especially apparent in our aging population, because their diet is often deficient in vitamins A and C. As older people find themselves without the economic means or the physical ability to prepare a meal for themselves, fresh fruits and vegetables are often the first items to be eliminated. They've been taught all their lives that if they're good, they get a piece of candy or cake, and now the sweet component too often becomes the only caress that remains. A gerontologist I know who visits older people has found, in some instances, the only food in the home to be sweets. How much more sense it would make nutritionally if these people had learned early in their lives to derive the same amount of pleasure from a piece of sweet fruit.

So far, I've been talking about a decline in fruit consumption, but what about people who are cutting fruits out altogether? Recently, a friend told me, matter-of-factly, that on his new regime, he was cutting out candy, cakes, *and* fruits. Although he had no medical reason (like diabetes) for his regime, his reasoning was that in eating fruits, he was eating some sugar in the form of fructose, and that was pretty much the same as eating a Milky Way.

I think it's great my friend was cutting down on sugar, but his cutting out fruits, too, was a misplaced good intention. Although the fructose in fruits eventually acts the same way in the body as sucrose in commercial sugar, in fruits, it is in a highly diluted state accompanied by a wide variety of useful minerals and valuable nutrients.

Fruits make a contribution to one's overall nutrition entirely different from eating a sweet candy or cake, which offers no significant amount of nutrients in addition to the sugar (for nutrients supplied by fruits, see chart, page 89).

Fruits also have such a high percentage of water that the effect of their sugar content is far less deleterious on the body, and on the teeth in particular, than the straight shot of sugar one gets from candy. Because of fruits' high water content, during the California drought, it was suggested somewhat facetiously that people eat melons instead of drinking water. For example, the casaba melon is 92 per cent water; the other 8 per cent is made up of minerals, nutrients, protein, and also some fructose. I think it would be really interesting if fruits were labeled to indicate their sugar content percent-

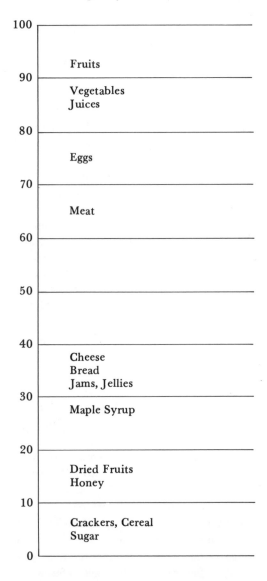

Percentage of Water Content

100	
90	Fruits
	Vegetables
	Juices
80	
	Eggs
70	
	Meat
60	
50	
40	
	Cheese
	Bread
	Jams, Jellies
30	Maple Syrup
20	
	Dried Fruits
	Honey
10	
	Crackers, Cereal
	Sugar
0	

age. They aren't. But common sense tells you a fruit has much less sugar than a candy bar because its high water content coupled with minerals and vitamins doesn't leave *that* much room for sugar.

One side benefit of eating more fruits is that you naturally decrease your consumption of other highly sugared products. Because fruits are often eaten for something sweet, they lend themselves to becoming desserts and snacks. Most everyone would benefit from developing the habit of reaching for a tangerine instead of a Hershey's chocolate bar.

 ## Buying Fresh Fruits

I find that the most seductive area in the fresh produce section in my neighborhood grocery store is the area where the fruits have been cut in half and displayed. Usually it's melons—honeydew, casaba, cantaloupe, watermelon—and the colorful mix of reds, oranges, and greens is a wonderful sight. How handy and convenient, one is apt to think when reaching for a precut fruit. Maybe you'll even be able to tell how ripe the fruit is.

But this routine practice of precutting fruits is something of a hoax on the consumer. You can see its color, but you still can't *taste* the melon, and by cutting it, the store is actually minimizing the nutrition in the product for the sake of a merchandising gimmick.

For display purposes, a peek at the fruit here and there is terrific. It's nice to see what papayas look like this season. But when it comes to buying, you're better off with the

Buy the size that's right for you.

whole fruit. The only clear-cut advantage in buying a precut fruit is with an extremely large fruit like a watermelon—you can buy the size that's right for you.

If, for example, a melon has been cut, refrigerated, wrapped with film to reduce the amount of air that gets in, held for only an hour before being sold, and used by the consumer immediately, then, and only then, the nutrient losses, especially the vitamin C, are minimized.

But usually these ideal conditions aren't met. One can't be sure how long the melon has been sitting after being cut, and if your grocery store is like mine, the display area for the cut fruit is not refrigerated.

No matter how fruits are displayed, the accompanying buying chart should be helpful in guiding you in their storage and selection. I also hope you will be willing to try some of the fruits your family doesn't normally eat the next time you see them in the store. The Nutritional Guide to Fresh Fruit is included to provide information on what nutrients are valuable plus practical cooking and nutritional tips.

Buying and Storage Guide to Fresh Fruits

Fruit	Peak Availability	Handling Notes and Storage Methods	What to Look for
APPLES	Year round. Peak: September-December, February-July—apples available from controlled atmosphere storage	Apples like cold and require constant refrigeration. Held at room temperature for just a few days, they will become mealy and overripe. Held at room temperature and in sunlight, they will ripen even faster.	Firm apples with no bruises. There are over 7,000 varieties. Be adventurous.
APRICOTS	June-July	Store fully ripened fruit in refrigerator.	The best-tasting apricots are tree-ripened, but these cannot be marketed commercially because they are too soft to move. Apricots must be shipped while still having a greenish hue. If the fruit is purchased greenish, store at room temperature until it colors to yellow-gold. Fruit should be plump, firm, and well formed.

Fruit	Season	Selection	Storage / Ripening
AVOCADOS	Year round	Free from bruises, bright and fresh appearing. Soft-skinned varieties with black spots will be soft and mushy. To test for ripeness: Cradle the fruit in the hand. If it yields and is soft to the touch, it's probably ripe.	To ripen a hard avocado, place in brown paper bag or wrap in foil and keep at room temperature. Once ripened, it can be held in refrigerator. Unused cut avocados should be wrapped airtight with seed replaced.
BANANAS	Year round	Choose bananas depending on use: Overripe ones are flavorful and useful for baking; perfectly ripened and colored are best for eating out of hand.	Ideal storage 57° F. Bananas are susceptible to chill; even 12 hours at a temperature below 45° F. will cause damage.
BLACKBERRIES, including Boysenberries	June-August	Bright, clean, fresh appearance. Overripe berries are usually dull and soft and leaking on container. Because of their perishable nature, many berries never make it out of the state in which they are grown. If you don't live in Oregon, Washington, Texas, Alabama, Michigan, California, North Carolina, or Oklahoma, you may have to settle for these berries in the frozen form.	Highly perishable. Refrigerate.
BLUEBERRIES	July-August	Plumpness, uniform size, clean, free from leaves, and of full color. Handle carefully—blueberries bruise easily.	Refrigerate.
CHERRIES	Peak: May-August.	Fresh cherries are available for a very short season so buy quickly or they'll be gone. Should be fresh, firm, and not leaky or sticky. Avoid immature fruit that is light in color.	Very perishable. Refrigerate.
CITRUS Grapefruit	Year round	Firm, but springy to touch. Relatively heavy fruits will be thin-skinned and have more juice. Surface blemishes do not affect flavor or quality.	Refrigerate.
Lemons	Year round	Buy without soft spots.	Moderate refrigeration is good, but not essential.
Limes	Year round	Immature limes will have a tendency to become blackened, dry, and hard.	Refrigerate.
Oranges	Year round. Peak: December-May	California oranges never need to have color added. Where necessary, color is added to Florida oranges.	Refrigerate.

Buying and Storage Guide to Fresh Fruits (continued)

Fruit	Peak Availability	Handling Notes and Storage Methods	What to Look For
Tangelos (hybrid of tangerine and grapefruit)	Peak: November-December	Refrigerate.	About the same size as common sweet orange, it's most distinguishing characteristic is its drawn-out neck and stem. They are usually more highly colored than oranges.
Tangerines	Peak: November-January	Constant refrigeration.	More delicate than oranges, a quality tangerine will be heavy, puffy, and deep orange.
COCONUTS	Year round	Room temperature for 2 weeks.	Test coconuts for quality by the "slosh test" to ensure that the coconut has milk. The 3 eyes at the base should not be wet or pierced.
CRANBERRIES	October-December	Refrigerate. Can keep refrigerated for 2-3 months.	Plump, lustrous, and firm. Poor quality indicated by low skin luster and shriveled appearance. Before they are marketed, cranberries must pass a bounce test. Each berry must bounce 7 times over 4" high wooden barriers. See if the berries you've brought home are still bouncing. Discard any that may be soft.
GRAPES	Peak: August-September	Refrigerate.	Avoid grapes that are soft or wrinkled as they may have been frozen or overdried. A bleached area around stem end indicates injury and poor quality.
MANGOES	May-August	Refrigerate.	Choose mangoes by feel, not color. Soft to the touch means ready to eat. Black spotting may indicate stringiness.
MELONS Cantaloupes	June-September	For all melons listed, refrigerate, but keep dry. Mold tends to form when melons are exposed to dampness. If you live far from growing areas, melons will probably be shipped in firm and immature. To ripen, let stand at room temperature until soft. When fully ripe, store at 50° F. (warm part of refrigerator or cool room).	Look for smoothly rounded, depressed scar at the tip end. If tip end is rough with portions of stem remaining, the melon was harvested too early and it didn't have a chance to mature adequately on vine. They are ready to eat when they feel springy and give off a fragrance.
Casabas	September		Chartreuse-yellow rind, creamy white, juicy flesh.

	Season	Storage	Selection
Crenshaws	August-September		Rich golden pink flesh. Skin is golden at peak of ripeness.
Honeydews	June-October		Rind is creamy yellow at peak of ripeness. Flesh is delicate green and very juicy. If dead white with greenish tint, it is unripe. A hard, smooth feel also indicates an unripe condition.
Persians	August-September		Mauvish in color when ripe. Flesh is thick and pale orange. Not as well known as other melons and may be mistaken for large cantaloupes.
Watermelons	July-September. Mexico: December-June	Refrigerate, but not below 50°F. At 50°F. or lower, tend to lose color and are subject to chill injury.	Melons should have a yellowish underside where the fruit contacted the ground. If the melon is very pale green on underside, it is probably immature.
NECTARINES	July-September	Ripen nectarines at room temperature (65°-70°F.). When ripe, refrigerate.	Rich color, slight softening. On the average, nectarines are smaller and sweeter than peaches. Most nectarines sold in grocery stores will take 2-3 days to ripen by holding at room temperature.
PAPAYAS	May-June, October-December	Refrigerate after ripening. If papaya is purchased in green state, keep at room temperature for 2-3 days until it turns golden.	Firm, green-skinned papayas will ripen fully only if there is slight yellow tinge at larger end of fruit. Look for it. Avoid papayas with dark spots on skin—may go far beneath skin's surface.
PEACHES	June-September	Refrigerate. Ripen at room temperature.	Peaches are of 2 general varieties: clingstone and freestone. Clingstone have flesh firmly attached to the stone and are primarily used for processing market; freestones have flesh that is easily separated from stone and dominate the fresh market. Peach color should be yellowish or creamy. A green ground color suggests peach was picked immature and will not ripen. Avoid bruises.
PEARS	August-November	Pears develop best when they are ripened off the tree. Once ripened, refrigerate.	Pears should be uninjured by cuts or bruises and fairly firm. An overripe condition is indicated by obvious softness and discoloration. The test of whether a pear is ready to eat is whether it yields to gentle pressure near the stem end.
PERSIMMONS	October-February	Extremely delicate skin; easily bruised with fingernails.	Resemble large ripe tomatoes, but brilliant orange in color. Fruit must have stem cap *attached*. In theory, it is desirable to select fruits soft as jelly, perfumey, and ready to eat. In practice, such soft persimmons would be damaged in handling. When buying, select firm, fully colored, with stem cap attached, and hold at room temperature until they are soft.

Buying and Storage Guide to Fresh Fruits (continued)

Fruit	Peak Availability	Handling Notes and Storage Methods	What to Look For
PINEAPPLES	Year round. Peak: March-June	Room temperature.	There is some confusion at the retail level as to when a pineapple is ripe. The physiology of a pineapple is such that it cannot sweeten or ripen after harvest. A pineapple can never be any sweeter than when picked. As time goes on, the shell changes color and the fruit becomes soft, but this is a reflection of deterioration, not ripening. There is nothing to be gained by holding a pineapple in the hope it will improve. The sooner eaten, the better. Crown leaves should be deep green. Fragrance is a good sign, but since most pineapples are stored too cold to be fragrant, this is a moot point. Avoid pineapple with yellowish appearance, or "eyes" that are dark and watery. Always turn upside down and check base for mold.
PLUMS and PRUNES*	Plums: May-September. Prunes: July-October	Refrigerate after ripening at room temperature.	Quality characteristics for both are very similar. Avoid those with skin breaks, punctures, or brownish discolorations. Should be well colored.
POMEGRANATES	September-December	Refrigerate.	As fruits go, this one, with its hard brownish-yellow to red rind, isn't going to attract customers because of its exterior beauty, so it's even more important to know how to select the best. Look for fruit with no unbroken rind, with no sign of decay, and with a fresh, dried outlook.
RASPBERRIES	July-August	Delicate, highly perishable. Refrigerate.	Another fruit that's becoming almost extinct in its fresh form. When you find raspberries fresh and they aren't too exorbitantly priced, look for full firm berries with no leakage.
STRAWBERRIES	Year round Peak: June	Perishable. Must be refrigerated.	Berries should be fresh, clean, and bright. Caps should be attached.

*Originally, the terms "plum" and "prune" were used synonymously, but now *prune* designates a variety that is normally dried without the pit, and to confuse matters, refers to both the fruit in its fresh state *and* the dried product. Plum specifies a variety used for purposes other than drying.

Nutritional Guide to Fresh Fruit

Fruit	Amount	Calories	Protein (gm)	Carbo-hydrate (gm)	Iron (mg)	Sodium (mg)	Vit. A (I.U.)	Vit. C (mg)
APPLES	1 medium, 3" diameter	96	.3	24.0	.5	2	150	7

Crisp apples cleanse the teeth and are recommended by the American Dental Association. Studies in Britain showed that children who ate apples had much less tooth decay and gum disorders than a control group that ate none.

Fruit	Amount	Calories	Protein (gm)	Carbo-hydrate (gm)	Iron (mg)	Sodium (mg)	Vit. A (I.U.)	Vit. C (mg)
APRICOTS	3 raw	55	1.1	13.7	.5	1	2,890	11

Even as small a quantity as 3 apricots supply about the half the day's need of vitamin A. Since apricots are grown only in California and the growing season is short, these luscious fruits are expensive.

Fruit	Amount	Calories	Protein (gm)	Carbo-hydrate (gm)	Iron (mg)	Sodium (mg)	Vit. A (I.U.)	Vit. C (mg)
AVOCADOS	1/2	188	2.4	7.1	.7	5	330	16

Some people stay away from avocados because of their high fat content, which is unusual in fruits. For comparison:

	Fat Gms	Fat saturated
1/2 avocado	18.5	3.7
1 cup lean beef	19.5	9.4
Tuna	13.1	3.5

Fruit	Amount	Calories	Protein (gm)	Carbo-hydrate (gm)	Iron (mg)	Sodium (mg)	Vit. A (I.U.)	Vit. C (mg)
BANANAS	1 medium whole, 8" long	101	1.3	26.4	.8	1	230	12

The banana is a good source of potassium.

Fruit	Amount	Calories	Protein (gm)	Carbo-hydrate (gm)	Iron (mg)	Sodium (mg)	Vit. A (I.U.)	Vit. C (mg)
BLACKBERRIES (including Boysenberries)	1 cup raw	84	1.7	18.6	1.3	1	290	30

Frozen blackberries compare favorably nutritionally, but not aesthetically. The freezing process turns once plump, firm berries into limp shadows of their former selves.

Nutritional Guide to Fresh Fruit (continued)

Fruit	Amount	Calories	Protein (gm)	Carbo-hydrate (gm)	Iron (mg)	Sodium (mg)	Vit. A (I.U.)	Vit. C (mg)
BLUEBERRIES	1 cup raw	90	1.0	22.2	1.5	1	150	20
	Follow this easy way to freeze extra: Place berries on a flat tray in a single layer and freeze solid. When frozen, put into an airtight storage container. When frozen, berries will pour out freely like marbles and and will not stick together. Do not wash berries before freezing because washing causes berries to mat together; wash frozen berries just before serving.							
CHERRIES, Sweet	1 cup raw	82	1.5	20.4	.5	2	130	12
CITRUS								
Grapefruit	1/2 raw white, 184 gm	40	.5	10.3	.4	1	80	37
Lemons	1 medium, 130 gm	24	1.0	7.1	.5	2	20	46
Limes	1 medium, 80 gm	19	.5	6.4	.4	1	10	25
Oranges	1 whole, 180 gm	64	1.3	16.0	.5	1	260	66
Tangelos	1 medium, 170 gm	39	.5	9.2	—	—	—	26
Tangerines	1 large, 136 gm	46	.8	11.7	.4	2	420	31
COCONUTS	1 cup loosely packed meat fresh, raw	277	2.8	7.5	1.4	18	—	2
	To open: Pierce the 3 soft spots or indentations with an ice pick, let the milk drain. With a hammer, tap all over until the shell begins to crack apart. Eat coconut meat fresh from shell or grate it for cooking purposes.							
CRANBERRIES	1 cup cooked cranberry sauce	404	.3	103.9	.6	3	60	6
DATES	10 dried, with pits	219	1.8	58.3	2.4	1	40	0
FIGS	1 medium, raw, 2¼" diameter	40	.6	10.2	3	1	40	1
	Fresh figs are exquisite to eat out of hand with no cooking and no preparation other than gentle peeling. Unfortunately, 90 percent of the fresh figs in this country are sold where they are harvested, in California, so are unavailable to most people unless they have their own trees.							

GRAPES, American-type slip skin Concord, Delaware, Niagara, Catawba	1 cup raw, approximately 38	70	1.3	15.9	4	3	100	4	Halved seedless grapes make a refreshing addition to many fish dishes and curries.
MANGOES	1 whole, raw	152	1.6	38.8	.9	16	11,090	81	An outstanding source of vitamin A, this fruit has been mislabeled by some as fattening. Compare the calories yourself.
MELONS Cantaloupes (musk melons)	1 cup raw	48	1.1	12.0	.6	1.9	5,440	53	Good source of vitamins A and C. A half cantaloupe makes an edible natural bowl for other fruits in season: strawberries, blueberries, watermelon balls.
Casabas (Golden Beauties)	1 cup diced	46	2.0	11.1	.7	20	50	22	
Honeydews	1 cup diced	56	1.4	13.1	.7	20	70	39	
Watermelons	1 cup diced	42	.8	10.2	.8	2	940	11	
NECTARINES	1 medium, raw	88	.8	23.6	.7	8	2,280	18	Nectarine consumption in the United States has doubled since 1960. Contrary to consumer belief, a nectarine is not a fuzzless peach; it is a nectarine; but it can be used in any recipe that calls for peaches.
PAPAYAS	1 medium, raw	119	1.8	30.4	.9	9	5,320	170	The papaya is an excellent source of vitamin A, with 1 whole papaya supplying an adult with total vitamin A needs for the day. Unlike some light-colored fruits, papayas do not lose color after cutting, so they are easy to prepare in advance.
PEACHES	1 medium, raw	38	.6	9.7	.5	1	1,330	7	If today's peaches don't seem as fuzzy as you remember them, you're right. Now peaches are defuzzed with nylon brushes to improve(?) their appearance and to remove pesticide residue.
PEARS, Bartlett	1	100	1.1	25.1	.5	3	30	7	Serve pears cool, but not too cold. As with most fruits, when too cold they lose their bouquet.

Nutritional Guide to Fresh Fruit (continued)

Fruit	Amount	Calories	Protein (gm)	Carbo-hydrate (gm)	Iron (mg)	Sodium (mg)	Vit. A (I.U.)	Vit. C (mg)
PERSIMMONS	1 raw	129	1.2	33.1	.5	10	4,550	18
	Because of their sourness, persimmons are called the "pucker" fruit. Let them ripen and become softer and they will be less sour. When fully ripened, they can be eaten with a spoon, or frozen, cut into sherbetlike slices.							
PINEAPPLES	1 cup diced, raw	81	.6	21.2	.8	2	110	26
	To prepare: Cut the pineapple in half lengthwise, leaving the green leaves attached; with a sharp knife remove the bony central core and discard. Cut remaining pineapple into large chunks and serve in the half shell. If you add any other fruits that normally turn brown (apples, bananas, etc.), the pineapple juice will keep them white.							
PLUMS and PRUNES	Plums: 10 raw, 1″ diameter	66	.5	17.8	.5	2	300	—
	Prunes: 10 medium, dried	215	1.8	56.9	3.3	1,350	.14	—
POMEGRANATES	1 medium	97	.8	25.3	.5	5	—	6
	This fruit has limited popularity because of the difficulty of eating it out of hand. The edible portion is the reddish juicy pulp around each seed.							
RASPBERRIES	1 cup raw	700	1.5	16.7	1.1	1	160	31
	The raspberry has vitamin C content similar to oranges and lemons.							
STRAWBERRIES	1 cup whole, raw	55	1.0	12.5	1.5	1	90	88
	Strawberries are an excellent source of vitamin C, but since a large portion of that vitamin C is readily oxidized when the strawberries are uncapped, leave them capped as long as possible or, better yet, serve them with their green caps as an extra-pretty bonus.							

SOURCE: Compiled from *Nutritive Value of American Foods*, Handbook #456, U.S. Department of Agriculture.

WAXING

Both fruits and vegetables are waxed, but it's more noticeable on fruits. When you see an extraordinarily shiny apple—looks too good to be true—often it is. Nature was clever in giving apples a coat of natural wax for protection, but today by the time apples are commercially harvested and cleaned, that natural wax has been removed. So the processors put a wax back on the apples to duplicate what was there before. The growers say they use so little that 1 gallon polishes 5 tons of apples.

Because fruits and vegetables are composed of 85–90 per cent water (see chart, page 82), they are subject to dehydration, which leads to deterioration of quality and loss of nutrients. Waxing helps prevent some of this by reducing the rate of evaporation by as much as 90 per cent.

Most commonly waxed produce: Apples, cucumbers, rutabagas, sweet potatoes, tomatoes, melons, oranges, green peppers, lemons, squash, eggplant, limes, parsnips, pumpkins.

Unfortunately, most of the time you can't tell if produce has been waxed or not, but with cucumbers and apples you can often scrape a layer of wax off with your fingernail. If you think the produce you've purchased is waxed and you don't want it that way, there are three things you can do:

* Prepare and eat with the skin peeled off.

* Run very hot water over the produce to melt off most of the wax.

* With a wet brush, scrub off the wax under hot water.

There's no harm in eating the wax; however, because the wax is chemically inert, it is not digested by your body, but just passes through, so it does not provide any nutritional advantages either.

Consumers Who Don't Want Waxed Produce

Waxing is one of those processes that some customers feel is unnecessary; they feel it doesn't contribute to better health and is a technique done basically for cosmetic reasons that allows food processors to make extra profit.

In some states where consumers have been vocal, growers have actually changed their processing techniques. I was speaking with an industry representative of the apple growers of the East Coast and he was stumped to come up with the name of one grower who was still waxing his apples. He said that because of the consumer outcry against this practice, the growers stopped it. I think what makes more sense than isolated growers waxing or not waxing is that produce that has been waxed be so labeled. But this will never happen unless consumers demand it. (Consumers in New York State demanded that "Color Added" be labeled on oranges and it is.) With proper labeling, we can all have free choice to select between produce that is labeled "waxed" and that without labels, which we can assume has what's left of its natural coating.

Waxing

Although this labeling may sound far out, it isn't. It's already been implemented in Germany. In addition to the price sticker posted on vegetable bins in Germany, by law the grocers must supply information on how the produce was grown, what pesticides were used, what chemicals and colorings added. German consumers can make their purchasing decisions based on information presented in full view.

One note on the economics of waxing or not. Because waxing does help protect the produce, I've been advised that if consumers demand more unwaxed produce, they should be willing to pay more. Pay more for not getting something that's currently included?

Yes, because the shelf life of the produce will be shortened. You'll either pay at home by discarding produce that doesn't last as long, or you'll pay at the grocery store when higher prices are passed on to you because of the higher discard rate.

TIP

* When using the rind of a lemon or orange, remember citrus is routinely waxed. Wash the fruit in hot water to remove the wax. That way you can be sure you don't have a thin film of wax along with the rind.

 Organically Grown: *Are They Better?*

By now, the term "organic" is commonly accepted to mean a fruit or vegetable that is grown without synthetic pesticides, fertilizers, or chemicals; in soil that is enriched only by the addition of natural matter. The general consumer acceptance of this meaning further perpetuates the confusion since there is no legal definition set by the FDA on what can be called organic.

In fact, plants can only use the organic material from the soil after it's been broken down into its inorganic parts. The idea that there's something different or special about an atom of iron when it's from an organic compound has no factual basis.

The big question with organically grown and fertilized foods is: are they in any way superior, other than price? A USDA study revealed organic foods cost from 1⅓–1⅔ times as much as regular foods. A market basket made up of a unit of each of twenty-nine organic foods available in all the stores cost $20.39 at a supermarket, $21.90 at a health food store, $17.80 at a natural food store, and the same regular foods at the su-

permarket just $11. What are you getting for that increased price? Probably not much.

You should at the very least be getting more nutrition, more vitamins and minerals if you are paying more for organic foods. But studies done by the USDA, Rutgers University, and the U. S. Plant, Soil, and Nutrition Laboratory have failed to show consistent differences that favor either form of fertilization.

The principal factor in the nutrient content of any food is its genetic make-up. Thus, an orange with a high vitamin C content has that content because it is an orange and not necessarily because of the amount or kind of humus in the soil.

This does not mean that soils and fertilizers have no effect on the nutritional value of plants. They do. But in tests done by the U. S. Plant, Soil, and Nutritional Laboratory, it was found that whenever a mineral deficiency was so severe as to reduce a plant's vitamin A content, the plant became discolored and normally green leaves yellowed. Since mineral deficiencies that result in plant discoloration usually lead to very low crop yields or even to complete crop failure, there is very little chance that plants of abnormally low carotene content would ever be commonly used in human diets.

It's up to you. Without evidence, do you want to pay 39¢ a pound for peaches or $1.25 a pound for ones organically grown, 49¢ for a bag of carrots or $1.05 for those labeled organic? Since there is no definition of what constitutes an organic product and there is no enforcement to make sure the products marketed as organic are indeed grown under organic conditions, for now the benefits of organically grown produce seem dubious.

 # Extending the Fresh Fruit Season

In the past few years, you've probably noticed that fresh produce that was once available only during short, well-delineated growing seasons now crops up almost year round. What's happening is that the seasons are being extended. So far, it's most apparent with strawberries, but you can see it with other fruits as well, and to a lesser extent with some vegetables. How scientists are able to stretch the seasons depends on the crop; whether the consumer is the beneficiary or not depends on your point of view.

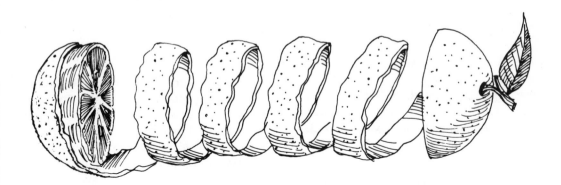

The Strawberry

Probably the most extravagant success story resulting from extended seasons is the strawberry. Dr. Royce Bringhurst of the University of Southern California told me that, since 1953, he's been experimenting with the genetics of strawberries to extend their fruiting periods. He has been so successful that it's now possible to buy strawberries fresh every month of the year except January.

To say that, after all these years, Dr. Bringhurst is still enthusiastic about his strawberries is an understatement. A colleague of his told me, "You can't start any conversation with Dr. Bringhurst, but in 5 minutes, it's back to strawberries."

He's extended the strawberry growing season by genetically manipulating them to prolong their fruiting periods. Now off-season fruiting is normal.

Even though Dr. Bringhurst is wildly

enraptured by his pet strawberries, he told me there are some problems with off-season fruits. First, they never color as intensely as fruit grown with full, hot summer sun. With the strawberry, that means they don't get as bright red and usually have white shoulders. Although Dr. Bringhurst breeds these from wild strawberries, with a full flavor taste, without the hot summer sun, the taste often isn't as robust as when the fruit is grown during the normal summer season. But one aspect that is startlingly better is that some of the varieties grown off-season have from 10–100 per cent more vitamin C. Since strawberries are a good source of vitamin C anyway, this makes these off-season strawberries quite an extraordinary source. The scientists don't know why this bounty happened, but they are investigating.

There's practically no way to tell on the retail level if the strawberries you're purchasing are the ones that have been found to be exceptionally high in vitamin C. (I would be surprised if produce managers could even identify strawberries by their variety.) But on the home front, if you're planting strawberries, you could select these varieties to plant:

Toro: Very high in vitamin C.
Aiko: High in vitamin C.
Cruz: High in vitamin C. Full flavor.
Tioga: Old stand-by, with traditional amounts of vitamin C—comparable to the amounts of vitamin C found in Valencia oranges.

The same day I spoke to Dr. Bringhurst, I went out for dinner at a fancy Los Angeles restaurant for a Christmas celebration with some friends. After we'd ordered the dinner, we debated on what flavor of hot soufflé to order for dessert. Having spent the day talking about strawberries and knowing they were available, I ordered a strawberry soufflé. The waiter took the order, came back and said, "Sorry, but the chef refuses to make a strawberry soufflé. The strawberries don't look so good." I pleaded with the waiter to have the chef taste one of the strawberries and if they didn't taste right, then I'd agree.

I explained to him that at this season the strawberries were bound not to *look* too great (the business about the white shoulders), but that they should be very flavorful nonetheless and perfectly good to make into a soufflé. The chef wouldn't be budged. This incident points out one of the problems with marketing a food that in any way differs from the expected: the consumer's expectations don't change quickly. The chef expected a strawberry to conform to a traditional picture of a strawberry and since a winter strawberry is not going to resemble a summer strawberry in many ways, he drew the line.

Peaches, Nectarines, Plums, Melons, Pears

With other fruits such as peaches, nectarines, plums, melons, and pears, the seasons have been extended by breeding earlier and later varieties. Melons in this country used to have a very short season, restricted almost to summer. Now, the early part of the season they are grown in Mexico and the later part they are imported from Central America, so the marketing season here is extended.

Kiwis

Some seasons are extended just because a crop is being grown here for the first time. To obtain the kiwi fruit—the sweet green fruit with the bright black patterning of seeds inside—we used to have to depend on its importation from New Zealand. Now, it's grown in the San Joaquin Valley of California and is stored 6–9 months. What was once a delicacy for only a few short months a year is much more available, and at a more affordable price.

Cranberries and Apples

The seasons can also be extended by storage. Cranberries were once available only immediately after their fall harvest in time for Thanksgiving, and the last of the crop in time for Christmas. Now, because of their popularity, some of them are put in controlled-atmosphere cold storage and are not marketed until Easter. And, of course, apples are available year round because of the miracle of cold storage.

Consumer Reaction

Robert Kasmire, a marketing expert from the University of California at Davis, says there is some consumer reticence to buying off-season fruits. People remember back to their childhood experiences of strawberry patches in the summer and they are reluctant to buy the fruits in the winter.

Aside from the emotional response, there are also other practical problems that affect the consumer. Because off-season produce is grown under less than optimum conditions, its shelf life is reduced and it has to be handled more carefully than produce grown under the best conditions. And, of course, off-season fruits sometimes are priced higher. Sometimes the price is extraordinarily high and other times there's no difference. One winter in New York City, supermarket strawberries were going for 89¢ a box; street-corner vendors sold two boxes for $1.00, which pretty much matches their price during the summer.

When I asked Mr. Kasmire about consumer resistance he said that there are some

Some fruits stay close to home.

people who are reluctant but there are always enough people who will buy.

The important point here is not who has to buy off-season strawberries—obviously no one does. But this points up an important new trend. Illustrated very clearly with the fruit market, scientists and farmers are beginning to have the ability to produce a year-round agricultural market. The problem with this scientific advance is that it does not always mean better produce for the consumer. Just look at the "progress" of the tomato.

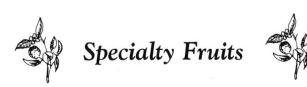

Specialty Fruits

The Specialty Fruits section is one of my favorites in any food store. I'm always on the lookout for unfamiliar produce, something new and different. A honey papaya. A pineapple quince. I take the new-found prize home and experiment and see how I and everyone else likes it. Perhaps you don't share my feeling of instant euphoria upon encountering an unfamiliar fruit for the first time. Maybe your feelings are more: What would I do with *that?* A prickly pear. A manzano banana.

In most cases, the solution with specialty fruits is even easier than with specialty vegetables. What you do with them is eat them fresh, out of hand. With a few exceptions (quince, currants, and crab apples, all of which have recipes for cooking accompanying them in the specialty list that follows), most of the fruits are best when eaten as they are. Just peeled, if necessary, and sliced.

I've compiled the specialty list here to introduce you to some favorites. I've included suggestions on how to enjoy them best. The

Specialty Fruits

list is not definitive but concentrates on fruits that are regularly available in this country. When available, the nutritional information is included and is given for 100 grams raw unless otherwise stated (100 gm is equal to ½ of a medium-size apple).

My hope is that this will inspire you to include more specialty fruits as part of your everyday meals. When you're looking for a special dessert, maybe you'll look beyond that sugary double-decker German chocolate cake, and give fresh lychees or mangosteens a try. Some of these, like the loquat, have such a short season in our market (3 weeks), don't pass them by when you first see them. By the time you've decided to try them, they may be gone for the year.

FRUIT TASTING

People have been having wine tastings for years, sitting around tasting wines and munching on crackers and cheese. I like to orchestrate fruit tastings. After dinner, instead of serving a dessert, I bring out a huge platter of beautiful fruits that I think will be new introductions to at least some of my friends. The platter should be artfully arranged with all the fruits prepared ready to eat. For example, prickly pears should be cut into slices; kiwis should be peeled and sliced; chunks of honey papaya could be placed in a bowl with raspberry purée on top. Garnish with mint sprigs, dried figs, and apricots. You also could serve a fresh fruit sherbet, like grapefruit, but this is totally optional.

You can have different fruit tastings each season of the year because there's always another fruit appearing on the market.

Apple Pear: Also called Asian Pear, this green apple-looking fruit is prized by the Chinese and used to celebrate their New Year. I thank Frieda Caplan (who specializes in importing and growing specialty produce in Los Angeles) for my first taste of an apple pear. The only way to describe this remarkable fruit is to say it combines the best textural and taste qualities of both the apple and the pear. Eaten out of hand, it is delightfully refreshing and when available (California-grown, August–December, Washington-grown, September–April) it should not be passed by. Select those that are very firm—almost hard—to the touch.

Banana, Manzano: These are also called baby or apple banana because they look like a short, stubby banana. They are imported from Mexico, eaten like a regular banana, and are available year round.

Banana, Red: These are red-skinned and come from Guatemala. So far in this country there is limited availability because of limited demand.

Nutritional Value:*

Calories	Protein	Carbohydrate	Iron
118	1.6 gm	30.7 gm	1.0 mg

Sodium	Vitamin A	Vitamin C
1 mg	520 I.U.	13 mg

Like all bananas, this is a good source of potassium.

* 1 each 7¼"

Cherimoya: I was first introduced to the cherimoya, or custard apple, when my friends, Jinny and George Elbert, returned from a trip to Spain. They regaled me with stories of their eating cherimoyas like children eat candy. The outer green part is not eaten, and the inside white custard literally melts in your mouth. This is a good source of vitamins, thiamin, and niacin and is available November–May.

Nutritional Value:

Calories	Protein	Carbohydrate	Iron
94	1.4 gm	24 gm	0.5 mg

Sodium	Vitamin A	Vitamin C
—	10 I.U.	9 mg

Crab apple: Tiny, usually only 1″–1½″ in diameter, their sour taste makes them more suitable for cooking than eating fresh. Ever since I can remember, my mother, who likes their sharp tangy taste, has decorated the holiday turkey platter with bright red crab apples. For sentimental reasons, I like to do this, too, but canned crab apples are now heavily dosed with chemicals and that bright red color comes artificially, so I suggest making your own spiced crab apples, in the late summer–fall when they are available fresh.

Nutritional Value:

Calories	Protein	Carbohydrate	Iron
68	.4 gm	17.8 gm	.3 mg

Sodium	Vitamin A	Vitamin C
1 mg	40 I.U.	8 mg

SPICED CRAB APPLES

From Dr. George York of the University of Southern California at Davis, I got the following advice on how to make spiced crab apples. This has several steps to it, but it's mostly passive work; you do one step and then wait. Don't be put off by the multiple steps. It's worth it.

Ingredients:

Crab apples

Salt

Vinegar

Sugar

Ginger

Cinnamon

Cloves

Canned beet juice (optional)

1. Place crab apples in a salt solution of 1 quart water and 2 tablespoons salt for 2–3 days to allow better penetration of the vinegar mixture. Make enough salt solution to cover the amount of crab apples you are spicing.

2. After 3 days, remove fruit and rinse with water. Make a 2½ per cent vinegar solution. Since household vinegar is 5 per cent, dilute it with water, i.e., 1 quart vinegar to 1 quart water. Add fruit to vinegar solution.

3. Add sugar to mixture. You add as much sugar as you have vinegar. If you've used 1 quart vinegar (4 cups), add 4 cups sugar. If your hackles go up at the thought of adding this amount of sugar (as mine ordinarily would), remember what we're concocting here isn't going to be served as a main course, but as a garnish with perhaps one small apple to a person. Heat mixture about 5 minutes until apples begin to soften. Cool.

4. Add spices such as ginger, cinnamon, and cloves. Taste for seasoning.

5. Let sit in refrigerator 5–7 days. This can either be canned or eaten immediately. Commercially prepared crab apples are colored with Red Dye #40 or beet powder. If you want a brighter red color, use juice from canned beets to color; this is a matter of personal preference since the naturally colored golden-red apples are also nice.

Currants: Gooseberries and red and black currants are from the same botanical family. They've fallen into disfavor in recent years since the plants act as a host to a fungus that attacks the valuable white pine trees. There are now federal and state laws which regulate where they may be grown. On my first trip to Germany, I had Rote Gruitze, a dessert with a soft custard-like texture, made with currants and raspberries. This is a summer dessert—prepared from June–August when fresh currants are available.

Nutritional Value:

Calories	Protein	Carbohydrate	Iron
54	1.7 gm	13.1 gm	1.1 mg

Sodium	Vitamin A	Vitamin C
3 mg	230 I.U.	200 mg

ROTE GRUETZE

Ingredients:

¾ pound red currants

¼ pound raspberries

¼ cup sugar

½ cup cornstarch

Serves 4

1. Cook ¾ pound red currants and ¼ pound raspberries in 3 cups water until currants are tender—about 8 minutes.

2. Pass though sieve and discard seeds.

3. To fruit, add sugar and cornstarch. Cook again, stirring until it thickens, about 5–10 minutes.

4. Refrigerate and serve cold, topped with milk or cream.

Guava: This pale green tropical fruit varies in size, shape, and flavor, most often being strawberry- or pineapple-flavored and about 2″ oblong. The guavas I've tasted in Southern California have soft custard-like meat and have been very sweet. Eaten fresh, preserved, or pickled, they can be an extraordinary souce of vitamin C. They are available in the fall months, from September to December.

Nutritional Value:

Calories	Protein	Carbohydrate	Iron
62	.8 gm	15 gm	.9 mg

Sodium	Vitamin A	Vitamin C
4 mg	280 I.U.	242 mg

Kiwi: The kiwi fruit is sometimes called the ugly fruit, but not by those who know what internal beauty it possesses. The outside is khaki green and furry, while the inside is crystalline green, surrounded by patterns of black seeds. It has a sweet, refreshing taste. I like it slightly chilled, peeled, and sliced. With the recent increase in volume and its year-round availability, prices have lowered, and its popularity may one day move it from specialty status to just another everyday, beloved fruit.

Nutritional Value:

Calories	Protein	Carbohydrate	Iron
36	.79 gm	7.3 gm	—

Sodium	Vitamin A	Vitamin C
—	—	56 mg

Kumquat: At Christmas, my sister and I offer the Buddha sculpture who resides in my living room a few kumquats. These bright golden-orange baby (1″–2″ long) citrus fruits make a fitting offering for a 15″ Buddha. In Japan, regular-size Buddhas are offered regular-size citrus, so we thought our small offering was just right for our diminutive Buddha thousands of miles from his home, residing next to a Christmas tree, of all things.

I ate my first kumquats not in China, from where they originate, but in Molly Sidi's hospital room when she was recuperating from an automobile accident. All the months she was in traction she hankered for kumquats and so, whenever I visited, we ate them together. Their pronounced bitter taste may not make them everyone's favorite. You can either eat them fresh, or capitalize on their brilliant gold-orange color and use them as part of your decorations during the holidays. Kumquats can be held and refrigerated for several weeks and are available December–May.

Nutritional Value:

Calories	Protein	Carbohydrate	Iron
65	.9 gm	17.1 gm	.4 mg

Sodium	Vitamin A	Vitamin C
7 mg	600 I.U.	36 mg

Fruit Tasting

Lady Apple: About the size of an apricot, these tiny apples are grown in California and Washington. They have red-gold coloring, are eaten raw out of hand, and are available December–May.

Loquat: This is a small fruit, about the size of a walnut, with yellow to orange skin. Some have a slightly "downy" surface. Loquats do not develop sugar after picking so they should be purchased ripe (when they are slightly soft) and ready to eat. I think they have a sublime delicacy. Loquats are usually eaten out of hand; if you prefer, peel, remove seed, and slice. They are available in April and May. The loquat is high in vitamin A and potassium—100 gm has 1,216 mg of potassium.

Nutritional Value:

Calories	Protein	Carbohydrate	Iron
168	1.4 gm	43.3 gm	1.4 mg

Sodium	Vitamin A	Vitamin C
—	2,300 I.U.	3 mg

Lychee (Litchi): This fresh fruit is rightfully considered a delicacy in the Far East. Many years ago, I was on a bus in Hong Kong and as we went down a steep hill the driver pulled to the road's edge and motioned for us to reach out and pick the fruit of a nearby tree. The lychee I picked was one of the most delicious fruits I've ever tasted. It's slightly larger than a walnut, with a hard, crinkly shell that you crush in your hand; then you eat the delicate, fleshy white meat inside. The fruit of the lychee is unmatched in its lightness and delicacy. Probably if I had to pick only one fruit for my Last Supper, it would be a fresh lychee. They

are also an excellent source of vitamin C, but that wouldn't matter for a Last Supper. Chinese restaurants in America often list lychees as a possible dessert choice; unfortunately, what they are usually offering is the sickly sweet, flabby-fleshed, canned variety. My advice is to stay away from the canned; they give the fresh a bad reputation and taste nothing like the real thing. The fresh are available in limited supply from March–early August and usually only at stores specializing in oriental foods.

Nutritional Value:

Calories	Protein	Carbohydrate	Iron
174	2.4 gm	44.6 gm	1.1 mg

Sodium	Vitamin A	Vitamin C
—	8 I.U.	113 mg

Mangoes: In New York City, on upper Broadway, I always know it's summer when the colorful crates of mangoes start showing up on the sidewalk fruit stands. To some people, the mango might seem exotic, but to most Spanish-Americans, it's an inexpensive summer staple. One 3-ounce serving—about a 2″ wide wedge—has 1½ times the daily requirement of vitamin A.

With unfamiliar fruits, sometimes it's difficult to tell if they are ripe. With the mango, the main thing is *feel*. When ripe, they are soft to the touch. It used to be thought that color was the primary indicator, with solidly golden-red mangoes being the

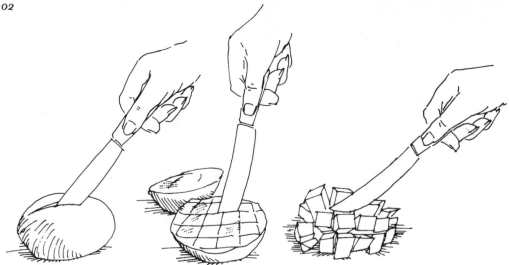

ripe ones. But looking only at color can lead you to pass up some nice soft ones that are ripe, but haven't colored.

Black spots that sometimes appear on older varieties may look objectionable, but they are in no way dangerous. A grower told me that the black spotting often may be an indicator that the mango is stringy. I've not found this to be consistently accurate, but I pass it along, for what it's worth. (See pages 86 and 91 for nutritional information and Buying and Storage Guide.)

MAGNIFICENT MANGO

Because the mango has such a wonderful unique flavor, bright color, and texture, I think it stands on its own just fine and needs very little help from me in the way of cooking to make it more interesting. My way with a mango is to cut it so it literally stands by itself on a plate. Because this can be a bit tricky and messy, the first time, I suggest experimenting when mangoes are cheap. Buy extra and practice.

Ingredients:

1 mango

Fresh mint leaves

Kiwi slices (optional)

Serves 1

1. Start with a full, firm, medium- to large-size mango at least 5″ long. Be sure the mango is firm because a mushy overripe mango won't stand up to this process. Starting at one end with a very sharp knife, slice the mango in two separate halves on each side of the seed. Now you have two mango halves and a center section containing the seed, which you can use for some other purpose.

2. Now comes a delicate task. Holding the mango in the palm of your hand, cut the meat in a checkerboard pattern. There are a couple of cautionary points here: First, if you cut too deep, you'll cut through the skin of the mango and you'll be holding mango pieces in your hand instead of a whole shell. Second, if you cut the squares too small, you won't be able to accomplish Step 3. So, be generous—make the squares about ½″ or ¾″.

3. There's always a stage where you reap the rewards of diligent effort and this is it. Very gently, press up on the mango skin and pop the fruit to stand out and up. The mango should look hemispherical sitting on a plate with pieces jutting out in porcupine fashion. If you're doing this in advance of the meal, do Steps 1 and 2 and refrigerate the scored mango halves. Do this last step when you're ready to eat. To serve, place the mango in the center of a lovely plain-colored plate. The brilliant orange mango looks glorious when accompanied by vibrant green kiwi slices on one side and fresh mint leaves on the other.

Mangosteen: I have eaten luscious mangosteens in France that have been imported from Thailand, but until recently they were not available in this country. Now it looks like the United States will start importing this fruit on a limited basis from Mexico. This native of the Far East has been described as having a taste between a mango and a lychee. The diagram below shows the easiest way to prepare them for eating out of hand.

Nutritional Value:

Calories	Protein	Carbohydrate	Iron
57	0.5 gm	14.7 gm	0.5 mg

Sodium	Vitamin A	Vitamin C
1 mg	—	4 mg

Passion Fruit (Granadilla): The fruit is the size and shape of an egg, has a tough purple skin, and the meat is yellow with many edible black seeds. It is generally eaten fresh, spooned out of the hard shell. Unlike most fruits freezing does not detract from the flavor of this fruit. So you can buy from March–May when available and store in the freezer for use later.

Nutritional Value:

Calories	Protein	Carbohydrate	Iron
90	2.2 gm	21.2 gm	1.6 mg

Sodium	Vitamin A	Vitamin C
28 mg	700 I.U.	30 mg

Prickly Pear: Sometimes called cactus fruit, Indian fig, or tuna fruit, this has been a standard item in California markets for many years. About the size of a flat pear, when fully ripe the prickly skin is discarded

and the deliciously sweet, vibrant, purple-red pulp is eaten. The outstanding fluorescent purple color of the fruit makes them worth at least one try. If you get one that is dry, mealy, and tasteless, try again. Used by American Indians in jams and jellies, by the rest of us they are most often eaten out of hand. They are available from September–December, most often in Mexican markets.

Nutritional Value:

Calories	Protein	Carbohydrate	Iron
84	1.0 gm	21.8 gm	.6 mg

Sodium	Vitamin A	Vitamin C
4 mg	130 I.U.	45 mg

Quince: An autumn fruit whose strong flavor is used primarily in jellies and preserves, there is now a pineapple variety that is edible without cooking. This new variety still has a sharp, tart, distinctive quince taste. I've made sautéed quince as a dessert snack and it is delicious and unusual. It's a little like Chinese fried apple rings.

Nutritional Value:

Calories	Protein	Carbohydrate	Iron
158	1.1 gm	42.3 gm	1.9 mg

Sodium	Vitamin A	Vitamin C
11 mg	—	40 mg

CARAMELIZED QUINCE

Ingredients:
   8 quinces
   Oil
   1–2 tablespoons brown sugar
            Serves 8 hungry dessert eaters

1. Peel and core the quinces; slice thinly as you would apples for a pie.
2. Sauté sliced quinces in skillet with oil.
3. Caramelize the quince slices as they cook with 1–2 tablespoons brown sugar. Serve warm.

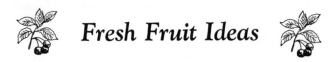

Fresh Fruit Ideas

CHERRIES SWIMMING IN A BOWL

Once while in France I was eating in a small village in one of those restaurants that the French do so well, the kind with the crisp white tablecloth, the flowers, and the gleaming silver. It was summer, and the cherries were at their peak. For dessert, people were being served fresh cherries swimming in water in individual glass bowls about the size of a small soup bowl.

What a pretty way to enjoy cherries instead of baking them in a pie. If you decide to try this, figure ¼ pound per person and keep the stems attached, as they help retain the moisture and look pretty.

ADULT ICE CREAM SUNDAE OR RASPBERRIES AND ICE CREAM

Ingredients:

1 (12-ounce) package frozen raspberries, thawed and drained
1 quart vanilla ice cream
1 cup crushed pralines or peanut brittle
¼ cup kirsch
1 (8-ounce) box fresh raspberries (optional)

Serves 6

This is an elegant ice cream sundae for adults. It tastes complicated, but takes less than 5 minutes to assemble.

1. Thaw and drain frozen berries. Reserve liquid for other purposes. (Use 12 ounces of fresh berries—if they are available and priced right.)

2. In a large bowl, mix vanilla ice cream with raspberries, crushed pralines or peanut brittle, and kirsch.

3. Spoon ice cream mixture into large, elegant individual serving dishes and, if available, sprinkle fresh raspberries on top. Garnish with sprigs of fresh mint. Serve immediately.

I have varied this depending on what berries are available. Sometimes I've used a combination of strawberries and raspberries, sometimes only strawberries or blueberries. Next, I'm going to try it with kiwi.

FRUIT AND CHEESE WITH LEAVES

Ingredients:

Assortment of fresh fruits
Assortment of cheeses
Fresh green leaves

Fruits and cheese go wonderfully together; to make them look even more special, try serving them on a platter that's been lined with fresh leaves. I came up with this idea when the florist sent over too many greens. I laid the leaves on the platter and they made a natural background for the fruit and cheese. Use large, glossy, flat leaves. To make sure they stay put, place a little Scotch tape under the leaves as you overlap them on the platter. After the leaves have been laid out, arrange the cheese and the fruit. It should look gorgeous.

ORANGES

Ever wonder if the oranges you are buying are naturally orange, or if they've been helped along artificially? The color of the orange depends on the night temperature of where it was grown. California oranges have a natural orange color from the cold nights. In Florida, the night temperature is warm enough so that the oranges stay blotchy and green and it takes a boost of artificial coloring to give them that familiar orange look.

Florida growers say if consumers didn't demand such a cosmetically perfect product, they'd market the oranges, natural green blotches and all, except, they claim, nobody buys green oranges. Here are two ways to tell about Florida oranges:

1.   If you're buying them in a bag or carton, it's easy. Read the label. The container in which they leave Florida must be marked.

2.   If you're buying them loose, look at the stem scar. Naturally, this is a whitish yellow in color. But if the orange has been artificially colored, the stem scar will be a giveaway pinky color.

Oranges

SPIRALED ORANGES

The nicest thing to do with oranges I learned from the Japanese. The Japanese have a way of feeding the eyes as well as the stomach and I've found their simple tricks are often worth incorporating into daily habits.

Mrs. Kinue Nakamura taught me to make spiraled oranges. It takes less than 3 minutes per orange. Start with an eating orange. You'll need as many oranges as people you are serving. Don't use juice oranges for this, as they won't have enough skin.

Ingredients:

   1 orange per person

1.   Cut away a piece of the round bottom to make a flat base for the orange to stand on. With a very sharp knife, starting at the top and working down, cut a large spiral (about 1″ in width) away from the fruit. You should now have the fruit exposed with the skin cut and the spiral still attached at the very bottom. With the bottom platform attached to the spiral, cut the spiraled peel away from the orange sections.

2.   You now have a peeled orange. Cut the orange into sections or slices so that it can be reassembled into its original shape. I've usually cut the orange into vertical sections, but it could also be cut horizontally into slices. However you cut the orange, the sections or slices should be totally separated from each other. You could fancy this up a bit at this stage with a dash of raspberry purée or the thinnest slice of fresh kiwi placed between the horizontal sections, but I've never found that this needed anything else other than the orange and possibly a sprig of mint on the side for garnish.

3.   In your hand, reassemble the cut orange slices into their original shape. Rewind the peel in the spiral shape, making a nest-like platform. Arrange orange slices in nest, and assemble remainder of spiraled peel tightly around. The effect, if one doesn't look closely, is of a whole, uncut, fruit. Chill until it is icy cold. This makes a wonderfully refreshing cold dessert.

If you, who feel all thumbs, pale at the thought of spiral cutting, try it just once and I guarantee you'll be surprised how easy it is and how pretty it looks when you're finished. Once you get the hang of it, figure it should take less than 3 minutes per orange.

CRANBERRIES

There are three fruits truly native to North America: blueberries, concord grapes, and the cranberry. The one I love the best is the cranberry; without question it's because my memories of cranberries are associated with all the holiday feasts of my childhood. And it's true with their brilliant red color they look like someone created them especially for Christmas.

But they've also been used for serious purposes as well. American clipper ships and whaling voyagers carried barrels of cranberries with them. Back then, they didn't yet know they were high in vitamin C, they just knew they kept away scurvy.

The fall is the peak harvesting period. They grow on low-lying vines in shallow bogs that are flooded with water. The berries are gently knocked off the vines and float to the surface of the water. If you ever have the opportunity to see a cranberry bog at harvesttime, don't miss it; it's truly a beautiful sight.

When I was a child, my aunts used the canned variety. I was given the important task of pouring it out of its can just so into a glass dish and making sure it never lost its molded shape. Even though I liked the ceremonial canned cranberries, I wonder why all those years my aunts never once deviated and tried the fresh, especially since we lived in Washington, one of the biggest cranberry-producing states.

Many years later, I know that when it comes to using the fresh berry or the already prepared varieties, there's no comparison between the sharp taste of the fresh and the oversweetened taste of the processed. Cranberries should taste bold—slightly tart. They don't need to be masked behind sugar. It seems most cranberry manufacturers have elected to cater to America's sweet tooth instead of respecting the cranberry's natural, piquant taste.

Another good thing about the fresh is that if you purchase extra, they can be easily frozen in a plastic bag for the time when they aren't available fresh in the stores. But if you know in advance you want to purchase in quantity to freeze, it's better to purchase the commercially frozen berries. The commercial freezers can freeze better and faster than you can.

CRANBERRY CONSERVE

Every year in the fall, as Thanksgiving approaches, I traditionally make cranberry conserve. I usually multiply the recipe many times to make enough to see me and my friends through the holidays and into spring. I put this into Mason jars, and keep them refrigerated. It goes wonderfully with turkey and poultry, but also try it with beef. If you compare cost, my cranberry conserve is probably double the cost of the canned variety, but you'd never bring a can of that to someone's house as a present and this makes a perfect gift.

Ingredients:

  1 pound fresh cranberries
  1 cup water
  ½ cup sugar
    or
  ¼ cup honey
  ½ cup raisins
  1 orange, cut into chunky pieces
  ½ cup sliced pineapple (optional)
  ½ cup walnuts

Makes about 5 cups

1. Bring the berries to boil in the water and simmer till they pop open (about 3–5 minutes), but watch that they are still firm and not getting mushy.

2. Stir in sugar, raisins, orange pieces. Simmer for about 15 minutes. If you like your conserve extra sweet, you could add ½ cup pineapple slices, but I think the pineapple detracts from the special tart taste of the cranberry. If this is too tart for you, add more sweet oranges, or a dash more sugar, but be prepared for this to taste boldly of

cranberries and not of cranberries in sugary syrup the way the canned product does.

At this stage, your house is filled with the most wonderful fragrance. It's probably worth it to make cranberry conserve just for the side benefit of the wonderful scents that waft through the rooms.

3. Stir in the walnuts. The ½ cup is enough, but I usually add extra for more crunch.

If you compare nutrition, we've made this recipe more flavorful and nutritious than its commercial counterpart by adding the raisins and nuts. The vitamin C that was in the raw berry was approximately 10 mg per cup; this has been cut to approximately 6 mg by the cooking process, but since cranberries are never eaten in their raw form, it doesn't serve much purpose to compare them to an unobtainable ideal.

Be prepared for this to grow on you as this mixture improves with age. With age might come mold, also, although the sugar content combined with the acid content usually will safeguard against the formation of mold. If you do notice some mold, it's not toxic; don't go overboard and feel you have to sacrifice the whole container of delicious cranberry conserve. With a clean instrument (a knife is easiest), scrape away the mold and be careful not to contaminate the other parts. (However, if you ever notice mold on breads, nuts, or cereals, that mold is toxic and the food should be thrown away immediately.)

CRANBERRY BREAD

I also like to make a special bread with cranberries. Taking advantage of the cranberry's new availability, I've made this in the spring. As in the cranberry conserve recipe, this also features cranberries with oranges.

Ingredients:

  2 cups whole wheat flour
  1½ teaspoons baking powder
  ½ teaspoon baking soda
  1 teaspoon salt (optional)

¼ cup shortening

¾ cup orange juice

1 tablespoon grated orange rind

1 egg, beaten

1 cup chopped nuts

2 cups coarsely chopped cranberries

Makes 1 (9″×5″) loaf

1. Mix together the flour, baking powder, soda, and salt. (Salt is used in baking for flavor. Contrary to myth, it has no special properties that help in the making of bread, so if you prefer, eliminate it.) Cut in the shortening.

2. In a small bowl, combine orange juice and grated rind with the beaten egg. Pour the liquid into the dry ingredients to dampen.

3. Add nuts and cranberries. The cranberries should be barely chopped. You want their effect in the bread to be of bright spots of color, rather than a blanket of solid color.

4. Grease the pan well. Push mixture into pan evenly and let it rest while oven heats up to 350° F. Bake for 60 minutes, or until toothpick comes out clean and dry.

5. Gently release loaf from the pan . . . often breads like this taste better when they are a day old . . . but I wouldn't know. This always gets eaten the first night at my house.

APPLES

Apples are one of the great pleasures of fall. With their shiny, gleaming skin (for more on that, see Waxing, page 93), they've come to be associated with good health. You know the business about keeping that doctor away? They are much more likely to keep the dentist away. They don't have any special nutrients in abundance, but they do provide good roughage and they are nature's best toothbrush, cleansing your teeth and gums as you eat.

The average apple has just 90 calories and 1 mg of sodium per 100 gm, making it suitable for people on low sodium diets.

There are over 7,000 varieties of apples grown in the United States. By far the most popular is the Delicious, followed by McIntosh.

If you're a purist and you want your apples fresh-fresh, then you'd better buy them in the fall when they're harvested. Although apples are available the rest of the year, after November 1, virtually all apples come from cold storage. But you needn't be overly concerned about cold storage because when it's done correctly at the right temperature and humidity the apple loses very little nutritionally.

Aside from eating apples fresh, I like mine in applesauce (see chapter 1, Vegetables, for recipe Heaven and Earth—applesauce served with potato pancakes), in juice, or baked.

APPLE JUICE

Using a juice extractor, you'll know for the first time what truly fresh juice from apples tastes like. Although manufacturers of juice machines would have you believe you get more nutritionally when you eat a fruit or vegetable in juice form, it just isn't so . . . you can't get *more* than was originally present in the natural fruit, unless something else is added.

Professionals making apple cider blend the juices of several kinds of apples, which is also a nice idea even if you're only making a few glasses of juice at home. There's a Foodmart grocery store in Corning, New York, that for the past 20 years, each fall, offers seventeen varieties of apples. In many areas, you don't have such a selection. It's either Delicious or Golden Delicious and/or maybe McIntosh. But if you are presented with a selection, choose one from each group to make a more interesting mix of flavors:

Sweet-Subacid	*Aromatic*
Baldwin	Delicious
Hubbardston	Golden Delicious
Rome Beauty	Ribston
Stark	McIntosh
Delicious	Winter Banana
Grimes	
Cortland	

Mild to Slightly Tart	*Astringent*
Winesap	Florence Hibernal
Jonathan	Red Siberian
Stayman	Transcendant
Northern Spy	Martha
York Imperial	
Greening	
Newton-Pippin	

1. Depending on the type of juicer you have (with some juicers you don't have to peel fruits or vegetables; the peel is extruded), prepare the apple for juicing by cutting into pieces and coring. In a moment, you have fresh juice. It may take 2–3 medium-size apples to make one 8-ounce glass of juice.

2. You can either take your apple juice straight, or I make mine fizzier with a combination of 2 parts apple juice to 1 part naturally carbonated water.

BAKED APPLES

Elaine Rose Ruderman, who is with the Nutrition Department at Cornell University, described the microwave oven to me as a freezer accessory and that for the most part is exactly what it is. A fancy, very expensive gadget for defrosting foods quickly. I think its one other good use is in baking whole fruits or vegetables, like apples and potatoes. Here it's a miracle worker. What used to take a drawn-out 45 minutes now takes less than 5. With the advent of the microwave,

Baking apples

sometimes as a midafternoon snack in fall or winter, I take a break and microwave an apple for myself and eat it smilingly as I read a book next to the fire. What could be more pleasurable?

Ingredients:

  1 tablespoon raisins

  2 tablespoons rum, brandy, or cognac

  1 tablespoon chopped dried apricots (optional)

  1 baking apple (I select from mild to slightly tart group, above)

  1 tablespoon chopped walnuts

  Dash cinnamon

  2–3 tablespoons white wine, dry or sweet

Serves 1

1. Soak raisins in liquor for 10 minutes to plump them. You could also soak a few chopped dried apricots if you wanted to, but that's optional.

2. Prepare the apple by coring it and removing 1″ of skin surrounding the top hole. Make the cavity sufficiently large to drop in the goodies.

3. In a pretty dish that you'll serve the apple in, stuff the apple with raisins, nuts, and pour in any remaining liquor. Sprinkle cinnamon into cavity. The raisins and nuts should be heaped generously so they are coming out the top. Spoon 2–3 tablespoons of white wine over the apple and onto the dish to keep the apple moist.

4. Bake in microwave with care because a minute extra turns this into mush. My microwave takes 3 minutes for one medium-size baked apple, but yours may take more; or bake for 45 minutes in a regular oven at 325° F. For each additional person, double the microwave cooking time and the ingredients.

Most standard recipes for baked apples also call for sugar and butter. Sugar mixed in with the cinnamon and raisins and then butter to keep things moist. Apples themselves are sweet, raisins are sweet, and the liquor is sweet, so with additional sugar you've got another case of sugar overkill. As for the butter, skip it. The wine will keep the apples moist.

Baked apples are often served with a mound of whipped cream on top, but since this already has a mound of nuts and raisins, it doesn't need the cream, too. If you find you can't resist the urge, see Chapter 6, Protein, and try the nonfattening, nondairy cream.

 # Processed Fruits

The nutritional comparisons of frozen, canned, and dried fruits follow the same trend as with vegetables, but with the big difference being that fruits by their nature have soft tissues so they don't freeze as successfully as vegetables. Another disadvantage of processed fruits is that they are usually processed with additional sugar, either as a preservative or for sweetness; however, with diligence, it is possible to persevere and find processed fruits packed in their own unsweetened juices.

a way that hides their loss of texture: in a purée, jams, jellies, instances where the fruit won't be exposed naked by itself.

Sometimes, for economic reasons, it also makes sense to mix frozen fruits with fresh. For example, I use frozen raspberries in a purée that tops an otherwise more traditional strawberry shortcake. Since once they are puréed it's impossible to tell if the berries were fresh or frozen, this is a natural way to economize.

THAWING TIPS

* Thaw as close to serving time as possible.

* One pint frozen fruit takes 30 minutes

* Thaw unopened to avoid darkening.
to 1 hour in cold water to thaw; 2–4 hours at room temperature; 5–8 hours in refrigerator.

The Frozen Orange

The most popular frozen fruit is the orange in frozen orange juice. Because for some people it's too time-consuming, too messy, or too sticky to eat a fresh orange, they gulp a glass of juice instead. That's better than nothing, but in terms of what an orange could contribute, eating the whole orange you're getting much more. The edible yield of an orange as juice is only 2/3 to 3/4 that of the whole orange eaten as fresh fruit.

Although economically frozen orange juice is a good buy, and nutritionally you're getting an amount of vitamin C equivalent to squeezing the oranges yourself, there are some other nutritional losses that consumers have either come to accept or have never

Processed Fruits

FROZEN FRUITS

The only frozen fruits I've had any luck with are berries—raspberries, boysenberries, strawberries—packed in plastic bags with all berry and no juice or syrup added. Most fruits if not frozen this way, but in a liquid, turn mushy, almost slimy. Recently, to experiment, I bought several jars of frozen cantaloupe and honeydew balls. They were squishy, and waterlogged, just what one doesn't want a melon to be. If you must use frozen fruits, most of them should be used in stopped to consider. For example, when you juice an orange, no matter how well you squeeze there's still orange left over. In commercial processing, the valuable fiber and roughage are thrown out and sold to the cattle houses to become part of cattle feed. When I asked the Sunkist people why they didn't include the pulp in their juice, they said consumers found it objectionable. I wonder if that's the real reason, or if it makes their processing machinery cleaner and easier to operate to have juice with a uniform texture and no pulp. A few brands do contain some pulp, but it's almost as if it has been thrown in for cosmetic flair and it's never as much as if you'd squeezed it yourself. And if you're squeezing fresh orange juice at home, don't strain it unless you're feeding it to a baby.

Orange juice, no matter how you make it, as long as it's properly stored in a refrigerator, retains most of its vitamin C for up to 48 hours. Ever wonder, when you put a lid on the container, if you're helping to keep the vitamin C locked in? Lid or no, it makes no difference, but it's a good practice to keep out off-flavors.

CANNED FRUITS

My strongest remembrance of canned fruit is fruit cocktail from grade school. Canned fruit cocktail is a plague that shouldn't be served to anyone, let alone to unsuspecting kids. The mixture itself is one of the few standardized by federal law that gives a definite proportion for each of the fruits. Because the fruits become pale in the canning process, artificial color is added, and a heavy sugary syrup is added for sweetness. By the time the manufacturers are finished, their version of a fruit cocktail doesn't so much resemble fruit as something else: soft chunks of artificially colored squares of sugar.

If you search diligently, you can find canned fruits that do not have the sugar added. Some companies, like Del Monte, make one product several ways. But of their whole repertoire, they still offer only two canned fruits that don't have sugar added

. . . grapefruit sections and pineapple. I think that's a deplorable record.

When I was doing a special investigative series on school lunches I spent a lot of time perusing the pantry shelves of public schools in New York City, and almost always I found the gallon containers of fruits were packed in heavy syrup. Why, I asked? The dietician for the food system told me "that's what the children like, and what we're accustomed to; that's what we've been ordering and receiving for years from the federal government."

DRIED FRUITS

Another way to buy fruits is dried. Dried fruits are always available, they don't spoil, and they're a concentrated source of nutrition. What does a concentrated source of nutrition mean? Here's one way to look at it as it relates to dried fruits. Raisins are the dried fruit of fresh grapes and almost all the nutrition of 4½ pounds of grapes is concentrated into 1 pound of raisins. The nutrition of 6–8 pounds fresh apricots is concentrated into 1 pound dried. You would probably never sit down and eat a pound of grapes, but you might eat 4 ounces, or ¼ pound, of raisins. You also get more fiber by weight from dried fruits since the moisture has been removed.

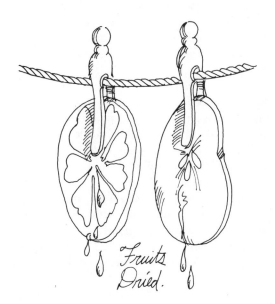

Fruits Dried.

With dried fruits you're getting a nutritionally denser product, with more calories, and the only nutrients that are lost are those that are subject to oxidation—primarily vitamin C and thiamin.

There's a variety of drying processes available, from the oldest technique of sun-drying, to the newest—freeze-drying, a technique that preserves the greatest nutrients. Scientists originally developed the freeze-drying technique of compacting the most amount of food and nutrition into the smallest and lightest package for our astronauts. It's a technique that has filtered down to supplies made for long distance campers, who need lightweight, compact food. Unfortunately, because it is such an energy intensive process, it's very expensive and right now probably suitable only for rich campers. A 3″ round ⅛″ thick package of freeze-dried green beans rehydrates to make a quart of beans and can cost an astounding three dollars, but the results are dramatic. When rehydrated with boiling water, the beans have their normal fresh green color, all the nutrients that were originally present in the fresh form, and even retain a somewhat crisp texture. Fruits are not yet commonly available in this form, but even if they were you'd be paying up to ten times more money for the compact size, and for home storage, unless you have the world's smallest pantry, that's an unnecessary expense. You're much more likely to be buying them sun-dried. Then the concerns are whether to buy fruits that have been sulfured or have potassium sorbate added. First, the sulfur dioxide question.

Sulfur dioxide is a chemical historians have traced back thousands of years to when the Romans and ancient Egyptians used it as a preservative in wine. In light-colored dried fruits, it is used to prevent discoloration. It helps keep apple slices white and apricots orange.

Some say that perhaps it's an unnecessary practice to gas fruit for cosmetic reasons, but the sulfur dioxide also helps preserve vitamins and discourages insects. On the negative side, it's not good to breathe it, but that's primarily an industrial consideration rather than a practical at-home concern.

Even so, Hadley's, a store which specializes in dried fruit that's a landmark on the highway near Palm Springs, advises their customers to open a bag of dried fruit and let it air for 2–3 minutes before sticking your hand in for a piece. They say that a little airing lets any excessive sulfur dioxide dissipate.

Fruits Usually Sulfured	*Fruits Not Usually Sulfured*
Apples	Dates
Apricots	Figs
Peaches	Prunes
Pears	Raisins
Golden raisins	

Sometimes dried fruits are dipped in honey to preserve their color, but since none of us need extra sugar in our diet, and the sweet taste of the fruit is concentrated in the dried form, honey-dipping is unnecessarily gilding the lily.

Potassium Sorbate is used in fruits high in moisture content that would turn moldy without it. It's considered one of the safest food preservatives since it's a food itself that's found naturally in rowanberries.

The Expense

Dried fruits are expensive. A bag of dried apricots is usually over three dollars a pound,

but when you think it takes from 6–8 pounds of apricots to make just 1 pound of the dried, you begin to understand what you're paying for better. And apricots, because of their short growing season, are the most expensive of the dried fruits. Fresh fruits, when they are in season, are the better buy economically and nutritionally. Dried fruits, which used to be much cheaper (what didn't?), are now more expensive because the price of fresh fruit has increased and the processing is labor intensive. But there are ways to save money when buying dried fruits.

* You pay for moisture; the more moisture in the fruit, the more expensive. Buy the more leathery dried fruits (they are just dryer and not less nutritious) and add the moisture at home yourself by soaking the fruit in warm water before eating.

* If you like your dried fruit (raisins) in little boxes to give to the kids or take to the office, since you pay more for raisins in those little boxes, buy raisins in the more economical big box and put them in recycled little boxes yourself.

* If you have your own garden and you're harvesting any of these fruits, invest in a small home dehydrator. A hiker friend of mine who can't lug around regular weight food does his own drying and recommends a Dri-Mor home dehydrator, available from Cache Manufacturers, Box 692, Logan, Utah 84221.

* Make your own dried fruit by-products such as fruit leathers. Fruit leathers can be made from the same range of fruits that are appropriate for jams or jellies, but my favorite is apricot. I first sampled apricot leather in a typical New York delicatessen, and when it's made right, it falls into the category of a good snack. The apricots are high in vitamin A, and if you make your own, you can use very little sugar and you can also do away with any preservatives the commercial makers use. I now find most commercially available fruit leathers are too sweet for my taste. Another reason to make your own: it's often cheaper.

APRICOT LEATHER

Ingredients:

1¾ cups dried apricots (about 11 ounces)
Water
½ cup sugar (or less)
½ teaspoon each cinnamon, cloves, and
   nutmeg

Makes 2 (12″) squares

1. Place apricots in a medium saucepan with enough water to cover. Bring to boil. Cover and simmer 15 minutes. Remove from heat and drain thoroughly. Blend into a purée in food processor or blender.

2. In saucepan, combine other ingredients with apricot purée. Simmer over low heat for 10 minutes, stirring constantly.

3. Remove from heat. Cool 15 minutes. Spread mixture in a thin even layer on two lightly greased pieces of waxed paper, each measuring 12″ square. Let stand uncovered in a warm, dry place about 48 hours.

4. The final cutting can be varied. Delicatessens sell large square pieces rolled up diagonally and you break off as much as you like. You could also make smaller pieces by cutting ½″ wide strips and rolling each strip into a pinwheel.

5. Stored in a cool dry place, this will keep 3 weeks.

TIPS

* If you notice sugar crystals on your dried fruits, that's from the natural sugar in the fruits. Don't get rid of the fruits; get rid of the crystals by heating the fruits in a medium oven for a moment to dissolve the crystals.

* It is best to store dried fruits in airtight containers such as home canning jars or freezing bags.

* Dried fruits should retain their flavor, color, and nutritive value up to 2 years if, once opened, they are stored in the refrigerator.

* They can be kept even longer if frozen. Yes, *frozen* dried fruits are a possibility. They thaw quickly at room temperature.

Ways to Use Dried Fruits

Bake Them—in applesauce, spice or carrot cake, rolls or muffins. For apricot bran muffins, add ⅔ cup diced dried apricots to your favorite recipe for 12 muffins.

Stir Them—into yoghurt, custard, rice puddings.

Sprinkle Them—on cold cereal or with chopped nuts on ice cream. I remember as a child having to eat so much cereal just to get a few raisins; why not add a few more to start with?

Soak Them—in rum or brandy and serve flaming over crepes or ice cream for dessert.

Gorp Them—into snacks. Gorp stands for "good old raisins and peanuts," but you can put in more ingredients, and most people do. Mix raisins and dried apricots with equal amounts of peanuts or other nuts, coconut, sunflower seeds, packaged cereals, and granola.

Ways to Prepare:

Cooked Method: Bring equal amount of fruit and water to boil. Cover and simmer 5–10 minutes. (Less for pitted fruit.)

Soak Method: Cover fruit with equal amount of cold or boiling water (may substitute fruit juice). Cover and let stand overnight.

Soak and Cook Method: Cover fruit with cold water and soak 8 hours or more. Bring fruit and water to a quick boil and then simmer 5 minutes.

Steaming Method: Steam fruit over boiling water 30 minutes.

To Purée: Cover with hot water. Cover and cook 5–10 minutes. Drain, then press through a strainer or whirl in blender until smooth.

BUYING WHOLESALE AND PICKING YOUR OWN:
Dollars and Sense

I n addition to buying fresh produce at your supermarket or green grocer, there are many other ways for you to get wonderfully fresh, wholesome produce and have a lot of fun at the same time.

 ## Pick Your Own

The way some people can't pass a McDonald's, I find I can't pass a "Pick Your Own" patch without longing to stop. I try to plan these forays in advance and turn them into a festivity with friends and kids brought along to enjoy the fun. Depending on the season and locale you can pick your own almost anything—ranging from the standard apples and strawberries to pumpkins, cherries, and peaches. Part of this picking your own business also contributes to gaining a respect for food . . . where it comes from, what's involved in growing and harvesting it. It gives us city dwellers a heightened appreciation for the items we often purchase in tidy plastic-wrapped packages under fluorescent lights.

Expect the prices to be about one third or less what you would pay in the stores, but sometimes the farmers add a small extra charge when novices pick because inexperience often leads to extra waste for the growers (more apples on the ground than in the basket sort of thing). If you're less athletically inclined, you can usually buy what the farmer has already picked, but has not yet sorted and often this is the cheapest way of all.

The system for inquiring about picking your own (where, when, etc.) varies from state to state, and some states offer more and fancier information than others, but it follows a basic pattern. If you call or write your

State Department of Agriculture, Direct Marketing Program, they will make available to you more information than you'll ever be able to use. One fall, I was planning a trip with some friends up the Hudson River to pick apples and gather pumpkins. The information I received from the New York State Department of Agriculture was so complete and tempting, we extended the trip, including other farms with different produce.

You can usually expect to receive a booklet free of charge listing all the farms in your area that allow pickers, their addresses, phone numbers, and their facilities, such as

Call the Dept. of Agriculture

picnic areas, recreational areas for children, etc. The pamphlets list seasons and produce usually available. The state of California during the summer even has a hot line phone number you can call to locate which farms have bountiful crops which day.

So, you've had the fun of picking your own, but now what do you do with the stuff? After you've eaten what you immediately want to consume, depending on the produce, you can freeze or can it (for specific techniques and suggestions see Chapter 2, Processed Vegetables); or, if it's apples, you can refrigerate them, if you have the space. Last year, 30 pounds of hand-picked apples saw me through the winter, and while they lasted, they were stored in the bottom bin of an extra refrigerator.

 # Farm Stands

Often in connection with the pick your own operations, farmers put a farm stand out on the road. In my family, nothing causes such a squealing of brakes at 50 mph **as a farm stand** that looks great.

Beware the farmer trap

There's a popular feeling that you're getting the freshest product when you buy from a stand and not from the corner grocery. Well, it depends. If the farm stand is located near the growing fields and if they have adequate refrigerated storage space, then you probably are getting a superior product. However, the local farmer who picks his produce in the morning, lets it sit in the sun half the day wilting before getting it to the stand, is doing you no great favor.

Keep in mind that big companies, when picking fresh produce, usually have the ability to whisk that produce immediately into waiting refrigerated trucks, which slows down their rate of respiration and nutrient loss. And if the produce is delivered to the stores within a short period of time, that properly refrigerated produce will have more nutrients remaining and will be "fresher" than the produce some hot, poorly organized farm stands might try to sell.

DIRECT MARKETING UNITS

Spurred by federal grants, at least twenty-two states are now exploring alternate ways of moving fresh produce quickly from the farmer directly to the consumer. What used to be called farm stands are now bureaucratically referred to as "Direct Marketing Units." The farmer is happy—he gets a higher price than he would normally; and usually the consumer is happy—he receives the freshest produce. Expect to see more Direct Marketing Units (direct from farmer to the consumer) cropping up, located in a wide variety of places ranging from the traditional side of the road to the more unconventional urban parking lot, where farmers sell produce out of their trucks for only a few hours a week. Your State Department of Agriculture has complete lists of where these farmers' markets are located. Because of their popularity, these lists are updated each season for the most current information and produce availability. If you have last year's list, get another one for this year.

TIPS

* *Don't buy produce that's displayed in the sun.*
It's wilting every minute it's out there. At least, the farmer could put up an umbrella.

* *Expect the produce may* look *different.*
Since local producers generally do not choose varieties for the mass, long-distance market, their produce may be quite different in appearance from what you're used to in the grocery store. Tomatoes, for example, probably won't be so uniform in size or color.

* *Only purchase corn from a cool area.*
Corn, to be sweet, must be cooled immediately after picking. If the farm stand doesn't have corn in a refrigerated unit, or at least a shady corner, I wouldn't buy it. The sugar will have turned to starch and you will be disappointed.

* *Farmers are not retailers.*
It pays to bring along shopping bags and small change.

* *Ask if produce is* locally *grown.*
You're shopping at a farm stand to purchase *local* produce, but that's not always what's offered. I was at a stand in Arizona where the produce looked so questionable I asked where it was from. The lady said proudly it was exactly the same goods as in the grocery stores, which meant at that season of the year, it was from Mexico. So what was the big advantage of her farm stand, except dust?

* *Consider the price.*
Some farm stands, like some stores, are rip-off operations. They'll charge an arm and a leg if they can. Be calm. Don't let yourself be so seduced by the sights and fragrances that you forget to check how competitive prices are. While produce is freshest and variety most plentiful early in the day, bargains are most often available at the end of the day.

* *Watch the seasons.*
To get the best from farm stands, take advantage of local, seasonal specialties. Be knowledgeable about what produce your area grows and in what season. Use your common sense. If it's August in New Jersey, buy the tomatoes and corn and be prepared to skip the grapes (they've got to be imports). If it's December in South Texas, buy grapefruit, but skip the apples.

 Buying Wholesale

Another alternative is to buy wholesale. Some people form co-ops with their friends, and in exchange for a little work, get the benefits of fresh produce at discount prices.[1] Although I've been intrigued by the co-op idea and know of people who have benefited from it (I especially like the idea behind co-ops formed to aid elderly people on fixed incomes), I've never found that my schedule allowed me the time to participate.

[1] If you want to form a co-op, write to American Friends Service Committee, Room 370, 407 South Dearborn Street, Chicago, Illinois 60605. Ask for their directory of co-ops across the country. Or, write for information from Food Cooperative Project (Loop College), Center for Continuing Education, 64 East Lake Street, Chicago, Illinois 60601.

Buy Wholesale

But depending on my needs and the season, I've found buying wholesale even for my small family can make sense.

Buying wholesale is easy to do. There are no secrets involved. It's not a private club and it just takes a little *chutzpa* the first time when everyone else comes in a big truck and looks like they belong there and you feel like an outsider.

If you're a type, like me, who lingers at the produce counter, loving the sight of it, be prepared for wholesale shopping, with blocks after blocks of nothing but fresh produce, to be an intoxicating experience. All the colors and smells make for a delicious dilemma of what to buy. I guarantee—the first time you'll be tempted to buy *everything*. And part of the fun is looking, smelling, squeezing, and even a little tasting as you go along.

Every large city has its wholesale market. (See list at end of chapter. If your city is not included in listing, check your State Department of Agriculture or consult the Yellow Pages under Fruits and Vegetables, Wholesale.)

The markets are usually easy to get to. In New York City, the Hunts Point wholesale market is a 15-minute car ride from midtown Manhattan. In Los Angeles, the Seventh Street and Central Avenue Produce Terminal is in the center of downtown Los Angeles.

The markets function pretty much the same way from city to city. The produce terminals are divided into individual stalls owned by private companies. Each stall specializes in a few kinds of similar produce. Most of the produce is warehoused in the back in cardboard boxes for immediate ship-

ment, but there are usually a few display cases out front.

HERE ARE SOME DO'S AND DON'TS:

* *DO bring your own transportation.*
If you go on public transportation, you're going to have an impossible time hauling your purchases home.

* *DON'T expect much personal service.*
These people are in business to service large chain stores. They are accommodating you by selling to the small customer, so don't ask for extra favors—it creates a bad climate for the next small customer who comes along.

Do's and Don'ts.

* *DON'T expect them to break large quantity boxes or cartons for you.*
Be prepared to buy in bulk (50-pound bags of carrots, potatoes, 30 pounds of tomatoes), or don't go to a wholesale market.

* *DO pay with cash.*
At the very least pay with a personal check. Don't expect to charge. This is probably the last bastion that doesn't take Master Charge.

* *DO dress appropriately.*
With a few exceptions, this is mostly a man's business and the atmosphere here sometimes tends to be a little like men on a construction site. To keep the cat calls to a minimum, women should wear utilitarian clothes and be business-like.

Stalls close early

* *DO go early in the morning.*
Check list for times in your area. By early afternoon, most stalls are closed.

* *DON'T feel intimidated because you aren't the A&P.*
Even though your purchases won't make a dent in their inventory, as the morning wears on it's better for them to sell highly perishable items at some price than to have to eat them.

Pay in cash.

* *DON'T buy sight unseen.*
Even though you're buying in large, usually boxed quantities, open the boxes and poke around and see what you're getting.

* *DO question the price.*
Often prices are somewhat flexible and a little bargaining helps.

* *DON'T think you're buying wholesale to get better produce.*
It's the same stuff you'll find in your neighborhood stores just a few hours later. The only difference is you might be able to afford a better quality wholesale than in your neighborhood store because it costs less.

* *DO go on a slack day of the week, like Wednesday.*
They won't be as busy and will be more able to take care of you.

Question the price.

* *DO seek out smaller dealers.*
Some of the bigger stalls have their accounting tied up with fancy computerized systems and they can't sell to you even if they wanted to. The smaller stands may even welcome your business.

* *DO go during the summer.*
Go anytime, but during the summer when lots of soft fruit is ready for market all at the same time, you can get the best buys.

Select smaller dealers

I make my wholesale shopping pilgrimages at least three times a year, usually to buy enough tomatoes so I always can have lots of freshly made sauce on hand. One of my favorite wholesale buying stories took place one August morning.

My husband and I set off on a tomato-buying spree at Hunts Point, the wholesale market in New York. The purpose of the trip was to buy Italian plum tomatoes, which had been hard to find and expensive that summer in the retail stores. We got to the market early, for us, around 9 A.M., which was late for the produce people. The market had been open since late at night and, unbeknown to us, their supplies of Italian plum tomatoes were already scant by the time we arrived.

I found some tomatoes I liked, but not the price. So I wandered away leisurely, looking for more of a bargain. After all, part of the reason to buy wholesale is to get a bargain, right? Later, after wandering around fifty or sixty stalls, we decided the original vendor's price was probably okay, but by the time we returned he had sold out his tomatoes. It turned out the tomatoes were in short supply and were moving faster than we were that morning. The moral of the story? If you want something that you sense is scarce, buy it when you see it; the price will still be better than retail.

Saddened over our defeat with the toma-toes, which were the reason for the trip, my husband, who is the original impulse buyer, went on a spree and we wound up with 50 pounds of carrots and a dozen mangoes. I'll never buy that many carrots again. There is only so much carrot cake one can eat and carrot juice one can drink! But the dozen mangoes inspired me to make chutney for the first time and it turned out to be some of the best chutney I'd ever tasted. Because I'd made it in such quantity and it keeps practically forever, some of that mango chutney became Christmas presents for friends.

When does wholesale shopping make sense? Buying wholesale for one family only makes sense when you have a real reason for buying an item in quantity and if you also have the storage space. Some of the less perishable commodities that make sense to buy this way are:

> Potatoes
> Juice Oranges and Grapefruits
> Onions
> Nuts
> Tomatoes for sauce

Sometimes wholesale produce purchases unexpectedly make terrific gifts. Close to Thanksgiving one year I was researching a story in Los Angeles at the main Produce Terminal and I bought a case of spaghetti squash. A spaghetti squash tied with a ribbon with the cooking directions attached became my Thanksgiving present that year. Because I had bought it wholesale (the case of a dozen squash sold for one eighth the price in the stores), I could afford to be generous and share my new find with friends.

WHOLESALE TOMATO SAUCE

The only bulk recipe I've chosen to include is Wholesale Tomato Sauce. This recipe is included for several practical reasons:

* *It is versatile.*
At some time or other, almost everyone can use more good tomato sauce.

* *It is easy.*
Although the amounts are large (28 pounds tomatoes), the steps are simple and easy to

follow. The entire process is completed in about 2 hours.

* *It isn't costly.*

You can save over 75 per cent of what you pay for commercial tomato sauce.

* *It keeps.*

When you have a *lot* of something, it's good to know that it keeps well until you're able to use it.

You can figure your savings this way. Recently I purchased 28 pounds of tomatoes for $5.00. That comes out to 17¢ a pound. Stores in my area were selling the same tomatoes for 79¢ a pound. That's a difference of 62¢ a pound over the neighborhood price, or $17.36 in all. Or, if you usually buy your tomatoes for sauces canned, compare the cost of 17¢ a pound with canned tomatoes at over $1.00 a pound.

This whole procedure, using a food processor, takes about 2 hours from beginning to end. That includes 1 hour of free time when everything is simmering on the stove. I would not contemplate doing this without the help of a food processor or blender.

Ingredients:

    28 pounds[2] tomatoes, Italian plums or
       regular sweet, but fully ripened
    4 large onions, chopped finely
    1 whole bunch garlic, about 14 cloves,
       mashed
    3 tablespoons oil
    5 large carrots, chopped
    3 stalks celery, chopped
    ¼ cup chopped fresh basil
    ¼ cup chopped fresh parsley
    ¼ cup chopped fresh oregano
    ¼ cup chopped fresh tarragon
    5–6 sprigs fresh mint, chopped, about
       ⅓ cup

Makes 14 quarts

1. For cooking 28 pounds of tomatoes, you'll need at least two, possibly three,

2 In the wholesale market, tomatoes are usually sold in 28-pound boxes.

heavy-bottomed pans. Mix the onions and garlic together and divide between the pans. Sauté in oil till onion is wilted. Add the carrots and celery and cook till soft.

2. A traditional Italian recipe will now instruct you laboriously to peel and take the seeds out of the tomatoes. In the days before I questioned every step in a cooking procedure, I'd blindly go through the interminable process of taking off the skins and then trying to get all the seeds out, too. This is an example of a traditional habit that is nonsense. Tomato skins taste fine and when processed in a food processor are certainly as edible in a sauce as the rest of the tomato. When you throw out the tomato skins, you aren't losing as much nutrition as you would with cucumber, zucchini, or potato skins, but by saving them you're gaining in several respects. First, there's less waste in general. And second, though the nutritional contribution of this one act with the tomatoes may be somewhat negligible, this kind of thinking, carried through in the preparation of all fruits and vegetables, establishes a good habit.

If you decide to use the skin and the seeds, you *will* have extra liquid in the sauce. To compensate for this, when you take your sauce out of the freezer, you will have to cook it a little longer to reduce it to a thickness you like, but that's a small price to pay for salvaging an extra 12 per cent of the tomato.

So, skip traditional Step 2 and go on to Step 3.

3. Rinse tomatoes, and with a sharp paring knife, remove small crusty stem scar and slice tomatoes into halves. Put tomatoes, skin and all, into food processor and purée.

You'll have to do this in many stages because obviously all the tomatoes won't fit in the bowl of your processor at once. Divide tomato purée between cooking pans.

4. Add seasonings fresh from your garden, window sill, or the fresh produce department of your grocery store.

Because part of the pleasure of this sauce is opening this later and having the fragrance of the fresh herbs waft out, I can't imagine making this with dried herbs.

5. Often, at this stage, traditional recipes

will instruct you to add sugar. If your tomatoes are sweet, you don't need sugar, and with carrots being naturally sweet, I've found the addition of sugar to be unnecessary.

For a certain special sweet taste, nothing compares to the flavor and aroma of adding fresh mint.

6. Simmer gently for 1 hour, uncovered, so you can savor the smell throughout the house.

7. Let cool. Put in quart-size containers to freeze. I use glass containers and allow 2″ breathing space at the top. I use glass because I like the way it looks; you could also use soft plastic containers. If you're like me, you'll go through at least two stages at this step. First, you'll wonder where to put *all* the sauce and then you'll feel like you should be going into the restaurant business. But don't panic. After filling six or seven containers, you'll wonder where it all went.

Since I freeze very little food in general, I don't have need for a separate big freezer and I put this in the freezer attached to my refrigerator and, surprisingly, it doesn't take up all that much room. This could keep in your freezer for a year, but mine never lasts longer than a few months at most.

TERMINAL MARKETS

ARIZONA

Phoenix
  Central Wholesale Terminal
  323 East Madison (85004)
    Tel. 253-6787
  Hours: 6:30 A.M.–1:40 P.M., Mon.–Sat.

CALIFORNIA

Los Angeles
  Los Angeles Union Terminal ("Seventh Street")
  746 South Central Avenue (90021)
    Tel. 627-9767
  City Market of Los Angeles ("Ninth Street")
  San Pedro between Ninth and Twelfth Streets (90015)   Tel. 764-0646

Central Wholesale Market
  1211 East Olympic
    Boulevard (90021)   Tel. 623-1930
  Hours: 4 A.M.–2 P.M., Mon.–Fri.

San Diego
  Bulk of wholesale activity in four-block area between K, North Island, West Fifth and Seventh Streets
    Tel. 232-3871
  Hours: 6 A.M.–1 P.M., Mon.–Fri.

San Francisco
  San Francisco Produce Terminal
  Islias Creek area
  2095 Jerrold Avenue (94124)
    Tel. 826-7133
  Golden Gate Produce Terminal
  131 Terminal Court (94080)
    Tel. 583-4886
  Hours: 4 A.M.–12:30 P.M., Mon.–Fri.

COLORADO

Denver
  Denargo Market
  Twenty-ninth and
    Broadway (80216)   Tel. 837-4570
  Hours: 4 A.M.–12 P.M., Mon., Wed., Fri.;
    5 A.M.–12 P.M., Tues., Thurs.

FLORIDA

Miami
  Miami Produce Center
  2140 N.W. Twelfth
    Avenue (33127)   Tel. 324-6794
  Hours: Closed Sat., Wed.

GEORGIA

Atlanta
  State Farmers Market
  Forest Park (30050)   Tel. 366-6910
  Hours: 6 A.M.–2 P.M., Mon.–Fri.

HAWAII

Honolulu
  Ala Moana Market Center
  1020 Auahi Street (96814)
    Tel. 533-4278
  Iwilei Road Market
  918–920 Iwilei Road (96817)

Hours: 5:30 A.M.–5:30 P.M., Mon.–Fri.;
5:30 A.M.–12 noon, Sat.

ILLINOIS

Chicago
South Water Market
1425 South Racine
Avenue (60608)   Tel. 226-7560
Hours: 4 A.M.–2 P.M., Mon.–Fri.

INDIANA

Indianapolis
Indianapolis Produce Terminal
4101 Massachusetts
Avenue (46204)   Tel. 574-5301
Hours: 3 A.M.–10 A.M., Mon.–Fri.;
6 A.M.–8 A.M., Sat.

KENTUCKY

Louisville
Louisville Produce Terminal
(40218)   Tel. 454-3740
Hours: 4 A.M.–2 P.M., Mon.–Sat.

LOUISIANA

New Orleans
French Market
French Market Place (70116)
No established hours.

MARYLAND

Baltimore
Maryland Wholesale Produce Market
7460 Conowingo Avenue (20794)
Tel. 799-3880

Maryland Wholesale Food Center
Authority
201 West Preston Street (21201)
Tel. 383-2000
Hours: 3 A.M.–9 A.M., Mon.–Fri.

MASSACHUSETTS

Boston
New England Produce Center
Chelsea (02150)
Hours: Starts 5:30 A.M. Mon., 6 A.M.
Tues.–Sat.

Boston Market Terminal
34 Market Street.
Everett (02149)   Tel. 387-6500
Hours: Starts 5:30 A.M., Mon.–Fri.

MICHIGAN

Detroit
Detroit Union Produce Terminal
7201 West Fort Street (48209)
Tel. 841-8700
Hours: 6 A.M.–1 P.M., Mon.; 7 A.M.–12:30
P.M., Tues. and Wed.; 7 A.M.–1 P.M.,
Thurs. and Fri.

MINNESOTA

Minneapolis
The greater Minneapolis market centers
around the various railway tracks and
terminals as well as in the Hopkins and
St. Louis Park suburbs.
Hours: 5 A.M.–4 P.M., Mon.–Fri.;
5 A.M.–12 noon, on Sat.; opens 6 A.M. in
winter.

MISSOURI

Kansas City
Kansas City Market
Between Main and Walnut Streets and
Third and Fifth Streets (64106)
Hours: virtually 24 hours a day, 7 days a
week.

St. Louis
St. Louis Produce Market
45 Produce Row (63102)   Tel. 621-4383
Hours: 2 A.M.–12 noon, Mon.–Fri.

NEW JERSEY

Newark
Newark Farmers Market
Tel. 645-2636
Hours: 24 hours a day.

NEW YORK

Albany
Capital District Regional Market
Menands (12204)   Tel. 465-1023
Hours: 4:30 A.M.–1 P.M., Mon.–Fri.

Buffalo
  Niagara Frontier Food Terminal
  Clinton and Bailey
    Avenues (14206)   Tel. 823-5294
  Hours: 6:30 A.M.–ca. 2 P.M., Mon.–Fri.

New York City
  New York City Terminal Market
  Hunts Point, Bronx
    County (10474)   Tel. 328-9100
  Hours: 5 A.M.–8 P.M., Mon.–Fri.

  Bronx Terminal Market
  150th and Exterior Streets (10451)

  Brooklyn Terminal Market
  Foster and Remsen Avenues

NORTH CAROLINA

Raleigh
  State Farmers Market
  1301 Hodges Street (27604)
    Tel. 733-7417
  Hours vary with company.

OHIO

Cincinnati
  Plum Street Yards
  Plum Street (45202)   Tel. 684-3193
  Hours vary by company.

Cleveland
  Northern Ohio Food Terminal
  3800 Orange Avenue (44115)
    Tel. 881-5100
  Hours: 5:30 A.M.–12 noon, Mon.–Fri.

Columbus
  Columbus Produce Terminal
  4561 East Fifth Avenue (43219)
    Tel. 231-8727
  Hours: ca. 4 A.M.–ca. 3 P.M., Mon.–Fri.;
    4 A.M.–12 noon, Sat.

OREGON

Portland
  Most wholesalers and distributors located
    in the vicinity of Alder and Union
    Streets and S.E. Tenth Avenue and
    Belmont Street.
  Hour vary by company.

PENNSYLVANIA

Philadelphia
  Produce Center
  3301 South Galloway
    Street (19148)   Tel. 336-3003
  Hours: 4 A.M.–12 noon, Mon.–Fri.

Pittsburgh
  Pittsburgh Market
  Twenty-second Street to Thirteenth Street
    from Penn Avenue to the Allegheny
    River (15222)   Tel. 644-5847
  Hours: 4 A.M.–12 noon, Mon.–Fri.

RHODE ISLAND

Providence
  Produce Terminal
  Harris Avenue (02903)   Tel. 331-2955
  Hours: 4 A.M.–2 P.M., Mon.–Sat.

SOUTH CAROLINA

Columbia
  Columbia State Farmers Market
  (29201)   Tel. 758-3325
  Hours: 5:30 A.M.–3:30 P.M., Mon.–Fri.
    There are shorter hours on Sat.

TENNESSEE

Memphis
  Farmers Market
  814 Scott Street (38112)   Tel. 327-8828

TEXAS

Dallas
  There is no terminal market but receivers
    are in a three-block area on South Pearl
    Street and South Central
    Expressway. (75201)
  Hours: 5 A.M.–2 P.M., Mon.–Fri.;
    5 A.M.–12 noon, Sat.

Houston
  Houston Produce Center
  3100 Produce Row (77023)
    Tel. 928-2481

San Antonio
  San Antonio Produce Terminal
  1500 South Zarzamora
    Street (78207)   Tel. 223-4301

Hours: 5 A.M.–5 P.M., Mon.–Sat.

WASHINGTON

Seattle
    Major terminal is located at 1500 block of
    Occidental Avenue. Other wholesalers
    and distributors are located around 900
    and 1200 Western Avenue and between

King Street and 2000 on Occidental.
Hours vary with company.   Tel. 764-3500

WISCONSIN

Milwaukee
    Market is centered in a two-block area
    between 300 and 500 on Broadway.
    Hours: 5 A.M.–3 P.M., Mon.–Fri.

SALADS:
Tossing It Together

Salads have gotten such good press recently, you'd think anything green and crunchy was good for you and packed with vitamins. Unfortunately, that's not quite the whole story.

People in this country generally could use more vitamin A and C and salads are a good opportunity to pick up these vitamins naturally, providing you know how to select the most nutritious ingredients. (For discussion of vitamin A and C, see Chapter 1, Vegetables, page 16, and Chapter 3, Fruits, page 89.) Since we don't yet have nutritional labeling on a head of lettuce or a head of cabbage, sometimes knowing what's the most nutritious choice is a tricky business for the average consumer. I also see the time in the not so distant future when labeling will go one step further and list the nutrients "as served" so it will be possible to understand the nutrient losses which occur up to the time of consumption.[1]

We eat salad for lots of reasons. Sometimes for variety, for the lovely contrasting colors, for terrific textures of varying crunchiness. And those reasons are okay, but if you want the best nutrition, use the Salad Score Sheet that follows on page 134 for the most nutritious combinations.

SALAD TIPS

* *Prepare only the amount of salad to be eaten at one meal.*
Prepared fruits and vegetables lose many of their nutrients as they stand waiting to be eaten again.

[1] For example, with this kind of labeling, if you were making a salad with cauliflower, you could quickly determine if you wanted to steam the cauliflower first (22 per cent vitamin C loss after 15 minutes steaming), or if you just wanted to use it raw (8 per cent vitamin C loss after cutting). More detailed labeling would give the consumer one more nutritional edge.

* *Don't prepare salad until you're ready to eat it.*
Nutrients are lost through exposed surfaces when vegetables are diced, shredded, cut, or torn, so minimize this loss by eating the salad as soon after it's prepared as possible.

* *Use a salad dryer.*
Available in a variety of styles, they spin the salad greens dryer faster, and with less work than any other method.

* *Serve a salad as the main course.*
Women seem to like salads naturally, but if you think the man of your house would scoff at eating just a salad and call it rabbit food, remind him what such food does for rabbits: the male rabbit is light on his feet, has no paunch, and maintains a lively romantic interest in the opposite sex.

* *Stuff a super salad into pita bread and make a super sandwich.*
Pita is a twin-sided flat Middle Eastern bread that in recent years has made its debut in American grocery stores. It makes a natural envelope for sandwiches.

* *Buy a new vegetable peeler yearly.*
After 1 year, the blade of a peeler is so dull, it's peeling away lots of the vegetable as well as the skin. Since most nutrients are found in higher concentrations in the outer layers, use a light touch.

* *Grow your own fresh herbs in big pots.*
When I lived in an apartment I almost gave up on fresh herbs until I discovered the secret of growing them indoors is to grow them in *big* (at least 10″) pots that give ample room for their root system. Of course, if you have outdoor garden space that's even better.

The Bowl

An important part of making a successful salad is choosing the bowl. The capacity of a salad bowl should be measured in gallons, even if you're not making gallons of salad. This way the greens have extra head space so they aren't mashed and suffocated. You, the salad maker, will also enjoy tossing a salad more with a bigger bowl because you won't have to stand guard catching the greens that inevitably fly out of a bowl that's too tiny.

Here's the way I figure it: the absolute smallest bowl I would consider for 2 people holds 1 gallon of water; the bowl I use for 6 holds 5 gallons. Don't think this means I serve extraordinarily large amounts of salad. I don't, but the process is done so much more gracefully with a large bowl.

Fill your current bowl with water and see how it measures up. I always select either glass or pottery. I shy away from "well-seasoned" wooden bowls. They usually smell well-rancid to me. If you can't find a conventional bowl that's large enough, have a local potter make one to your specifications.

The super salad bowl

Salad Score Sheet

The best way to put together healthful salads is to use the Salad Score Sheet. Here's one way to use the Score Sheet: 1 cup of celery, 1 cup of cucumbers, and 1 cup of radishes, if you could eat all that, would still furnish less than one third the vitamin C you get by eating just one green pepper. It's a little like a green pepper a day keeps Linus Pauling happy.

To fix the most nutritious salads, select ingredients from the SUPER group. It's easy to see that a coleslaw combination of chopped cabbage, sliced green peppers, and diced carrots is a SUPER salad, high in both vitamins A and C. It's also easy to see that America's favorite restaurant salad of head lettuce, mixed with radishes for color and celery for crunchiness, is pretty LOUSY nutritionally. You're getting roughage, but at those prices, you could be getting a good shot of vitamins, too.

Using the Score Sheet, you can quickly rate some classic salad combinations nutritionally:

* Sliced Cucumbers flavored with fresh dill
* Coleslaw (cabbage, green pepper, carrots)
* Tomatoes Provençale and Green Pepper
* Mushrooms à la Grecque (fresh mushrooms marinated)
* Caesar Salad (romaine leaves)
* Carrot and Raisin
* Half Papaya filled with Strawberries and Kiwis

Several thoughts should come to mind:

* Healthful salads are not necessarily synonymous with lettuce.

* If you want red color in your salad, why bother with the lowly radish; try a fresh red pepper instead.

* If you automatically add mushrooms to a spinach salad, look at their pathetic rating and you'll see you're getting very little nutrition for all that expense. If you like white crunchy things in your salad, try cutting cauliflower into slices of cauliflower "mushrooms."

* If crunch in a salad means celery to you, for a change, try fennel. Fennel looks like a hairy celery and, like celery, it has a lot of crunch and unfortunately very little nutrition. They both cost about the same, but at least with fennel you have the fun of adding an interesting flavor to your salad: licorice.

* Use the Score Sheet to judge if a new salad recipe is worth the effort from a nutritional point of view.

* Gardeners can use the Score Sheet to assess how well they're selecting their salad crops.

* Until you get the hang of it naturally, make a copy of the Score Sheet and use it as a guide when you're shopping.

This is not in any way to suggest that we should give up those fruits or vegetables on the Lousy end of the Salad Score Sheet. There are some tastes one loves regardless of their nutritional rating and since these are all at least natural foods, they aren't going to harm us. But, with the incredibly high prices one has to pay for fresh produce, the Score Sheet gives a rather dramatic perspective from which to make purchases more knowledgeably, based on something other than just taste and price.

One of my first converts to the Salad Score Sheet was my husband. When we first met, he was on a self-administered lunch-time diet of half a head of lettuce sprinkled with fresh lemon juice. He was doing a lot of chewing with almost no nutritional benefits. So, today when he wants to lose weight, he chews on fresh green peppers, or a handful of watercress, both of which are always on hand in the refrigerator. These two offer plenty of chewing for the dieter, along with vitamins and very few calories. It's important for everyone to eat well, but for dieters who are

Salad Score Sheet*

VEGETABLES

VITAMIN C mg per 1 cup edible portion		VITAMIN A I.U. per 1 cup edible portion	
Super C		Super A	
Peppers, red bell	204	Dandelion Greens	12,290
Broccoli	140	Carrots, deep color	12,100
Peppers, green	128	Spinach	8,100
Watercress	99	Watercress	6,130
Arugula	99	Parsley	5,100
Cauliflower (chopped)	90	Peppers, red bell	4,450
Cabbage, red	55	Spinach	4,300
Spinach	51	Chicory Greens	4,000
Asparagus, green	45	Broccoli	3,880
Cabbage, white	42		
Good C		Good A	
Tomatoes	40	Scallions	2,000
Peas, green	39	Curly Endive, Escarole	1,650
Potatoes (cooked)	36	Tomatoes	1,580
Scallions	32	Asparagus, green	1,220
Zucchini	25		
Chicory Greens	22		
Bean Sprouts, mung	20		
Lousy C		Lousy A	
Beans, green (cooked)	15	Lettuce:	1,050
Corn (cooked)	12	Loose-leaf, Grand Rapids,	
Radishes	12	Salad Bowl, Simpson,	
Cucumbers	12	Romaine, Dark Green,	
Celery	11	White Plains	1,050
Artichokes (cooked)	10	Peas, green	930
Lettuce:	10	Beans, green (cooked)	680
Loose-leaf, Grand Rapids,		Corn (cooked)	660
Salad Bowl, Simpson,		Peppers, green bell	420
Romaine, Dark Green,		Zucchini	420
White Plains	10	Cauliflower	339
Beets (cooked)	10	Celery	320
Carrots	9	Cucumbers	260
Fennel	9	Artichokes (cooked)	180
Lettuce:		Cabbage	120
Crisphead, Iceberg, New York,		Beets (cooked)	30
Great Lake	5	Bean Sprouts, mung	20
Lettuce:		Radishes, Mushrooms,	trace
Butterhead, Boston, Bibb	4	Potatoes (cooked),	
Sunchokes	4	Chicory (Belgian Endive)	
Mushrooms	2		
Chicory (Belgian Endive)	trace		

*Although the vegetables and fruits rated on the Salad Score Sheet may be useful sources of other vitamins and minerals, because a fresh salad is one of the easiest ways to obtain the needed amounts of vitamins C and A, the Score Sheet takes only these two important vitamins into account. For other vitamins and minerals, see Nutritional Guide to Fresh Vegetables and Nutritional Guide to Fresh Fruits.

*Salad Score Sheet** (continued)

FRUITS

VITAMIN C mg per 1 cup edible portion		VITAMIN A I.U. per 1 cup edible portion	
Super C		Super A	
Guavas	242	Mangoes	7,920
Oranges, navel	88	Melon: cantaloupe	5,440
Strawberries	88	Apricots	4,190
Grapefruits, red	87	Papayas	2,450
Papayas	78	Peaches	2,260
Mangoes	58		
Kiwis (Chinese gooseberry)	56		
Melon: cantaloupe	53		
Good C			
Melon: honeydew	39		
Raspberries, red	31		
Pineapples	26		
Raspberries, black	24		
Melon: casaba	22		
Avocadoes	21		
Apples	18		
Apricots	16		
Lousy C			
Bananas	15		
Cherries, sweet	12		
Peaches	12		
Watermelons	11		
Grapes	4		
Figs	2		

SOURCE: Compiled from *Nutritive Value of American Foods*, Handbook #456, U. S. Department of Agriculture.

Recommended Daily Dietary Allowances[†]							
Infants 0-1	Infants 1-3	Children 4-6	Children 7-10	Adult Men	Adult Women	Pregnant Women	Lactating Women
Vit. A (I.U.)	1,400	2,000	2,500	3,300	5,000	4,000	5,000	6,000
Vit. C (mg)	35	45	45	45	60	60	80	100

[†]SOURCE: Recommended Daily Dietary Allowances, Revised 1980, Food and Nutrition Board, National Academy of Sciences-National Research Council.

trying to eat less, it's especially important to know which of the few foods they allow themselves to eat are really beneficial.

A few general salad hints: You can't tell by taste if more nutrients are present, but if you have a choice between dark and light vegetables or fruits, choose the dark unless, of course, you're in France when the white asparagus are up. Then you'll eat the cool white asparagus for the pure taste pleasure of it, but privately you'll know that the bleached asparagus has very low vitamin A where dark green asparagus is a good source. This light versus dark works with lettuce and cabbage as well. There is 1.5 to 3 times as much iron, 1.5 times as much vitamin C, and *21* times as much vitamin A in green leaves as in the bleached.

Often when preparing a salad, you're faced with a choice between using the leaf only, or the leaf attached to the stem-stalk. Making your decision based on taste and texture, usually the tough stem gets thrown out. Although it can be saved and puréed into sauces and soups, don't feel too bad about the lowly stem. The leaves contain from two to over six times as much vitamin C as the stems, more minerals and iron, and up to 99 per cent of the vitamin A.[2]

And when it comes to salad making, don't forget the kids. Salads make for terrific kiddie cuisine, especially for their first "cooking" experience. There is no danger of getting burned and a salad involves lots of activities kids enjoy: sloshing water (washing the greens), making whirling sounds (spinning the salad dryer), and unbounded creativity. And then, of course, this great surge of creativity is rewarded with adult praise as the salad is being eaten.

I'll never forget my first "salad." As is often the setting for childhood experimentation, my parents were gone and my brother and I took what seemed like dozens of cans down from my mother's rainy day pantry. With wonderful abandon and feigned innocence, we opened them all and poured them into one big aluminum pan, which became our "salad bowl." I never have forgotten the sight and sickly sweet

Kids love to eat leaves

smell of all those pears, peaches, and cherries sloshing around. We were jubilant over our wonderful fruit salad, if not the end result it brought from our parents when they returned. But it did teach me a dramatic boldness in salad making that is still with me today.

Aside from that bout with the cans, my present delight with salads grew out of another early childhood salad-making adventure. As a youngster living in Seattle, Washington, I had an aunt and uncle who always had an enormous vegetable garden that covered several acres. Since Seattle has a perfect growing climate, the garden was lush and prolific (unlike my sad allotment garden in Manhattan, which was always run down and would grow only onions and basil). It was the usual thing to pick greens from the garden. My aunt would make a hot dressing, then she and I would play grownup and sit down to a wilted lettuce salad just minutes from a garden.

---

[2] The parents who force their kid to eat the whole vegetable might actually be accomplishing more by concentrating on the leaves if the child has a limited appetite for vegetables as many kids do.

Recipes

Using the Salad Score Sheet as a guide, develop any nutritious combinations you like; following are some of my favorites.

FAVORITE FAMILY WATERCRESS SALAD

My favorite family salad is without question a combination of watercress, Greek feta cheese, and oranges. Depending on what's at hand, sometimes I add only the oranges, and not the cheese, but the three together make a delightful combination.

I was recently in a store buying watercress for just this salad, and the teen-age check-out clerk said to me, "That's a sad-looking assortment of stems"—meaning, I guess, that I was buying cheap green stems (watercress in Southern California is bargain priced) because I didn't know enough or have money enough to buy the more conventional head of lettuce. I explained the nutritional advantages of watercress, that it has ten times the vitamin A as head lettuce and 12 times the vitamin C. Then she was skeptical about the taste. So I snapped off a leaf and we had a tasting at the check-out counter. I'm not sure she was convinced, but at least she now had *tasted* watercress.

I use commercially available watercress and it has a pleasant, just faintly sharp taste. I think some people, the check-out clerk among them, get the taste of watercress confused with other cresses that are often sprouted in home sprouters, such as mustard cress, which do have an exceptionally heavy taste and are used for an accent, but never for a whole salad.

Ingredients:

3 bunches watercress

1 large orange

1 cup crumbled fresh Greek feta cheese

Tulip Orange Vinaigrette (see page 142)

Serves 4 as a salad

1. Wash the watercress. Cut off the stems. If you feel badly about not using every precious piece of the vegetable, add stems to your vegetable soup pot. These stems are tough to chew so it makes them unlovable in your salad and besides, most of the nutrients are concentrated in the plant leaf.

2. Dry the watercress in a salad dryer and place in salad bowl.

3. Peel orange. Remove all the white. Cut into chunks and add to watercress.

4. Add 1 cup feta cheese, crumbled. You can see by the Score Sheet that combining watercress with oranges you get a SUPER combination of vitamins A and C. The feta cheese is added for its distinctive flavor not for the minuscule amounts of protein or calcium that it contributes when ¼ pound is shared by 4 people.

I read somewhere that oranges in a green salad take a bit of getting accustomed to. I loved the combination immediately and most people I've served it to over the years have commented on the refreshing complement of flavors, colors, and textures.

CHICK-PEA VINAIGRETTE

To me, this icy-cold salad is indelibly associated with summer and can be the most refreshing food around in a sweltering August heat wave.

Although the chick-pea has a whimsical sound to it, it's a serious source of protein and has been for centuries. Depending on what part of the country you live in, chick-peas are also called garbanzos. You can save some money by cooking the dried peas yourself, but since this is an inexpensive salad anyway, I use the canned, already-cooked chick-peas for convenience.[3]

[3] Using their protein value as a guide, there is no significant nutritional difference between the canned and dried chick-peas.

Ingredients:

2 (1-pound) cans chick-peas

1 cup red wine vinegar

⅔ cup safflower oil (or less)

4 cloves garlic, mashed

½ sweet onion, diced

Dash paprika

1 cup grated carrots

1 cup chopped green pepper

1 cup chopped tomato

1 cup grated zucchini

Serves 8 as main course

1. Add the drained chick-peas to a pan with the vinegar, oil, garlic, onion, and dash of paprika. Bring to boil and cook for just a moment.

2. Chill till icy cold. Now you have chick-pea vinaigrette, but to make it a SUPER salad, add the carrots, green peppers, tomato, and zucchini.

One of the SUPER ingredients here is the carrot, and since the skin of the carrot is especially rich in thiamin, niacin, and riboflavin, peel, if necessary, with a very light touch. I find this is best accomplished with a specially designed vegetable peeler a German chef gave to me when I was filming in Munich. It delicately takes off less than half the amount other peelers seem to rip off. I've never found my special peeler for sale in the United States, but a standard peeler works as well if it is replaced often so its blade is sharp.

Because we're using many SUPER ingredients, we're adding the grated zucchini for its unique, almost spaghetti-like texture when it's been grated in the food processor.

Because the protein from the chick-peas is not a complete protein, you need to eat a little animal protein in the same meal to complement the chick-peas. I think a nice way to do this is to have some cheese for dessert or a glass of nonfat milk.

In addition to being a SUPER source of vitamins C and A, this salad provides a hefty 41 gm of protein per serving (the average

daily requirements are 30 gm for children, 46 gm for women and 55 gm for men).

A nice adaptation is to substitute 4 cups of cooked kasha (buckwheat groats) for the chick-peas. And then instead of protein, you're loading up on B vitamins.

AMERICAN HERO SALAD

I call this an American Hero Salad because I created it to celebrate the Tall Ships sailing into New York Harbor for the Bicentennial Fourth of July.

Ingredients:

4 tomatoes, cubed

1 green pepper, sliced

1 red onion, sliced

1 small bunch radishes, sliced

1 (2-ounce) can anchovy fillets, drained and chopped

1 (3-ounce) jar capers

20 pitted Greek olives, chopped

1 cup crumbled feta cheese

3 cloves garlic, pressed

¼ cup olive oil

½ cup vinegar

Serves 4 as salad

1. Toss the fresh vegetables together gently with the anchovies, capers, olives, and crumbled cheese. The use of anchovies is suggested not for their nutritional contribution, which is slight, but for that spark of distinctive flavor they add when used in the right proportion. Some people object to anchovies as being too strong, and they *can* have an overpowering taste when one uses too much. In this recipe, though, they add a necessary spike.

2. Toss with garlic, oil, and vinegar.

This can be served either as a main course salad, or stuffed into hollowed-out French bread and made into a very elegant hero sandwich for a picnic.

AMERICAN HERO SALAD
SANDWICH

1. To hollow out a French baguette, cut
the bread in half lengthwise and pull the inside crumbs out very gently, leaving a sturdy
wall of bread crust. Add the bread crumbs to
the salad if you like.

2. Pile the lower half of your bread boat
high with salad so the top just fits on. Secure
with a string tied in several places.

3. Wrap with foil and refrigerate for several hours before the picnic. The foil
wrapped with string makes a secure, handy
carrying case and keeps the salad sandwich
well chilled as it travels from the refrigerator
to a picnic site.

You can do virtually the same thing with
individual rolls as well, whole wheat rolls,
sesame seed buns, but if you intend to put
this salad inside bread, go very light on the
oil, or you'll have soggy bread.

4. To serve the large baguette, slice
through the crust and you have the wonderful surprise of a rainbow of color.

SLICED TOMATOES IN
AUGUST

There is probably nothing better than vine-
ripened tomatoes, with fresh herbs sprinkled
on top. Although the tomato has modest nutritive value, with water representing more

than 90 per cent, the natural preference for a
vine-ripened tomato has solid nutritional
backing. Studies show that vine-ripened tomatoes contain 25–33 per cent more vitamin
C than tomatoes that are picked green and
ripened off the vine. (Ripening on the vine
doesn't always produce higher vitamin content, but with tomatoes it does.) Plant
breeders who breed a redder tomato (or a
more orange carrot) are increasing the nutritive value as well. Here I am not talking
about foods that are more colorful because of
chemically induced dyes, but foods that in
this instance are bred to have more carotene,
vitamin A.

One way to get vine-ripened tomatoes any
season of the year is to buy hydroponic tomatoes. These are grown in a water-nutrient solution and are shipped vine-ripened. So far,
hydroponic tomatoes are in good supply only
around the Phoenix area where the hydroponic people are headquartered, but it is
predicted that in the near future 10 per cent
of the tomatoes sold in supermarkets will be
hydroponic. You can tell if the tomatoes
you're buying are hydroponic by the identi-
fying sticker.

Remember to buy tomatoes with the stem
attached, as it helps retain moisture.

TOMATO IDEAS

*   Thickly sliced tomatoes dipped in seasoned bread crumbs and broiled until warm.

*   Cold whole tomatoes stuffed with shrimp,
or chicken, or tofu (see Chapter 6, Protein).

*   Tomatoes cubed and cooked with fresh
okra.

SUNCHOKE SALAD

As a departure from concentrating on vitamins A and C in salads, I'm including a new
salad possibility: the Jerusalem artichoke or
sunchoke. Although the sunchoke is not a
good source of A or C, it is a good vegetable

source of iron, is inexpensive, and has a surprising light taste. A 1-cup portion of this simplest of salads furnishes 3.4 mg iron or approximately 25 per cent of the day's requirement.

Ingredients:

1 pound sunchokes, peeled

½ cup Tulip Orange Vinaigrette (see

page 142)

1. Grate the sunchokes into thin strands in a food processor, or cut into julienne strips by hand.
2. Place the grated sunchoke in a bowl of water with vinegar added to prevent discoloring.
3. When ready to serve, drain and toss with vinaigrette dressing.

Another adaptation, which makes for a slightly less crunchy salad, is to steam the sunchokes for a moment and let them get a bit tender before grating.

SALAD SOUP

Salad leftovers needn't be thrown away because they look too wretched to be used out in the open. Often good food becomes trash because someone does not know what to do with it. The University of Arizona in their Garbage Study found that the average house throws out eighty to one hundred dollars' worth of food every year. I suspect that's a low figure. Leftover salad greens and vegetables suffer an exceptionally high fatality rate.

True, the longer produce hangs around the more nutrition it loses (after 24 hours of refrigeration chopped tomatoes lose 40 per cent of their vitamin C), but it still doesn't deserve to end up in the garbage and you deserve more for your food dollars than refuse.

Salad soup is one solution. It can be made either hot or cold from leftover salad or the remains of the vegetable bins.

COLD GAZPACHO

Ingredients:

Any leftover salad with dressing

Any leftover vegetables

Tomatoes or tomato juice

Any broth or gravy, chicken or beef

Chopped cucumbers

Yoghurt (optional)

1. Blend salad with its dressing in food processor or blender.
2. Add extra tomatoes or tomato juice. Process as you go and add as much liquid as you like until it looks like soup. Chill.
3. To serve, pour into soup bowls and float chopped cucumbers on top.

HOT GAZPACHO

1. Blend salad or leftover vegetables in food processor or blender (don't purée).
2. In saucepan sauté chopped vegetables until barely soft in a scant amount of water.
3. Add as much broth or tomato juice as you have vegetables.
4. Bring to boil.
5. To make the texture more creamy before serving, fold in a generous spoonful of yoghurt.

VIETNAMESE LETTUCE ROLLS

This delightfully light dish falls somewhere between a vegetable platter and a salad.

There is a wonderful Vietnamese restaurant in Paris on the same street as the Sorbonne where the food is prepared and served as artistically as if art students were creating still-lifes. Their lettuce rolls are one of my very favorites. The contrasts of tastes makes each bite a little different from the last.

This can either be served as an appetizer, or—as I prefer on a hot summer day—

served as a main course; guests usually seem relieved to be served something so light.

Ingredients:
Lettuce leaves, dark and large and
    flexible—about 8 per person
1 cup fresh mint leaves
1 cup fresh parsley
½ cup fresh cilantro[4]
1 cucumber, very thinly sliced
About 20 pieces citronella (lemon-like
    grass available in Haitian produce
    stores)

FILLINGS

Shredded Chicken
2 chicken breasts
1 cup water
½ cup dry white wine
½ onion, chopped
½ cup chopped carrots

Barbecued Shrimp
1 dozen medium shrimp, butterflied
1½ cups Bar B Cue Sauce (see recipe,
    Chapter 6, page 178)

SAUCE
½ cup Nuoc Mam (commercially
    available Thai fish sauce)
¼ cup lemon juice
¼ cup white vinegar
Strips of lemon rind
                    Yields 1 cup sauce

        Serves 4 amply as main course

[4] Cilantro is a Spanish herb whose seed is called coriander when it's dried. Fresh, its parsley-like leaf has a very strong flavor.

TO MAKE FILLINGS:

Shredded Chicken
1. Poach chicken in water, wine, onions, and carrots for 10 minutes or until done. Let cool.
2. With your fingers shred cooked chicken into fine pieces.
3. Arrange shredded chicken in a pile on a small serving dish. If this is done in advance, before serving, rewarm chicken to room temperature in a 350° F. oven.

Barbecued Shrimp
1. Cut shrimp down the center to butterfly.
2. Marinate in Bar B Cue sauce for an hour and grill 1½ minutes per side. Serve warm from the grill, or if done in advance, reheat prior to serving.

TO MAKE SAUCE:

For authenticity, use Nuoc Mam, a Thai fish sauce that's available in most oriental grocery stores. It has an anchovy fish extract base that is mixed with salt and water. If Nuoc Mam is not available, you could use soy sauce spiked with lemon and orange rind.

To make the traditional sauce, mix all ingredients together and add enough lemon rind to impart a citrus zest.

TO ASSEMBLE:

1. With an artist's eye, arrange fresh ingredients in neat individual piles on a large platter or in a flat basket. The small mounds of lettuce, mint, parsley, cilantro, and cucumber should be beautifully assembled— maybe with a few fresh flowers scattered among them. Although the fresh mint is essential, you can vary the other ingredients depending on availability: for example, try fennel leaves or dill instead of cilantro. The citronella, which adds an unusually pungent lemon flavor, is not necessary if unavailable.
2. Each guest places a large lettuce leaf in his or her palm and fills it with a sampling of the above ingredients, almost as one would

fill a crepe. Then either a barbecued shrimp or a small portion, a tablespoon or so, of the shredded chicken filling is added to the center of each leaf.

3. The lettuce leaf is rolled together, sausage-like, and dunked in the sauce. Everyone should have individual saucers with sauce.

This is great for those who feel they often end up eating too large a portion of protein. The main part of this meal is the fresh produce and the small piece of chicken or shrimp is for flavor. It's also nice for the cook who feels he or she doesn't have time to prepare anything. You put out the ingredients, prepare only the shrimp and chicken fillings and the sauce and the guests do their own preparation as part of the fun.

SALAD DRESSINGS

Once you have salad you need to dress it, right? Unless you're on a strict diet and a squeeze of lemon is all you're allowed (which is okay, too), you'll probably want something a little jazzier.

I hate making salad dressing. Although I get pleasure from most tasks in the area of food preparation, to me making salad dressing is a royal bore. It seems the dinner is almost ready and there I am scurrying back to the kitchen to start fiddling with a dressing. To avoid this situation, I try to have a few staples on hand already made up. In an incident my younger sister Wendy will never let me forget, on one of her visits to New York, I cajoled her into making me gallons of salad dressing. She was mixing oils and vinegars and seasonings for hours. I thought that would solve my salad dressing dilemma for a year. It didn't. The gallon-size batches never tasted quite right to either of us.

Here are my basic dressings.

WENDY'S BUTTERMILK AND BLUE CHEESE DRESSING

This is a creamy dressing, but with no heavy cream. Instead, this dressing gets its thick consistency from the buttermilk and the blue cheese.

Ingredients:

   ½ quart buttermilk made from skim milk
      (read the label on the carton)
   6 tablespoons blue cheese

Makes 3 cups

Combine ingredients in blender and chill. It's great over dark-green leafy salads.

TULIP ORANGE VINAIGRETTE

Lucy Simon Levine introduced me to the idea of adding fresh orange juice and zest to a traditional French vinaigrette. The orange adds a wonderful lightness.

Ingredients:

⅔ cup oil

⅓ cup red wine vinegar

2 cloves garlic, pressed

2 shallots, minced

Juice and zest from 1 orange

Makes 1½ cups

Mix ingredients. Note this uses less oil than more traditional ratios of 3 to 1. This is especially good with a slightly tart salad made of watercress or endive.

STRAWBERRY DRESSING

This is a reminiscence from my college dorm days when Miss Emma, the cook, used to make a rendition of this to top slices of fresh fruit. Back then, at the University of Texas, this was a strawberry *cream* dressing made with either sour cream or a combination of whipped heavy cream and mayonnaise. My lighter, healthier adaptation uses the best locally available yoghurt.

Ingredients:

½ cup plain yoghurt

½ cup sliced strawberries (or papayas, mangoes, or raspberries)

1 teaspoon honey

Makes 1 cup

Combine ingredients in blender. If you use strawberries, the dressing should be pink in color and rich with fruit. Try the other suggested fruits for variety.

MICHEL ROSTANG'S DRESSING

Spanish sherry wine vinegar

The simplest dressings are often the best and can also be the most unusual. During the mid-seventies, while traveling in France, my husband and I became friendly with the young owner of a two-star restaurant near Grenoble, Michel Rostang.

His salad dressing was like nothing we had ever tasted before. When we left, Michel mischievously presented us with a bottle of his "secret." To my amazement, it was nothing more than vinegarized Spanish sherry. At that time it was a novelty to us, but now it is sometimes available in fine gourmet cook shops in the United States. With such a distinctive vinegar, you can dress salad greens with just a sprinkle of it and nothing else, or you can use it with a smattering of oil and herbs.

TOFU DRESSING

This pleasant-tasting dressing has no fat and gives you some protein from the soybean, which you don't usually get from a salad dressing.

Ingredients:

1 (2″ square) fresh soybean custard, tofu[5] (obtainable in Japanese food stores and recently in produce departments of grocery stores)

¼ cup vinegar

Makes ½ cup

Put the soybean custard in a blender or food processor. Add the vinegar. Can be served as is, or used as a base to which to add spices, varying from curry and mustard to basil and oregano. Also makes a great topping over freshly steamed asparagus.

POPPY SEED DRESSING

People often request this recipe when I serve it. It's so simple, but it's a show-stopper. It is delightful when it is served chilled over fruit salads and the combination of the grated onion and the mustard tends to fool people's

[5] Do not attempt this with canned tofu. The tinny flavor of canned tofu does not lend itself to this use.

palates . . . some guests have even guessed it has coconut in it!

The traditional southern recipe calls for so much sugar, it's like dripping candy over fresh fruit. This recipe keeps the essence of a good poppy seed dressing, but does away with its excesses.

Ingredients:

2 tablespoons mustard

1 cup oil

⅓ cup red wine vinegar

⅓ cup sugar or honey

⅓ medium onion, grated (a red onion gives a reddish tinge to the dressing)

2 tablespoons poppy seed

Makes 2 cups

Mix well the mustard, oil, vinegar, and sweetener in a food processor or blender. Add the onion and poppy seed. The onion is one of the crucial ingredients. Too much makes this taste oniony. Be careful.

I have made this in large batches and saved it in my refrigerator for 6 months, and it improves with age.

PROTEIN:
A Little Goes a Long Way

olf and Kim Ekeus are husband and wife members of the Swedish diplomatic corps; I affectionately refer to them as my Swedish poster family because they, along with their two little ones, Helena and Oscar, are tall, blond, and gorgeous. After taking a look-see trip to The Hague, before being posted to Holland, they shared a curious food story with me that left them somewhat embarrassed, since they didn't know if what they had seen would be expected of them, too. To me their story uniquely illustrates the important role protein plays in people's lives.

After the war, it seems that the people in The Hague were so pleased to eat meat again that they would display a whole ham in the window, when they had one, for all their neighbors to see. A ham in the window became a status symbol, a sign that the family was doing well. Eventually, the story goes, everyone wanted a ham and the solution that my friends thought was curious, and which continues to this day, was the creation of beautifully painted, lifelike pottery hams, made expressly for window-sitting. It was a very practical solution as it posed no damage to the real thing.

What this story illustrates to me is how protein-conscious people are. For those people in The Hague, after the hardship of war, the window-sitting ham was undoubtedly a sign of having something substantial to eat for a change. Since the tradition has lingered long past the war years and continues today, I think it also touches on people's desires to show off with food—especially protein foods, since they are often the most expensive.

Being able to eat expensive animal protein has long been looked on as a desirable thing to strive for by many people. There's the archetypical man who works hard to put meat on the family's table. But there's a transition happening in some sectors of our society and because of this change, increasingly, the *type* of protein you eat labels you, but in

Pick the protein of your choice

totally reverse ways from the past: Now the vegetarians are at the top. In this chapter I will look in depth at the important health implications of this transition.

Briefly, let's look at what protein is. The people in The Hague were seeing a representation of protein with those hams. If on a more basic level, we could actually *see* protein, it would make it easier to understand what it is. But you can't. What you can see around you are protein-rich foods (meats, poultry, fish, cereals, dairy foods) that after digestion yield a combination of twenty-two amino acids. These amino acids are important because they are the principle materials from which our body cells are composed— our bone cells, brain, muscle, skin, intestine, nerve, and lung cells.

In this chapter, I discuss what kinds of protein you should eat to get the correct amino acid balance, or if this balance is even important. Should you select from animal sources, vegetable sources, or a combination of both? If you're on a vegetarian diet, do you have to be a scientist to calculate if you're getting enough protein and whether or not it's the right kind? I'll also look at which sources of protein are the cheapest and suggest a practical way to figure your specific needs.

 # What Kind? A Personal Choice

What *kind*—red meat, poultry, fish, vegetable protein—and does it matter? This is a highly personal question involving health, religious and moral convictions, and personal aesthetics, in addition to what tastes delicious to you.

I started changing my personal use of protein eight years ago when I was exposed to three factors simultaneously: cancer, fats, and an extended trip to the South of France. The first factor involved a documentary film I produced for Public Television on cancer. In 1973 I traveled around the country interviewing the country's top oncologists. They frequently could not agree on the method of treatment, but most of them did agree on one thing: they had stopped eating processed meats preserved with nitrites. (Nitrites are chemical compounds used to preserve color and flavor in luncheon meats, bacon, ham, pickled pigs feet, corned beef, and cured fish; they have been suspected of causing cancer.) I felt if our country's leading cancer specialists had stopped bringing home the bacon, probably my husband and I should, too, especially since my husband's mother had just died of cancer. Out of our diet went meats processed with nitrites—most luncheon meats, Canadian bacon and ham, unless we could find a butcher who cured his own without nitrites. This decision certainly simplified our diet; there are whole rows in supermarkets we don't even go near. (For the current situation on nitrites, see Chapter 7, Demons and Other Additives.)

Carrying this cancer-causing connection a step further, many oncologists also told me they were decreasing the consumption of all red meats (whether nitrite preserved or not) in their diets because of the emerging correlation between the consumption of red meats and a higher incidence of cancer. According to T. Colin Campbell, Professor of Nutritional Biochemistry at Cornell, one of the more popular theories in this vein is that "the high and prolonged intake of beef and certain other meat have been shown to give rise in the G.I. tract to microflora which may promote or induce tumor formation."

The second factor in my personal decision about protein concerned saturated fats and cholesterol. Cholesterol levels may reveal a predisposition to heart disease. (To find your levels, have an easy, painless, inexpensive cholesterol-triglyceride test done, for which it takes 5 minutes to have the blood drawn. See page 182.)

Because tests over the years show my cholesterol levels to be low and no one in my family has ever had heart disease, it appears I don't have a problem and could probably eat red meats of any kind, and saturated fats like butter and nuts in moderation. However, the story doesn't end there. My husband has an entirely different picture, with raised cholesterol levels. For his health, we made the personal decision of eliminating most saturated fats high in cholesterol. Except for an occasional splurge at Hamburger Hamlet, out of our diet went fatty red meats and even some beloved French cheeses. (For a discussion of whether diet *can* affect cholesterol levels, see page 181.)

The third factor was the most fun to experience. We went on an extended holiday to the South of France. Because of the wide variety of seafood available, we ate practically nothing but local fish for weeks as we worked our way from Provence across the Riviera. With the sun shining on us in Marseilles, we ate bouillabaisse with racasse. In the open-air market in Nice, we'd have fish grilled over charcoal. Loup (Mediterranean sea bass) grilled over fennel twigs was featured in Monaco. On the Italian border in Ventimiglia it was cold marinated mussels.

Essentially, we were eating a diet of light fish and locally grown vegetables, and sometimes, if poultry was a specialty of the chef, we'd have a local chicken or hen. Upon returning home to New York, we realized it had been weeks since we'd eaten any red meat and we hadn't missed it. The variety of tastes available with the fish, poultry, and vegetables had become more satisfying. We also made another discovery; we found that if all the senses are catered to—if the food *looks* beautiful, if it *smells* wonderful, and if it *tastes* delicious—then you can eat much *smaller* portions and still feel more genuinely satisfied than if you sat down to the traditional chunk of red meat.

Some people returning from France complain of the heavy cream sauce sickness. I returned that summer with an appreciation of how light food can be when it is simply prepared with the freshest ingredients. (And this was years before the French started their nouvelle cuisine, inspired by health spas.)

Living now on both the Atlantic and Pacific Coasts, our acquired food preferences are easy to implement on a practical basis. In fact, it's even easier in California since we have our own vegetable patch. I admit it would be much less easy and less interesting if we didn't live near areas where fresh fish is in abundance, or where gorgeous fresh produce isn't easily grown or readily available. I certainly don't hold our dietary regime to be the perfect or even necessary answer for everyone. My father, who is in his sixties, is in excellent health, is athletically trim and spry, and there are no health reasons to indicate he should change from his lifelong diet of meat and potatoes. And he *likes* meat and potatoes. But for us, especially for my husband, ours *feels* like a good regimen and over the years I continue to receive medical and research information that reassures me that what we're doing is right and healthful for *us.*

People sometimes ask if I'm fanatic about adhering to this regimen. I'm not. If I go to someone's house and they're serving pot roast, I eat it and perhaps enjoy it more because it's something we never have at home. At home, I stick to no red meat and serve small portions of protein. Other people are more rigid in their behavior. I will never forget the time I went to Santa Barbara to interview Nathan Pritikin, the maverick inventor turned nutritionist, who runs a fine clinic primarily for heart disease patients. Pritikin's basic tenet is that heart disease and other circulatory diseases can be cured by the use of proper diet and exercise.

He met me at the door of his sprawling house, which overlooks islands of Japanese gardens and cool, lily-pad pools, with a bowl of day-old kasha in his hand. During our interview, he sat monklike, eating his lunch of cold, dried-up kasha. A lot of his philosophy is probably right (he says no fats, no sugar, no salt[1]), but I'm not as strict as he is. Dried-up kasha for lunch doesn't satisfy my sense of aesthetics. I would feel deprived. And besides, I know you can change to a better, more healthful diet and still eat beautifully prepared foods. (See recipes at end of chapter.) Apparently Pritikin knows this now, too, because in a recent visit to his Los Angeles headquarters, the food looked terrific.

[1] For more information, see his book *Live Longer Now,* published by Grosset & Dunlap.

Complete Versus Incomplete

Nutritionists used to teach that some proteins were complete unto themselves (animal proteins—meat, fish, and poultry), while others, especially proteins from vegetables and grains (beans, rice, and nuts) were incomplete and needed to be supplemented to be fully useful to the body. This rigid regimentation probably caused many people to stick with animal proteins: they didn't want to chance getting shortchanged.

The idea of complete versus incomplete emerged in the early 1900s in studies Osborne and Mendel carried out with rats. The rats were fed various proteins one at a time and their growth was measured. If the rats

Complete vs. incomplete protein

grew well on one protein source, it was called complete and if they did not grow, the protein was called incomplete. Some were also called partially incomplete (growth stopped but life was not impossible). From these studies there emerged a curiously titled Rat Biological Value calculation that for obvious reasons has since been shortened just to BV, Biologic Value. The BV reflects the completeness or incompleteness of various protein sources. Rats grew well on an egg diet, thus the BV of eggs is 94 per cent; on potatoes, they didn't do quite so well, thus potatoes got a BV of 67 per cent.

Using the BV calculations, proteins of ani-

mal origin, such as those found in eggs, dairy products, and meats, yield a mixture of amino acids that are well balanced, with none of the amino acids lacking or found only in small amounts. They are therefore said to be of higher biological value than proteins from vegetables and beans. (You can see why the meat and dairy industries have long favored the idea of complete versus incomplete. Viewed from this perspective, their industries come out smelling like roses.)

Unfortunately, some popular authors using this antiquated complete-incomplete idea have contributed to making vegetable proteins seem unnecessarily complicated. Frances Moore Lappé, author of *Diet for a Small Planet,* created a career based on the exaggerated idea of complete and incomplete protein. Her book on how to eat lower on the food chain by using more vegetables is essentially a complex set of directions on how to complete vegetable proteins successfully to avoid protein deficiency. Except, in general, even among vegetarians, we don't have a condition of protein deficiency in this country. Although her book became a bestseller and was thus read by a mass audience, Lappé's elaborate calculations are really of value only to the tiniest group of purists on *strict vegetarian diets,* eating *no* protein from any animal sources, including dairy sources.

As Doris H. Calloway, Professor of Nutrition at the University of California at Berkeley, has said to me, "It is hard to eat a diet unbalanced in protein in this country." Our American diets have over 50 per cent of their protein derived from high quality animal sources, whether this is from meat, or dairy sources like milk and cheese. Even most vegetarians get *twice* as much protein as they need. I focus on this issue of complete versus incomplete proteins because to my mind it has received much misplaced publicity. We are not rats eating only one protein food in isolation from all others. In our varied diets, there is little danger of protein deficiency from lack of *completion*. (For more information on vegetable sources of protein, see page 171.)

The idea of combining different protein foods in the same meal does have its place, but most Americans do this combining naturally: beans *and* rice, cereal *and* milk, macaroni *and* cheese, baked beans *and* brown bread. Let's look at one example. Cereals and grains tend to be lower in the amino acid lysine, but rich in sulfur-containing amino acids. Milk is rich in lysine, but low in sulfur. Therefore, by doing what comes naturally and tastes best, eating cereal *with* milk, by custom and preference, the consumer gets the proper scientific balance.

 # How Little?

Although an awareness about the importance of protein exists, on a practical level there is little consciousness of how *much* protein is necessary for good health. Since most Americans eat from *two* to *five* times the amount of protein they need and, as mentioned earlier, even vegetarians get *twice* what they need, I prefer to think of the protein requirement in terms of how *little* we need, rather than how *much*.

The protein publicists have done such a good job of promoting the value of protein foods that the American public generally feels the more you eat, the better. But protein in excess of what we need doesn't go to vital organs or essential growth; it is burned for calories, converted to fat, or excreted in the urine. That's what's meant when it's said we're a country with very expensive urine.

Is too much protein dangerous? Aside from the obvious fact that excessive protein consumption is expensive, high protein diets are usually associated with high fat and cholesterol intakes, and high calories. It is these aspects which many experts feel are helping Americans dig their graves with a knife and fork.

One side effect of high protein intake currently under study is calcium depletion. At the University of California at Berkeley and at the University of Wisconsin, the departments of Nutritional Science are investigating the relationship between high protein intakes and increased calcium excretion in the urine. Currently, the data suggests that a relatively high protein diet leads to a loss of calcium, which can cause one of the serious problems of aging: development of osteoporosis—a reduction in the quality of bones that is associated with frequent fractures. (For more on this, see Chapter 11, page 359.)

On the other hand, getting too little protein (protein deficiency) is rare in this country, except in extreme cases of poverty, catastrophe, or crazy dieting. Usually, if adults are getting enough calories, the protein requirement takes care of itself.

But how is one to know the correct amount of protein that *is* required? Perhaps,

How little?

for example, you want to eat less protein to save money or calories, how do you know how little is still enough? Since the requirements for a specific individual can be determined only through elaborate metabolic studies, it has been necessary to devise general estimates of amounts needed that will be safe for the entire population. We now have a variety of ways of expressing protein needs for adults (for children, see chart, page 153): A study done in 1920 by H. C. Sherman calculated that adults need 0.5 gm of protein per kilogram of body weight and a summary of information available in the seventies still supports Sherman's estimate; the National Academy of Science's figure of 0.8 gm of protein per kilogram of body weight has become the Recommended Daily Allowance for the nation; and the Senate Select Committee on Nutrition suggested 10–14 per cent of calories should be from protein. (When computed, this recommendation reflects a protein consumption that is substantially higher than the RDA indicates is necessary.)

Here's one way to look at the amount of protein suggested for a 154-pound man (74 kg).

Method	Measure Grams of Protein/ kilograms body weight	Daily Protein Need of 154-pound man
Sherman	0.5 gm/kg	35 gm
National Academy of Sciences	0.8 gm/kg (RDA)	56 gm
Dietary Goals	12 per cent of calories	81 gm

But all this is only so much gobbledygook unless you, sitting in your home, have some practical way of calculating how *your* protein intake compares. When you eat a hamburger, cottage cheese, or rice and beans, you know you are eating protein-rich foods, but you probably don't know how rich.

To help, I've composed an easy to use Protein Intake Guide. For comparison, I've contrasted the RDA figure (which has a built-in safety margin of 50–100 per cent more protein than you need), with Sherman's lower figure. I am not suggesting the minimum amount, but it's included to show how *little* some scientists think we can get by on. If you stick with the RDA, you'll certainly be on the safe side.[2]

The only people who need more than the RDA requirement are pregnant women, who should increase their protein intake by 30 gm a day in the second and third trimester, and lactating women, who should increase their protein intake by 20 gm a day. During recovery from illnesses, stress, or trauma, or from any other condition in which new tissue must be synthesized, requirements for protein are elevated, but a generally bigger food intake automatically includes more protein and naturally fills this need. There is also the commonly held belief that for muscular work you need to increase your protein intake particularly while muscle tissue is developing. In fact, you should increase your complex carbohydrates (see Chapter 12, For the Life of You: Exercise).

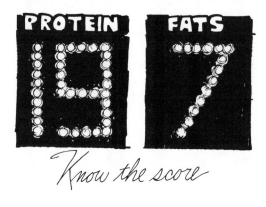

Know the score

Although checking your protein intake is not something you would want to do every day, doing it at least once will enlighten you about how much protein you consume versus how much it is suggested you *need*. The

[2] The RDA should be viewed as a *guideline* figure that has been developed to satisfy the needs of 98 per cent of the population. It is too often interpreted as a concrete *requirement,* rather than a suggested guide that is subject to individual differences among people.

process is simple. First, find your body weight on the Protein Requirements chart and check the protein recommendation for you. Record this in the Protein Need space on the Protein Intake Guide. Then, using the Protein Index, (page 155), select the items you might typically eat in one day and record the numbers of grams of protein. (If you eat a lot of vegetables, see chart on page 16 for their protein contribution.)

Protein Requirements for Women (19⁺ years)

WEIGHT		PROTEIN INTAKE (GM/DAY)	
lbs.	kg	Sherman*	RDA†
100	45	23	36
110	50	25	40
120	55	28	44
130	59	30	47
140	64	32	51
150	68	34	54
160	73	37	58
170	77	39	62
180	82	41	66

Protein Requirements for Men (19⁺ years)

WEIGHT		PROTEIN INTAKE (GM/DAY)	
lbs.	kg	Sherman	RDA
130	59	30	47
140	64	32	51
150	68	34	54
160	73	37	58
170	77	39	62
180	82	41	66
190	86	43	69
200	91	46	73
210	95	48	76
220	100	50	80
230	105	53	84
240	109	55	87
250	114	57	91

* Based on requirement set by H. C. Sherman, 1920.
"A summation of all data available 50 years later supports Sherman's estimate, and indicates the normal individual variability to be within ± 15 percent of that value." From *Nutrition and*

Protein Requirements for Children

	AGE (YEARS)		WEIGHT		PROTEIN
	From	up to	lbs.	kg	(gm)
Infants	0	½	13	6	13.2
	½	1	20	9	18
Children	1	3	29	13	23
	4	6	44	20	30
	7	10	62	28	34
Males	11	14	99	45	45
	15	18	145	66	56
Females	11	14	101	46	46
	15	18	120	56	46

Age. Because their tissues are growing, infants and children require two to three times more protein per unit of body weight than do adults.

SOURCE: Recommended Daily Dietary Allowances, revised 1980, Food and Nutrition Board, National Academy of Sciences–National Research Council.

After you've recorded the grams of protein you typically eat, compare it with what the chart shows you need. If you are like most Americans, you will find you're eating much *more* protein than your body requires. The aim of this exercise is to make you conscious of how *little* protein is enough. For example, a 120-pound woman needs 44 gm of protein a day. For me, it turns out that a turkey sandwich (20 gm), a glass of low fat milk (10 gm), and ½ cup of cottage cheese (15 gm) satisfies my protein requirement.

Since high protein foods are also high calorie foods, if I get hungry after eating what I know to be my quota of protein, to keep my weight at its present level, I nibble on low calorie vegetables, rather than last night's leftover chicken. If more people thought in terms of what their bodies need, instead of whimsical cravings for food, we'd be a thinner nation.

Physical Fitness, Bogert, Briggs, and Calloway.

† Extrapolated from Recommended Daily Dietary Allowances, revised 1980, Food and Nutrition Board, National Academy of Sciences–National Research Council.

Easy-to-use Protein Intake Guide

EXAMPLE: WEIGHT: 190-lb. Man

One Day's Food Intake	Item	Protein gm
Breakfast: Toasted muffin	Muffin	2.0
w/cheese. Glass of milk.	Cheese	7.1
Coffee.	Milk	8.8
Lunch: Egg salad sandwich on	Egg	6.5
whole wheat bread. Yoghurt	Bread	2.5
topped w/fruits.	Yoghurt	7.7
Dinner: Broiled fish.	Fish	25.0
Broccoli. Tomato salad	Broccoli	3.0
w/slices of mozzarella cheese.	Tomato	1.5
Watermelon.	Mozzarella	7.0
	TOTAL:	71.1

NOTE: This man's food intake is quite prudent, yet it easily fulfills his protein requirement.

For You to Use: YOUR WEIGHT: _____   YOUR PROTEIN NEED: _____

One Day's Food Intake	Item	Protein gm
Breakfast:		
Lunch:		
Dinner:		
	TOTAL:	

Protein Index *

	Amount	Protein (gm)	Calories	Fat (gm)
DAIRY PRODUCTS:				
Milk				
Whole (3.5% fat)	1 cup	8.5	159	8.5
Low Fat (2% fat)	1 cup	10.3	145	4.9
Skim	1 cup	8.8	88	0.2
Condensed (sweetened)	1 cup	24.8	982	26.6
	1 fl. oz.	3.1	123	3.3
Evaporated (unsweetened)	1 cup	17.6	345	19.2
	1 fl. oz.	2.2	43	2.5
Dry (nonfat instant)	1 cup	8.2	82	0.2
Human	1 cup	2.4	192	9.6
	1 fl. oz.	0.3	24	1.2
Eggs	1 large raw or cooked	6.5	82	5.8
Yoghurt				
from partially skimmed milk	1 container net weight 8 oz.	7.7	113	3.8
from whole milk		6.8	140	7.7
Cheese				
Cheddar (prepackaged)	1 oz.	7.1	113	9.1
	1 slice (13 gm)	3.3	52	4.2
Cottage Cheese				
Dry curd with creaming mixture, 4.2% milk fat, large or small curd	1 cup	30.6	240	9.5
Dry curd without creaming mixture, 0.3% milk fat	1 cup	25	125	0.4
Cream Cheese (regular, packaged)	1 tbsp. 1 oz. = 2 tbsp.	1.1	52	5.3
Swiss (prepackaged)	1 oz.	7.8	105	7.9
	1 slice (14 gm)	3.9	52	3.9
Pasteurized Process Cheese, American	1 oz.	6.6	105	8.5
	1 slice (13 gm)	3.0	48	3.9
Pasteurized Process Cheese Spread, American	1 oz.	4.5	82	6.1
	1 slice (14 gm)	3.2	52	4.2
GRAINS, CEREALS, FLOUR:				
Bread				
Corn, from mix	1 slice	2.5	95	3.0
French/Vienna	1 slice	2.0	70	0.7

Protein Index (continued)

	Amount	Protein (gm)	Calories	Fat (gm)
GRAINS, CEREALS, FLOUR (continued):				
Rye	1 slice	2.0	55	0.3
White	1 slice	2.0	60	0.7
White, enriched (slightly more vitamins)	1 slice	2.0	60	0.7
Whole Wheat	1 slice	2.5	55	0.7
Cereals				
Ready to Eat				
Bran Flakes	1 cup	4.0	120	0.7
Corn Flakes	1 cup	2.0	95	0.1
Puffed Rice	1 cup	0.8	55	0.1
Wheat Flakes	1 cup	3.0	90	0.4
Puffed Wheat	1 cup	2.0	45	0.2
Cooked				
Oatmeal	1 cup	4.8	132	2.4
Farina	1 cup	3.2	105	0.2
Rice				
Brown, long grain	1 cup cooked	4.9	232	1.2
White, enriched	1 cup cooked	4.1	223	0.2
Precooked, instant	1 cup cooked	3.6	180	trace
Noodles				
Egg, enriched	1 cup cooked	6.6	200	2.4
Unenriched	1 cup cooked	6.6	200	2.4
VEGETABLES:				
Beans				
Garbanzos	1 cup cooked	6.0	110	1.0
Snap Beans	1 cup cooked	2.0	31	0.3
Soybeans	1 cup cooked	19.8	234	10.3
Mung Beans	1 cup sprouted raw	4.0	37	0.2
Broccoli	2/3 cup boiled	3.0	25	0.3
Carrots	1	0.6	20	0.1
Cauliflower	1 cup flower buds	2.5	25	0.2
Celery	1 cup diced or 2 large sticks	0.9	15	0.1
Chard, Swiss	1 cup cut-up stalk and leaves	4.0	40	0.4
Dandelion Greens	1/2 cup boiled, drained	2.0	35	0.6
Kale	1/2 cup boiled, drained	2.5	20	0.4
Kohlrabi	1/2 cup diced, boiled, drained	1.5	20	0.1
Lettuce, iceberg	1/5 head	0.8	12	0.1
Mushrooms	3½ oz. raw	2.5	30	0.3
Olives, green	1 large or 2 small	trace	5	0.6
Onions	1 raw	1.5	40	0.1
	3-4 small boiled	1.0	30	0.1

Protein Index (continued)

	Amount	Protein (gm)	Calories	Fat (gm)
VEGETABLES (continued)				
Peas, green	1 cup raw	9.1	122	0.6
	1 cup drained cooked	8.6	114	0.6
Peppers, green	1 raw	0.8	15	0.1
Potatoes	100 gm of each:			
	1 medium baked	2.5	95	0.1
	1 medium boiled, pared before boiling	2.0	65	0.1
	20 pieces french-fried	4.5	275	13.0
Frozen	20 pieces french-fried	3.5	220	8.0
Mashed	Milk and fat added, 1/2 cup	2.0	95	4.0
Squash				
Summer	1/2 cup boiled, drained	0.9	15	0.1
Winter	3½ oz., baked	2.0	65	0.4
Sweet Potatoes	1 small baked	2.0	140	0.5
Tomatoes	1 medium fresh	1.5	35	0.3
Watercress	10 average sprigs raw	0.2	2	trace
FISH:				
Cod	4 oz. before cooking, baked	28.5	170	5.0
Fish Sticks	5 sticks	18.0	195	10.0
Flounder/Sole	4 oz. before cooking, baked	30.0	200	8.0
Haddock	4 oz. before cooking, fried	19.5	165	6.0
Halibut	3½ oz. broiled	25.0	171	7.0
Salmon				
Fresh	3½ oz. broiled	27.0	180	7.0
Canned, pink	1/2 cup	23.0	155	7.0
Sardines, packed in oil	3 oz. drained	20.5	175	9.0
Tuna				
in oil	5/8 cup drained	29.0	195	8.0
in water	5/8 cup solid and liquid	28.0	125	0.8
POULTRY:				
Chicken				
Light meat, without skin	100 gm, or 3½ oz. roasted	32.0	166	3.4
Dark meat, without skin	100 gm, or 3½ oz. roasted	38.0	176	6.3
Flesh and skin	100 gm, or 3½ oz. roasted	27.0	250	15.0
Fryers				
Breast	100 gm or 1/2 breast fried	32.5	203	6.4
Thigh and drumstick	100 gm or 1 of each fried	29.0	235	11.0
Back	100 gm or 3½ oz. fried	30.0	347	21.0
Drumstick	100 gm fried	33.0	235	10.2
Neck	100 gm fried	27.0	289	17.4
Thigh	100 gm fried	29.0	237	11.4
Wing	100 gm fried	29.0	268	15.0

Protein Index (continued)

	Amount	Protein (gm)	Calories	Fat (gm)
POULTRY (continued)				
Duck (for raw)				
Flesh only	100 gm, or 3½ oz.	21.4	165	8.2
Turkey				
Light meat, flesh only	3½ oz. or 3 slices roasted	33.0	175	4.0
Dark meat, flesh only	3½ oz. or 3 slices roasted	30.0	205	8.0
MEAT:				
Beef				
Hamburger				
Lean, about 20% fat	4 oz. raw	20.0	235	16.6
	2.9 oz. broiled			
Extra lean, about 10% fat	4 oz. raw	23.0	186	9.6
	3 oz. broiled			

(NOTE: There is variation from market to market as to the fat content of different grades of chopped meat. State and federal regulations give ranges of fat content for different grades, but each market has its own quality control.)

	Amount	Protein (gm)	Calories	Fat (gm)
Roast				
Chuck				
Choice Grade				
Lean with fat (69% lean + 31% fat)	3 oz. braised	19.0	363	31.2
Lean trimmed of separable fat	3 oz. braised	25.0	212	12.0
Good Grade				
Lean with fat (73% lean + 27% fat)	3 oz. braised	20.6	320	25.8
Lean trimmed of separable fat	3 oz. braised	25.0	186	8.7
Rib				
Choice Grade				
Lean with fat (64% lean + 36% fat)	3 oz. roasted	16.9	374	33.5
Lean trimmed of separable fat	3 oz. roasted	24.0	205	11.4

(NOTE: Choice grade has more internal fat than lower grades. If you trim the fat off meat, you reduce fat intake significantly.)

	Amount	Protein (gm)	Calories	Fat (gm)
Steak				
Round				
Lean with fat (81% lean + 19% fat)	3 oz. broiled	24.3	222	13.1
Lean trimmed of separable fat	3 oz. broiled	26.6	161	5.2

Protein Index (continued)

	Amount	Protein (gm)	Calories	Fat (gm)
MEAT (continued)				
Sirloin				
Lean with fat (66% lean + 34% fat)	3 oz. broiled	19.6	329	27.2
Lean trimmed of separable fat	3 oz. broiled	27.4	176	6.5
Flank				
100% lean	3 oz. broiled	26.0	167	6.2
Pork				
Chops				
Lean and fat	1 medium, 66 gm (about 2.4 oz.) broiled	15.0	245	20.0
Lean only	1 chop, 48 gm (about 1.7 oz. of meat) broiled	13.5	110	6.0
Loin				
Lean and fat	2 slices, 90 gm (about 3.2 oz.) roasted	20.0	335	28.0
Lean only	2 slices, 70 gm (about 2.5 oz. of meat) roasted	20.0	165	9.0
Ham, cured				
Lean with fat	2 pieces (3 oz.) baked or roasted	18.0	246	19.0
Lean without fat	2 pieces (3 oz.) baked or roasted	22.0	159	7.5
Bacon	3 strips (1 oz.) broiled, drained	8.0	155	13.0

(NOTE: Yield from 1 lb. of bacon is about 5 oz.)

Sausage	3 links, cooked	11.0	285	27.0

Luncheon Meats				
Bologna	1 oz. or 1 slice	4.0	85	7.0
Salami, dry	1 oz. or 1 slice	7.0	135	11.0
Corned beef, canned	1 oz. or 1 slice	7.0	65	3.4
Roast Beef	1 oz. or 1 slice cooked	8.0	68	3.8
Turkey				
White meat	1 oz. or 1 slice	9.0	30	1.0
Dark meat	1 oz. or 1 slice	8.5	58	2.4
Hot Dog	1 average cooked	6.0	150	14.0

SOURCES: *Nutritive Value of American Foods*, Handbook #456, U. S. Department of Agriculture. L. Jean Bogert, George M. Briggs, and Doris H. Calloway, *Nutrition and Physical Fitness*, 9th ed. (Philadelphia: W. B. Saunders Company, 1973).

*In addition to protein content, the fat and calorie contents are also listed on this chart. This additional information is included because some foods may be very similar in the amount of protein they provide, but may vary widely in their fat and calorie contents.

Dairy Sources of Protein

Dairy products ranging from milk and eggs to cheese and frozen yoghurt supply one fifth of the protein in our diets, along with supplying calcium, riboflavin, and other valuable nutrients. For the lacto-ovo vegetarians, who eat eggs and cheese and no other animal sources of protein, the dairy group supplies the largest part of the protein in their diets. The dairy group, with its rich supply of calcium, should also assume a more important role in the diets of both teen-age girls and women, since the USDA's consumption survey published in the summer of 1980 revealed that these two groups are not getting enough calcium.

Dairy products

EGGS

It has been said eggs are nature's prepackaged masterpiece. They are one of the richest sources of protein, furnishing all the amino acids essential for building and maintaining body tissues. Their versatility in cooking is almost unmatched—they can be used for any meal from breakfast to lunch and dinner and for snacks in between. This versatility is further enhanced by their reasonable price.

Price

Eggs are one of the few food bargains left. They *are* a bargain because people are eating fewer and fewer of them so their decline in sales keeps their price down.

To get the best price when buying eggs, choose small and medium eggs in the fall when they are plentiful and are usually more economical than large eggs. In the spring large eggs are plentiful and may cost less than smaller sizes on the basis of the cost of a pound of eggs.

Color

Egg color is determined by the breed of the hen laying the egg and it may vary from white to deep brown. Color is a breed characteristic. I have a friend who drives miles to buy brown eggs to use in baking. She swears they cook better, so maybe, for her, they do. But, in fact, brown- and white-shelled eggs have no different cooking properties, no nutritional difference. The only difference is the color of their shell and usually their price. Because consumers often mistakenly *think* brown eggs are superior, the seller is able to capitalize on this and charge more. The best reason I can think of to buy brown eggs is as a means of keeping eggs sorted in the refrigerator. If you alternate your purchases between brown and white eggs, you can use up last week's brown eggs before this week's white eggs.

Eggs are everything they're cracked up to be.

Eating Less

Americans are producing eggs on a massive scale, even exporting millions of dozens to the Arab countries, where it's too hot for large-scale egg production, but we are eating fewer and fewer ourselves. In the last 10 years, our consumption has dropped 20 per cent. Egg consumption is down because of its cholesterol content and its connection with the diet-heart controversy. In some circles the egg has been condemned as a public enemy, a potential killer right up there with cigarettes and DDT. (See cholesterol discussion this chapter, page 182.)

MILK

Milk is the backbone of the dairy group and in addition to supplying calcium and riboflavin it is still one of the cheapest sources of protein. One 8-ounce glass of skim milk provides almost 9 gm of protein or about 20 per cent of the day's entire protein requirement. Some nomads in West Africa live for months exclusively on milk. Although I wouldn't suggest that, milk's usefulness in the diet is without question. (For problems in drinking milk, lactose intolerance, see Chapter 10, Children, page 308.)

Milk Labeling

In grocery stores it is easy for the consumer to get confused by the vast array of milks for sale. Their labels *seem* so similar, yet the products are different. But how different? The following definitions should clear up some of the confusion concerning terminology, fat content, and introduce you to some new milk products on the market.

Whole Milk

Whole milk is the old stand-by. It is rich in flavor, is 3.5 per cent fat, and has a heavy, milky-white color. One cup has 159 calories. Whole milk is the type of milk recommended for infants and small children, who need all its calories and nutrients. Increasingly for adults, other kinds of milks are recommended.

Low Fat Milk

Low fat milk is a category many people find misleading. Low fat milk usually has 2 per cent milk fat, which places it, fat-wise, *between* skim and whole milk. Calorie-wise, it is closer to whole milk with 145 calories per cup. Because its flavor is so close to whole milk, it's often the intermediate route taken by people who are trying to wean themselves off whole milk onto skim milk.

Skim Milk or Nonfat Milk

Skim milk has recently become the darling of the milk crowd. Even though technically it has some fat (less than .5 per cent), skim milk is milk from which as much fat as technologically possible has been removed. If the skim milk is fortified with vitamins A and D, it contains almost all the valuable nutrients found in whole milk, but without the extra calories and fat. You also get an extra protein bonus with skim milk. To enhance the flavor and texture, manufacturers add one extra gram of protein powder per glass. Skim milk is often labeled nonfat milk; they are one and the same thing.

TIPS

* If you're one of those people who don't like the color of skim milk, or its *lack* of color, try drinking it in an opaque glass.
* If at first you don't like its watery flavor, to make it thicker try mixing in a teaspoon of instant nonfat dry milk powder in each glass.

Nonfat Dry Milk

Nonfat dry milk is made from skim milk and has the equivalent food values as the milk from which it's made. In some instances where it is fortified with vitamins A and D, it will have more of these two vitamins. The home use of nonfat dry milk is up 30 per cent and for good reason: you can save at least *50 per cent* of the price of liquid milk by buying the powdered form. I've found that if it's made in advance and well chilled, it tastes fine and it also makes an indistinguishable substitute for liquid milk in baking and cooking. I always keep a few envelopes on hand in case I run out of liquid milk. The packages have a shelf life of 1 year. It can also be added in its dry form to the diets of people needing more calcium. For example, ½ cup added to a small meatloaf gives more calcium without changing the taste.

NONFAT WHIPPED TOPPING

One idea that's fun to do with nonfat dry milk is to make a low calorie whipped topping that you can use on desserts instead of whipped cream. It has a light, airy consistency.

Put ½ cup cold water in bowl. Add ½ cup nonfat dry milk. Beat until stiff. Add sweetener of your choice—sugar, brandy or rum, or perhaps some vanilla or cinnamon. Beat only until well mixed. Makes 2½ cups. Use same day; the following day, this will be flat.

CANNED MILK

Condensed Milk (sweetened)

Canned milk comes in two forms: condensed (sweetened) and evaporated (unsweetened). Condensed milk is a thick, rich-tasting product whose high sugar content (42 per cent) makes it suitable for use in dessert-type cooking. In the last decade, consumer use of both condensed milk and evaporated milk has drastically decreased as people opt for powdered milk instead.

Evaporated Milk (unsweetened)

Evaporated milk is a canned milk product that pours more like the fresh product than its condensed counterpart. It has undergone a heating process that extends its shelf life well over a year. It is used primarily in bread and candy making. Although it is most often a whole milk product, it is possible to find evaporated skim milk.

Cream

Traditionally, creams have not had nutritional labeling because their serving size is so small—usually a tablespoon per person. Used in these small quantities, the dairy industry felt cream didn't make enough contribution to the diet to warrant individual labeling. The significant differences between creams are their *fat* and *calorie* content:

	% Fat	Calories in 1 Tbsp.
Half and Half	11.7%	20 calories
Light (coffee/table)	20.6%	32 calories
Light Whipping Cream	31.3%	45 calories
Heavy Whipping Cream	37.6%	53 calories

WHIPPING NOTE: All creams and milk products *can* be whipped whether or not they are so labeled. The higher the fat content, the longer they stay puffy and inflated. If the product is labeled "whipped" cream, that means emulsifier has been added to keep it inflated after it's whipped.

Cultured Milks

Cultured milks are usually, but not always, skim milk with a bacteria culture added that gives them their distinctive taste.

BUTTERMILK

Buttermilk is the most familiar cultured milk. Years ago, buttermilk was simply the liquid left in the churn after making the butter. Although the taste remains pretty much the same, today, buttermilk is made with specially prepared cultures and pasteurized at higher temperatures and for a longer period of time than other fresh fluid milks. Because of the "butter" in its name, weight watchers may be needlessly staying away from it. A cup of buttermilk has only 88 calories and is usually made from skim milk. Because salt is added to bring out its tangy flavor, buttermilk may be a problem for people on a sodium-restricted diet.

ACIDOPHILUS

Acidophilus is a newly introduced cultured milk product, but without the sour taste. It is simply milk—either whole or skim, but each quart has approximately 6 billion microorganisms of bacteria added. All the claims for what those organisms can do for the intestinal tract have not yet been proven. If you're healthy, you already have a good supply of useful bacteria in your intestinal tract and since it costs a few cents more than regular milk, you can decide if it's worth it to you.

KEFIR

Kefir is another old milk product that has recently been introduced in our stores. It originated in the Caucasus, the area in Russia where people live so long, supposedly because they eat mostly yoghurt. Kefir is essentially drinkable yoghurt and comes in a variety of flavors.

MILK FACTS

* *Milk can be frozen.*
You have too much milk; what to do with it? Freeze it. Frozen milk has the same nutritional values and once thawed has the same consistency.

* *Make cream last a long time.*
For maximum shelf life, do not return unused cream from a pitcher to its original container. Store it separately in the refrigerator. Try to pour only the amount needed at one time.

* *Ultra-pasteurized milk does not need refrigeration.*
Ultra-pasteurization is a process widely used in Europe and may gain in popularity here if people can reconcile themselves to buying fresh milk that's not refrigerated. Ultra-pasteurization sterilizes milk at 280° F. to remove organisms that cause it to sour. The process eliminates the need for refrigeration until the container is opened.

* *Cut calories and cost in cream sauces.*
To cut calories in cream sauces, trying using full-strength canned evaporated milk. It has the same texture as cream, but half the calories and is less expensive.

Whole Milk

	Calories	Protein (gm)	Fat (gm)	Carbohydrate (gm)	Calcium (mg)	Phosphorus (mg)	Iron (mg)	Sodium (mg)	Potassium (mg)	Vitamin A (I.U.)	Thiamin (mg)	Riboflavin (mg)	Niacin (mg)	Vitamin C (mg)
1 cup	159	8.5	8.5	12.0	288	227	.1	122	351	350	.07	.41	.2	2

Evaporated Milk (unsweetened)

	Calories	Protein (gm)	Fat (gm)	Carbohydrate (gm)	Calcium (mg)	Phosphorus (mg)	Iron (mg)	Sodium (mg)	Potassium (mg)	Vitamin A (I.U.)	Thiamin (mg)	Riboflavin (mg)	Niacin (mg)	Vitamin C (mg)
1 cup	345	17.6	19.9	24.4	635	517	.3	297	764	810	.10	.86	.5	3

Low Fat Milk

	Calories	Protein (gm)	Fat (gm)	Carbohydrate (gm)	Calcium (mg)	Phosphorus (mg)	Iron (mg)	Sodium (mg)	Potassium (mg)	Vitamin A (I.U.)	Thiamin (mg)	Riboflavin (mg)	Niacin (mg)	Vitamin C (mg)
1 cup	145	10.3	4.9	14.8	352	276	.1	150	431	200	.10	.52	.2	2

Skim Milk or Nonfat Milk

	Calories	Protein (gm)	Fat (gm)	Carbohydrate (gm)	Calcium (mg)	Phosphorus (mg)	Iron (mg)	Sodium (mg)	Potassium (mg)	Vitamin A (I.U.)	Thiamin (mg)	Riboflavin (mg)	Niacin (mg)	Vitamin C (mg)
1 cup	88	8.8	.2	12.5	296	233	.1	127	355	10	.09	.44	.2	2

Nonfat Dry Milk (Reconstituted)

	Calories	Protein (gm)	Fat (gm)	Carbohydrate (gm)	Calcium (mg)	Phosphorus (mg)	Iron (mg)	Sodium (mg)	Potassium (mg)	Vitamin A (I.U.)	Thiamin (mg)	Riboflavin (mg)	Niacin (mg)	Vitamin C (mg)
1 cup	88	8.8	.2	12.5	296	233	.1	127	355	10	.09	.44	.2	.2

Condensed Milk (sweetened)

	Calories	Protein (gm)	Fat (gm)	Carbohydrate (gm)	Calcium (mg)	Phosphorus (mg)	Iron (mg)	Sodium (mg)	Potassium (mg)	Vitamin A (I.U.)	Thiamin (mg)	Riboflavin (mg)	Niacin (mg)	Vitamin C (mg)
1 cup	982	24.8	26.6	166.2	802	630	.3	343	961	1100	.24	1.16	.6	3

Buttermilk

	Calories	Protein (gm)	Fat (gm)	Carbohydrate (gm)	Calcium (mg)	Phosphorus (mg)	Iron (mg)	Sodium (mg)	Potassium (mg)	Vitamin A (I.U.)	Thiamin (mg)	Riboflavin (mg)	Niacin (mg)	Vitamin C (mg)
1 cup	88	8.8	.2	12.5	296	233	.1	319	343	10	.10	.44	.2	2

YOGHURT

Yoghurt is a custard-like product created by fermenting milk with a special culture. It is usually made from homogenized, pasteurized whole milk, but may be made from skim milk or partly skimmed milk. It has the same nutritive value as the milk from which it is made.

Often yoghurt is sweetened and fruit-flavored. You do better buying plain yoghurt and adding your own natural fruit slices.

YOGHURT FACTS

* If yoghurt appears to have separated, stir the liquid back into the yoghurt.

* Unopened yoghurt, plain or fruit-flavored, may be stored in a freezer up to 6 weeks. To defrost, let stand at room temperature for 3 hours.

Bring home a little culture from abroad.

* If you're traveling abroad and find a yoghurt that you particularly like the flavor of, bring some of it back and use it as a base for your yoghurt-making here. Contrary to popular thought, it is not illegal. It is illegal to bring in meat products, fresh fruits, and vegetables. According to John Bruhn, extension food technologist, University of California at Davis: if the culture selected is fresh, you could probably keep it unrefrigerated for three days and still find it in good shape when you arrived home.

Frozen Yoghurt

The most popular form of yoghurt is, without question, frozen yoghurt. When it was first introduced in Manhattan several years back, people lined up in throngs to buy the stuff. The crowds surprised me because they included many people who would never be caught dead eating ice cream—too fattening and too sweet. They told me they felt virtuous licking their frozen yoghurt cones. After all, they said, "It's yoghurt," implying it's natural and good for you.

I wondered. Most tasted less like yoghurt and more like candy. I sent samples from three of the most popularly sold frozen yoghurts in New York City to laboratories for analysis. Although some of the brands may vary across the country, what holds true for frozen yoghurt sold in Manhattan probably holds true for frozen yoghurt sold around the rest of the country as well.

DANNON

In my comparison tasting, Dannon came out as the most natural frozen yoghurt around.

They add only gelatin and the sugar used in preserving the fruits. You can tell the difference by its taste. It tastes like chilled yoghurt, not like some of the other more candied products.

Even though this was the least sugary-tasting, I was suspicious about frozen yoghurt products in general so I had a laboratory do a sugar analysis. Dannon's frozen vanilla yoghurt tested out to be 17.8 per cent sugar. Most plain ice cream is 15–16 per cent sugar.

FROGURT

Frogurt is a nationally distributed frozen yoghurt. In an effort to meet their consumers' expectations, the Frogurt people told me they've been trying to make their product more natural. The artificial ingredients are gone, but too much sugar still remains. The frogurt alone, without any toppings, tested out to be 20.9 per cent sugar. Yet many customers eat theirs embellished with candied chocolate sprinkles, colorful confetti dips, or marshmallow swirl.

JOHANNA FARMS

Johanna Farms uses both artificial flavors and colors. A spokesman said their strawberry yoghurt would look gray without a little dye and besides their customers like it as is, so they are in no rush to make a more natural product.

Whether you prefer the natural product, or like yours spiced artificially, there are some generalizations that can be made about frozen yoghurt based on the three frozen yoghurt products I tested.

FROZEN YOGHURT HAS:

* 5–6 per cent more sugar than plain ice cream.

* about the same amount of calories as ice cream (250 in an 8-ounce serving of vanilla-flavored).

* less fat; frozen yoghurt is 2 per cent fat and ice cream is often 10 per cent.

* 20–40 per cent air whipped in, so you're actually eating less real product.

* double the carbohydrates of ice cream because of its high sugar content.

CHEESE

Cheese is a highly concentrated form of milk. In the last 10 years, the yearly consumption of cheese in this country has nearly doubled, from 3.4 pounds per person to 6.2 pounds. A 1-ounce serving of cheese provides the percentage of the Recommended Daily Allowances shown in the chart at the top of page 167. (A 1-ounce slice of cheese is a 2″×4″ piece, ¼″ thick.)

Cheese Labeling and Low Fat Cheese

The traditional full-fat cheeses are labeled with familiar names like Gruyère, Camembert, Colby, or Brie. But the labeling often gets misleading when it comes to selecting a *low fat* cheese. The three most common descriptive labels are: "low fat cheese," "cheese made from skim milk," or "cheese made from part skim milk."

Beware the low fat cheese trap

CHEESE MADE FROM PART SKIM MILK

I think the most misleading label is "cheese made from part skim milk." It sounds like

Nutritional Contributions of Five Popular Cheeses

	Cheddar	Swiss	Pasteurized Process American	Edam	Cream
Protein %	15	15	15	15	4
Vitamin A %	4	4	4	4	6
Riboflavin %	6	4	6	4	2
Calcium %	20	25	15	15	2

SOURCE: National Cheese Institute.

this would be low in fat, right? Wrong. The difference between cheese made from part skim milk and from whole milk is minute.

Trying to cut down on fat intake, my husband thought he was doing a good thing when he bought cheese made from part skim milk. But as you can see below, the term "part skim milk" doesn't mean much in terms of cutting down fat content. Also, as the fat and calorie contents of cheese decline, so does the per cent of protein and other nutrients.

	Cheese	% Fat
Part Skim Milk	Edam	28%
	Swiss	27%
	Parmesan	26%
Whole Milk	Cheddar	32%
	Colby	31%
	Provolone	26%

LOW FAT CHEESE

You *will* be getting less fat when you select a cheese whose label reads, "low fat," or "made from skim milk." These have less than 10 per cent fat; however, be prepared for less taste and texture, too. A low fat cheese goes against the concept of cheese. Cheese by its nature has high amounts of fat and that amount of fat largely determines its texture and taste. I taste-tested a group of low fat cheeses: Slim Cheese Australia, Tilsit Slim, Swiss, and Echterharzkase, to name a

few. They were rubbery, dry, hard, and undistinguished in flavor. Because they have more moisture, most had a glassy, transparent appearance. If they weren't totally bland, they were overly strong like the Echterharzkase, a soft German cheese.

Low fat cheeses that have a more acceptable taste are the soft cheeses that are naturally low in fat, like cottage cheese and pot cheese or hoop cheese. These range in fat content from 1–4 per cent. The low fat varieties of cottage cheese have as little as ½ per cent fat. There is such a demand for low fat cheese that the "biggies" like Borden and Kraft have gotten into the market; both now market a low fat cheese that has one third the fat of their regular products, or 11 per cent fat. Another point to keep in mind is that, as a general rule, the process cheese foods and cheese food spreads do have less fat (and flavor) than the natural cheese they imitate. Process American cheese foods are low in fat (23 per cent fat) compared to whole milk cheeses (30 per cent fat). Most slicing cheeses, like Muenster and Monterey, have 20–30 per cent fat.

If you're looking for a way to lower the fat in your diet, I'd suggest eating less of the real thing, rather than sticking to the lower fat skim milk cheeses, or the imitation process by-products.

Although what follows is certainly not a complete listing of cheeses, some of the more popular cheeses are classified into fat categories. As you see the full fat cheeses are the most popular.

High Fat Cheese: Enriched with cream.

    Cream cheese   Double Creme
    Petit Suisse   Boursin

Full Fat Cheese: Generally made from whole milk or partially decreamed milk.

    Cheddar   Gouda
    Brie   Natural Gruyère
    Raclette   Reblochon
    Blue   Provolone
    Limburger   Ramadur
    Appenzeller   All Swiss, i.e.,
    Tilsit   domestic, Jarlsberg,
    Muenster   Baby Swiss

Partial Fat Cheese: Usually made from milk which is more decreamed or skimmed than milk for full fat cheese.

    Parmesan   Mozzarella
    Romano   Myost

Low Fat Cheese: Contain from 0–15 per cent fat. Very few such natural types are produced.

    Cottage Cheese   Skim milk Cheddar
    Sapsago (Hoop)   Ricotone
    Gammelost   St. Otho

Process Cheese

There are four main categories of cheese: natural, process, cheese foods, and cheese spreads. Process cheeses differ from the natural cheese in two principal ways: the manufacturer has the advantage of composing cheese from many different batches; emulsifiers are added to keep the fat from separating and to extend the shelf life. A process cheese is more uniform in taste and texture than a natural cheese. For example, a natural Cheddar characteristically changes in flavor as it ages, while a process cheese does not. A process cheese food is a cheese that has water and nonfat dry milk added. The process cheese spread has gum added to make it spreadable, and even more water. With both the cheese food and the cheese spread, the product is less flavorful, softer, and you're getting less cheese and more water than in its natural counterpart. Cheese facts are included for you to use as a handy reference in comparing some familiar cheeses to see how they rank in relation to protein, sodium levels, and fat. I've not included calories because, although there are some variations in caloric content, cheese generally has about 100 calories to an ounce.

Cheese Facts

For 1 oz. (28 gm)	Flavor	Basic Ingred.	Protein (gm)	Sodium (mg)	Cholesterol (mg)	Fat (%)	Lipids Total	Fatty Acids Sat.	Fatty Acids Unsat.
Blue	piquant, spicy	Whole milk	6		21	29	8.3	5.4	2.6
Brick	mild	Whole cow's milk	6.5		N/A	29	8.2	5.0	2.8
Camembert	mild to pungent	Whole cow's milk	5.5		20.2	26	7.3	4.6	2.4
Cheddar	mild to sharp	Whole cow's milk	7	196	28.7	32	9.2	5.7	3.0
Colby	mild	Whole cow's milk	6.7		26.6	31	8.6	5.4	2.7
Creamed Cottage	mild, slightly acid	Skimmed cow's milk and cream added	3.5	64	3.9	4	1.1	0.7	0.3
Uncreamed Cottage	mild, slightly acid	Skimmed cow's milk	4.9	81.2	1.9	—	0.1	0.06	0.03
Cream	mild, slightly acid	Whole cow's milk and cream	2.1	70	30.5	34	9.5	6	3
Edam	mild, nutlike	Partly skimmed cow's milk	7.2		25	28	7.8	5.1	2.3
Mozzarella (low moisture part skimmed)	mild, delicate	Partly skimmed cow's milk	7.8		15	19	5.4	2.9	1.4
Neufchâtel	mild	Whole cow's milk	3.3		N/A	24	6.8	4.3	2.2
Parmesan	sharp, piquant	Partly skimmed cow's milk	10.8	205	20.5	26	7.4	4.7	2.3

Cheese Facts (continued)

For 1 oz. (28 gm)	Flavor	Basic Ingred.	Protein (gm)	Sodium (mg)	Cholesterol (mg)	Fat (%)	Lipids Total	Fatty Acids Sat.	Unsat.
Provolone	mild to sharp and piquant, usually smoked	Whole cow's milk	7.3		19.3	26	7.3	4.6	2.3
Ricotta	bland but semisweet	Whey and whole, part skimmed	3.1		N/A	9	2.4	1.5	0.8
		Skimmed	3.3		N/A	15	4.1	2.6	1.3
Swiss	sweetish, nutlike	Partly skimmed cow's milk	8.1	199	24.1	27	7.7	4.9	2.5
Pasteurized Process American			6.5	318/	N/A	29	8.1	5.0	2.7

SOURCES: "Flavor, Basic Ingredient, Sodium, Milk Fat," from *Newer Knowledge of Cheese*, 2nd ed. National Dairy Council of Chicago, 111 North Canal Street, Chicago, Ill. 60606. "Protein, Cholesterol, Fats," from *Dairy Council Digest*, Vol. 46, No. 3 (May-June 1975), National Dairy Council of Chicago, 111 North Canal Street, Chicago, Ill. 60606.

Vegetarian Diet Guide

The most difficult dietary problem for vegetarians or for people contemplating becoming vegetarians is where to get their protein and how to get enough. The Vegetarian Diet Guide devised by Jo Ann Hattner, R.D., at Stanford University is designed for basic vegetarians who use dairy products. As you can see from the guide, if you choose foods thoughtfully, it is easy to get more than enough protein from vegetable sources.

Vegetarian sources of protein

Milk Group: Include daily 3 servings of milk and milk products. (3 servings supply an average of 30 gm of protein)

- 1½ ounces American cheese
- 1 cup buttermilk
- ½ cup creamed cottage cheese
- 2 cups ice cream
- 1 cup milk (skim, low fat, or whole)
- 1 cup plain yoghurt made with low fat milk

Peas and Beans: Include at least 1 (¾-cup) serving each day.
(¾ cup cooked provides an average value of 8 gm protein)

Fresh

| Black-eyed peas | Lima beans |
| Green peas | Sprouted mung beans |

(½ cup cooked provides an average value of 8 gm protein)

Dried

Black-eyed peas	Soybeans
Great Northern beans	Split peas
Lima beans	Red kidney
Navy beans	beans

Nuts: Include daily at least 1 (¼-cup) serving of nuts or peanut butter. (¼ cup supplies average value of 6 gm protein; 2 tablespoons peanut butter supplies 8 gm protein)

Almonds, shelled whole	Pecans, shelled
Cashew nuts, roasted	halves
Peanuts, roasted	Walnuts, black

Breads and Cereals: Include daily at least 3 servings of bread (1 serving=1 slice) and cereals (1 serving=¾ cup). (Whole wheat, other whole grains, or products made from enriched flours provide 2–3 gm protein in each serving.)

Fruits: Include daily 3 servings.
At least 1 serving of citrus or other fruit rich in vitamin C.

¼ cantaloupe	½ cup orange juice
½ grapefruit	1 cup red raspberries
½ cup grapefruit juice	1 cup strawberries
	1 large tangerine
1 orange	1 cup tomato juice

At least 1 serving of fruit rich in iron.

½ cup dried uncooked apricots	¾ cup cooked prunes
	½ cup prune juice
¾ cup dates	¾ cup raisins
7 large dried figs	¾ cup dried cooked peaches
½ cup dried uncooked peaches	

Vegetables: Include daily 3 ½-cup servings. At least 1 serving green or yellow vegetable.

Beet greens, cooked	Mustard greens,
Carrots, raw	cooked
Collards, cooked	Squash, winter,
Spinach, cooked	baked
Kale, cooked	
Pumpkin, canned, cooked	

At least 2 ½-cup servings of other vegetables, including potato or substitute. Some suggestions:

Bean sprouts	Macaroni
Beets	Mushrooms
Broccoli	Noodles
Brussels sprouts	Onions
Cabbage	Peas
Cauliflower	Potato
Celery	Rice
Cucumber	Spaghetti
Eggplant	Tomatoes
Green beans	Turnips
Lettuce	

Sample Daily Food Pattern

3 servings milk and milk products.
1 serving peas and beans.
1 serving nuts.
3 servings breads and cereals.
3 servings fruit.
3 servings vegetables.

Typical Day's Menu

Morning: *Sample*
1 serving citrus fruit   ½ grapefruit
1 serving bread   1 slice w/margarine
1 serving cereal   ¾ cup oatmeal
                               w/honey
1 serving milk   1 cup low fat milk

Noon:
½ serving milk   ¼ cup cottage
                               cheese
1 serving vegetable   Lettuce
1 serving bread   1 slice w/margarine
1 serving fruit   1 banana

Snack:
1 serving milk   1 cup low fat milk
1 serving nuts   ¼ cup peanuts

Evening:
1 serving   1 cup cream of
  green or yellow   spinach soup
  vegetable
1 serving   ½ cup kidney
  peas or beans   beans on
1 serving   1 cup rice
potato or
  substitute
½ serving milk   ½ cup yoghurt

Snack:
1 serving fruit   ½ cup prune juice
  (rich in iron)

This diet provides approximately:

Calories:	1,800
Protein:	75 gm
Fat:	60 gm
Carbohydrate:	250 gm
Calcium:	1.4 gm
Iron:	17 mg
Thiamin:	1.8 mg
Riboflavin:	2.2 mg
Niacin:	14.0 mg
Vitamin C:	100 mg
Vitamin A:	10,000 I.U.

SOYBEAN CAKES

One of my favorite vegetarian sources of protein are soybean cakes. With soybean curd, you get all the good things in soybeans—in a pleasant custard-like package: the soybean has 9.4 gm of protein in a 2″ square, no cholesterol, practically no saturated fat, and it's cheap. (Most squares sell for about twenty cents each and one cake serves 1 person adequately.)

Soybean cakes are made by mashing soybeans into soymilk and pressing the resulting soybean curd mixture into a solid cake. (When figuring soybean cakes on the Vegetarian Diet Guide, they fall into the milk category; one cake equals one 8-ounce glass of milk.) These cakes, called tofu (pronounced toe-fu), are available at most stores selling Japanese, Chinese, or Korean produce and, increasingly, they are sold in fresh vegetable markets, in health food stores, and now I see them regularly in big grocery store chains.

Soybean cakes can be purchased in several forms:

Japanese-style 2″ thick squares usually sold in water. Very soft, delicate, and fragile in this form. Best suited for dishes in which the soybean cake is added tenderly at the last moment.

Chinese-style 1″ thick with some water pressed out. More durable; can be cut into strips and will keep its form.

Pressed[3] ½″ thick with all water removed. Sold dry. A tougher texture suited for dishes that involve cooking and stirring. Can be cut into thin strips like pasta.

Pressed and Spiced Same as above, only preseasoned with spices.

I love the versatility of cooking with tofu because this bland substance takes on the flavor of whatever it is cooked with. If you cannot find fresh bean curd, do not use the canned instead; it tastes tinny and in no way is an adequate substitute for the real thing. The fresh stays good refrigerated for 1 week. Some people keep meat in their freezer in case company drops by unexpectedly. I try always to have at least one container of tofu on hand. With tofu in the fridge, I'm always ready for unexpected guests.

BEAN CURD AND VEGETABLES

Ingredients:
  1 tablespoon oil
  1 tablespoon ginger (best if fresh)
  4 scallions, chopped
  ¼ cup chicken broth or stock
  4 bean curd cakes, cut into thin slices
    (Chinese-style bean curd; the
    Japanese-style will fall apart)
  1 uncooked chicken breast, slivered
  4 tablespoons soy sauce, low salt

[3] If pressed soybean cakes are not sold in your area, you can do the pressing yourself by wrapping the custard in cheesecloth and leaving it in the refrigerator overnight with a heavy object on top. I put the tofu on a plate with another plate on top to weight it down. Be sure the bottom plate has a rim to catch the water. You end up with a nice firm cake that's easy to work with.

  1 teaspoon cornstarch
  3 cups leftover vegetables (e.g., broccoli
    flowerets, lightly steamed)
  ½ cup lettuce leaves
                    Serves 4 amply as main course

1. Heat oil in a wok or skillet. Add ginger, scallions, chicken broth and cook for 2 minutes. Add bean curd cakes and chicken.
2. Mix soy sauce with cornstarch and pour over bean curd mixture.
3. Add leftover vegetables. I like to add lightly steamed broccoli, although you can add practically any vegetables. Be sure to select bright-colored ones that vividly contrast with the white tofu. It's ready when chicken, bean curd, and vegetables are well mixed with the sauce.
4. At the last minute, add lettuce and cook only until lettuce is warm. I like romaine because of its dark green color and its crackly crunchiness. Serve immediately.

BROCCOLI STEM SALAD

One way to make use of broccoli stems—too often thrown out—is in a salad. This salad is a good accompaniment to the previous recipe.

Ingredients:
  2 cups thin pieces broccoli stems, steamed

DRESSING
  1 tablespoon soy sauce, low salt
  1 tablespoon sesame oil
  ½ tablespoon sugar

Toss the broccoli stems with dressing. Line up stems in one direction on serving platter. Serve chilled.

                                    Serves 4

SCRAMBLED TOFU

For people who have to cut down their consumption of eggs, and for others who love the taste of tofu, here's an idea that looks exactly like, and tastes somewhat like, scrambled eggs.

Ingredients:

    4 cakes bean curd, Japanese-style, drained
       of excess water

    Dash turmeric

    1 clove garlic, pressed

    ½ cup minced scallions

    ¼ cup chicken broth

    4 slices whole wheat toast

Serves 4

1. In a medium-size bowl, combine first five ingredients.

2. To hot skillet, add couple of drops of water, then the tofu mixture. Break up tofu into a scrambled egg consistency. Cook until heated through.

3. Serve hot with slices of whole wheat toast.

SCRAMBLED TOFU VEGETABLE STUFFING

An unexpected way to use Japanese-style tofu is to make a stuffing for vegetables such as artichokes or tomatoes. The custard-like texture of the tofu goes wonderfully with vegetables.

Ingredients:

    1 bean curd cake, Japanese-style

    1 teaspoon chives

    1 teaspoon sesame seeds

    ½ teaspoon ginger

*Makes stuffing for 1 large artichoke or
1 large tomato*

1. In skillet over medium heat, warm all ingredients together. Break up tofu with a fork until it has the consistency of frothy scrambled eggs.

2. Stuff into hollowed-out tomato and bake in 325° F. oven until tomato is cooked, about 8 minutes.

3. If stuffing artichoke, hollow out artichoke and steam until tender, about 40 minutes. When artichoke is cooked and still warm, fill with stuffing and serve immediately.

 # How Much Does Protein Cost?

When I ran away from home as a young child, I packed peanut butter sandwiches. They were supposed to last me for the rest of my life. My choice of peanut butter made sense both economically and nutritionally: 2 tablespoons, which is plenty for a sandwich, still costs only about six cents, and is a good source of protein to sustain you out in the woods or wherever you happen to be.

Protein is usually the most expensive part of any meal and buying it prudently can be tricky because the price per pound doesn't tell the whole story. Someone trying to select thrifty sandwich meats may be buying bologna only to find, other nutritional considerations aside, it's no bargain.

Cost of 20 Grams of Protein
From Specified Meats and Meat Alternates at June 1980 Prices

Food	Market unit	Price per market unit *	Part of market unit to give 20 grams of protein†	Cost of 20 grams of protein
Dry beans	lb	$0.59	.24	$0.14
Eggs, large	doz	.77	.25	.19
Peanut butter	12 oz	.91	.23	.21
Bread, white enriched**	lb	.47	.51	.24
Chicken, whole, ready-to-cook	lb	.67	.37	.25
Beef liver	lb	1.03	.24	.25
Turkey, ready-to-cook	lb	.86	.33	.28
Pork, shoulder, smoked, bone in	lb	.89	.32	.29
Milk, whole fluid ‡	half-gal	1.07	.29	.31
Ham, whole, bone in	lb	1.15	.30	.34
Bean soup, canned	11.25 oz	.37	.96	.36
Chicken breasts	lb	1.31	.29	.38
Tuna, canned	6.5 oz	.98	.44	.43
American process cheese	8 oz	1.16	.38	.44
Pork loin roast, bone in	lb	1.33	.33	.44
Ground beef, lean	lb	1.89	.25	.48
Chuck roast of beef, bone in	lb	1.50	.35	.52
Ham, canned	lb	2.20	.24	.53
Liverwurst	8 oz	.94	.60	.56
Frankfurters	lb	1.63	.36	.59
Pork sausage	lb	1.13	.52	.59
Salami	8 oz	1.21	.50	.61
Round beefsteak, bone in	lb	2.70	.23	.62
Ocean perch, fillet, frozen	lb	2.21	.29	.63
Bacon, slices	lb	1.22	.52	.63
Pork chops, center cut	lb	1.87	.35	.65
Rump roast of beef, bone out	lb	2.53	.26	.66
Sardines, canned	4 oz	.73	.94	.69
Haddock, fillet, frozen	lb	2.43	.29	.71
Bologna	8 oz	1.09	.73	.79
Rib roast of beef, bone in	lb	2.54	.33	.84
Sirloin beefsteak, bone in	lb	3.06	.28	.86
Veal cutlets	lb	4.48	.23	1.05
Porterhouse beefsteak, bone in	lb	3.59	.34	1.22
Lamb chops, loin	lb	4.08	.32	1.31

*U.S. average retail price of food item estimated using information provided by the Bureau of Labor Statistics, (U.S. Department of Labor) and U.S. Department of Agriculture.

†One-third of the daily amount recommended for a 20-year-old man. Assumes that all meat is eaten.

**Bread and other grain products, such as pasta and rice, are frequently used with a small amount of meat, poultry, fish, or cheese as main dishes in economy meals. In this way the high-quality protein in meat and cheese enhances the lower quality of protein in cereal products.

‡Although milk is not used to replace meat in meals, it is an economical source of good-quality protein.

SOURCE: U.S. Department of Agriculture, Science and Education Administration, Human Nutrition, Consumer Nutrition Center, Hyattsville, Maryland 20782.

Look at the figures on the preceding chart and you'll see that an 8-ounce package of sliced bologna sells for $1.09. Chicken breasts are $1.31 a pound. If you're being thrifty, you'd opt for the bologna for luncheon sandwiches, right? Wrong. When you figure out how much of the market unit you have to eat to get roughly one third the protein you need for the day, you can see from the chart that about one quarter of a pound of breast of chicken fills one third of your protein requirements at a cost of *38¢*. With the bologna, you would have to eat closer to one third of a pound (it's unlikely you'd eat that many slices) at a cost of *79¢*.

There are ways to save money when purchasing protein, and often these suggestions benefit your health as well.

* Use expensive animal protein as a condiment rather than as the main attraction.

* Serve more appropriately sized portions.

* Use inexpensive sources of vegetable protein: dried peas and beans.

* Shop seasonal sales. In summer, fish is less expensive than in winter.

* Dairy prices are rising at a slower rate than meat prices, so rely on protein from dairy sources: milk, cheese, yoghurt.

* Chicken and turkey provide protein at a lower cost than just about all red meats, with the exception of ground beef and liver.

* When buying poultry, buy the less expensive parts such as turkey legs and chicken livers.

* Buy a different *grade* of meat. Americans have a love affair with juicy, fatty meats in the Prime and Choice grades. If you buy the Good grade instead, you get:

> 15 per cent less calories
> 25 per cent less fat
> And you save money.

If you don't see the Good grade marketed in your area, ask for it. The USDA Good grades are out there, but many stores don't market them because they say the consumer demand isn't there. The only drawback is that juiciness is a function of fat and the Good grade has less fat, so it can be overcooked more easily.

FISH

Doctors, nutritionists, and congressmen have all been urging the American public for health reasons to eat less red meat and more fish and poultry. Despite the high price of fish in general, there are still some affordable fish around if you know how to buy. Summer is often the best time to buy fish, because the weather is good and the fishermen are able to catch more. Expect the price to be 25–30 per cent less than in the previous winter or spring.

Another way to cope is to stay away from the high-priced fillet and to buy the *whole* thing. The price of the whole fish is usually one third to one quarter the price of the fillet. So, you can count on saving much more than 100 per cent of your seafood dollar when you stay away from the fillet. When I suggested this to a fellow reporter and noncook, she said, "But what would I do with all those *bones?*"

Usually I buy the whole fish and I ask the fish man to debone it for me (most fish stores don't charge for this extra service), leaving the head and tail on. When I suggested this in a TV story once, a viewer wrote in saying that then you have a fillet. Not true. You simply have a whole fish, but without the bones that many people find objectionable and hard to handle. I find the whole fish with the head and tail on much juicier than its filleted friends, which tend to dry out quickly. And besides, when you serve it, it *looks* like a fish.

Sometimes an unfamiliar-sounding fish can be a good buy and delicious. The summer of '79, the prices of cod were up very high, so knowledgeable fish people were substituting tile fish instead (that's right, like kitchen tile). I was somewhat amused as I dined in Manhattan restaurants that summer when I observed that restaurants were often making this substitution, too. It was too hard for them to make a profit with some of the other more traditional fish fare, so they offered tile as their specialty. What other fish might be a good buy? Ask your fish man. Tell him you're open to trying something other than just snapper, sea bass, or flounder and, depending on the season, I bet he'll have some suggestions for fish you've never tried before.

 # Can You Cook Away the Protein?

Ordinary cooking temperatures used at home have little or no effect on the protein quality. There are some problems with the high temperatures and dry heat used in the processing of cereals, but Dr. Calloway of the University of California at Berkeley, feels these small changes in cereals are not very important since most people eat a wide variety of protein foods anyway. (However, one can always cook and prepare one's own cereals, such as oatmeal and granola. (See Chapter 10, Children, page 310).

In fact, there are some *advantages* to heating and cooking proteins. With meat, poultry, and fish, cooking kills any harmful micro-organisms and the slight protein breakdown that occurs may make the protein more digestible. After I did a story about hard-boiled eggs, I received a letter from a viewer scolding me for suggesting hard-boiled eggs for anything because boiling eggs congealed the protein and made it unavailable. That's another myth. In fact, cooking eggs, especially the whites, may make them *more* digestible.

NONCOOKING

What about eating protein that has not been fully cooked—is there any advantage to this?

The Masai in Africa eat raw meat, the Eskimos and Japanese eat raw fish, and, increasingly, so do Americans—in sushi bars. Some people claim they get a protein "rush" from eating raw meat. In research, this protein "rush" has not been documented. Dr. C. E. Bodwell of the Department of Agriculture says that with rats there is a slight nutritional advantage to raw protein foods, but with humans this is insignificant.

The real problem with raw protein foods, whether it's steak tartare or sashimi, is the potential for bacterial contamination. Be very careful about sanitary conditions.

Although the Japanese have a national tradition of eating chicken raw, in general it is suggested poultry should not be eaten uncooked, because the risk of salmonella (a type of bacteria that causes food poisoning) is much greater.

Did you know that after handling raw protein foods, especially chicken, you should wash your hands, whatever implements you used, and the cutting surface you were working on with hot soapy water? The reason for this is that if, for example, the chicken is contaminated with salmonella, you can transfer it through your hands or other implements and contaminate other foods or areas in the kitchen. If the chicken has salmonella, the heat of the cooking process destroys it and makes the poultry safe to eat.

THE OUTDOOR BARBECUE— FUN AND HEALTH PROBLEMS

One of the most flavorful ways to cook meats, poultry, fish, or vegetables is to barbecue them outdoors. A barbecue, whether it's for 2 or 20, by its nature is a festive occasion. I'm such a fan of barbecuing that summers before I had a house with a backyard barbecue area, I always carried a small hibachi grill in the trunk of my car. Wherever I stopped to rest or swim, out came the hibachi.

I like my barbecuing traditional. The following recipe for barbecue sauce comes from my sister-in-law Libby, whose family has a ranch on the Texas-Mexican border near McAllen, Texas. At the ranch, they do old-fashioned barbecues of whole steers. This sauce is about as authentic as you can get.

BAR B CUE SAUCE

Ingredients:

1 onion, diced

2 cloves garlic, pressed

½ cup oil

½ cup catsup[4]

Dash Worcestershire sauce

¼ cup red wine vinegar

¼ cup brown sugar or honey

Lemon juice (optional)

Makes 2 cups

---

[4] If you're wondering how healthy catsup is, all catsup, whatever the brand, must, by federal law, have certain ingredients. The main ingredient is tomatoes; catsup also has vinegar, salt, and spices, which act as natural preservatives. And that sweet taste doesn't all come from the tomatoes. There's also sugar and that's why some people object to catsup. They say it's just another junk food. But since catsup is primarily a condiment, used in small doses, I like to think of it this way: A little bit probably won't hurt you. *But a lot may not be better.*

1. Sauté onion and garlic in oil until soft. Add catsup, Worcestershire sauce, red wine vinegar, and the brown sugar or honey. Perhaps add a squeeze of fresh lemon juice for tartness.

2. Simmer for 10 minutes or until the flavors are blended. (You may want to simmer this longer just because it smells so delicious when it's cooking.)

To see me through a summer of barbecuing, I multiply this recipe many times and make it up in quart batches and refrigerate.

MEDITERRANEAN MARINADE

I've found one of the simplest and easiest ways to do fish, especially shrimp, is to follow a Mediterranean tradition. At least 1 hour before grilling, marinate the fish in a mixture of: olive oil, garlic, fresh oregano, fresh rosemary, and lemon juice. Use whatever portions please you. I go heavy on the garlic and herbs. For 1 cup of marinade I use: ½ cup oil, 4 cloves garlic, pressed, ¼ cup each fresh oregano and fresh rosemary, juice of 1 lemon. When grilling, continue basting with the marinade. The fish can either be placed directly on the grill and basted, or placed in a classic fish-shaped steel grill. I prefer using the fish grill as it makes the job of turning the fish so much easier.

Using a Charcoal Grill

Too often perfectly good food is burned to a crisp because the heat from a charcoal grill is uncontrollable. Here are some helpful things to know before putting food on the grill.

* Begin by stacking the charcoal briquets in a pyramid so they will ignite easily. Sprinkle charcoal lighter fluid over the briquets to start the fire, or, better and easier—use an electric starter element if you have an outlet handy.

* Before you put the food on the grill, be sure to have a bed of *evenly* burning coals. It will take about 20–40 minutes for the coals to burn to the right stage. When they are ready, they will be covered with a layer of gray ash. At this stage, use tongs to spread the pyramid of briquets into a single layer of coals . . . and you are ready to cook.

Barbecue Japanese-style

The Japanese idea of a barbecue is distinctly different from ours. From the Japanese we can learn several significant lessons that make barbecuing at home more fun. And their ideas are also helpful in keeping the weight down. (Aside from Sumo wrestlers, how often have you seen a fat Japanese?)

The Japanese have a saying that if the eyes and the nose are not charmed, then the food does not taste good. The Japanese elevate barbecuing to an art form. In Texas, to barbecue means to take the biggest piece of meat possible and grill it for hours. It's an open invitation to stuff oneself without limitation. In contrast, the Japanese version seems positively delicate.

The Japanese feel that the outside and inside of the food should cook at the same time so they purposely choose thin, small pieces, about 2″ square, that cook evenly. The Japanese grill thin slices of vegetables (carrots, potatoes, green peppers, etc.) along with similar-size pieces of meat, poultry, or fish. I like the Japanese way of doing things. When these vegetables are served separate and distinct by themselves, you begin to notice how orange a carrot looks, how green a green pepper is, and by cooking them the shortest amount of time possible, you can really appreciate the contrast of texture of a sweet potato, a slice of fresh corn on the cob, a slice of onion, or a mushroom. The Japanese use no spices in barbecuing, just a smattering of oil on a hot grill, and soy sauce to dip the pieces of food in after they've been grilled.

Barbecuing With a Solar Cooker

When Carter was giving tax breaks for people using solar energy in their houses, I tried solar outdoor cooking. I didn't get a tax break and didn't get my food cooked very well, either.

The solar cooker I tried was a 12″ long grill with an aluminum reflector that angled to the sun. It was advertised as the perfect answer to the energy problem. Except it didn't work when it was windy or when it was cloudy and it didn't work very well when it was sunny either. On a bright sunny day, it took over 20 minutes to cook a 9″ long vegetable shish kebab and it required constant jiggering from me to keep the kebab and the grill in proper alignment with the sun. These solar cookers are gimmicks playing off our current interest in solar energy. Until they are improved and made more substantial, they are more gimmicky than workable.

Barbecue Health Hazards

Despite my acknowledged fondness for barbecuing, there are some health hazards associated with it that you ought to be aware of in advance. With this information in hand you can decide how you wish to proceed.

Warning: Barbecue Smoke May Be Dangerous To Your Health

The high temperature cooking of foods, especially meats with high fat content, results in the formation of benzopyrene. Inside the body, after being metabolized by the enzyme system, benzopyrene (BP) has been shown to be carcinogenic. The source of the BP is the melted fat which drips on the hot coals. As the smoke rises, the BP is deposited on the meat. And the smoke doesn't have to "touch" the meat, but just be in the air surrounding the meat. A 1-pound steak has been found to contain as much BP as found in 270 smoked cigarettes.

In a study reported in *Science,* researchers Tijunsky and Shubik reported beef steaks cooked by the following two methods contained varying amounts of BP:

Cooking Method	Amount of Benzopyrene (Parts per billion)
Gas Flame	2.0–4.4 ppB
Smoky Fire	12.6–86.4 ppB

There is a strong correlation between incidence of stomach cancer and levels of benzopyrene consumed. In Japan, where people consume large amounts of smoked fish, the levels of BP are believed to be at least partially responsible for the high incidence of stomach cancer. Subsequent studies in Iceland have also shown a high incidence of stomach cancer. However, this is not a clear-cut issue. Dr. L. F. Bjeldanes of the Department of Nutritional Science, University of California at Berkeley, cautions that so far there is no definitive evidence which proves that BP directly causes stomach cancer in humans.

Until more definitive answers are in, I am personally going to continue barbecuing, but with caution and moderation.

TIPS

* Put your meat, poultry, fish, on the coals after the smoke subsides. The less smoke, the less BP generated.

* Use only lean meats, well trimmed of all fat. Less fat on the meat means less fat drips on the coals, less smoke, less BP.

* Barbecue in the open air if possible. Do not barbecue with the lid on, as this increases the smoke. If barbecuing inside, keep kitchen vent on.

* Wrap food in aluminum foil to avoid contact with the flame. This does not mean placing food on aluminum foil and letting the smoke curl up around the foil. Food must be entirely wrapped by foil to be protected.

What it sizzles down to is this: If you can taste the barbecue flavor, then you are probably ingesting BP.

Speaking of barbecue *flavors,* what about that smoky flavor you get in commercially made barbecue sauces? The manufacturers get the smoky flavor by generating smoke and letting it dissolve in water, and then collecting the smoky water and adding it to their sauces. I wouldn't be alarmed about these products. First, they are used in small quantities and second, there is no evidence so far that they contain significant levels of benzopyrene.

This is all a question of degree. Most of us don't barbecue every day; it's something that's done on special occasions, usually just during the summer. To those who argue that man has been smoking his meats and eating over fires since the beginning of time, so what's to worry, I add that primitive man's food supply didn't have the multiplicity of environmental factors to take into consideration that we have today.

Fat and Cholesterol:
Your Heart Doesn't Have to Attack You

In the last decade eighteen major organizations concerned with health and nutrition (among them the United States Departments of Agriculture and Health, Education and Welfare, the National Institutes of Health, and the American Heart Association) have advised Americans to eat less saturated fat and less cholesterol as a means of reducing the risk of heart disease.

The count of cholesterol

As people are becoming more health conscious, an important reason for selecting one kind of protein instead of another increasingly may have to do with its fat and cholesterol content. Yet another decision may pertain to the way the protein is cooked: what sort of oils are selected—margarine, butter, olive oil, leftover bacon drippings—and which are preferred?

In this complicated and often controversial fat-cholesterol area, I stress practical guidelines to provide you with the information to make intelligent decisions not only about which proteins to eat, but how to cook them as well. For example, let's say you select a striped bass and then decide to cook it in coconut oil to give it an exotic flair. By how much have you increased the fat content of the once lean fish by the oil you selected, and does it matter? We'll see.

FAT

Fat is necessary in the human body. It provides the body's greatest energy reserves, is an essential part of cell membranes that regulate nutrient passage in and out of cells, and insulates and protects organs such as the kidney and the heart. Subcutaneous fat (the fat directly under the skin) is what helps keep us warm. Fats transport and aid absorption of essential fat-soluble vitamins A, D, E, and K. They have satiety value—making us feel full. Fats in the diet improve palatability of foods; any good cook knows this as he or she puts a little butter here, a little oil there.

The problem is that the American diet has 31 per cent more dietary fat now than it did 60 years ago. The overconsumption of fats in the diet in general, and of certain types in particular, have, rightly or wrongly, come to be associated with heart disease, but more about that controversy later.

According to the Dietary Goals—1977, issued by the Senate Select Committee on Nutrition, most Americans eat about 42 per cent of their calories in fat. The Dietary Goals recommended an over-all decrease in fat consumption to about 30 per cent of daily calories, with 10 per cent in the form of saturated fat, 10 per cent monounsaturated, and 10 per cent polyunsaturated. On the extreme end, Nathan Pritikin of the Longevity Research Institute suggests that only 10 per cent of calories should be derived from fat.[5] The American Heart Association recommends an upper limit of 30–35 per cent.

Saturated, Monounsaturated, and Polyunsaturated

There are more than forty fatty acids found in nature and more than twenty commonly appear in foods. These are classified into three major categories: *saturated, monounsaturated,* and *polyunsaturated.*

Why the concern with differentiating between fats? Because some populations that consume much saturated fat seem to have more heart disease. Experiments suggest a relationship between the *type* of fat eaten and the condition of the blood vessels and the heart. It appears that diets high in fat can lead to above normal amounts of lipids in the blood. (Lipids include triglycerides, fatty acids, cholesterol, and other fatlike substances.) *Saturated* fatty acids *increase* the level of cholesterol in the blood, *monounsaturated* fatty acids have little effect, *polyunsaturated* fatty acids *decrease* the level. Dietary cholesterol (cholesterol taken in as part of food consumed) may raise cholesterol in the blood (serum cholesterol).

CHOLESTEROL IN THE DIET

If you're concerned about the relationship between diet and heart disease and you're designing a diet to decrease fat consumption, remember the intake of *both* saturated fats and cholesterol must be lowered.

[5] Pritikin's regimen, and other regimens which severely restrict fats, may have a possible effect on growth and hormone production which makes such diets questionable for pregnant or nursing women and for children. As reported in Harvard Medical School *Newsletter,* January 1980, exactly why a rapid loss of body fat is accompanied by a failure to ovulate is not known, but it has to do with changes in female hormones, particularly estrogens, since fat tissue is responsible in part for estrogen production.

Dietary cholesterol first became an issue in 1908 when Russian research revealed rabbits developed hardening of the arteries after eating a diet heavily laden with saturated fats and cholesterol. In virtually every society studied since, scientists have found that the more fat and cholesterol in the diet, the higher the average blood cholesterol level in the people and the higher the death rate from coronary heart disease.

Cholesterol is a waxy substance found in every cell of the body, where it is an essential component of cell membranes. It is found only in foods from animal sources, not plant sources. Recently Dr. John Gofman, at the University of California at Berkeley, discovered there is "bad" cholesterol and "good" cholesterol. The cholesterol-containing lipids (blood fats) can be separated into four classes of lipoproteins, defined on the basis of their density upon blood centrifugation. Two of these classes, LDL, low density lipoproteins, and HDL, high density lipoproteins, are now being used as clues in establishing the relationship between cholesterol and heart disease. (Request that your physician do a cholesterol-triglyceride test, or go directly to a laboratory. However you have the test done, make sure the lab is equipped to fractionate triglycerides into high density lipoproteins and low density lipoproteins. The HDL and LDL levels are helpful in diagnosing people who have difficulty handling fats.) For once, a high level of something, high density lipoprotein (HDL), is all to the good. It's been shown that a person with a high HDL has a lower risk of coronary heart disease. This means that the HDL form of cholesterol can be beneficial. It is just the opposite with the second major class of fat in the blood, low density lipoprotein (LDL); the higher the LDL, the greater the risk of coronary heart disease. High blood levels of a third class of fat, very low density lipoprotein (VDL), increase the risk of coronary heart disease. In terms of cholesterol, research suggests raising HDL and lowering LDL and VDL. The tricky question is: How do you accomplish this raising and lowering, or can you, and can it be accomplished by diet?

Diet-Heart Controversy

This brings up the great diet-heart controversy which was refueled in June 1980, when the august Food and Nutrition Board of the National Academy of Sciences issued a twenty-page report, "Toward Healthful Diets," which disputed the widespread opinion that cholesterol intake should be restricted. The report made the front page of the New York *Times* and every wire service. In sharp departure from recent dietary recommendations the Board found no reason for the average healthy American to restrict consumption of cholesterol, or reduce the intake of fat except as necessary to achieve and maintain normal body weight. The Board said that seven large scale studies in which diets were modified to alter the incidence of heart disease had shown only a "marginal decrease" in the rate of heart attacks, but no effect on over-all mortality.

As expected, the report received widely mixed reactions: it was greeted with confusion by the American public, was praised by the affected food industries (the meat, milk, and egg industries whose food products are known to be high in cholesterol), met with approval by the American Medical Association, and was attacked with a fire storm of criticism by groups like the American Heart Association and the United States Department of Agriculture, which called it irresponsible.

Those opposed to the report said that the Board had ignored a vast body of convincing evidence, especially an independent study developed by a Norwegian cardiologist which had been presented as testimony at hearings for the Dietary Goals recommendations of the Senate Select Committee on Nutrition and Human Needs. As part of the Norwegian independent study a questionnaire was sent to 215 leading lipid researchers from twenty-one countries: 98.2 per cent agreed that there is a direct relationship between diet and the development of heart disease; 97 per cent felt there is a positive relationship between dietary cholesterol and serum cholesterol; and 98 per cent indicated a strongly positive relationship between serum cholesterol levels and the development of heart disease.

William Connors, M.D., professor of medicine and director of the Lipid Atherosclerosis Laboratory in the department of Medicine at the University of Oregon and a member of the American Society for Clinical Nutrition panel, said in an interview in the Los Angeles *Times* that the Food and Nutrition Board acted without a "perspective for human illness. The U.S. male population has one of the highest mortality rates in heart disease in the world and it's not going down all that much. Of 100 people, 80 die of heart disease. And that's still a problem."

Questions Remain

The relationship between nutritional factors and coronary heart disease is not definitely and unquestionably established for a variety of reasons. One reason is the complexity of the disease process itself. Conditions closely associated with the development of heart disease are varied, but they include such personal characteristics as heredity, sex, and age; personal habits such as smoking, exercising, eating habits and food patterns; metabolic changes, such as overweight and elevated serum lipids, reduced glucose tolerance, and increased blood pressure.

Dietary Changes for Whom?

If the evidence increases in support of dietary remedies for heart disease, the most important question will become: for *whom?* Should *everyone* be concerned about saturated fat and cholesterol? Or just those at risk for heart disease? The Dietary Goals said that *all* Americans should reduce cholesterol intake to about 300 mg per day, and reduce fat intake to about 30 per cent of calories. I attended the 60th Annual Meeting of the American Dietetic Association and the following views were presented that reflect three approaches on the diet-heart issue.

* *Everybody* should be concerned.
A strict approach. The strictly styled ap-

proach was represented by Robert E. Hodges, M.D., from the University of California at Davis. He agrees with the American Heart Association that the *entire* population should reduce total fat consumption to 30–35 per cent of their total daily calories and reduce cholesterol intake to around 300 mg per day.

* *Some* people should be concerned.
A moderate approach. The moderate-style approach is backed by Dr. Roslyn Alfin-Slater, U.C.L.A. Her position is that there is a segment of the population that is genetically disposed to heart disease; this group should, therefore, limit its dietary cholesterol intake, but this should not apply to the population as a whole. Her approach is based on a study she did in which extra eggs were fed as a source of cholesterol on top of an otherwise normal diet. She found no significant changes in serum cholesterol levels resulting from the additional eggs; thus, contrary to the anti-egg people, she says most people can eat eggs and other cholesterol-rich foods in moderation.

* *Not everyone* should be concerned.
A loosely styled approach. Dr. Raymond Reiser, with Texas A&M, feels there is a normal spectrum of blood serum values and that normal persons do not develop pathological levels upon eating eggs and other cholesterol-containing foods.

EXAMPLES OF FOODS CONTAINING SATURATED FATS:[6]

One way to remember quickly which foods are high in saturated fats is to remember that most saturated fats are of *animal* origin, and are solid at room temperature.

Red Meats: Beef, lamb, pork, and ham all contain saturated fat. Veal contains less satu-

[6] Partially excerpted from *A Change for Heart*, by James M. Ferguson, M.D., and C. Barr Taylor, M.D. Published by Bull Publishing Company, 1978.

rated fat than beef (see Protein Index, page 155). The lean part of a steak contains most of the protein, minerals, and vitamins. The fat in and around the meat generally supplies only calories so you can trim away the visible fat with no nutritional loss.

It is not well known that the more expensive the grade of meat, the more fat it contains. Meats are graded partially on fat content:

Prime grade generally has the highest proportion of fat (as high as 50–60 per cent of the total weight). These meats are expensive and are generally bought by restaurants and hotels.

Choice grade contains about 35–40 per cent fat, is widely available and less costly than Prime grade meats.

Good grade has less fat than the other grades (about 25–35 per cent) and is available in some markets. Although less tender, these meats are flavorful, and as tender as the other grade meats when prepared properly.

Ground Meats are usually prepared from the trimmings of other meat cuts. They can contain a very large amount of fat. Since ground meat is very popular, it is important to recognize the different fat contents:

* *Hamburger* or "regular ground meat" contains 30–35 per cent fat. Much of this can be rendered or melted out during cooking and discarded, but this is wasteful and more expensive in the long run.

* *Lean ground beef* is generally prepared from such cuts as chuck or rump, and has about 20–25 per cent fat. This is probably the best buy for your money.

* *Extra-* or *super-lean ground beef* contains the least fat. It generally contains about 15–20 per cent fat.

There are different amounts of saturated fat in different cuts of beef. Chuck, rump, and round are generally low while prime rib, sirloin, and porterhouse are high in saturated fats.

Sausage, Bacon, Cured, and Luncheon Meats: Most of these meats contain large quantities (about 35–40 per cent) of saturated fats and probably should be used infrequently.

Poultry: Chicken, turkey, and game hens all have less saturated fat than red meats and are excellent sources of protein. They are all similar in cholesterol content. Their fat content can be further reduced by removing the skin and underlying fat before cooking.

Game: Most wild birds and animals are low in fat and are good sources of protein; however, domestic ducks and geese are very high in fat content.

Fish: Fish are excellent sources of protein, minerals, and vitamins. Although they have almost the same cholesterol content as lean red meat, they are generally much lower in saturated fat.

Dairy Products: Milk is one of the most nutritious foods available. It is rich in all types of nutrients: protein, carbohydrate, fats, minerals, and vitamins. However, whole milk has a relatively high cholesterol and saturated fat content compared to nonfat (skim) milk.

Cream: All creams contain large amounts of saturated fats and cholesterol. Most powdered cream substitutes are made with coconut oil and contain saturated fats. However, some are made with soy oil, or cottonseed oil, which contain no cholesterol and very little saturated fat—read the labels before you buy a cream substitute.

Butter: This is a concentrated milk fat with the largest amount of cholesterol and saturated fat per ounce of all commonly used fats. (For substitutions, see chart, page 189.)

Ice cream: Regular ice cream generally contains 10–12 per cent fat. Iced milk and frozen milk desserts are usually less than 10 per cent fat. They are recommended as a substitute for ice cream. Sherbet does not usually contain milk or saturated fat.

Cheese and Cheese Products: These are highly concentrated forms of whole milk and almost all have a high saturated fat and cholesterol content. (See Cheese section of this chapter, page 167, for discussion of low fat cheeses.)

Cheese products such as process cheese foods (Velveeta) and cheese spreads are softer and lower in total fat because they are made from water and skim milk solids. Despite this, they are still 20–30 per cent saturated fat.

Cream cheese generally contains 50–60 per cent fat. This cheese is a highly concentrated source of cholesterol and saturated fat.

The accompanying chart shows the breakdown for the fat and cholesterol content of some of the commonly consumed foods just discussed. A quick comparison might be helpful in deciding which foods you might want to include more of and which you want to include less of.

COOKING OILS

We know that certain dietary fats have higher proportions of polyunsaturated to saturated fats. This is called their P/S value. The higher the saturated fat, the lower the value. Animal fats such as beef tallow and butter contain very high proportions of saturated fatty acids while most vegetable oils are rich in polyunsaturated fatty acids, which have a high P/S value. (This isn't true of all vegetable oils—see coconut and palm oil on chart on page 188.)

TIPS

* Polyunsaturated fats (the good guys) are in highest concentration in *liquid* vegetable oils.

* The ratio of polyunsaturated to saturated fat should be at least 2:1. That's at least 2 gm of polyunsaturated fat for every gram of saturated fat.

* When buying a margarine, look for a product that lists *liquid* vegetable oil as its first ingredient. If the first item is a partially hydrogenated vegetable oil, or a hydrogenated vegetable oil, it means it is a more saturated product.

Fat Content, Major Fatty Acid Composition, and Cholesterol Content of Selected Foods Per 100 Gm Food Item

	% Total Fat	% Total Saturated	% Total Monoun-saturated	% Total Polyun-saturated	Mg Cholesterol in 100 gm Edible Portion
FISH					
Cooked Salmon, sockeye	8.9	1.8	1.5	4.7	(47)
Striped Bass	2.1	0.5	0.6	0.7	
Haddock	0.7	0.1	0.1	0.2	(60)
SHELLFISH					
Eastern Oyster, raw flesh	2.1	0.5	0.2	0.6	50
Alaskan King Crab, cooked, legs and claws	1.6	0.2	0.3	0.6	100
Shrimp, raw flesh	1.2	0.2	0.2	0.5	150
Scallop, raw flesh	0.9	0.1	—	0.4	35
BEEF					
T-bone Steak, broiled 56% lean + 44% fat	43.2	18.0	21.1	1.6	(94)*
Lean, trimmed of separate fat	10.3	4.4	4.3	0.6	(91)*
Rump Roast, roasted 75% lean + 25% fat	27.3	11.4	13.1	1.2	(94)*
Lean, trimmed	9.3	3.9	3.9	0.5	(91)*
Round Steak, 81% lean + 19% fat	14.9	6.3	6.9	0.7	(94)*
Lean, trimmed	6.4	2.7	2.7	0.4	(91)*
LAMB					
Shoulder of Lamb, Roasted 74% lean + 26% fat	26.9	12.6	11.0	1.6	(98)*
Lean, trimmed	5.6	2.3	2.1	0.3	(100)*
Leg of Lamb, roasted 83% lean + 17% fat	21.2	9.6	8.5	1.2	(98)*
Lean, trimmed	9.6	4.0	3.7	0.6	(100)*
VEAL					
Foreshank, stewed 86% lean + 14% fat	10.4	4.4	4.2	0.7	(71)*
PORK					
Loin, roasted 79% lean + 21% fat	28.1	9.8	13.1	3.1	(88)*
Lean, trimmed	13.9	4.7	6.3	1.5	(88)*
Ham, cured, roasted 84% lean + 16% fat	22.1	7.8	10.4	2.4	(88)*
Lean, trimmed	8.8	3.0	4.0	0.9	(88)*
Bacon, cooked	49.0	18.1	22.8	5.4	85
LUNCHEON MEATS					
Corned Beef	22.7	8.7	11.3	1.2	43
Knackwurst	27.2	10.0	12.9	2.6	58

Fat Content, Major Fatty Acid Composition,
and Cholesterol Content of Selected Foods
Per 100 Gm Food Item
(continued)

	% Total Fat	% Total Saturated	% Total Monoun-saturated	% Total Polyun-saturated	Mg Cholesterol in 100 gm Edible Portion
LUNCHEON MEATS (continued)					
Luncheon Meat	32.1	11.5	15.1	3.7	55
Dry salami	33.0	11.8	16.7	3.1	79
Summer Sausage	29.0	11.1	13.6	2.8	68
POULTRY					
Chicken, roasted					
Dark Meat	9.7	2.7	3.2	2.4	91 (without skin)
Light Meat	3.5	1.0	0.9	0.9	79 (without skin)
Turkey, roasted					
Dark Meat	5.3	1.6	1.4	1.5	101 (without skin)
Light Meat	2.6	0.7	0.6	0.7	77 (without skin)
DAIRY					
Cottage Cheese					
Creamed	4.0	2.6	1.1	0.1	19
Uncreamed	0.4	0.2	0.1	—	7
Cheese					
Cheddar	32.8	20.2	9.8	0.9	99
Swiss	27.6	17.6	7.7	1.0	100
Mozzarella (part skim)	16.4	10.2	5.3	0.5	66
American	28.9	18.0	8.5	1.0	(90)
Yoghurt					
Whole Milk	3.4	2.2	0.9	0.1	13
Part Skim Milk	1.5	1.0	0.4	—	6
Milk					
Whole, 3.5% fat	3.5	2.2	1.0	0.1	14
Low Fat, 2% fat	2.0	1.2	0.6	0.1	9
Skim, 1% fat	1.0	0.6	0.3	—	6
Eggs, raw, whole, fresh	6.6	3.4	4.5	1.4	504, or 1 egg approx. 250 mg

SOURCES: *Dietary Goals for United States*; Consumer & Food Economics Institute, (USDA, Agricultural Research Ser͞ ͞ ͞, Hyattsville, Md.; 1977) "Comprehensive Evaluation of Fatty Acids in Foods," *Journal of American Dietetic Association* (May, July, August, October 1975; March, July, September, November 1976; January 1977). Ruth M. Feeley et al., *Cholesterol Content of Foods*, Institute of American Dietetic Association, August 1972).

( ) Figures in parenthesis denote imputed value.
— means less than 0.005 gm.
*Composite of all retail cuts.

SKIMMING OFF THE FAT

The following suggestions are simple changes that can be easily implemented to reduce one's fat intake:

* Use skim milk or low fat milk instead of whole milk.

* Use smaller amounts of butter. Or, use margarine, which has the same total amount of fat, but the saturated fat is reduced by one third.

* Trim meat of all outside fat. A 3½-ounce portion of steak trimmed of fat can reduce fat intake by a whopping 75 per cent.

* Use leaner ground meats.

* Eat the white meat of chicken without the skin. The skin of the chicken contains most of the fat.

* Pay attention to the difference in cooking oils. Corn or safflower oils are recommended.

Fatty Acids in Typical Food Fats
(Per cent of Total Fatty Acids)

COOKING OILS	Poly- unsatd.	Mono- unsatd.	Satu- rated	P/S Value
ANIMAL FATS				
Beef Fat	2	44	54	< 0.1
Butter	4	37	59	< 0.1
Chicken Fat	27	29	44	0.6
Lard	14	46	40	0.4
VEGETABLE OILS				
Coconut	2	6	92	< 0.1
Corn	60	26	14	4.3
Cottonseed	52	19	29	1.8
Olive	15	69	16	9.9
Palm	10	37	53	0.2
Peanut	35	45	20	1.8
Safflower	78	11	11	7.1
Soybean	58	27	15	3.9
Spec Proc Soybean	47	38	15	3.1
Sunflower	70	18	12	5.8

ANSWERS TO PRACTICAL QUESTIONS REGARDING CHOLESTEROL AND FAT

* *Does cooking affect cholesterol?*

There is little information available, but from studies on cooking chicken and meat, it appears that cholesterol is not affected by heat any more than protein is.

* *What about shellfish?*

At one point, the American Heart Association cautioned people on low cholesterol diets not to eat shellfish. They have now softened their position somewhat, saying shellfish can be eaten in moderation, but shrimp should be eaten in even more moderation. In a recent report, the USDA reported the following amounts of cholesterol in a 3½-ounce serving:

Oysters = 50 mg   Shrimp = 150 mg
Lobster = 85 mg   Clams = 50 mg
Scallops = 53 mg   Crab = 100 mg

* *How do butter and margarine compare?*

Both have about 100 calories per tablespoon and both are about 80 per cent fat. Whether you personally want to use margarine instead of butter will depend on a lot of factors. In a well-publicized statement Dr. Joan Dye Gussow, Chairman of the Nutrition Department at Teachers' College of Columbia University, said, "I trust a cow or chicken more than I do a chemist. When I spread something on my bread I want it to be butter . . ."

The fatty acid picture looks like this:

	Polyun- saturated	Monoun- saturated	Saturated
Butter	3%	23%	50%
Margarine	23%	39%	14%

Margarines vary according to fatty acid composition, though all are derived from vegetable fat. There is also a difference in the *shape* they are sold in. *Sticks* of margarine usually contain a relatively low proportion of polyunsaturated fat. That's because when a larger amount of liquid oil is used to increase the proportion of polyunsaturated acids, it cannot be formed into a stick and is usually packaged in a bowl or tub. Not all soft or tub margarines are formed in this way. Some "diet" margarines may be soft because they contain large amounts of water.

For a look at specific brand differences, see chart below:

Some Margarines, Oils, and Dressings

Content per Serving (1 tbsp. about 14 gm)	Total Fat (gm)	Poly-unsaturated (gm)	Saturated (gm)	Cholesterol (mg)	Total Calories	Type of Oil
MARGARINES						
Blue Bonnet	11	4	3	0	100	soybean, cottonseed
Blue Bonnet (soft)	11	4	2	0	100	soybean, cottonseed
Chiffon (soft)	11	3	2	0	100	soybean
Fleischmann's (soft)	11	5	2	0	100	corn
Fleischmann's (diet)	6	2	1	0	50	corn
Imperial	11	3	3	0	100	soybean, palm
Imperial (soft)	11	4	3	0	100	soybean, palm
Mazola	11	3	2	0	100	corn, soybean, cottonseed
Mazola (diet)	6	2	1	0	50	corn
Mrs. Filbert's Golden Quarters	11	1	2	0	100	soybean
Mrs. Filbert's Golden (soft)	11	3	2	0	100	soybean
Mrs. Filbert's Corn (soft)	11	5	2	0	100	corn
Mrs. Filbert's (diet)	6	2	1	0	50	corn
Nucoa	11	3	2	0	100	soybean, cottonseed
Nucoa (soft)	10	3	2	0	90	soybean, cottonseed
Parkay (soft)	11	4	2	0	100	soybean
Promise	11	5	2	0	100	cottonseed, soybean, safflower, or sunflower
Promise (soft)	11	7	2	0	100	cottonseed, peanut, safflower, or sunflower
OILS AND DRESSINGS						
Crisco Oil	14	5	2	0	120	soybean
Fleischmann's Corn Oil	14	8	2	0	120	corn
Kraft Safflower Oil	14	10	1	0	120	safflower
Mazola Oil	14	8	2	0	120	corn
Planter's Oil	14	5	3	0	126	peanut
Bright Day Imitation Mayonnaise	6	4	1	0	60	soybean and others

Some Margarines, Oils, and Dressings (continued)

Content per Serving (1 tbsp. about 14 gm)	Total Fat (gm)	Poly-unsaturated (gm)	Satu-rated (gm)	Choles-terol (mg)	Total Calo-ries	Type of Oil
OILS AND DRESSINGS (continued)						
Hellmann's Real Mayonnaise	11	5	2	10	100	vegetable
Kraft Real Mayonnaise	11	6	2	5	100	soybean
Mrs. Filbert's Mayonnaise	11	6	2	10	100	soybean
Miracle Whip Salad Dressing	7	4	1	5	70	soybean
Mrs. Filbert's Salad Dressing	6	3	1	10	65	soybean

SOURCE: *The Medical Letter*, vol. 18 (September 24, 1976).

NOTE: If you are purchasing oil that has a generic labeling, such as vegetable oil, and not a specific label, such as safflower oil or corn oil, read the back panel to identify the composite of the oil used and to see its combined polyunsaturate content.

* *What is hydrogenated fat and is it bad for you?*

It is a fat which has reacted with hydrogen in a process known as hydrogenation. It increases the stability of the fat against rancidity and may convert a liquid polyunsaturated oil to a more solid form; however, this process always *decreases* the polyunsaturate content of the fat, but because it may be stopped at the monosaturated stage, hydrogenation does not necessarily result in a marked increase in saturates.

* *After cooking, sometimes if I have oil left over, I reuse it later. Does reheating vegetable oils affect the degree of polyunsaturation?*

A study in England[7] showed that after corn oil was reheated seven times, there was no appreciable difference in the degree of saturation. Reheating oil at normal home cooking temperatures does not increase the degree of saturation.

 Futuristic Protein Possibilities

There is much talk about the necessity of cutting our intake of animal protein because of the changing world food supply and the fact that we can't go on eating so high off the hog. But to me it seems that convincing the public there's a food shortage is a more difficult task than selling the energy crisis.

The majority of people feel there's enough for their families to continue eating the way they are accustomed, a roasted chicken here, a lamb chop there, a steak on Sunday.

[7] The Lancet, August 20, 1977, Little, Brown and Company, Boston, Massachusetts.

Futuristic protein possibilities

Food scientists feel the population of the earth may reach a point where agriculture becomes insufficient or uneconomic as a source of food. Then, out of necessity, we'll have to turn to other sources of protein, but so far the audience in America isn't ready for this information. This crisis still seems too far removed.

Much of the present research in protein centers around the concept of providing a *less expensive* source of protein to replace more expensive ones and using vegetable proteins to extend or replace meat proteins. One of the most successful has been the use of Texturized Vegetable Protein.

TEXTURIZED VEGETABLE PROTEIN

Much of the research in new protein sources involves texturizing vegetable proteins; the plant sources may be soybeans, peanuts, wheat, or cottonseed, but most come from soy. It's a process where vegetable protein is changed into forms that are acceptable to the populations involved. I was at the Meals for Millions laboratories in Santa Monica, California, one day when American experts were showing professionals from developing countries how to produce low-cost, highly nutritious protein-based foods. One of the professionals from Ghana learned how to use a suitcase version of a hand texturizer that changed iron-enriched soybean dough into a

protein-rich crepe that could be used to scoop up traditional beans.

Unfortunately, Americans have a tendency to look condescendingly at these people with their portable suitcase protein-makers and say fine for them, but we don't need it, thank you. Right now in the United States it is hard to build a strong argument for portable cereal extruders or even for these cereal products at their most commercial level: TVP, or Texturized Vegetable Protein.

As long as the supply of animal and vegetable protein is adequate and available to the consumer, TVP is a product whose time has yet to come. But in the future, if animal protein gets too expensive, then TVP—used primarily in combination with meat as an extender—will have a real place in this country.

Ground Beef and Texturized Vegetable Protein

During the recession of '73, when food prices first started their dramatic escalation, an interesting thing happened: TVP entered the retail market premixed in packages of hamburger meat. The proportion was two-thirds meat to one-third soy extender. Research revealed consumers would purchase the blended product when they considered savings substantial enough. But a short time later, when beef prices came down, the demand for the soy blend fell, too. When beef becomes scarce, soy extenders will have another field day.

I saw this happen again in the spring of '78, when beef prices skyrocketed and meat departments on the West Coast started offering soy blends. Many West Coast supermarkets took out full-page ads introducing "Beef Patty Mix. A controlled blend of Ground Beef and Textured Vegetable Protein." The savings were about 30 per cent over ground beef.

Of course, you don't have to wait for beef prices to escalate to start using soy blends, and if the supermarkets in your area don't do the blending for you, you can do it yourself. Some of the soy mixes available are: Vita Burger from Loma Linda Foods; Make a Better Burger by Lipton; and Vegetable Pro-

Super soybean burger

tein Mix by Sahadi Kitchens. These are made from soybeans and unfortunately they are heavily preseasoned and salted. What should also be marketed is just plain Texturized Vegetable Protein, and you could add your own seasonings.

WHAT ARE THE ADVANTAGES?

The most obvious is price. These mixes average a few pennies a burger and since you need 30 per cent less meat, they save you 30 per cent on your ground meat bill. A less obvious advantage is health. You're substituting a vegetable protein for part of the animal protein. You're ending up with virtually the same amount of protein, but with less saturated fat, less cholesterol, and about 20 per cent less calories (see comparison below).

As far as taste goes, as long as the mixture is no more than 30 per cent TVP, the taste is fine. If you like your burgers with onions, celery, tomato sauce, covered with pickles and cheese and lettuce, I doubt if you'll even be tasting any difference.

Although these mixes are usually marketed to be used with beef, they can be blended with other meats—veal, lamb, pork—equally as well. In addition to their standard use in burgers, they can be used in spaghetti sauce, meatloaf, sloppy Joes, and meatballs.

WHAT ARE THE DISADVANTAGES?

With TVP by itself, you get less fat; however, when combined with meat, as in a hamburger patty, meatloaf, or meatballs, the TVP tends to absorb fat and hold it in rather than letting it drain off. You might not want the salt and other flavorings used in the preseasoned mixes, so check labels carefully. Sometimes the burger doesn't hold together; however, if you follow directions on the package carefully, this shouldn't be a problem.

TVP—Meat Analogs

Cornell University has predicted, I think optimistically, that vegetable protein meat analogs (products that are manufactured from vegetables to resemble traditional sources of protein) may reach 10 per cent of the total domestic meat consumption by 1985. Large

A 3½-ounce Burger

	Calories	Protein gm	Fat gm	Carbohydrate gm	Iron mg	Thiamin mg	Riboflavin mg	Niacin mg
ALL BEEF	268	17.9	21.2	0	2.7	.08	.16	4.3
BEEF-SOY BLEND	223	17.7	16	2.5	2.8	.11	.17	4.5

(The fat content of ground beef may be higher, depending on whether the fat is drained off.)

Vegetarian Steak

companies like General Mills, Worthington Foods, Ralston Purina, Swift, and Archer Daniels are trying to make meat analogs that approximate the sensory characteristics of meat, fish, or poultry. So far, only one TVP product, BacoBits, imitation bacon-flavored bits, has had much visible impact on the retail market. This is one instance where the consumer knows a product is TVP and is buying it anyway. Unknowingly, consumers are eating TVP in a wide variety of other foods, from chili con carne to bread, in which the manufacturer uses the TVP for its functional properties (i.e., improving the texture of bread), but the consumer gets an extra dose of protein as well.

Other products like TVP chicken chunks (an imitation chicken-flavored product that is chickenless chicken) have been unsuccessful because their taste and appearance aren't up to par, yet. And even their names—ISP, Texgran, edi Pro—so far sound more like dog food or fuel, but hardly like people food.

Although I've been tasting these meat analogs as they've been developed, I didn't want my previous experience to prejudice me in judging them. So, in the interest of fairness, one afternoon I assembled a group of neutral friends who had never seen a meat analog, for the purpose of a tasting. These are the results:

TVP Meat Analogs

Name of Product	Resembles	Company	Comments
Stripples	Bacon	Worthington	Comes in very pink and beige strips, looks like an art director's idea of bacon. The flavor tasted like bacon, but the texture was way off.
Breakfast Links	Sausage	Morningstar Farms	This tasted pretty good and looked like you would expect sausage to look. In fact, one woman on my tasting panel thought it was delicious and wanted more of my limited supply!
Wham	Ham	Morningstar Farms	This has a pink-green tinge with a paperlike consistency. You couldn't cut this one, but could shred it apart as you would wet cardboard. None of my tasters wanted to go near it. After the mandatory bite, it stayed on the counter.
Breakfast Strips	Bacon	Morningstar Farms	This handles more like bacon than the first bacon product sampled. The taste wasn't too bad, but no one was crazy about it.
Breakfast Patties	Sausage	Morningstar Farms	This was excellent. It had an authentic flavor and the best texture of the products sampled.

My sampling could have gone on to include products like Tuno, Skallops (the worst), and Staklettes, but from what was sampled, some general conclusions can be drawn:

1. Although soy protein is a good source of protein, it is not complete unless essential missing amino acids are added. In most instances, the manufacturers add egg white solids. With the egg white solids added (this

is marked on the label) these products can be used as one would use traditional sources of protein.

2. Without exception, all the products are too salty. During the testing we were repeatedly reaching for water.

3. All are made with artificial colors and flavors. The manufacturers say natural colors are problematic in that they oxidize and turn brown.

4. The prices are too high, sometimes costing as much or more than the items they are designed to replace. One company told me their prices could go 20–25 per cent below beef, but not until the volume gets bigger.

5. All products are energy intensive, involving sophisticated spinning of vegetable proteins into a fiber similar in production to spun rayon or nylon products.

6. Chemical preservatives and additives were used in almost all the products.

7. Over-all quality of most products—including taste, appearance, aroma, textures—leaves a great deal to be desired.

Comparison of Protein, Fat, and Carbohydrate in Soy Products and Traditional Protein Sources

Product	Amount	Weight (gm)	Protein (gm)	Fat (gm)	Carbohydrate mg	Calories
Beef-style Soy Product	1 slice	28	4.5	4.0	2.0	60
Beef Rump Roast, lean	1 slice	28	6.6	7.7	0	97
Chicken-style Soy Product	1 slice	28	4.5	5.5	1.0	70
Light Meat Chicken, without skin	1 piece	28	9.0	1.7	0.3	55
Stripples (bacon)	1 slice	8.3	1.3	1.8	0.8	25
Bacon, drained	1 slice	8.3	2.2	4.3	0.3	49
Wham (ham imitation)	1 slice	23	3.3	3.0	1.3	47
Ham, baked, lean	1 slice	23	4.8	5.1	0	66
Prosage Links	1 link	23	3.7	4.0	1.7	60
Pork Sausage Link	1 link	23	4.2	10.1	Trace	110

SOURCE: Traditional protein nutritional values from *Nutritional Value of American Foods*, Handbook #456, U. S. Department of Agriculture. Soy protein information furnished by manufacturers of soy products.

Peanut Flakes and Minced Fish

Possibilities for futuristic protein foods are coming from a variety of unexpected sources. Two that I have personally had experience with are peanut flakes and minced fish. Scientists at Clemson University steam, dry, and grind peanuts, ending up with a bland, light-colored, high-protein product they call peanut flakes. (In texture, they remind me of Ivory flakes.) I was sent several packages of these flakes with directions on how to turn them into high-protein brownies, casseroles, and cocktail dips. My taste-testers and I unanimously agreed that the cheese-flavored dip was horrible in every respect. The chocolate brownies were okay, but our national need for an additional way to make protein-rich brownies doesn't seem to be so pressing. Another package of flakes was to be combined with seasonings and vegetables to make a casserole, but by that time I lost my interest. Peanut flakes were touted as the food of the future. Thank goodness they fizzled out before they got started.

Another futuristic development that has been considerably more successful is minced fish flesh. (Try to say *that* without stumbling!) Minced fish provides a better answer to the problem of what to do with tons of fish that are caught each year and are thrown back because they are low in commercial value. Maybe it's too difficult to remove their skins or they are too bony, but they are still a good source of protein, *if* there were an easy way to get at that protein. Dr. Robert Baker of Cornell University (developer of the chicken frankfurter, among other new foods), enters the picture. He developed a special deboning process where the end product—minced fish flesh—can be used in a variety of items ranging from chowders and fish sticks to, maybe in the future, fish hot dogs and fish sausages. The advantage is that it's fish—so it's low in cholesterol and fat, and in comparison to beef, lower in calories, too.

To produce a minced fish product, controversial mechanical deboners are used. There was a consumer outcry when these mechanical deboners were used for meat. Consumers

thought they were getting shortchanged, paying for more bone and getting less meat. When it comes to fish, the regulating agency allows for a tolerance of less than 1 per cent bone and often *none* ends up in the final product. But historically, with fish, we've been merrily eating soft salmon and sardine bones for years. So as long as the minced fish is at least 99 per cent flesh, I don't see a problem.

In test markets in New York, the minced fish flesh was sold frozen in 1-pound packages. I combined a package with fresh bread crumbs, an egg, and seasonings and made fish balls. It took 5 minutes and I was surprised at how pleasant it was. It didn't taste like fresh fish, but then neither do frozen fish sticks. It was quick, easy, and as a convenience item, which is what this is, it's worth looking into. Its worth is also enhanced by its versatility: it can be used in everything from fish casseroles and chowders to fish croquettes and even a hot fish sandwich.

In New York, during its test run, it was introduced at selected supermarkets at 89 cents a pound. It could have been priced significantly lower, but Dr. Baker was afraid that if it was priced lower, people wouldn't take it seriously. I take it plenty seriously, but I think since it *can,* it *should* be priced lower.

Here's one food developed to satisfy our protein needs in the future that's here today. If you're interested in finding out when minced fish might be available in your area, write to Dr. Robert Baker, Rice Hall, Cornell University, Ithaca, New York 14853.

Recipes

The recipes that follow feature primarily fish and poultry, often in combination with unusual grains like kasha, couscous, and wheat pilaf. The recipes are geared to the person or family who wants to use healthful sources of

protein in more appropriate portions, prepared in healthful ways. For the most part the recipes are not geared for the strict vegetarian, although some could be adapted.

STEAMED WHOLE FISH WITH FERMENTED BLACK BEANS

This is one of my favorite ways to cook a whole fish and make it special yet very easy. The distinctive flavor, which I experienced for the first time in Hong Kong, comes from fermented black beans, which can be purchased inexpensively in stores selling oriental products. Their powerful flavor goes a long way, so a small bag (approximately 2 cups of beans) lasts me many years. At point of purchase the beans are precooked, fermented, and ready to use.

There are elaborate ways to cook a whole fish that require endless stuffing and then sewing the fish back together again. This recipe is every bit as special in flavor, and much *easier* in preparation.

Ingredients:

1 (2½-pound) whole fish, cleaned and deboned, with head and tail on

SAUCE

2 tablespoons fermented black beans

4 tablespoons soy sauce, low salt

6 tablespoons Chinese rice wine or sherry

1 tablespoon oil

1 scallion, cut into matchstick-like pieces

1 tablespoon finely shredded fresh ginger root

Serves 3–4 as main course

1. The Chinese like to use sea bass, but if it's out of season or out of your budget, try any other firm white fish, like tile, for example. Wash and dry the fish inside and out. Using a sharp knife, make 2″ horizontal slits down the length of the body. These slits should pierce the skin so that the sauce has funnels through which to seep.

2. Using a mortar and pestle, combine the beans with the soy sauce, wine, and oil. Let beans "puff up" and absorb liquid for 5 minutes. Blend well into a paste consistency.

3. Wrap enough aluminum foil around the fish to catch the sauce.

4. Fish should be cooked in a fish poacher or any other kind of cooking implement where fish can be steamed over water. Pour water into bottom of fish poacher, being careful that water does not reach cooking rack. Lower fish into poacher. With fish in place, spoon on bean sauce mixture. Add scallions in pretty cross-wise bunches, making xxxx's across the top of the fish. Arrange finely shredded slices of fresh ginger on top. Put on lid and steam. (I find the easiest way to steam using my 18″ long poacher is across two cooking units on the top of the stove.) Steam until fish is firm to the touch, about 15 minutes.

5. To serve, lift fish out of poacher and place on long flat serving platter. Gently pull away aluminum foil. Serve with rice and spoon on extra sauce with each serving.

WHOLE GRILLED FISH STUFFED WITH ELDA UNGER'S WHEAT PILAF AND DAVID LEVINE'S SUMMER TOMATO SAUCE

In the summer, Southern California is a mecca for houseguests. The most appreciated are the ones like David Levine, who enthusiastically pitch in and cook up wonderful concoctions like this simple summer sauce.

Ingredients:

1 (3-pound) whole fish, cleaned and deboned with head and tail on

STUFFING

1 (8-ounce) package wheat pilaf mix (a commercially available product)

¼ cup chopped onion

2 cloves garlic, pressed

¼ cup chopped fresh parsley

1 tablespoon oil

½ pound shrimp, chopped (optional)

SAUCE

3 fresh tomatoes, chopped

6 shallots, finely minced

3 cloves garlic, pressed

4 tablespoons sherry vinegar or, if not available, red wine vinegar

¼ cup dry white wine

3 tablespoons chopped thyme

Serves 6–8

1. Select any firm-fleshed fish. On the West Coast, I use white fish. Dry inside of fish.

2. In medium-size pot, cook wheat pilaf mix according to directions on package for firmer wheat. In skillet, sauté onions, garlic, and parsley in oil. You can add chopped shrimp, but it is not necessary and for many, the additional cholesterol count of the shrimp makes it an undesirable option. Sauté onion mixture about 2 minutes, and add to wheat pilaf mixture.

3. Fill cavity of fish with stuffing mixture. At first, there may seem to be more stuffing than will fit into the fish, but very gently, starting at one end, sew up the fish with needle and thread and you'll see that all the stuffing does fit.

4. Grill fish over hot coals about 20 minutes, 10 minutes per side. To avoid having fish stick to the grill, lightly brush fish with oil as it cooks. (This can also be baked in a 350° F. oven for 15–20 minutes, but the grilling singes the skin and makes it crusty in a delicious way.)

5. While the fish is grilling, prepare the sauce. With a sharp knife, chop fresh tomatoes into small cubes. In small saucepan, cook shallots and garlic in vinegar and wine with thyme. Sauce should be well cooked in about 2 minutes. The essence of this sauce is that the tomatoes are not cooked, but added to the sauce after the 2-minute cooking and warmed through.

6. Serve fish whole on large platter. Remove thread as you make individual servings. Serve sauce separately.

MUSSELS

People complain about the high cost of seafood, yet there are two kinds of seafood that are always reasonable: one is the mussel, the other is squid. Both are big favorites of mine.

The common blue mussel, with its sweet-tasting orange meat, has one of the highest protein contents of anything from the sea. Europeans have long coveted the mussel and for good reason. It is delicious *and* inexpensive. They sell for one half or one third the price of oysters and clams. On the Atlantic Coast, mussels are available year round.

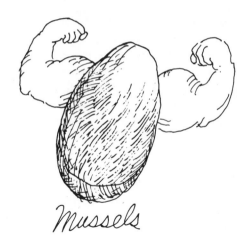

Mussels

They deliver good nutrition at a reasonable cost.

One classic use of mussels is to serve them over pasta as a main course dish. This is also a good method for those of you who think, "My family would never eat mussels." Most people I know, especially children, can't resist pasta, so by combining an unknown, the mussel, with something well loved, like pasta, you've made the whole thing acceptable.

MUSSELS AND PASTA

Ingredients:

4 pounds mussels

1 cup clam juice or mussel juice

3 cloves garlic, pressed

⅓ cup chopped parsley

Juice 1 lemon

1 pound pasta

Serves 4

1. Even if you ask the fish man to clean the mussels (which you should), they always need some last-minute attention. Under cold running water, go over the shells with a copper scouring pad, the kind that comes without soap. Cut off the "beards" (the hairy part that sticks out) with scissors.

2. In a large covered pan, over high heat, steam mussels in a few inches of water until they open, about 3–5 minutes. (The less water you use, the more concentrated is the juice you get from the mussels. You can

steam them over white wine, too.) Discard the shells that don't open.

3. Reserve a few whole mussels for garnish. With a sharp knife, remove the meat from the shells and put in a small frying pan. I use half whole meat, because it looks pretty, and half chopped, because it adds its flavor to the sauce more quickly. It can be quickly chopped in a food processor or blender.

4. Add either 1 cup of juice from the mussels, strained through a cheesecloth, or 1 cup of store-bought clam juice.

5. Add pressed garlic and the parsley; I prefer the flat Italian variety of parsley. Add the juice of one lemon and cook for a moment to heat all ingredients.

6. Toss with steaming hot pasta. Serve on a large platter decorated with a few mussels in their shells.

This festive-looking dish is very reasonably priced and feeds four people elegantly. You also have the fun of knowing that what you've very easily created is a classic dish. The French call it *spaghetti aux moules,* the Italians—*vermicelli con le cozze.*

SQUID TOULON

Although squid rivals the mussel in being one of the best buys at the seafood counter, it has the added bonus of being even easier to prepare. Some people order it in Italian restaurants (*calamari*), but they would not think of cooking it at home. When I asked a few friends why not, they said they thought it would be too time-consuming or too difficult, so they save it for eating out. As you'll see, there's nothing complicated about preparing fresh squid.

Ingredients:

   1 pound squid, cleaned[8]

   1 cup tomato sauce (see page 122)

   1 pound pasta

Serves 3–4

[8] If you live in an area where fresh squid is not available, here's an instance where the frozen will do just as well.

1. Ask your fish man to clean the squid for you. They do this at no extra charge and it is a time-consuming thankless task to do yourself. When you get the squid home, check to see that all traces of black ink have been cleaned out. If there is any ink left, rinse the squid in cold water. With the cleaned squid, you should have two parts: the hood and the tentacles. Cut both into 1" pieces so they will cook rapidly.

2. In a frying pan big enough to hold the squid, warm the tomato sauce. When the sauce is bubbling, add the squid and cook until it turns from its raw, gray-white color to its cooked, beige-white color. This color change should take no longer than 3–4 minutes at the very most. If it cooks longer, it will end up tough and rubbery. Serve immediately with hot pasta.

FISH KEBABS

On a thrifty budget, you may be staying away from the expensive fish fillet. But there is a practical way to use the fillet in combination with other foods. You can buy just what you need and there are no wasted leftovers. Try turning the traditional shish kebab into a fish kebab. A fish kebab requires much less fish per person than you would normally buy because you are threading the fish on the skewers *with* vegetables and fruit. I've found almost all fish works well with this technique: halibut, sole, flounder, cod, whiting, bluefish, the list is endless.[9]

Here are a few points to keep in mind when making fish kebabs:

* The skewers are easier to cook if a 10" skewer has no more than 6" of food on it.

* Keep an artistic color palette in mind when threading the kebabs. Red cherry tomatoes look pretty in between the fish as do alternating thin strips of red and green peppers. Round green grapes are also a nice contrast.

[9] Some people have been astonished that the fish doesn't flake or fall apart when cooked this way, but in my experience, it never has.

* Remember, whatever vegetables or fruit you thread on the skewer should cook in the same amount of time as the fish—which is only 2 minutes per side. A hard vegetable like summer squash, unless it's already cooked, will not work.

* Figure ½ pound fillet makes 4 skewers, and feeds 2 people.

Ingredients:

½–¾ pound fish fillet

1 cup cut-up vegetables or fruits of your choice (cherry tomatoes, grapes, red and green peppers, etc.)

MARINADE

¼ cup olive oil

4 tablespoons soy sauce, low salt

3 tablespoons dry white wine

2 tablespoons bread crumbs

Grated rind 1 lemon

1 tablespoon chopped thyme

2 tablespoons red wine vinegar

Serves 2

1. Cut fillets into thin strips approximately 3″×¾″, or into chunks about 1″ square. (Try for the strips, they are prettier, but cod and bluefish work best in chunks.) Combine marinade ingredients and marinate fish strips at least 1 hour. I sometimes marinate the fish overnight to let the marinade really seep in.

2. Roll the fish into curls and thread onto thin wooden skewers. (Grocery stores sell them 100 for about fifty cents.) Alternate the fish with attractive color combinations of raw vegetables and/or fruits.

3. Grill over hot coals or in broiler until fish is brown and crusty, about 2 minutes per side. Spread extra marinade on fish while it's cooking. This looks spectacular served on a bed of yellow Summer Rice.

SUMMER RICE

Although this can be made and served any season of the year, I like to make it in summer when I can use fresh peas from the garden as an accent.

Ingredients:

½ cup chopped onion

3 cloves garlic, pressed

1 tablespoon oil

1 cup raw rice

2 cups chicken broth

1 tablespoon turmeric

½ cup fresh green peas

Serves 4

1. In a medium-size pan, sauté onion and garlic in oil until wilted. Stir in 1 cup rice and cook until grains are coated with onion-garlic mixture. Add 2 cups of boiling chicken broth. Add turmeric. Cook covered over low heat for 15 minutes. (If using brown rice, cook covered for 35 minutes.)

2. Add fresh peas during the last 2 minutes of the cooking process.

PAPER-WRAPPED FISH

This is delicious, and as easy to prepare as it is to serve. Although I often do this with salmon, this technique can be used with other fish just as successfully.

Ingredients:

1 fish fillet per person (¼ pound or less per person)

Parchment paper or aluminum foil

Vegetable mixture (about ¼ cup per fillet; green peppers, celery, carrots, onion, cut into short julienne strips)

Butter or oil (1 tablespoon per fillet)

Dash pepper

White wine (1 tablespoon per fillet)

1. Preheat oven to 350° F.

2. Put individual fillet in center of square of either aluminum foil or parchment paper. Whichever you use must be large enough to enclose the fish and the vegetables fully.

3. On top of each fillet, place a mound of julienne vegetables (about ¼ cup). On top of the vegetables, place a tablespoon of

butter or oil. Add a dash of pepper and 1 tablespoon white wine.

4. Enclose fish by bringing the long ends of the foil or paper together over the fish and roll downward. Tuck the sides in. You want to make this package as airtight as possible to keep all the juices in. The folding should also look pretty because the fish will be served in this package.

5. Bake for approximately 15 minutes. Serve each person an individual package. This and a salad make a lovely light dinner.

PICKLED SALMON WITH DILL MUSTARD SAUCE

This is one of those exceptional dishes that even nonfish eaters enjoy.

Ingredients:

1 (4–5-pound) salmon

1–2 large red onions

½ cup olive oil

1 cup red wine

Dash pepper

Wine vinegar (at least 32 ounces)

4 pounds serves 10 as first course

1. Have your fish man debone a 4–5-pound piece of salmon. You will probably receive two pieces of equal size and that's fine. Wrap the salmon carefully in cheesecloth and poach in 1″ of boiling water for 20 minutes, or until the fish begins to flake. Since the salmon is going to be pickled, don't overcook it and let it dry out.

2. Remove from poaching water. Unwrap cheesecloth and let cool. When cool, with a knife gently remove skin.

3. Place fish in large flat glass or ceramic dish with sides at least 2″ high. Add paper-thin slices of red onion on top. (When you serve this, the red onion adds a nice contrast against the pink of the salmon and the green of the sauce.) Add the olive oil, the red wine, a dash of pepper, and enough red wine vinegar to cover. This will probably take at least one 32-ounce bottle of red wine vinegar.

4. Cover tightly and refrigerate over-

night. Remove fish from pickling liquid and serve well chilled with pickled red onions on top and a healthy dollop of dill mustard sauce on the side. (The pickling liquid can be reserved and refrigerated for future use.)

If I'm not having one large party, I like to make this in a week when I have two groups of guests. I divide it between the two evenings and it's less work.

DILL MUSTARD SAUCE

Ingredients:

6 tablespoons mild mustard

4 tablespoons white vinegar

2 tablespoons sugar

1 cup oil

1 cup chopped fresh dill

Makes 1½ cups

1. In a blender or food processor, mix mustard, vinegar, and sugar.

2. Add oil and blend in dill. This should have a heavy almost pasty consistency. Can be saved almost indefinitely in the refrigerator.

SEATTLE CLAM CHOWDER

When I was growing up in the Pacific Northwest, a special family weekend included clamming for goey ducks (a big clam used in chowders) very early in the morning and returning in time for a fried clam breakfast. As little kids, we used to wait until the very last moment to race the tide back in; part of the thrill of clamming was that we sometimes got stranded out too far, up to our waist in water, and had to be rescued. On my return visits to Seattle, I always try to include at least one clamming expedition.

Two nights before I got married, with relatives descending from all over the country, I made a batch of this clam chowder. On a winter's night, everyone felt well-fed, warm, and happy. Most of all, *I* was happy because this is so little work for so much pleasure and nutrition.

My version differs from many traditional recipes in that there's no cream and no bacon, and I guarantee this is so delicious these ingredients are not missed.

Ingredients:

48 clams, chowder or razor

2 cups clam broth

1½ pounds potatoes

3 tablespoons margarine, or butter

1 cup chopped onions

3 cups skim milk

Salt and pepper

Serves 8

1.   Clean clam shells of sand and place in large pot with 2″ of water. Bring to rolling boil until clams open.[10] Discard any that do not open.

2.   Drain clams and strain the liquid through cheesecloth to filter out sand particles. The liquid should be about 2 cups. With a sharp knife, remove clams from their shells.

3.   Put clams in a blender or food processor and chop coarsely.

4.   Cut peeled potatoes into large bite-size chunks.

5.   In the margarine or butter, brown the chopped onions in a large kettle. Add the clam broth, potatoes, chopped clams. Simmer 35 minutes.

6.   Add milk and salt and pepper to taste. Bring to boil and serve hot.

This freezes very well. During the winter, I often double or triple this recipe so I have something warm on hand when friends drop in unexpectedly.

CEVICHE

This is the perfect recipe for summer when nobody wants to hang around a hot kitchen.

[10] It is also possible to purchase clams already shelled. If you're so lucky, proceed immediately to Step 3. If they haven't come with enough of their own liquid (usually they do, though), make up the difference with store-bought bottled clam juice.

What could be more convenient than fish that cooks itself?

Ceviche is the name for any fish that is marinated in lime juice. When I lived in Chile, we ate it all the time: at nightclubs with small pieces of bread; on the beach as part of a picnic; or as a main course dish by itself.

Ceviche originated farther north in Peru, where it's usually served as an appetizer because they like it so peppery hot that's all you can eat of it. My adaptation is much more Chilean and milder.

If this is going to be an appetizer served as a dip with crunchy bread, then all the ingredients (fish, green pepper, and onions) should be chopped finely. If it's to be a course served by itself, eaten with fork and knife, cut the ingredients into strips. The instructions here are for serving the ceviche as a course by itself; the directions are the same for the other, only the cutting is different.

Ingredients:

1 pound lean firm white fish, filleted and
   skinned

1 green pepper

1 sweet onion

½ dozen each lemons and limes or 12
   limes

3 tomatoes, chopped (optional)

Black pepper

Dash cayenne pepper

Serves 6 as first course

1.   Cut raw fish into uniform strips, about ½″ wide and 2″ long.

2.   Arrange strips on the bottom of a flat glass or ceramic dish.

3.   Cut green pepper into thin strips and place over the fish.

4.   Cut onion into paper-thin slices and place over fish.

5.   Cover fish with lime juice. Or with a mixture of half lemon and half lime. You will probably find, depending on how juicy your limes and lemons are, that you'll need the juice of about a dozen limes (or ½ lime, ½ lemon). In Southern California, this is a

cheap dish to make when the limes are on the backyard trees.[11]

6.   Season lightly with pepper and a dash of cayenne.

7.   Refrigerate for at least 3 hours. When the fish turns opaque white, it is "cooked" by the acid in the lime and lemon juices. It is just as cooked as if it had been grilled over a fire or poached with wine.

8.   It's served cold. I like it as a first course, the way the Peruvians eat it, with a thin round slice of cooked corn on the cob and a couple of pieces of warm baked sweet potato.

LOBSTER FRA DIAVOLO

This is one of those glorious dishes that people die over. I swear sometimes my sister-in-law, Hilda, stays on good terms with me just to be able to eat this once again.

Ingredients:

6 (1½-pound) live lobsters

¼ cup olive oil

½ cup finely chopped onion

6 cloves finely chopped garlic

1½ cups dry white wine

1–1½ cups chopped green pepper

½ cup finely chopped parsley

4 tablespoons finely chopped fresh basil

2 tablespoons chopped thyme

1 bay leaf

2 tablespoons fresh oregano

3 tablespoons tomato paste

5 cups cut up tomatoes (canned are okay)

Hot red pepper flakes to taste

1 pound enriched white pasta

1 pound spinach pasta

Serves 10 with leftovers

1.   On a thick bed of newspapers, kill

lobsters by piercing them at the back of their necks with a sharp knife. I find this is done with less mess outdoors on a stoop where it's most easily cleaned up afterward. When the lobsters stop moving, break off the claws, and with a hammer, crack them. Cracking at this stage makes them easier to eat after they are cooked. With scissors, cut off the eight little "legs" and discard. With a sharp knife, cut the tail into two or three sections. Cut off the head and discard. With a spoon, scoop out roe from interior of body. This roe may be discarded or reserved and added after Step 4 to the sauce.

2.   Into a large, heavy-bottomed pot (at least 8-quart capacity), add the oil. When the oil is very hot, add lobsters and cook until pink.

3.   Sprinkle onions and garlic on top and add white wine. Cook over high heat until most of the wine evaporates.

4.   Add green pepper, parsley, basil, thyme, bay leaf, oregano, tomato paste, and tomatoes to mixture in pot. Sprinkle lightly with hot pepper flakes. Cook for ½ hour to let ingredients seep in. This recipe is best when it is prepared through Step 4 in the morning, then left all day to rest in the refrigerator, letting the flavors seep in, and reheated when it's time to eat.

5.   In a large pot, add pasta to boiling water and cook until done; drain.

6.   In a large deep-sided serving dish (I use a 22″ oblong copper dish), pour lobsters and sauce on top of pasta. Serve immediately.

PHEASANT IN APPLE CIDER

Pheasant is not usually considered everyday fare, but it's a healthy choice if you want to cook something exotic. In contrast to duck and geese, the pheasant is low in fat and a good source of lean protein. (Pheasant is available from mail order sources if you cannot find it at your local markets.)

This is a wonderful, robust dish that's easy to assemble and could be done with a large chicken if no pheasant is at hand. For the cook in a hurry, the stuffing can be consid-

---

[11] If this is too tart for you, I've also included the option of adding chopped tomatoes. Although the addition of tomatoes is not traditional, I've found it can make the dish appeal to more tastes.

ered optional. Apples and celery inside the cavity will suffice, but the stuffing is so delicious I wouldn't pass it up.

Ingredients:

   1 (about 4 pounds) fresh pheasant

   16 ounces apple cider

   2 oranges, peeled and cut in thick slices

STUFFING

   1 cup wild rice

   ¼ cup chopped onions

   ½ cup chopped celery

   2 cloves garlic, pressed

   3 tablespoons oil

   ½ cup chopped walnuts

   ½ cup seedless grapes

   ½ cup chunks fresh apple

BASTING SAUCE

   ½ cup soy sauce (low salt)

   3 tablespoons honey

   ¼ cup oil

   2 tablespoons sour cream

Serves 6

1.   Preheat oven to 375° F. Prepare stuffing. Cook wild rice according to directions on package. At the same time, sauté onions, celery, and garlic in oil until soft. Add onion mixture to cooked rice along with walnuts, grapes, and apples.

2.   Stuff the pheasant. With needle and thread, sew cavity closed.

3.   Place pheasant in roasting pan and surround with 1″ of apple cider, about 16 ounces. The cider creates a blanket of fragrance that keeps the pheasant moist as it cooks. Float orange slices in the cider. Cut orange slices thick enough so they don't fall apart as they cook. Place pan in oven.

4.   In small pan, heat together ingredients for basting sauce. This mixture gives a nice golden color and a slightly sweet flavor to the bird. Baste with sauce every 10 minutes or so. I use this sauce on turkeys, chickens, any bird that is baked in an oven.

5.   Figure cooking time at 15 minutes for every pound of pheasant. When the pheasant

is cooked, remove stuffing and place bird on serving platter surrounded by stuffing and orange slices. Put roasting pan with the drippings onto the stove and boil juices until cider is reduced by one third. Whip in sour cream and serve sauce separately. (Note the small amount of sour cream that will suffice to make this sauce creamy.)

TURKEY SCALLOPINI

Most people think of scallopini as meaning *veal* scallopini, but the word *scallopini* is Italian for scallop, and means any very thinly sliced piece of meat. You can make your own scallopini from turkey and chicken and save money in the process.

1.   Use a breast from a turkey no larger than 16 pounds. The breast will be 4–5 pounds. It's cheaper if you buy the whole turkey, but depending on your needs, it might be more convenient to buy only the breast. Since turkey is most readily available frozen, you can use a frozen turkey for this. The advantage of using a fresh turkey is that you can freeze any leftovers.

2.   If you have a whole turkey, thaw it enough to separate breast from the bone. As in illustration, using a very sharp knife, start at the wishbone and cut meat away from breastbone at all sides. Lift the meat away from breastbone. Do this with both sides of breast. You should have two nice pieces of turkey to work with. (The rest of the turkey can be cooked however you like.)

3.   Put turkey breast back into freezer—not to refreeze, but to firm up. (It's impossible to cut a turkey at room temperature into thin slices.) When it's hard to the touch, it's ready. Start at the point where the wing was attached. The grain of the meat runs the long way. To make the scallopini as tender as possible, cut across the grain, holding the knife at a 30° angle. The goal here is to cut the scallopini thin enough so that after they are pounded they are ¹⁄₁₆″ thin or thinner. If it's much thicker, you've cut a cutlet, not scallopini. You can also do the same thing on a smaller scale with chicken breasts.

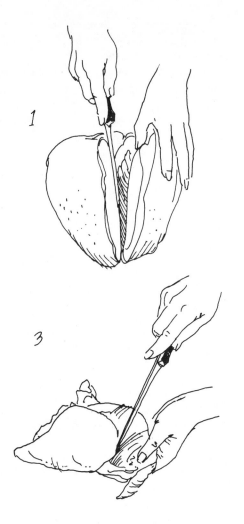

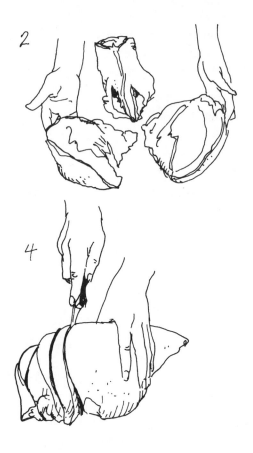

4. Put the slices on wax paper covered with another sheet of wax paper and pound with a meat pounder to make the surface smooth and thin.

5. This turkey can now be used for any of your favorite recipes that call for scallopini. Remember it needs to be cooked only a minute per side. If you cook it longer, it will be tough.

TURKEY SCALLOPINI AL LIMONE

This delicious dish takes less than 10 minutes to prepare and is at least one third the price of its veal counterpart. There are two tricks: one, pound the turkey very thin; two, pay close attention to the *short* cooking times.

When prepared according to these directions, the turkey scallopini will be as soft and tender as veal.

Ingredients:

1 pound turkey scallopini (should be about 2 large pieces per person)

Flour seasoned with pepper

4 tablespoons oil

½ cup white wine

½–¾ cup beef stock

12 slices lemon

1 pound fresh pasta, cooked

Serves 4 amply

1. Dip scallopini in flour and shake off any excess. In large, heavy skillet heat oil. When oil is very hot, add scallopini and

brown quickly, about 1 minute per side. Set scallopini aside on paper towels to drain.

2. With heat on high, add wine to skillet and loosen any pieces of scallopini clinging to skillet. Add stock and boil for 1 minute.

3. Return scallopini to skillet. If sauce doesn't cover scallopini, add more stock. Arrange lemon slices on top of scallopini and reheat.

4. To serve, place hot pasta on large platter, arrange scallopini pieces on top, pour sauce from pan over, and use lemon slices for garnish.

CURRY—CHICKEN OR SHRIMP (OR VEGETABLES, TOO!)

This easy curry is pleasantly mild. I make it most often with chicken, but if you have neither chicken nor shrimp on hand, you could make it all vegetable, starting with potatoes and adding zucchini, carrots, peas, and whatever else you have.

Ingredients:

¼ cup margarine, or butter

4 onions, chopped

Garlic, pressed

3 cups skim milk, mixed with

2 cups unsweetened shredded coconut

4 potatoes, peeled, cut into pieces

3 tomatoes (canned is fine)

1 cup chopped celery

1 tablespoon shredded fresh ginger root

3 tablespoons curry powder

2 apples, peeled and cut into large pieces (small pieces will cook too quickly and get mushy)

4 pounds chicken, cut up

   or

3 pounds raw shrimp

Serves 6 hungry people

1. In a skillet large enough to hold all the ingredients, heat the margarine or butter; add onions and as much garlic as you like. Cook until barely browned. Add the coconut-milk mixture to the skillet and

bring to a boil. Add potatoes, tomatoes, celery, and fresh ginger.

2. Mix curry powder together with enough water to form a paste. Add to skillet. Taste. If you like your curry spicier, add more powder directly to skillet.

3. Simmer mixture about 20 minutes. Add the apples. Stir in the apples gently so they remain whole, distinct pieces. If you are using chicken, add the pieces now. Cook an additional 20 minutes, or until chicken is cooked and apples are barely soft.

4. If using shrimp, add after sauce has cooked 40 minutes in all. Cook until shrimp is pink, probably less than 5 minutes.

For parties, this can be made a night in advance, refrigerated, and warmed up. If anything, it's better the second day. It can also be frozen and it reheats just fine.

Along with this, I serve almost anything colorful I can get my hands on: a variety of chutneys, slivered almonds, chunks of fresh papaya, mangoes and pineapples, shredded coconut, and always plenty of Cool Yoghurt and Cucumber Salad.

COOL YOGHURT AND CUCUMBER SALAD

Ingredients:

2 cucumbers, peeled and thinly sliced

1½ cups yoghurt

3 tablespoons finely chopped fresh mint leaves

Garlic

Put sliced cucumber into a medium-size mixing bowl. Add the other ingredients and as much garlic as you like. (In Morocco, they add a *lot.*) Serve chilled. The coolness of this salad contrasted with hot curry is delightful.

CHICKEN COUSCOUS

Some cultures are clearly more energy conscious than ours and have come up with ways of preparing whole meals using just one pot. Couscous is the Moroccan answer to a one pot delicious meal. It's cooked in a cous-coussier—a two-partition pot that looks a little like a huge double boiler. The chicken stews in the bottom half of the pot and its broth steams up and cooks the couscous grains in the top half. Another virtue of this dish is that it can be totally cooked in advance and reheated prior to serving.

Couscous is usually made from pellets of wheat—so it's one more interesting way of getting whole natural food into your diet. Look for it on the grocery shelves next to other grain products like rice, kasha, and pasta. The box often suggests you cook it like rice in boiling water. Don't you dare. It will become a gummy mass and you'll hate the stuff forever. The way I prefer cooking couscous is faster than the traditional way that takes hours and many washings and better than the modern answer of cooking it like rice.

Ingredients:

¾ pound couscous

¼ cup oil

1 large onion, sliced

1 (3–4 pound) whole chicken, cut into
    pieces, with skin removed

Pepper to taste

¼ teaspoon ground ginger

3 envelopes saffron

4 cups water

⅓ cup chopped fresh parsley

2 cups cut-up carrots or zucchini
    (optional)

ONION GLAZE

1 pound onions, thinly sliced

¼ cup oil

¼ teaspoon ginger

1 teaspoon cinnamon

1 envelope saffron

2 cups chicken broth

1 cup raisins, soaked in warm water

1 cup slivered almonds

Serves 6 handsomely

1. Wash couscous grains in a shallow pan and drain off excess water. With your hands, smooth the wet grains into a single layer and let them swell for 10–20 minutes. Now they are ready to be steamed.

2. In the bottom of a couscoussier, place oil, onion, chicken pieces, pepper to taste, ginger, and contents of 2 envelopes saffron; cook 5 minutes. (Couscoussiers in this country are usually made out of thin metal—so watch that the food doesn't burn. If you don't have a couscoussier, you could mock one up by using a 9″ high pot outfitted with a colander resting on top.)

3. Add water and parsley and simmer gently for 1 hour. Watch carefully as chicken pieces will be cooked in about 20 minutes. Remove them as they are done and set aside so they don't get overcooked. During the last 10 minutes add vegetables to the broth.

4. When broth and chicken in Step 3 begin to simmer, add couscous to top steaming section, cover pan, and let broth and couscous cook together, flavoring each other. Every so often, with a wooden spoon, separate the couscous grains so they don't clump together. After 15 minutes, stir saffron into the couscous. (The couscous should cook at least 30 minutes.)

5. While chicken and couscous are cooking, make onion glaze. In heavy-bottomed pan, cook onions in oil, covered, for 5–10 minutes. Add ginger, cinnamon, saffron. Continue cooking 15 minutes, then add 2 cups of chicken broth from couscoussier to the onions. Cook until onion glaze begins to thicken.

6. Add drained raisins and almonds to onion glaze.

7. I like to serve this wreath-style on a 16″ dark blue circular platter with the yellow couscous mounded in the middle encircled by the pieces of chicken and vegetables. Once assembled, pour the onion glaze over the pieces of chicken. Any extra broth should be poured over the couscous to moisten it. Serve immediately.

LO CALORIE CHICKEN

Ingredients:

1 (3-pound) broiler-fryer, cut into pieces

Pepper to taste, plus 1 teaspoon

3 teaspoons chopped thyme

3 teaspoons chopped marjoram

1 head lettuce, sliced horizontally

4 small onions, peeled and sliced

4 carrots, pared thinly and sliced

1 (10-ounce) package frozen peas

1 bay leaf

10 whole cloves

Chicken stock (canned or from bouillon cubes)

Serves 6

1. Dust chicken with pepper and 2 teaspoons each of thyme and marjoram; place on rack above 2″ of water in a Dutch oven to steam covered for 15–20 minutes. Save water.

2. Remove rack and place chicken directly in liquid. Cover the chicken with a layer of lettuce, onions, carrots, and peas. Sprinkle with 1 teaspoon each thyme, marjoram, pepper, and add 1 bay leaf and cloves. Add enough chicken stock to bring liquid up to cover vegetables. Cover and simmer only until carrots are barely tender, about 5–8 minutes. Spoon vegetables onto heated platter, top with chicken.

VARIATION: Use red cabbage, brussels sprouts, and carrots.

DALE'S CHICKEN IN CLAY

Some people think of chicken as a humdrum, reasonably cheap food that gets you through Wednesday night dinner, but not something special enough to serve guests. Dale Burg's dramatic Chicken in Clay proves this theory wrong. Dale bakes chicken in clay and brings it to the table; then with much ado and mal-

let in hand, she breaks it open before the amazed guests. It is a conversation piece and delicious.

Ingredients:

1 (3-pound) chicken, filled with stuffing of your choice (Dale uses rice, pine nuts, currants, and cloves)

3 tablespoons oil

Pepper, garlic, and paprika to taste

4–5 cabbage leaves

2 pounds wet earthenware clay, obtainable at any art supply store

Serves 4 amply

1. Preheat oven to 480° F. Sew chicken together with stuffing inside. Rub skin with oil and season with pepper, garlic, and paprika to taste. Place cabbage leaves in boiling water, briefly, until limp. Let cool. Drape limp leaves around chicken.

2. Using rolling pin, roll sheet of clay between layers of wax paper until ½″ thick. Wrap clay around chicken by placing chicken in center of large rectangle of clay, pulling up the sides; if necessary, put another smaller rectangle of clay over the top. With fingers, pinch seams together and cut hole in top for steam to escape. (In most areas, there will be a layer of cabbage separating the clay from the chicken, but if the clay touches the chicken, that's okay too.)

3. Place in preheated oven for 1½ hours or on outdoor grill with the cover on for at least 2 hours.

4. Bring chicken to table in clay and break through with a wooden mallet (or hammer) at the table, revealing the browned chicken. (The cabbage leaves stick to the clay.) After the dramatic presentation, Dale separates the chicken into pieces (it's too limp to carve), and arranges it over the stuffing.

NOTE: This should only be done in a well-ventilated kitchen or preferably on an outdoor fire. The cooking clay can be a bit smoky.

FINGER-LICKIN' GOOD CHICKEN WINGETTES

Chicken wingettes make an unusual and easy-to-do appetizer. You can either make them yourself or ask your butcher to do it for you.

Ingredients:

Oil

Chicken wings (2–3 per person)

Soy sauce, low salt

Honey

1. Take chicken wings and cut off the end of the wing from the tip of the wing to the second joint and save for broth, or stews. Then, with a sharp knife, push the meat from the second joint down to the third joint. (You can either do this with the skin attached or remove the skin first.) You will end up with something that looks like a midget drumstick.

2. In a large skillet, heat enough oil to brown the number of chicken wings you're cooking.

3. When slightly browned, add soy sauce and honey to coat the chicken with a syrupy glaze. (Half soy sauce, half honey . . . for 3 dozen chicken wings, you will need ½ cup soy sauce and ½ cup honey.) Cook until chicken wings are done and well coated with the sauce.

4. Arrange on platter and serve warm.

EGGS À LA PAT

This comes from my sister-in-law Libby's family, and it definitely can have that spicy south-of-the-border taste. Want it less spicy?

Use less canned jalapeño peppers. The first time I had eggs à la Pat (no one in the family remembers who Pat is) was at a bridal party for my future sister-in-law. This mixture was served on freshly made biscuits. I have since made it many times. (I often make this dish at Easter, as it is an excellent way to use all those hard-boiled eggs.) I prefer serving it inside round French puff-pastry shells. It's equally nice for a special breakfast or for a main course at lunch.

Ingredients:

1 dozen eggs

SAUCE

6 medium onions, chopped finely

3 medium green peppers, chopped finely

4 tablespoons oil

2 tablespoons flour

1 (½-ounce) tin jalapeño peppers

1 (28-ounce) can tomatoes

1 pound medium sharp Cheddar cheese, grated

10–12 biscuits or shells

Serves 10–12

1. Hard-boil eggs and let cool.

2. To make the sauce, sauté chopped onions and green peppers in oil.

3. When peppers and onions are lightly cooked, add flour, jalapeños, and juice from jalapeños. The wise person does this step with a light touch. What may not taste very spicy when it's added, will increase with ferocity after it's had a chance to cook. Caution is the word.

4. Add tomatoes and their juice and simmer over low heat for 25 minutes. Stir gently and often.

5. Add grated cheese and cook until cheese is thoroughly melted.

6. Shell eggs and cut into slices. Line bottom of prewarmed large flat serving platter. Pour steaming hot tomato sauce over eggs and serve immediately spooning eggs and sauce on top of hot biscuits or into pastry shells.

CHEESE FONDUE

On a winter's evening, there is nothing more cozy than cheese fondue. It takes very little time to prepare, and is fun to serve because everyone helps himself. An elaborate fondue setup is not necessary; in fact I prefer using a regular copper pot and just setting it on the table above the burner on a chafing dish. Although I usually serve this as a main course and accompany it with a salad, it also makes a nice appetizer for a party. I serve this with the traditional accompaniments for a Swiss raclette (melted cheese), the *cornichons* and pickled onions.

Ingredients:

1 pound cheese, French or Swiss Gruyère or Emanthal, mixed—shredded in food processor or blender

1½ tablespoons cornstarch

4 cloves garlic, pressed

Juice 1 lemon

2 cups dry vermouth or dry white wine

Cayenne pepper and pepper to taste

¼ to ½ cup kirsch

French baguette (long, hard French bread)

Serves 4

1. Off the stove, put cheese in a large, heavy-bottomed pan. Mix in the cornstarch. Add garlic, lemon juice, half the wine, and season to taste with pepper.

2. Simmer until cheese has melted and carefully add the last half of the wine. If it appears to be getting too thin, don't add all the wine. When cheese is well melted, and is a proper velvet consistency, add kirsch.

3. Serve immediately with bite-size pieces of hot, crusty French bread. Spear the bread with a long-handled fondue fork or regular fork and dip into hot fondue.

CALF'S LIVER AMALFI

For television I put together a series of budget gourmet meals that were each priced under one dollar a person. My criteria were that the food had to be nutritious (no saltine crackers for snacks, thank you), pretty to serve, delicious to eat, fairly easy to make, and require no specialized shopping expeditions to out of the way places. One of my favorites was Calf's Liver Amalfi; a meal and salad in one with an Italian flavor. The interesting twist is that the hot sauce from the liver is poured onto the spinach leaves to yield a delightful wilted spinach salad. Delicious.

Here are a few pointers to keep in mind when cooking liver:

* If you or your family aren't liver fans, it's probably because you've overcooked it in the past. Go easy; a few minutes per side is more than enough.

* When preparing liver for cooking, always remove any fat and all fatty connective tissue. You remove this fat because the liver is the central filter through which everything passes and if undesirable particles do get lodged in the liver, they will be in the fat.

* If you're told to go easy on cholesterol, go easy on all organ meats, including liver. Eat in moderation.

* If calf's liver is expensive in your city, substitute chicken livers. The fast food chains use all the other parts of the chicken except the livers, so there's a glut of chicken livers on the market, making them plentiful and cheap.

Ingredients:

½–¾ pound fresh calf's liver

¼ cup flour seasoned with pepper

1 medium onion, diced

2 fresh green scallions, diced

1 clove garlic

3 tablespoons olive oil

1 tablespoon thyme

1 tablespoon marjoram

2 tablespoons parsley

¼ cup dry white wine

1 tablespoon tomato paste

¼ cup chicken broth (you may need a
  little more)

2 tablespoons red wine vinegar

Juice 1 lemon

½ pound fresh spinach leaves, or other
  dark green leaves

Serves 2

1. Trim liver of all fatty connective tissues. Cut into strips 1″×3″. Sprinkle with
flour seasoned with pepper.

2. In medium-size skillet, sauté onions,
scallions, and garlic in oil until wilted. Add
spices and all other ingredients except spinach. Cook for 2 minutes to get all ingredients
well blended. (Add more chicken broth if
more liquid is needed.)

3. Add liver and cook no more than 2
minutes per side.

4. Wash and dry spinach leaves or other
dark leafy greens. Serve spinach on same
plate with calf's liver and pour extra sauce
from calf's liver, while it's still hot, on top of
spinach.

KASHA WITH . . .

Some people say the way to live forever is to
eat kasha, a dietary staple of some of the
longest-lived Russians. Whether that's true or
not, kasha, which is usually made from
cracked kernels of buckwheat (sometimes it's
called buckwheat groats) is a wonderfully
versatile whole grain that can elegantly extend a small portion of meat to feed many.

Kasha is a good natural fiber, has 20 per
cent more B vitamins than rice, and at about
five cents a serving, is affordable and delicious. Don't pay attention to the message on
the manufacturer's box that says you're eating kasha for protein. Here's one way to look
at it: 1 pound of kasha is equivalent in protein to over ½ pound of beef; however, if

you figure 1 pound makes 18 servings, that's
not much protein to go around. In my recipe, I add additional sources of protein with
slivers of beef, chicken, or lamb.

In Russia, kasha is used for breakfast,
lunch, or dinner, and depending on how it is
prepared it is used as a side dish with gravy,
as a flavorful addition to soups, or as a main
course dish. I prefer it as a main course for
dinner.

Ingredients:

  1 cup kasha

  1 egg, slightly beaten

  2 cups water or broth

  3 tablespoons oil

  1 cup finely chopped onions

  1 clove garlic, pressed

  ½ pound mushrooms

  1½ cups cut-up cooked chicken, beef, or
    lamb

Serves 6

1. In a heavy-bottomed frying pan, mix
egg with kasha kernels. Stir over high heat
until kernels separate and dry.

2. Add 2 cups boiling water or broth and
cook, covered, for about 20 minutes over low
heat.

3. Kasha is terrific by itself, but I like to
add a mixture of onions and mushrooms. In
a skillet, with 3 tablespoons oil, add onion,
garlic, and thinly sliced mushrooms. Cook
about 4 minutes until all is well cooked. (At
this stage, you can also cook in slivers of
whatever cooked meat you are combining
with the kasha.)

4. Add cooked kasha to cooked onion-
mushroom mixture and serve hot. Keeps for
days refrigerated.

The variations with kasha are endless. For
starters, in addition to or instead of the
onion-mushroom mixture, you can add grated
Parmesan cheese, or chopped green peppers.

7
DEMONS AND
OTHER ADDITIVES

It used to be that what you ate was your own business, but now it's become everyone else's, too. Scientists, engineers, food technologists, politicians, doctors, nutritionists, and food reporters are all concerned about what we're eating and how it's adding to, or detracting from, our ability to live healthy lives.

Sugar, salt, pesticides, and some *additives* and *preservatives* have been thoroughly publicized as demons, but often such an information blitz serves to confuse the important issues rather than clarify. My purpose is not to scare people from eating all and any food ever again, but to make you conscious of what the demons are, where they are present, and how in many instances the choice is still up to the consumer whether to include them in the diet or not.

 Salt

As often happens in life, when I began work on this chapter, a true-to-life incident happened that illustrated exactly what I was writing about. I hired a housekeeper, Mattie Pearl, who loves to cook everything from southern-fried chicken to Chinese vegetables. One day she showed me her three special little bottles that "makes food taste good." They were: seasoned salt, onion salt, and Beau Monde, a seasoning whose first ingredient is salt and whose second is sugar. In addition, she also had a big salt shaker next to the stove and she put a salt shaker on the table. It was a rare food that escaped being salted by Mattie at least *four* times. Make that *five* if you salted again at the table. And make that *six* saltings if the food was processed and arrived presalted.

I explained to Mattie that salt is a combination of sodium and chloride and that most Americans consume from six to forty times the amount of salt the body needs and that a link between excessive salt intake and hypertension exists, especially in black people. Hypertension affects as many as 35 million Americans and contributes to several hundred thousand deaths each year from heart disease and stroke. Studies indicate that hypertension could be alleviated or prevented in many people, if they consumed much less sodium. Mattie thanked me for my advice. I thought that was probably that. Mattie would go her way and I would go mine on the salt issue (although she stopped cooking food for us with salt), but several months later she told me I had made an impression

on her; she had cut back on salt and was convincing her friends to do the same. Mattie, a practical lady in her early fifties, felt it made more sense to break her own bad habit now, rather than wait, like some of her friends, until a doctor demanded that she do it.

By chance, Mattie pin-pointed the American dilemma with salt. We use too much of it, too often. We need salt to maintain the correct water balance in our bodies, for muscle contractions, and to prevent nervous irritability, but we don't need it in the quantities most Americans consume.

IT'S EVERYWHERE, EVEN IN THE WATER

In some areas of the country, the amount of sodium in the drinking water is of sufficient quantity to figure significantly in the total daily intake of sodium. To find out the sodium levels in your public water supply, call your local Department of Water and request the sodium concentration. Where I live on the West Coast, in the Pacific Palisades, it is 35 mg/liter, which, as you can see from the list below, is quite low in comparison with some areas in America.

City	Mg Sodium/liter of water*
Boston	3–4
Albuquerque	100
New Orleans	23
Chicago	5
Houston	100
Los Angeles:	
Owens River source	74
L.A. River source	50
New York City:	
Catskill source	2
Croton source	3

* The Environmental Protection Agency says there is no problem for people on a sodium-restricted diet if the sodium in the water supply is no higher than 20 mg/liter.

The sodium content of water is *not* regulated by the federal government and can vary enormously. It's reported that some individual home wells in California contain as much as 2,000 mg/liter. The Environmental Protection Agency is considering drawing up limitations of sodium in water.

So, the question is: should people be concerned about sodium concentrations in their water? There is a problem for some people with high blood pressure, or anyone who must restrict his or her intake of sodium, but most food contains more sodium than water does. I suggest that physicians ask their local water departments about the sodium levels so they can inform any patients who must be concerned. Another possibility would be to require the Water Department to include the sodium content as part of its monthly bill. For those people who can't drink their local water, distilled or bottled water is the answer and the amount of sodium is often listed on the side of the bottle. If it's not listed, write to the supplier of your favorite bottled water and ask what the sodium content is.

HOW MUCH IS TOO MUCH?

The average American uses 6–18 gm of salt a day. To combat this high use the Food and Nutrition Board, the Surgeon General's Office, and the United States Senate Select Committee have recommended limiting intake to 3–8 gm a day (3 gm, which is 3,000 mg, is a little more than half a teaspoon). Although this requirement may increase slightly for lactating mothers and for people working in hot, humid weather, generally as little salt as possible should be the rule. This is really a clear-cut case of less is more. Several years ago I stopped using salt. Now, on the rare occasion when I deliberately use salt, the salt crystals stand out vibrantly. I am no longer immune to its taste through overdosing.

SALT DIET RECOMMENDATIONS

Low	500 mg/day — Need to use salt-free milk, butter, etc.
Moderate	1,000 mg/day
Liberal	2,000 mg/day

These figures don't mean much if you don't have the practical means of equating them to your everyday diet. Compare these recommendations with the levels of salt in twenty-eight commonly eaten foods. You may be surprised. A cheese sandwich and a slice of Canadian bacon easily slips you out of the moderate-salt-user range into the high-rolling group of liberal salt users.

SALT IN FOOD

Item	Mg Salt
Hot dog, 1	542
Canadian Bacon, cooked, 1 slice	442
Bacon, raw, 1 slab or slice	76
Corned Beef Hash, canned, ½ cup	997
Ham, cured butt, cooked lean plus marbled, 1 slice	518
Beef TV Dinner, "complete dinner"	808
Ham TV Dinner	1,173
Haddock TV Dinner	1,319
Sauerkraut, canned, ⅔ cup drained	747
Pickle, 1 dill	1,428
Catsup, 1 tbsp.	177
Butter, 1 tsp.	49
2 tbsp.	138
7 tbsp.	987
Unsalted, 7 tbsp.	8
Cheese, process American, 1 oz.	318
American Cheese Spread, 1 oz.	455

Cheddar Cheese, 1 oz. (1×1×1″)	197
3½ oz. (2×2×1″)	700
Cottage Cheese, creamed, 6 tbsp.	229
1 cup	516
Tuna, canned, ¾ cup, in oil, (solid + liquid)	800
Tuna, canned, in water (solid + liquid)	41
Salt, 1 tsp.	2,361
MSG, 1 tsp.	750
Chicken Noodle Soup Heinz, 1 cup	868
Campbell's, 1 cup	754
Onion Soup, Campbell's, 1 cup	868
Bouillon Cubes, meat extract, 1 cube	424
Vegetable extract, 1 cube	245
Crackers Saltines, 1 lb.	4,990
5	220
Mustard, prepared, 1 tsp.	65
Olives, green, 2 medium	240
Potato Chips, 5	34
100 gm	may be as high as 1,000 mg
Soy Sauce, 1 tbsp.	1,319

As shown, table salt is not the only offender. Other salts like MSG, baking soda, and the high levels of salt found in club soda, meat tenderizers, and soy sauce also contribute to an increase in the sodium level. Unfortunately, it's often difficult to determine if sodium chloride *is* present in processed foods and, if present, how *much*. Currently only a few special dietetic foods list the sodium content on the package. The FDA is investigating the issue of salt labeling, but don't expect any quick action. The word in the food industry is that the FDA is handling this topic like a hot potato and is waiting for the correct time, politically, before making any proposals. Until the day that salt labeling is required on the package, here's a general way to look at the salt content of foods.

Protein Foods: Highest in salt: meat, fish, poultry, milk, and cheese.

Vegetables: Small amounts of salt in fresh and frozen vegetables. Exceptions are beets, carrots, celery, chard, kale, and dandelion greens, which are higher in salt than other vegetables. Canned vegetables have a higher salt level than frozen or fresh.
Peas: ½ cup raw = 1 mg sodium; frozen = 86 mg sodium; canned = 189 mg sodium

Fruits: Little amounts of salt.

HOW DO YOU AVOID USING TOO MUCH SALT?

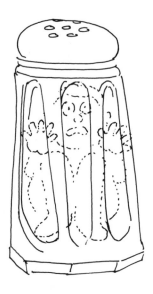

The best way to avoid the dangers and problems associated with high salt intake is to avoid using it in the first place. But how do you do that after you're already addicted?

This is what I recommend: First, recognize the fact that you gain nothing nutritionally by shaking salt on your food. We get all the salt we need naturally in foods. One painless way to decrease your intake of salt

easily is, if you must have some salt, eat foods that have only been salted once. Since most processed foods, and they range from TV dinners to slices of pizza, arrive already salted, don't resalt. If you add salt when you're cooking, don't add it again at the table when you're eating. Another trick is to use only coarse sea salt, the kind that needs to be ground in a little hand grinder. You get pleasure from grinding your own, and you probably use less than you would pouring it freely from a container.

Remember, alcohol and tobacco dull the taste buds. Don't try to overcompensate by seasoning fiercely with salt. Some people, by habit, have become lazy cooks, always reaching just for the salt shaker to flavor their foods. Try flavoring your foods with condiments other than salt.

Try These Salt-free Flavor Ideas

FOR MEAT, POULTRY, FISH, AND EGGS:

Beef: Bay leaf, dry mustard, green pepper, sage, marjoram, mushrooms, onions, pepper, scallions, thyme, wine, fresh or powdered ginger.

Chicken: Cranberries, mushrooms, lemon, paprika, parsley, cilantro, thyme, sage, onions, white wine, fresh or powdered ginger, garlic, curry.

Eggs: Curry, dry mustard, green pepper, jelly, mushrooms, onions, scallions, cilantro, chopped meat, parsley, tomatoes, chives, paprika.

Fish: Fresh or powdered ginger, scallions, wine, curry, lemon juice, lemon butter, bay leaf, pepper, mushrooms, oil, sweet/sour sauce (without salt or soy sauce).

Lamb: Curry, garlic, mint, pineapple, rosemary, wine.

Pork: Apples, applesauce, garlic, onions, sage.

Veal: Apricots, bay leaf, curry, currants, jelly, ginger, marjoram, oregano.

FOR VEGETABLES:

Asparagus: Lemon juice, fruit juice, vinegar/oil mixture.

Corn: Green pepper, tomato, mint leaves.

Green Beans: Marjoram, lemon juice, nutmeg, dill seeds, unsalted salad dressings.

Lettuce: Lemon juice, oil/vinegar, freshly ground pepper, fruit juices.

Peas: Onion, mint, mushrooms, parsley, cilantro, sweet peppers.

Potatoes: Onion, mace, green pepper, parsley, chives, paprika.

Spinach: Lemon juice, vinegar/oil.

Squash: Fresh or powdered ginger, mace, onion, cinnamon, fruit juices.

Tomatoes: Basil, marjoram, onion.

SOME COMMONLY ASKED QUESTIONS ABOUT SALT

* *What are the differences between kosher salt, iodized salt, sea salt, and regular table salt? Is one better than another?*

Salt is salt is salt.

Kosher salt has very coarse, squarish granules and is processed under strict rabbinical supervision to ensure there are no impurities. It is primarily used by Orthodox Jewish people to kosher meat (a process where the salt drains as much blood as possible from the meat). Commercially, kosher salt is often sprinkled over baked goods like pretzels.

Although kosher salt and *sea salt* have only an infinitesimal increase in minerals over the others, all sorts of health claims have been made for them that have not been substantiated. And be leery of fancy packaged sea salt. Often it's priced five to six times the price of regular table salt.

Recently I was sampling a new yoghurt chip and when I complained to the sales clerk that they were much too salty, she said, "But that's *natural* sea salt," implying that somehow it was more benevolent.

Cooking or table salt is still sodium chloride, but it's usually finely ground with impurities removed and magnesium carbonate added to make it flow freely. We'd be healthier if it didn't flow quite so freely.

Iodized salt is table salt with iodine added. Originally it was meant for people living in geographic areas like the Rocky Mountains, which are low in iodine. (Iodine is necessary for the thyroid gland to work properly.) People who live in areas such as the West Coast, where iodine is plentiful in their diets naturally don't *need* to use iodized salt, but since the iodine is added in such small doses there is no danger if they do.

* *Why is it often suggested to add salt to water before cooking vegetables, potatoes, spaghetti? Can you leave it out?*

Recipes almost always recommend this. Adding salt does raise the boiling temperature of the water, but only by about half a degree, so its temperature-raising property is inconsequential. The only reason you're adding salt to water is to season the food.

* *What about recipes for baked goods that call for salt?*

In the past, I thought maybe salt interacted in some chemical way with the yeast, helping the bread rise, but my investigation doesn't bear this out. In baking, salt is used once again just for seasoning and once you get accustomed to a less salty flavor, you can leave it out with equally good results.

* *Why are low salt products often more expensive?*

There is certainly no apparent reason why they should be, but manufacturers have told me they have to reorganize their equipment. Soy sauce is one startling example of the high cost of "equipment reorganization." Kikkoman low salt soy sauce is often two to three times the price of their regular soy sauce.

*   *If you want to add salt to meats or poultry, at what stage is it best?*

After cooking. Salting tends to dry the meat by drawing the juices out and thus losing flavor.

*   *Is it true there's sugar in salt?*

Yes. Hard to believe, isn't it? But sugar shows up everywhere, even in salt. According to a spokesman for Morton's, they've been adding a trace of sugar to table salt for years to "ensure optimum salt flavor characteristics," whatever *that* means.

*   *What about using a salt substitute to cut salt intake?*

The only prescribed use of salt substitutes, which can be purchased at drugstores, is to reduce sodium intake for patients with heart failure or hypertension. For normal people, there's no need to use them, and because of their high potassium level (salt substitutes are potassium chloride with less than 1 mg of sodium, which is considered dietetically salt-free), there is some question about getting too much potassium.

A friend of mine who was dieting and is a heavy salt user told me a fellow dieter suggested he use a salt substitute because he wouldn't retain as much water and miraculously he'd lose weight. There is no medical rationale for using salt substitutes to lose weight. You'll lose some water, not fat. They also cost astronomically more. Whether you buy them in a grocery store or in a drugstore, you pay on the average 75 cents for 3 ounces or 25 cents per ounce. One brand I bought was 80 cents an ounce. Compare this with table salt at 1.5 cents an ounce.

But if for medical reasons your doctor says you need a salt substitute, how do they taste? Not very good. The most acceptable ones in a taste test done at the University of Iowa were Neocurtassal, Morton's Salt Substitute, and Featherweight K.

*   *What about one of the brands called Lite Salt?*

Lite salt is half potassium and half sodium and is made especially for people who want to cut their sodium intake. Sold in grocery stores, it tastes more like regular salt, but it's three times as expensive as table salt. Lite salt can cut your salt intake, but this can also be accomplished by using regular salt, but just using less of it.

 Sweeteners

By now, you know sugar is added to everything from canned vegetables to salt. For even the most diligent, it's hard to escape the blizzard of sugar that lands everywhere in our food supply. Our consumption of sugar has actually declined recently, but it is still alarmingly high at about 115 pounds a year per person down from previous years' high of 125 pounds. The optimistic may attribute this decline to health reasons, but it's more likely economic, especially since the drop started after the price of sugar went sky-high several Christmases ago. Just as sugar consumption has been declining slightly, the

Sweeteners

consumption of artificial sweeteners has increased, so I think there's no danger that America is losing its sweet tooth.

One of the biggest problems with our high sugar consumption is our emotional attachment to sweet foods. Who doesn't remember a special lemon meringue pie from his or her childhood, or a cherry cobbler, or a chewy candy bar eaten on the way home from school? Sweets have a holding power. As a child, I liked *green* candies best. Once when I returned home from college, my nine-year-old sister had dutifully selected and saved the green Ju-ju fruits from her candy boxes. These green sweets were proudly stretched across the top of my dresser as my welcoming home gift.

Eating sweets traditionally has meant more than just another thing to eat—it's something special, a treat. Dr. Joan Dye Gussow, Chairman of the Nutrition Department at Teachers' College, Columbia University, told me of an incident that happened to her after she was quoted in the New York *Times,* saying she was glad sugar prices were up because then maybe people would use less of the stuff. A distraught woman wrote her asking how could she be so mean? It appears that during World War II, the letter writer was living in England and her husband was fighting on the front. Every afternoon she had tea with a lump of sugar and to this day a lump of sugar in her tea reminds her of her sweet husband who was killed in the war. So how could anyone dare to suggest

eating less of this marvelous, memory-provoking food?

If the only sugar our society was getting was a lump at teatime or coffee break, that would be one thing, but its use is widespread, and it is pervasive in foods not generally considered "sweets," like catsup and nondairy creamers.

PUTTING THE SUGAR CONTENT ON THE LABEL

The relationship between sugar consumption and health problems is becoming well known. Recently a group of ten professional and consumer organizations met with the Food and Drug Administration to urge the FDA to inform the public about the specific sugar content of foods. It is no longer just dentists who are concerned about sugar intake but now organized consumer and health-oriented groups are also aroused. In a battle for better labeling the Center for Science in the Public Interest was joined by the American Dental Association, and also by representatives from the American College of Preventive Medicine, American Diabetes Association, American Public Health Association, Society for Nutrition Education, Consumer Federation of America, Consumer's Union, and Food Research Action Center.

The organizations were asking the FDA to put words like: "contains 45 per cent sugar" on a label. It seems such a common sense idea, one wonders what the hullabaloo is about. The protesting comes from the food companies who used to be required only to list the ingredients in order of weight on the side of the package. So, although sugar was listed second or third on the side of a breakfast cereal box, it took intensive prying to find out, for example, that Trix, a General Mills cereal, actually contains 46.6 per cent sugar. Now the additional sugar information is on the box as well.

The following chart lists the sugar content of popular breakfast cereals. I suggest shoppers use it as a practical shopping guide.

Percentage of Sugar in Breakfast Cereals

KELLOGG'S
(information furnished by Kelloggs*)

All-Bran	14%
Apple-Jacks	56%
Bran Buds	25%
Cocoa Krispies	46%
Concentrate	11%
Corn Flakes	7%
Country Morning	25%
Country Morning, with Raisins, Dates	21%
40% Bran	18%
Froot Loops	53%
Frosted Mini-Wheats	28%
Frosted Rice	39%
Pep	14%
Product 19	11%
Raisin Bran	21%
Rice Krispies	11%
Special K	7%
Sugar Frosted Flakes	42%
Sugar Pops	39%
Sugar Smacks	56%

NABISCO
(information furnished by Nabisco)

Bran 100% with Prune Juice	17.2%
Cream of Wheat	1%
Cream of Wheat with Apple	24%
Cream of Wheat with Banana	25.3%
Cream of Wheat with Maple	22.4%
Shredded Wheat	2%
Shredded Wheat, spoon size	2%
Team Flakes	14.6%

GENERAL MILLS†

Boo Berry	45.7%
Buc Wheats	13.6%
Cheerios	2.2%
Cocoa Puffs	43%

GENERAL MILLS
(continued)

Count Chocula	44.2%
Frankenberry	44%
Lucky Charms	50.4%
Sir Grapefellow	40.7%
Total	8.1%
Trix	46.6%
Wheaties	4.7%

RALSTON PURINA†

Corn Chex	7.5%
Rice Chex	8.5%
Wheat Chex	2.6%

GENERAL FOODS
(information furnished by General Foods‡)

Alpha Bits	
Honeycombs	
Pebbles	38–49%
Super Sugar Crisp	
Bran Flakes	
Grape Nuts	10–20%
Grape Nuts Flakes	
Post Raisin Bran	

QUAKER
(information furnished by Quaker)

Cap'n Crunch	40%
Instant Quaker Oatmeal	1–3%
Life	20%
Old Fashioned Quaker Oats	1–3%
100% Natural Cereal	20%
Puffed Rice	3%

MISCELLANEOUS†

Alpen Natural	3.8%
Granola	16.2%
Granola with Almonds and Filberts	21.4%
Granola with Dates	14.5%
Granola with Raisins	14.5%
Heartland	23.1%

* Percentages calculated by the Center for Science in the Public Interest, Washington, D.C.
† Information furnished by Ira Shannon published in the *Journal of Dentistry for Children.*
‡ Complete information was unavailable for these products.

This precise sugar labeling information should be available for all foods, not just isolated listings of cereals, and perhaps it will be soon. If sugar labeling is mandated for all foods, it will have to be decided whether a statement of added sugar content or total sugar content is preferable, since sugars occur naturally in many foods. The "added sugar" method would exempt naturally sweet foods, such as orange juice and raisins, from being labeled even if they have more total sugar than foods made with added sugar.

The "added sugar" method also raises questions of compliance, since laboratory analysis cannot distinguish between added sugars and those occurring naturally. The New York State Department of Agriculture and Markets has testified that a mandatory labeling of added sugar would be unenforceable. The accuracy of "added sugar" information can only be checked by inspecting the packing plant or the processor's records.

Labeling the grams of sugar present in 100 grams of a particular food also distorts comparisons of foods. For example, the percentage of sugar in a powdered soft drink mix is considerably higher than the percentage of sugar in a liquid, although the amount of sugar per serving may be exactly the same. Labeling of sugar in grams per 100 grams might also be confusing to consumers since other nutrition information is based on common portion sizes, which are not usually 100 grams. So, the question remains, can consumers make the distinctions necessary to use this information correctly, once they have it?

KINDS OF SWEETENERS

There are two ways to get sugar. One is naturally, by eating starches and fruits (see Chapter 3, Fruits, page 79), and the other is from refined sources like granulated sugar, brown sugar, and honey. The problem is that increasingly we are getting less of our sugar from the first category and more from the second, which constitutes a loss since the starches and fruits offer other nutrients along with the sugar.

Our bowl and chain

The average American consumes about 600 calories a day of foods high in sugar. For the person with the sweet tooth, that's equivalent to eating:

4 chocolate chip cookies	206 calories
1 ounce chocolate candy bar	147 calories
1 piece apple pie	213 calories

But you'd have to eat this much fresh fruit to have almost the same amount of calories:

1 apple	96 calories
1 banana, medium	101 calories
2 oranges	128 calories
1 peach	38 calories
1 pear	100 calories
10 plums	66 calories
1 cup strawberries	55 calories

In choosing a sweetener, is one kind *better* than another? The following comparisons of honey, corn sweeteners, fructose, molasses, brown sugar, and white sugar should help you decide.

Honey

Honey, by many, is thought to be the purest and best kind of sweetener, and raw honey, well, that's even better. But I questioned honey's exalted place among the sweeteners: it's by far the most expensive and the most caloric, so what is its supposed nutritional edge?

I hadn't given this honey business much thought until I was interviewing Jane Frederick, the U.S. women's Olympic Pentathlon champion, and she said that when she was in training she had stopped using refined sugar and used only raw honey. Since she's an Olympic champion, she has access to the best coaches and nutritionists in the country. My interest was piqued. Was there a real scientific basis for preferring honey? When you're purchasing honey, should you go out of your way the way Jane does and search out a raw honey, or is strained or filtered just about the same at much less the price?

Strained, extracted, or filtered honey. Most of today's consumers want a honey that will not ferment, that will remain liquid, and that will have an attractive appearance; that's what these three types do.

Strained, filtered, or extracted are terms used for honey that has been separated from the comb by these techniques. These types should be free of visible crystals; if granulation does occur, let them stand in a 200° F. oven until liquid. In speaking with the Superior Honey Company, I got a better understanding of the differences between strained and filtered. Strained honey is heated to 135° F. to get the honey to move; then the impurities are removed by running it through a screening process which leaves the pollen food value in. Filtered honey is heated to 180° F., which removes the pollen. This high heat prevents granulation and extends the shelf life. Since filtering is a slightly cheaper process than straining, a filtered honey should be cheaper.

Crystallized honey is completely granulated or solidified and includes products that have a cloudy, creamy look, like spread-type honeys.

Raw comb honey. This is the kind Jane Frederick uses; it is honey that is contained in the cells of the comb in which it is produced. It is said that "raw" honey has not been filtered, strained, or heated. But 'tain't so. Most raw honey is strained to remove bee remains or pieces of wood and is heated to 100° F. to move the honey from the comb.

It can be purchased in several forms: section comb, individual comb, bulk comb, or chunk honey, which is cut comb honey packed in a container filled with liquid extract honey, so in a real sense this last is not really "raw" honey. Remember, the comb is not there for cosmetic purposes, it's edible. But honey with the comb in keeps the least well, and has a high price. Since it's not processed, raw honey should be cheaper, but it's the most expensive. Of the honeys, you're getting the most robust flavor with raw comb honey, if you can afford the price.

Those are the definitions of the different kinds of honey, but is raw comb honey *better* than strained or filtered honey? There's no conclusive answer. Filtration can diminish the vitamin content, but since honey is used in such small quantities the vitamin content of honey is of little practical importance. Dr. J. R. White, a honey expert with the Department of Agriculture, told me that properly manufactured honey should be as nutritious as "raw" honey although the flavor and aroma might be slightly altered.

So, various honeys don't differ that much nutritionally, but is *honey more nutritious than other sweeteners?* True, honey does contain some minerals, enzymes, and vitamins not present in some other sweeteners (see Sweet Facts chart, page 225–26), but the amounts are so small as to be insignificant. And if you want to get picky about it, dark honey is richer in minerals than light honey, but again the amounts are so minute that the differences are inconsequential. If you want to cut your sugar intake, don't plan on doing it by substituting honey.

A cautionary word about honey and infants: they don't mix. In fact, the Center for Science in the Public Interest has filed a petition with the Food and Drug Administration requesting that warning labels be placed on honey containers. The label would read: Do Not Feed to Infants Under One Year Old. Serious Illness May Result. According to the C.S.P.I. petition, honey, which may be added to the infant's formula by the mother, sometimes contains bacteria which, once inside the intestine, produce botulineal toxin, a poison that can cause intestinal disease and sometimes respiratory failure. The American Medical Association has also issued a warning to consumers against feeding honey to babies under one year of age.

HONEY TIPS

* Store in a dry place. Refrigeration hastens granulation.

* To replace other sweeteners. Replace 1 cup sugar with 1 cup honey. If recipe calls for additional liquid, omit ¼ cup. For example, if recipe calls for 1 cup sugar and ½ cup liquid, use 1 cup honey and only ¼ cup liquid.

Corn Sweeteners

A few years back at Christmas when sugar prices were high, it was the vogue to use corn syrup instead. Corn syrup is made from ground corn and the end result traditionally has been only three quarters as sweet as sugar. But the manufacturers are now producing a fructose corn syrup that is sweeter than sugar. Regardless of how sweet it is, corn syrup has never really caught on in home use and now that prices have stabilized, it probably won't. Most corn syrups consumed in this country are contained in processed foods such as baked goods and soft drinks.

Fructose

Fructose is made from naturally occurring sources of fructose (fresh fruits, for example, contain fructose naturally). According to Nutrition Action, regular sugar is just as natural as manufactured fructose. "Regular sugar could be called the type found in fresh beets and sugar cane." Fructose is 10–30 times the price of sugar and only tastes sweeter than sugar when used cold (in cold drinks and foods). Although fructose is marketed with misleading ads that tout its health advantages over other sweeteners, the FDA at

this point says they don't have the manpower to go after the companies who are making allegedly deceptive marketing claims. Since it is powdered like confectioners' sugar, you cannot substitute it for granulated sugar in recipes for baked goods.

Molasses

After years of declining use, molasses sales are on the upswing, probably because this sweetener carries the connotation of being better for you than sugar. Molasses, as you can see from the Sweet Facts chart, is high in iron. Sulfured molasses is molasses that has been treated with sulfur dioxide to preserve its color. It is a fraction more nutritious than the unsulfured because a fraction more iron is preserved. When used in cooking at home, the sulfur boils off.

For details on other sweeteners like granulated sugar, ultrafine sugar, powdered sugar, and brown sugar, refer to the Sweet Facts chart on page 225. Artificial sweeteners have purposely not been included on the chart because their legal status with the FDA changes so quixotically. I don't think people should be tricked into using artificial sweeteners as a way of using less sugar. Although you may not have some of the other complications associated with sugar consumption (cavities, overweight, acne), their oversweet flavor nurtures an even greater growth of the sweet tooth syndrome.

INTERPRETING THE SWEET FACTS CHART

In compiling this chart, I wanted to assess the different nutritional values, if any, the caloric differences, and the price spread among the sweeteners. It slowly became clear to me, taking all these considerations into account, that the best sweetener is brown sugar. Brown sugar has less calories than honey, slightly more nutrients than granulated sugar, and is reasonably priced.

When I need to use a sweetener, I use brown sugar for just about everything, but I wish you luck in convincing the unconverted. We have a friend whom we call the Sugar Man because he takes his sugar with a little coffee. I tried to persuade him to try brown sugar, but he longed for the real thing—those white granules. With him, it's hardly a question of type of sweetener he uses, but of the enormous quantity.

OTHER USES OF SWEETENERS

Other than as a flavor enhancer, sugar is also used as a preservative in jams and jellies. In canned fruits, packed in heavy syrup, the sweetener is there for flavoring because the concentration is too low to be useful as a preservative.

If you've purchased fruit in heavy syrup and you want to get rid of the syrup, just wash the fruit off. You will also be saving a lot in calories without the heavy syrup.

1 cup serving of pear halves
   in heavy syrup: 160 calories
    without syrup: 100 calories
1 cup serving of peach halves
   in heavy syrup: 170 calories
    without syrup: 115 calories

TIPS ON USING LESS SUGAR

* Think about what you're doing. When you find your hand automatically going to the sugar bowl, take a moment and look at that hand and rethink why your hand has traveled that route. I used to take sugar in my tea. One day, as a detached observer, I watched my hand habitually going from the sugar bowl into my teacup and I stopped to think, why? I now drink a slightly spicy tea and I haven't missed the sugar.

* Most sugar consumed comes from prepared foods and beverages. Less than 30 per cent of sugar is packaged for household use. Eat fewer prepared foods and beverages.

* Drink mineral water with a twist of lemon. Several years ago, I banned soda pop from the premises. Now on occasion, when someone offers me a swig, it tastes too heavy.

* Kids love the miniature 4-ounce bottles Welch's grape juice comes in. Save the bottles and refill them with other fruit juices. Next time they ask for a soda, give them this instead. This also makes sense from a recycling point of view; why throw away such sweet little bottles? If the kids miss the carbonation that comes with soda pop, add a drop or two of naturally carbonated water just before giving it to them.

* If you must have sugar in the house, keep it in a small quantity in an out-of-the-way hard-to-reach place, so that pulling out the sugar becomes rather like finding an ashtray in a nonsmoker's house.

* Do not buy presweetened foods. Do the sweetening at home and you'll add much less sugar than the manufacturers do. If children are given a bowl of cereal and a bowl of sugar, they will never add as much sugar as the manufacturer does.

* So much of the desire for sugar is for the added flavor it gives to food. Try spices to add that extra zing. Try baking breads, muffins, coffee cakes with allspice, cinnamon, cloves, ginger, nutmeg.

* Keep a spice blend on hand that can be used in preparing applesauce, dried fruit compotes, baked bananas, oranges, Bavarian custard, rice pudding.

Sweet Facts

Sweetener	Source	Nutritional Value	Uses	Calories per tbsp.	$ Cost per tbsp.	per lb.
SUGARS: Brown Sugar	1) refined sugar and molasses syrup; 2) boiling a syrup containing necessary flavor and coloring, spun in centrifuge	sucrose; traces of minerals present	light: baking, butter-scotch, condiments, glazes for hams; dark: gingerbread, baked beans	52	.011	.39
Granulated	sugar cane, sugar beets	sucrose	foods, beverages, table, baking	46	.01	.37
Powdered	sugar cane, sugar beets	sucrose, usually packed in cornstarch	icings, frostings, un-cooked candies	42	.007	.39
Raw Sugar	evaporation of sugar cane juice	96% sucrose contaminants (soil fibers, molds, yeasts, bacteria, lint waxes)	not available in U.S. due to these contaminants			
Turbinado	raw sugar, partially refined by washing in centrifuge	99% sucrose; slight traces of minerals present	same as granulated; slightly stronger, more molasses-like taste; may have different moisture content; closer to refined than raw			.86
Ultrafine	sugar cane, sugar beets	sucrose	special baking			
CORN SYRUP	product of corn	mixture of sugars, trace minerals, trace vitamins	mostly used in food processing, available to consumer as "Karo Syrup"	57	light: .022 dark: .018	.71/pint .57/pint

Sweet Facts (continued)

Sweetener	Source	Nutritional Value	Uses	Calories per tbsp.	Cost per tbsp.	per lb.
HONEY Strained	from nectar gathered by bees	depending on source of nectar, approximately: 38% fructose, 31% glucose, 1% sucrose, 9% other sugars, trace minerals, trace vitamins	sweetener, baking glazes	64	.048	1.06
MOLASSES	dark syrup derived from sugar cane stalks that are crushed, boiled, and the sugar crystals removed	sugar, minerals, vitamins	table syrups, baked beans, gingerbread, some cookies, dark breads	48	.038	1.21

SIMPLE SPICE BLEND

Ingredients:

    1 tablespoon ground cinnamon

    2 tablespoons ground nutmeg

    2 tablespoons ground allspice

    2 tablespoons ground ginger

Combine all ingredients and store in tightly covered jar.

EVEN SIMPLER SPICE BLEND

Ingredients:

    ¼ cup ground cinnamon

    2 tablespoons ground mace

Combine ingredients and store in tightly covered jar.

Additives

The problem with additives is that there are so many of them with so many names and initials that it's barely possible to keep the good guys separated from the bad. Additives are used for everything from artificial colorings and flavorings to antioxidants, flavor enhancers, color fixatives, stabilizers, texturizers, sweeteners, and antimicrobial agents.

The use of additives is a silent pact between consumers and manufacturers. As some consumers demand more unfood-like food: oranger oranges, redder red meat, manufacturers can't turn to nature, so they turn to their bag of additives to find the tricks. The distress over additives is not from a smattering of questionable food color here or there, but the fact that our entire food system is permeated with questionable amounts of questionable additives. A little here, a little there, is adding up to too much everywhere.

I do not mean to imply that in all instances additives are not safe. Some are safe (see Safety List of Common Food Additives, page 228), but in many instances manufacturers use additives so habitually and so unthinkingly that they continue to use them even in instances when they are clearly no longer necessary. To cite just one example, the Center for Science in the Public Interest in Washington, D.C., did a study of the unnecessary uses of one type of additive—antioxidants—and showed that for many kinds of foods, some manufacturers used BHT and/or BHA, while competing manufacturers did not use these or related antioxidants. The dry soup mix category looked like this:

Product	Antioxidant(s)
DRY SOUP MIX	
Lipton's Green Pea	—
Lipton's Chicken Noodle	—
Lipton's Chicken Rice	—
Mrs. Grass Chicken Noodle	BHA, BHT
Lipton's Cup-A-Soup, Tomato	—
Nestle's Souptime, Chicken Noodle	—
Giant Instant Chicken Noodle	BHA, BHT

C.S.P.I. concluded that these particular additives are rarely, if ever, actually *needed* in production of quality foods if manufacturers use good manufacturing practices.

Nitrite-free meat products are another example. In some products the additive nitrite has been removed and has not been replaced; there have been no dire consequences to either the economy of the meat processors or the health of the consumers.

On a limited basis, some meat products are now sold preserved by old-fashioned methods and cured without nitrites. But consumer beware, it is a tricky forest of labels and names. Although a product may be labeled "old-fashioned smoked meat," it is probably still made with nitrites if it is labeled "bacon," "frankfurters," and "hot dogs." When similar meats are made without nitrites the Department of Agriculture says they cannot be called by these familiar names. It is almost as if to punish this new nitrite-free industry, that nitrite-free bacon, for example, must be labeled "smoked uncured pork belly." Since this labeling situation is changing almost daily, if you're searching for products with no nitrites, look for packages labeled "no nitrites."

I think consumers sometimes feel unnecessarily helpless in situations where there are options still open to them. For example, let's look at caffeine, a well-known stimulant that the Safety List suggests should be avoided. Many popular soft drinks have caffeine added to the tune of 35–55 mg per 12-ounce bottle. If you drink those beverages, that's your choice; you selected that drink and the caffeine is right on the label. You can, of course, choose other beverages, soft drinks, fruit juices, mineral waters with no caffeine.

Since caffeine occurs naturally in coffee, Most teas,[1] and cocoa, you might throw up your hands and say, "Nothing to be done here," but 'tain't so. As chief coffee-maker and tea brewer, you have more control over the caffeine levels than you might think. In tea, with the exception of instant tea, the caffeine levels are directly related to brewing time; in coffee, to the different methods of preparation. The research done by Margaret McWilliams at California State College in Los Angeles looks like this:

TEA	Mg Caffeine per cup
Black Tea (ordinary tea, the kind usually served in restaurants)	
Brewed 1 minute:	19–35
Brewed 3–5 minutes	32–60
Other Tea (green tea, oolong)	
Brewed 3–5 minutes	19–40
Instant Tea	80–90
COFFEE	
Method of Preparation:	
Percolator	90–125
Dripolator	135–147

I'm a tea drinker, and I've never liked a heavily brewed tea anyway, but with this information in hand, I now drink an even more lightly brewed tea.

Caffeine is an easy example. With other additives it's hardly a question of brewing more or less of them, but there still are ways to avoid unnecessary additives and the main strategy is to rely less on already prepared foods that often contain additives. If this isn't a good solution for you, when you're purchasing convenience foods, take a moment to compare labels on several similar items and buy the product with the least additives, or none. This is still tricky because

[1] Only a very few strictly herbal teas such as peppermint, spearmint, and camomile are caffeine-free.

there are additives that are not listed, especially artificial colors and flavors. Now we're getting to the nitty-gritty. You start reading the label, but it looks like Martian language. That's where the following Safety List based on information supplied by the Center for Science in the Public Interest comes in handy. The Safety List is divided into three categories: Avoid, Caution, and Safe.

THE SAFETY LIST OF COMMON FOOD ADDITIVES[2]

Artificial Colorings:

Most artificial colorings are synthetic chemicals that do not occur in nature. Though some are safer than others, colorings are not listed by name on labels. Because colorings are used almost solely in foods of low nutritional value (candy, soda pop, gelatin desserts, etc.), you should simply avoid all artificially colored foods. In addition to problems mentioned below, there is evidence that colorings may cause hyperactivity in some sensitive children. The use of coloring usually indicates that fruit or other natural ingredients have not been used.

AVOID: *The additive is unsafe in the amounts consumed or is very poorly tested.*

Blue No. 1
Artificial coloring.
Beverages, candy, baked goods.

Very poorly tested; possible risk. Avoid.

Blue No. 2
Artificial coloring.
Pet food, beverages, candy.

Very poorly tested; should be avoided.

[2] The Safety List of Common Food Additives is based in large part on "Chemical Cuisine," a poster prepared by Nutrition Action, a project of Center for Science in the Public Interest. The full-color poster may be obtained for $2.00 from C.S.P.I., 1755 S Street N.W., Washington, D.C. 20009.

Citrus Red No. 2
Artificial coloring.
Skin of some Florida oranges only.

Studies indicate that this additive causes cancer. The dye does not seep through the orange skin into the pulp.

Green No. 3
Artificial coloring.
Candy, beverages.

Needs to be better tested; Avoid.

Red No. 3
Artificial coloring.
Cherries in fruit cocktail, candy, baked goods.

Studies suggest this dye may cause cancer. The FDA is concerned that if this iodine-containing dye is more widely used, it will contribute to undesirably high levels of iodine.

Red No. 40
Artificial coloring.
Soda pop, candy, gelatin desserts, pastry, pet food, sausage.

The most widely used coloring appears to promote cancer in mice. Americans consumed 1.8 million pounds of this dye in 1978.

Yellow No. 5
Artificial coloring.
Gelatin dessert, candy, pet food, baked goods.

The second most widely used coloring is poorly tested, with one test suggesting it might cause cancer. Some people are allergic to it.

Brominated Vegetable Oil (BVO)
Emulsifier, clouding agent.
Soft drinks.

BVO keeps flavor oils in suspension and gives a cloudy appearance to citrus-flavored soft drinks. Residues of BVO found in body fat are cause for concern. BVO should be banned; safer substitutes are available.

Butylated Hydroxytoluene (BHT)
Antioxidant.
Cereals, chewing gum, potato chips, oils, etc.

BHT is poorly tested, is found in body fat, and causes occasional allergic reactions. BHT is unnecessary in many of the foods in which it is used; safer alternatives are available.

Caffeine
Stimulant.
Coffee, tea, cocoa (natural); soft drinks (additive).

Caffeine may cause miscarriages or birth defects and should be avoided by pregnant women. It also keeps many people from sleeping.

Quinine
Flavoring.
Tonic water, quinine water, bitter lemon.

This drug can cure malaria and is used as a bitter flavoring in a few soft drinks. There is a slight chance that quinine may cause birth defects, so pregnant women should avoid quinine-containing beverages and drugs. Very poorly tested.

Saccharin
Synthetic sweetener.
"Diet" products.

Saccharin is 350 times sweeter than sugar and 10 times sweeter than cyclamate. Studies have not shown that saccharin helps people lose weight. Since 1951, tests have indicated that saccharin causes cancer. In 1977, the FDA proposed that saccharin be banned. Be wise—avoid saccharin.

Sodium Nitrite, Sodium Nitrate
Preservative, coloring, flavoring.
Bacon, ham, frankfurters, luncheon meats, smoked fish, corned beef.

Nitrite can lead to the formation of small amounts of potent cancer-causing chemicals (nitrosamines), particularly in fried bacon. Sodium nitrate is used in dry-cured meat, because it slowly breaks down into nitrite. Nitrite is tolerated in foods because it can prevent the growth of bacteria that causes botulism poisoning; it also stabilizes the red color in cured meat and gives a characteristic flavor. Companies should find safer ways of preventing botulism and in 1980 the USDA earmarked $2 million for research for a safer substitute.

In August 1980 the Food and Drug Administration and the Department of Agriculture jointly issued the following statement: "A group of independent pathologists has completed an extensive review of the study conducted at the Massachusetts Institute of Technology that led us in 1978 to consider the need to phase out nitrite as a preservative in cured meats and poultry . . . A committee of scientists has concluded that insufficient evidence exists linking sodium nitrite to cancer and therefore there is no basis to remove it from foods at this time . . . We will continue our efforts to eliminate preformed nitrosamines from foods.

CAUTION: *The additive may be unsafe, or it is poorly tested, or is used in foods we eat too much of.*

Yellow No. 6
Artificial coloring.
Beverages, sausage, baked goods, candy, gelatin.

Appears safe, but can cause occasional allergic reactions; used almost exclusively in junk foods.

Artificial Flavoring
Flavoring.
Soda pop, candy, breakfast cereals, gelatin desserts; many others.

Hundred of chemicals are used to mimic natural flavors; many may be used in a single flavoring, such as for cherry soda pop. Most flavoring chemicals also occur in nature and are probably safe, but they may cause hyperactivity in some sensitive children. Artificial flavorings are used almost exclusively in junk foods; their use indicates that the real thing (usually fruit) has been left out.

Butylated Hydroxyanisole (BHA)
Antioxidant.
Cereals, chewing gum, potato chips, vegetable oil.

BHA retards rancidity in fats, oils, and oil-containing foods. It appears to be safer than BHT (above), but needs to be better tested. This synthetic chemical can often be replaced by safer chemicals.

Heptyl Paraben
Preservative.
Beer.

Heptyl paraben—short for the heptyl ester of parahydroxybenzoic acid—is used as a preservative in some beers. Studies suggest this chemical is safe, but it has not been tested in the presence of alcohol.

Hydrogenated Vegetable Oil
Source of oil or fat.
Margarine, many processed foods.

Vegetable oil, usually a liquid, can be made into a semisolid by treating with hydrogen. Unfortunately, hydrogenation converts some of the polyunsaturated oil to saturated fat. We eat too much oil and fat of all kinds, whether natural or hydrogenated.

Monosodium Glutamate (MSG)
Flavor enhancer.
Soup, seafood, poultry, cheese, sauces, stews; many others.

This amino acid brings out the flavor of protein-containing foods. Large amounts of MSG fed to infant mice destroyed nerve cells in the brain. Public pressure forced baby food companies to stop using MSG. MSG causes "Chinese Restaurant Syndrome" (burning sensation in the back of neck and forearms, tightness of the chest, headache) in some sensitive adults.

Phosphoric Acid; Phosphates
Acidulent, chelating agent, buffer, emulsifier, nutrient, discoloration inhibitor.

Baked goods, cheese, powdered foods, cured meat, soda pop, breakfast cereals, dehydrated potatoes.

Phosphoric acid acidifies and flavors cola beverages. Calcium and iron phosphates act as mineral supplements. Sodium aluminum phosphate is a leavening agent. Calcium and ammonium phosphates serve as food for yeast in bread. Sodium acid pyrophosphate prevents discoloration in potatoes and sugar syrups. Phosphates are not toxic, but their widespread use has led to a dietary imbalance that may be causing osteoporosis.

Polysorbate 60
Emulsifier.
Baked goods, frozen desserts, imitation dairy products.

Polysorbate 60 is short for polyoxyethylene-(20)-sodium monostearate. It and its close relatives, Polysorbate 65 and 80, are sometimes contaminated with 1,4-dioxane, which is carcinogenic. These chemicals keep baked goods from going stale, keep dill oil dissolved in bottled dill pickles, and prevent oil from separating in artificial whipped cream.

Propyl Gallate
Antioxidant.
Vegetable oil, meat products, potato sticks, chicken soup base, chewing gum.

Retards the spoilage of fats and oils. It is often used with BHA and BHT because of the synergistic effect these additives have in retarding rancidity. Propyl gallate has not been adequately tested and frequently is unnecessary.

Sulfur Dioxide, Sodium Bisulfite
Preservative, bleach.
Sliced fruit, wine, grape juice, dehydrated potatoes.

Sulfur dioxide (a gas) and sodium bisulfite (a powder) prevent discoloration of dried apricots, apples, and similar foods. They prevent bacterial growth in wine and other foods. These additives destroy vitamin B_1, but otherwise are safe.

SAFE: *The additive appears to be safe.*

Alginate, Propylene Glycol Alginate
Thickening agents; foam stabilizer.
Ice cream, cheese, candy, yoghurt.

Alginate, an apparently safe derivative of seaweed (kelp), maintains the desired texture in dairy products, canned frosting, and other factory-made foods. Propylene glycol alginate, a chemically modified algin, thickens acidic foods (soda pop, salad dressing) and stabilizes the foam in beer.

Alpha Tocopherol (Vitamin E)
Antioxidant, nutrient.
Vegetable oil.

Vitamin E is abundant in whole wheat, rice germ, and vegetable oils. It is destroyed by the refining and bleaching of flour. Vitamin E prevents oil from going rancid.

Ascorbic Acid (Vitamin C), Erythorbic Acid
Antioxidant, nutrient, color stabilizer.
Oily foods, cereals, soft drinks, cured meats.

Ascorbic acid helps maintain the red color of cured meat and prevents the formation of nitrosamines. It helps prevent loss of color and flavor by reacting with unwanted oxygen. It is used as a nutrient additive in drinks and breakfast cereals. Sodium ascorbate is a more soluble form of ascorbic acid. Erythorbic acid (sodium erythorbate) serves the same functions as ascorbic acid, but has no value as a vitamin.

Beta Carotene
Coloring; nutrient.
Margarine, shortening, nondairy whiteners, butter.

Used as an artificial coloring and a nutrient supplement. The body converts it to vitamin A, which is part of the light-detection mechanism of the eye.

Calcium (or Sodium) Propionate
Preservative.
Bread, rolls, pies, cakes.

Calcium propionate prevents mold growth on bread and rolls. The calcium is a beneficial mineral; the propionate is safe. Sodium Propionate is used in pies and cakes, because calcium alters the action of chemical leavening agents.

Calcium (or Sodium) Stearoyl Lactylate
Dough conditioner, whipping agent.
Bread dough, cake fillings, artificial whipped cream, processed egg whites.

These additives strengthen bread dough so it can be used in bread-making machinery and lead to more uniform grain and greater volume. They act as whipping agents in dried, liquid, or frozen egg whites and artificial whipped cream. Sodium stearoyl fumerate serves the same function.

Carrageenan
Thickening and stabilizing agent.
Ice cream, jelly, chocolate milk, infant formula.

Obtained from "Irish Moss" seaweed, it is used as a thickening agent and to stabilize oil-water mixtures.

Casein, Sodium Caseinate
Thickening and whitening agent.
Ice cream, ice milk, sherbet, coffee creamers.

Casein, the principal protein in milk, is a nutritious protein containing adequate amounts of all the essential amino acids.

Citric Acid, Sodium Citrate
Acid, flavoring, chelating agent.
Ice cream, sherbet, fruit drinks, candy, carbonated beverages, instant potatoes.

Citric acid is versatile, widely used, cheap, and safe. It is an important metabolite in virtually all living organisms; especially abundant in citrus fruits and berries. It is used as a strong acid, a tart flavoring, and an antioxidant. Sodium citrate, also safe, is a buffer that controls the acidity of gelatin desserts, jam, ice cream, candy, and other foods.

EDTA
Chelating agent.
Salad dressing, margarine, sandwich spreads, mayonnaise, processed fruits and vegetables, canned shellfish, soft drinks.

Modern food manufacturing technology, which involves metal rollers, blenders, and containers, results in trace amounts of metal contamination in food. EDTA (ethylenediamine tetraacetic acid) traps metal impurities, which would otherwise promote rancidity and the breakdown of artificial colors.

Ferrous Gluconate
Coloring, nutrient.
Black olives.

Used by the olive industry to generate a uniform jet-black color and in pills as a source of iron. Safe.

Fumaric Acid
Tartness agent.
Powdered drinks, pudding, pie fillings, gelatin desserts.

A solid at room temperature, inexpensive, highly acidic, it is the ideal source of tartness and acidity in dry food products. However, it dissolves slowly in cold water, a drawback cured by adding dioctyl sodium sulfosuccinate (DSS), a poorly tested, detergent-like additive.

Gelatin
Thickening and gelling agent.
Powdered dessert mix, yoghurt, ice cream, cheese spreads, beverages.

Gelatin is a protein obtained from animal bones, hoofs, and other parts. It has little nutritional value, because it contains little or none of several essential amino acids.

Glycerin (Glycerol)
Maintains water content.
Marshmallow, candy, fudge, baked goods.

Glycerin forms the backbone of fat and oil molecules and is quite safe. The body uses it as a source of energy or as a starting material in making more complex molecules.

Gums: Guar, Locust Bean, Arabic, Furcelleran, Ghatti, Karaya, Tragacanth
Thickening agents, stabilizers.
Beverages, ice cream, frozen pudding, salad dressing, dough, cottage cheese, candy, drink mixes.

Gums derive from natural sources (bushes, trees, or seaweed) and are poorly tested. They are used to thicken foods, prevent sugar crystals from forming in candy, stabilize beer foam (arabic), form a gel in pudding (furcelleran), encapsulate flavor oils in powdered drink mixes, or keep oil and water mixed together in salad dressings.

Hydrolyzed Vegetable Protein (HVP)
Flavor enhancer.
Instant soups, frankfurters, sauce mixes, beef stew.

HVP consists of vegetable (usually soybean) protein that has been chemically broken down into the amino acids of which it is composed. HVP is used to bring out the natural flavor of food.

Lactic Acid
Acidity regulator.
Spanish olives, cheese, frozen desserts, carbonated beverages.

This safe acid occurs in almost all living organisms. It inhibits spoilage in Spanish-type olives, balances the acidity in cheese-making, and adds tartness to frozen desserts, carbonated fruit-flavored drinks, and other foods.

Lactose
Sweetener.
Whipped topping mix, breakfast pastry.

Lactose, a carbohydrate found only in milk, is nature's way of delivering calories to infant mammals. One sixth as sweet as table sugar, it is added to food as a slightly sweet source of carbohydrate. Milk turns sour when bacteria convert lactose to lactic acid.

Lecithin
Emulsifier, antioxidant.
Baked goods, margarine, chocolate, ice cream.

A common constituent of animal and plant tissues, it is a source of the nutrient choline. It keeps oil and water from separating, retards rancidity, reduces spattering in a frying pan, and leads to fluffier cakes. Major sources are egg yolk and soybeans.

Mannitol
Sweetener, other uses.
Chewing gum, low calorie foods.

Not quite as sweet as sugar and poorly absorbed by the body, it contributes only half as many calories as sugar. Used as the "dust" on chewing gum, it prevents gum from absorbing moisture and becoming sticky. Safe.

Mono- and Diglycerides
Emulsifier.
Baked goods, margarine, candy, peanut butter.

Makes bread softer and prevents staling, improves the stability of margarine, makes caramels less sticky, and prevents the oil in peanut butter from separating. Mono- and diglycerides are safe, though most foods they are used in are high in refined flour, sugar, or fat.

Sodium Benzoate
Fruit juice, carbonated drinks, pickles, preserves.

Manufacturers have used sodium benzoate for over 70 years to prevent the growth of micro-organisms in acidic foods.

Sodium Carboxymethyl Cellulose (CMC)
Thickening and stabilizing agent; prevents sugar from crystallizing.
Ice cream, beer, pie fillings, icings, diet foods, candy.

CMC is made by reacting cellulose with a

derivative of acetic acid. Studies indicate it is safe.

Sorbic Acid, Potassium Sorbate
Prevents growth of mold and bacteria.
Cheese, syrup, jelly, cake, wine, dry fruits.

Sorbic acid occurs naturally in the berries of the mountain ash. Sorbate may be a safe replacement for sodium nitrite in bacon. If potassium sorbate is more widely used, it should be tested more fully.

Sorbitan Monostearate
Emulsifier.
Cakes, candy, frozen pudding, icing.

Like mono- and diglycerides and polysorbates, this additive keeps oil and water mixed together. In chocolate candy, it prevents the discoloration that normally occurs when the candy is warmed up and then cooled down.

Sorbitol
Sweetener, thickening agent, maintains moisture.
Dietetic drinks and foods; candy, shredded coconut, chewing gum.

Sorbitol occurs naturally in fruits and berries and is a close relative of the sugars. It is half as sweet as sugar. It is used in noncariogenic chewing gum because oral bacteria do not metabolize it well. Large amounts of sorbitol (2 ounces for adults) have a laxative effect, but otherwise it is safe. Diabetics use sorbitol because it is absorbed slowly and does not cause blood sugar to increase rapidly.

Starch, Modified Starch
Thickening agent.
Soup, gravy, baby foods.

Starch, the major component of flour, potatoes, and corn, is used as a thickening agent. However, it does not dissolve in cold water.

Chemists have solved this problem by reacting starch with various chemicals. These modified starches are added to some foods to improve their consistency and keep the solids suspended. Starch and modified starches make foods look thicker and richer than they really are.

Vanillin, Ethyl Vanillin
Substitute for vanilla.
Ice cream, baked goods, beverages, chocolate, candy, gelatin desserts.

Vanilla flavoring is derived from a bean, but vanillin, the major flavor component of vanilla, is cheaper to produce synthetically. A derivation, ethyl vanillin, comes closer to matching the taste of real vanilla. Vanillin is safe; ethyl vanillin needs to be better tested.

For quick shopping, I've alphabetized the additives into one reference list that you can Xerox and fit handily into your wallet. When you are about to select an item, check its additives against the list.

Additives

Shopping List of Common Food Additives

Avoid:	Caution:	Safe:

ARTIFICIAL COLORINGS:
  Blue No. 1
  Blue No. 2
  Citrus Red No. 2
  Green No. 3
  Red No. 3
  Red No. 40
  Yellow No. 5
BROMINATED VEGE-
  TABLE OIL (BVO)
BUTYLATED HYDROX-
  YTOLUENE (BHT)
CAFFEINE
QUININE
SACCHARIN
SODIUM NITRITE,
  SODIUM NITRATE
	YELLOW NO. 6 (ARTIFI-
	  CIAL COLORING)
	ARTIFICIAL FLAVORING
	BUTYLATED HYDROX-
	  YANISOLE (BHA)
	HEPTYL PARABEN
	HYDROGENATED VEGE-
	  TABLE OIL
	MONOSODIUM GLUTA-
	  MATE (MSG)
	PHOSPHORIC ACID;
	  PHOSPHATES
	POLYSORBATE 60
	PROPYL GALLATE
	SULFUR DIOXIDE,
	  SODIUM BISULFITE
		ALGINATE, PROPYLENE
		  GLYCOL ALGINATE
		ALPHA TOCOPHEROL
		  (VITAMIN E)
		ASCORBIC ACID
		  (VITAMIN C),
		ERYTHORBIC ACID
		BETA CAROTENE
		CALCIUM (OR SODIUM)
		  PROPIONATE
		CALCIUM (OR SODIUM)
		  STEAROYL LACTY-
		  LATE
		CARRAGEENAN
		CASEIN, SODIUM
		  CASEINATE
		CITRIC ACID, SODIUM
		  CITRATE
		EDTA
		FERROUS GLUCONATE
		FUMARIC ACID
		GELATIN
		GLYCERIN (GLYCEROL)
		GUMS: Guar,
		          Locust Bean,
		          Arabic,
		          Furcelleran,
		          Ghatti,
		          Karaya,
		          Tragacanth
		HYDROLYZED VEGE-
		  TABLE PROTEIN (HVP)
		LACTIC ACID
		LACTOSE
		LECITHIN
		MANNITOL
		MONO- AND DIGLYCER-
		  IDES
		SODIUM BENZOATE
		SODIUM CARBOXY-
		  METHYL CELLULOSE
		  (CMC)
		SORBIC ACID, POTAS-
		  SIUM SORBATE
		SORBITAN MONO-
		  STEARATE
		SORBITOL
		STARCH, MODIFIED
		  STARCH
		VANILLIN, ETHYL
		  VANILLIN

Pesticides

I investigated pesticides as demons as a result of a comment by a colleague. He said, "You're always advocating fresh produce, fresh vegetables and fruits. Aren't people subjecting themselves to increased danger from pesticides by using more fresh produce?" His presumption seemed to be that processed foods, by the nature of the processing, had pesticides removed, but that fresh foods had a better chance of still having those pesticides clinging to them. I didn't know the answer, but I thought his was an interesting question.

I know firsthand that to feed a nation of 200 million people, there is an obvious need for pest control. When my husband and I moved into our first house, I had a plot set aside for a vegetable garden. The plot was large enough to feed the two of us, extra friends, and continual houseguests. It was lovingly planted with everything from edible soybeans to miniature carrots. Since I had no practical knowledge of garden pests, before I knew it the pests had feasted on the garden and there was nothing left for us. In a fit of rage, I dumped a box of pesticide over the entire garden. I was fed up. My reaction was one of, "Okay, you snails, you wanted the garden . . . here . . . take it all." What I did was make the garden not fit for man or pests.

Obviously, even if commercial growers feel like doing what I did, they can't throw in the towel the same way or they wouldn't have any crops to sell, or if they had crops, the levels of pesticides would violate tolerances for human consumption.[3]

Commercially, what evolves is a delicate balance between pesticides that are strong enough to do their job against the pests, yet weak enough not to cause any damage to man.

So back to my colleague's very real and practical question: From the standpoint of pesticides, are you better off eating fresh or processed produce? Does processing increase or decrease pesticide levels? Unfortunately, the pesticide question is one where there are the fewest clear-cut answers since much depends on the specific pesticide and the processing techniques used.

If you're the type who feels protected by governmental agencies, this is a good place to continue your faith in them, because, as you'll see, there isn't much else you can do.

The story goes like this: The Environmental Protection Agency sets levels for the amount of pesticide residue allowed and these tolerance levels are then enforced by the Food and Drug Administration. The EPA adjusts the tolerance levels on the basis of long-term consumption, maximum possible consumption, whether the produce is to be sold fresh or processed, on a mythical average daily intake, and the amount of pesticides in other foods. What it doesn't take into account is protecting anyone whose eating patterns are different from the norm . . . someone, for example, on a carrot binge.

The Environmental Defense League says that the high temperatures necessary in some kinds of processing may increase, decrease, or have no effect on toxicity. Some pesticides

[3] I have since learned to manage the snails. I use ashes from my fireplace to make an impenetrable barrier.

are so stable that temperature will not effect them and several others change drastically with temperature. The bottom line is this: if the tolerance levels are heeded, it doesn't much matter if the produce is fresh or processed, and many fruits and vegetables have no residues of pesticides.

The general rule is that the amount allowed as residue is no more than 1/100 of the smallest amount that has been found medically toxic. In the case of carcinogens, the tolerance is supposed to be 0, but as you'll see later, carcinogenic *by-products* are not so protected.

There are several levels of safety checks. The tolerance levels are set for the part of fruit or vegetable that is to be consumed. If only the pulp is used, the peel may have higher levels than if the whole fruit were to be consumed. In theory, there is an additional safety valve because the FDA can do a spot check on produce and confiscate those that are higher than tolerances. However, considering all the farms across America that use pesticides, it is obviously impossible physically to police all of them.

One of the side effects of FDA smugness about setting tolerances is that these amounts do not take into account the breakdown level of pesticides, which may be even more toxic than the original pesticide. For example, with processing, a common fungicide, EBDC, (ethylene bis dithio carbamate) breaks down to ETU, which in animal experiments has been shown to cause birth defects. A study comparing spinach reveals levels of ETU in canned vegetables.

SAMPLES:

Spinach	ppm ETU
Fresh:	0.12–0.36
Frozen:	0
Canned:	0.80

A monitoring program initiated in 1972 by the Canadian government found that 33 per cent of food samples contained detectable ETU residues. In particular, samples of canned spinach and orange peels had averages of 0.047 ppm and 0.083 ppm ETU, respectively.

A recent study of the effects of commercial food processing on residues of ETU appears to support findings that during commercial processing, as well as home cooking, EBDC residues on food are converted to ETU, causing a subsequent increase in ETU residues. This study is being reviewed by EPA scientists.

Although carcinogens used as pesticides are supposed to be set at 0 tolerance levels, the ETU situation is an example of a carcinogenic pesticide by-product escaping regulation because the breakdown into that by-product occurs during processing.

SOME COMMONLY ASKED QUESTIONS ABOUT PESTICIDES

* *What happens when you get too much pesticide?*

In the United States there have been no reported deaths of consumers caused by pesticides. There are, however, cases of accidental poisonings at the farm and manufacturing levels and many of these commercially used pesticides are also used by consumers in home gardening. So, if they don't get you in the grocery store, they can still get you in the garden. Products containing dieldrin, heptachlor, and chlordane are commonly used by home gardeners as well as commercial growers to control indoor and outdoor pests. These compounds do not wash away, but may last indoors for literally a lifetime. In heated rooms or in sunlight, the chemicals vaporize and become chronic poisons to be absorbed through the skin and eyes and by inhalation. The remarkable high dermal toxicity of chlordane was illustrated by the death of a factory worker a few hours after she spilled chlordane on her dress and skin. The footnote here is caution whenever you're using pesticides.

* *Is it necessary to wash fresh produce to remove pesticides that may remain?*

There's a variety of opinion on the usefulness of washing. A spokesperson for the United Fresh Fruit and Vegetable Association feels that it's a good practice to wash for general hygiene, but he also feels the tolerances are sufficiently stringent that washing will do little to affect pesticide levels. A spokesperson from the Environmental Defense Fund suggested washing produce in a solution of mild soap or in a mild acid solution of vinegar and water. But all the scrubbing or peeling you do may be for naught, depending on the type of pesticide you're trying to wash off.

There are two kinds of pesticides: the systemic, which is taken up by the plant tissue, and the contact, which works on the outer layer of the plant. For the consumer, there should be no difference, since both must comply with set tolerance levels. But for the consumer who is concerned, the contact pesticide residues can be totally removed by peeling the product, whereas there is no way to remove residues from the interior. Since the consumer has no way of knowing what kinds of pesticides were used, he or she can be scrubbing and peeling to no avail.

* *Are there practical alternatives to pesticides in the future, or are we stuck with this mixed blessing?*

One alternative that seems to be popular with the public is not to use pesticides at all anymore. In a Family Food Study conducted for *Woman's Day* magazine, half of the 1,188 respondents favored a ban on pesticides, even though this action might result in more expensive fruits and vegetables.

A more practical solution perhaps is that more and more farmers are switching from pesticides to integrated pest control and organic farming. An interesting study is being done by Barry Commoner, Director of the Washington University Center for Biology of Natural Systems, in which he's comparing yields, cost of production, and amount of labor with organic and chemical farms in the Midwest. Preliminary results show the yields are nearly equal and that organic farmers have the added advantage of lower costs since they don't need to buy pesticides.

EATING OUT:
A *Survival Guide*

As food service industry sales soar over $94 *billion* a year, the responsibility for providing adequate nutrition is shifting from the home kitchen to restaurants. By 1985, it is projected that, if the economy doesn't worsen, one out of two meals will be eaten out. (According to the Bureau of Labor Statistics if the head of the household is under twenty-five, chances are his family is *now* spending 50 per cent of its food budget eating out.) The type of food eating establishments serve and how it is handled is a nutritional concern, or should be. But often there is an astounding gap between attitudes about good nutrition in the home and what one does when one is eating out. In a nutshell: when people go out to eat, good nutrition tends to go out the window.

Dr. Howard Appledorf of the University of Florida points out an interesting angle—in the home most of us remember our parents telling us to "eat our vegetables." "But," asks Dr. Appledorf, "how would we respond if the waitress in a restaurant came by and said, 'You haven't finished your broccoli'?" You probably wouldn't like it.

The responsibility for providing good nutrition has shifted from a visible parent and an accepted authority figure to an unknown, invisible person, the chef (if you're lucky), preparing the meal in the restaurant kitchen, or to a large food processor that prepares giant quantities of food in advance and ships to restaurants on request. But how do you know what the food practices of a particular restaurant are, or what the nutritional consequences may be for you and your family?

In this chapter I describe some of the more devious tricks of the restaurant trade and suggest a game plan for survival that should help you order the most nutritious foods and then know if indeed you were served the food you ordered. I'll also examine some of the new trends on the horizon.

Because one naturally tends to think of the fast-food chains as nutritional bandits, they make too easy a target. First let's look at full-service, sit-down restaurants.

 ## Who Cares About Nutrition?

When I started investigating the restaurant scene, I was curious about the educational requirements of the people responsible for the food served to so many people. I wanted to know if people involved in the restaurant business—from administrators to chefs—received any nutrition education as part of their training, and if so, what kind. I wondered how likely it was that the information these students received, if they did, was practical enough and in-depth enough to actually be incorporated as a meaningful part of their everyday food experiences. I was curious if the schools were training new people to enter the food profession who would feel a responsibility to ask how can I make this dish more *nutritious,* as well as how can it be made cheaper, faster, tastier, and prettier.

I started with the venerable Culinary Institute of America. The most prominent professional cooking school in America, the institute trains some 1,500 students each year to go into the restaurant business. I received their curriculum and saw that in a first-term course called "Introduction to the Culinary Arts," topics like personal grooming, food service mathematics, food chemistry, and nutrition were lumped together. Theirs didn't seem to be an in-depth approach dealing with the wide range of nutritional concerns in institutional food situations. On my trip to Hyde Park, New York, to look over the Institute's facilities, never once was the subject of nutrition even mentioned as one of the hundreds of things one might learn.

The California Culinary Academy is located on the opposite coast, in San Francisco. Among food consultants, it is considered a good school. A spokesperson for the Academy told me on the phone that their nutrition course is "3 hours a week for 16 months." My skeptical side didn't let me believe that, so I sent for their curriculum. Sure enough, from "pulled sugar" to "the ancient art of clay cooking," their course catalogue didn't offer one course that could even be wildly construed as having to do with nutrition.

Something's missing from your education

Our country's two biggest schools, which turn out most of the people in the restaurant business (chefs trained at these institutes run restaurants ranging from Holiday Inns and Marriott Hotels to tiny bistros) are all but ignoring nutrition. Why?

A California-based food consultant, Leon Gottlieb, told me "Nutrition is an expensive process and the problem is that the training schools will not teach it unless the food service industry *demands* it." It's a chain of events. If the consumer demands that restaurants serve more nutritiously selected and prepared food, then restaurants will begin demanding that their chefs have this training. The schools will have to revise their curriculums to cater to this new consciousness on the part of the dining-out public.

PRIMARY AREAS OF CONCERN

Some of the most important areas for concern with regard to food served in restaurants are those in which nutritional abuse is blatant.

* Loss of nutrients in salads and vegetables. This relates to the methods of preparation, cooking, holding, and the span of time between preparation and consumption.

* Extremely high sodium content. This relates to salt added at various stages of the cooking process.

* Higher saturated fat content of restaurant food versus food cooked at home. This relates to the kind of food cooked, the way it is cooked, and the oils used.

* Food spoilage and food poisoning. This relates to poor food handling practices, the most common being food that is frozen, is partially thawed, and then refrozen.

* Large batch cooking. More waste and less taste.

* The *type* of equipment used in the professional kitchen is important because it can affect nutrient retention. The choices are:

Cooking equipment: e.g., kettles, ovens, steamers, fryers.

Holding equipment: (a) Cold: refrigerators, freezers; (b) Hot: e.g., insulated cabinets, heated cabinets.

Conditioning equipment: e.g., convection ovens, steamers.

Serving equipment: e.g., insulated containers, steam tables, infrared lamps.

THE PROFESSIONALS

But the training schools aren't the only ones with a difference of opinion on how important nutrition is. The professionals in the field, the food consultants who set up restaurants around the country and the world, are the theoreticians for the restaurant industry, and they differ sharply when it comes to the question of nutrition. Some care, most don't.

At the positive end of the spectrum is Dr. G. E. Livingston. Dr. Livingston, a professor of nutrition at New York University and a restaurant consultant with Food Science Associates in Dobbs Ferry, New York, has worked with restaurants ranging from fastfood places like Kentucky Fried Chicken and Nathan's Famous to military bases like Fort Lee and Fort Lewis. He says nutrition is the *last* factor considered. "Restaurants look at cost, labor productivity, capital outlay, energy consumption and sometimes, but not always, these hard commercial concerns are in conflict with good nutrition."

In Dr. Livingston's experience, the only attention the commercial food sector pays to nutrition is the "diet" meal. "But even these," he says, "are frequently not well planned from a nutritional point of view. The typical diet plate has a broiled burger that is high in fat, cottage chese that is often creamed and therefore high in fat, and canned peaches that are high in sugar. And the diet broiled fish is slathered with butter."

Why restaurants aren't doing better is probably because many people running them feel pretty much like George Lang, a famous New York-based restaurant consultant who is at the opposite end of the spectrum from Livingston. George Lang, who has set up some of the snazziest restaurants around the world, says, that for him, good nutrition, and even being concerned about it, has to do with a tasteless kind of food that he associates with being sick or recovering from a sickness. What he *is* interested in is a "juicy, dramatic, living dangerously attitude toward food."

These stories repeat themselves again and again. I was talking with a San Francisco-based restaurant consultant, Jay Perkins, and I asked him if in his many consultations over the years, nutrition was ever voiced as a concern of the restaurants he worked for. He said, "Never! Never!" I asked him if, in helping to set up restaurants, the restaurateurs ever asked him practical questions such as: What kind of utensils should I use for the best nutrient retention? How far in advance can I make my salads without an appreciable nutrient loss? What holding situations retain nutrients best over a long period of time? How does the common restaurant practice of reusing cooking oils affect my customers' health? Jay said not one restaurant in his 10 years in the restaurant consulting business had ever asked those questions. He said that sometimes, good nutrition wins out, but it's always in a convoluted way. Restaurants don't set out to achieve better nutrition, it sneaks in as part of something else. "One of the best examples of good nutrition sneaking in with technology," says Jay, "is the Vischer steamer unit. It's one of the most efficient ways for a restaurant to cook small amounts of vegetables very quickly. The customer ends up getting better nutrition, freshly steamed vegetables prepared moments before they are served." "But," Jay adds, "don't kid yourself—efficiency was the reason behind it."

Tricks of the Restaurant Trade

In trying to find out about restaurant practices, what they are doing right and what they could be doing better, I needed to discover the tricks of the trade.

Most restaurant consultants I spoke with said they didn't think consumers should be told these tricks of the trade. Mr. Leon Gottlieb of L.A. also agrees that consumers should not be informed, just as people go to a movie without knowing all the ins and outs of the movie-making business, he feels there should be magic in eating out, that the mystery should be retained. He is all for flambéeing entrees at the table for added excitement.

Tricks of the restaurant trade

To assure that restaurant suppliers and industry people would talk to me in a confidential way, a way they wouldn't talk to a writer, I decided to be one of them. For several weeks in Los Angeles, I posed as a would-be restaurateur. My "restaurant-to-be" was to feature health food, but I always indicated I was interested in taking any short cuts they had to offer, any processed foods that could pass as fresh. My menu would be salads, vegetables, poultry, fish. Since all the suppliers wanted to know how many my restaurant would seat (how big their sales would be), I said it would seat 100. I went so far in my charade as to find a location for

my restaurant on Main Street in Santa Monica and I named it Josie's, after my grandmother. I was ready to meet my suppliers.

What I learned from these meetings will never let me look at another restaurant in exactly the same way again. I was aware that some of what was disclosed went on, but the extent astounded me, and probably will astound you, too. Most of these tricks are done in the name of saving money and labor and end up fooling the consumer.

Since Josie's Restaurant was now in "business," I started searching industry publications like *Restaurant News* and *Food and Equipment Product News* to select suppliers who could show me some of the "short cuts." The ads alone in these publications reveal a fascinating story of where the restaurant industry is today. Try these:

From Presto Food Products: "You may never buy sour cream again. Presto Cater-S™ Sour Dressing can fool just about everyone into thinking it's real sour cream . . . Use it and make every taste bud tingle. Especially your bookkeeper!"

From Menu-Ready comes a Menu-Ready Tuna Salad: "Only Menu-Ready canned salad can offer uniformity in taste and texture. Price stability. A year's shelf life . . . the only surprise is great taste."

From Armour comes: "Pin-striped Pork Loin." The pin-striping is their way of saying it already has the grill marks on it so restaurants do not need to bother to grill it. They can microwave it in seconds.

THE FRESH PRODUCE TRICKS

With my disguise in order, I decided to start by meeting with a sales representative from Redi-Spuds of America, a company that supplies fresh produce to restaurants. I was especially interested in fresh produce because I thought how *much* can you do to a green salad? A green salad can't be frozen or canned, so it must be pretty pure, no? Since I didn't represent a major new account for my salesman (too few seats), and he was moving more toward the catering side of the business, he was more candid than other salesmen I was to meet in the future.

He walked in the door lugging a $3' \times 1'$ plastic bag of precut tossed green salad. He started the conversation immediately by presenting me with this 10-pound bag of salad and telling me that when I got my restaurant rolling, this was how I could purchase salad. Ordering it this way would substantially reduce my labor and materials cost. How could I compete with an already prepared 10-pound bag at $2.30, if I had to buy the ingredients and hire someone to wash, dry, and cut the greens? Besides, all my competitors were doing it! His firm's policy was to deliver on Monday and their salads lasted through Friday. If the salads went bad by Friday, he'd come and replace it. That's 5 days for salad to stay fresh and crunchy.

I wanted to know *how* they did it. The trick, he revealed, is that their fresh produce is treated with a preservative so that it will last from *7 to 10 days* under refrigeration. The preservative is sodium bisulfite,[1] but as the salesman said, "just one tenth of one per cent," that's all that's allowable by law.

I tasted his pretossed green salad, the all too familiar kind that's served in many restaurants, mostly pale leaves with a few strips of purple cabbage thrown in here and there

Sodium Bisulfite or how to fix a salad.

for color. When I commented on how almost unnaturally crunchy it was, he said, "Yes, and that's after it's been sitting in my hot car for 5 hours before I got here." (Compare that to the average salad made at home that often wilts before dinner is over.)

His salad *did* last for six days in fine shape in my refrigerator. On the seventh day, the edges started turning yellow and brown, but if I had been in the restaurant business that would have posed no problem. I could have sprinkled on White-All, a preservative that gets rid of the darkening colors and leaves the salad supposedly still salable.

As you know from Chapter 5, Salads, and the Salad Score Sheet, we eat salads and greens for a variety of nutrients, mostly vitamins A and C, both of which oxidize over a short period of time. For that reason they should be prepared as close to when they are eaten as possible. It seems ironic to me that in restaurants, especially salad-bar type establishments, a customer often selects a salad because it's a healthy food item, but if it's days old, filled with preservatives, and then has preservatives sprinkled on top, too, how does that salad hold up nutritionally? Not very well, I'm afraid. (And you thought the only things with preservatives came in cardboard boxes?)

My salesman told me restaurants don't have a choice. "The restaurant business is a whore's business and you're competing for every penny. A salad is a high profit item and it can cost the restaurateur as little as

---

[1] Sodium bisulfite is listed by the FDA as a GRAS substance—generally recognized as safe at permitted levels of usage. It is now under review as part of the current FDA review of all GRAS substances. Its presence in restaurant salads is questionable, not because the additive may not be safe for consumption, but because adding preservatives to supposedly fresh foods without informing the consumer represents a questionable practice. John Taylor, who is with the legal branch of the FDA in Washington, D.C., told me that although food served in restaurants falls under State jurisdiction, he felt that there should be some indication on the menu that the restaurant was using preservatives.

10¢ for a dinner salad my way and he can charge $1.39 or more. All the salad bars use this." Jay Perkins, the restaurant consultant, has since told me that from a cost and nutrition standpoint, there is no excuse for restaurants *not* making their own salad.

Stunned by the salesman's long-lived tossed salad, I proceeded down the list of other salads Redi-Spuds had to offer. He informed me their potato salad and macaroni salad both have a shelf life of 6–8 *weeks*. Their coleslaw lasts only 1 week. Their raisin and carrot salad, which was a new offering catering to the health food crowd, lasts 1 month (wouldn't the health crowd die to know *that?*). All the while this discussion was going on, he proceeded to drop the names of high and mighty, fancy and not-so-fancy restaurants and delicatessens that use his prepared produce in Los Angeles.

His company also handles carrot sticks. They are prepared the same way as the salad with the same preservatives and last for 1 week to 10 days under refrigeration. How nutritious could these carrot sticks possibly be? "Well," he said, "hospitals use them." No wonder patients are often malnourished.

My salesman revealed another standard trick of the restaurant business: prepared foods. As we moved from salads into other vegetable items, he gleefully told me about a party he had just catered for Jack Lemmon, the actor, in which he "fooled everyone." For appetizers he served pre-prepared breaded frozen vegetable products—zucchini sticks, stuffed mushrooms, and bell pepper rings, all frozen. When the party-goers asked him if he made all the food, he said, "Well, my chef did." (Meaning, I suppose, the chef back in some food factory in Indiana.) In telling me the story, he was ecstatic that he had fooled the guests with his frozen wares. I've since tasted these frozen, breaded, deep-fried vegetables, and if they are properly handled— thawed and cooked according to directions— they can be quite tasty and nutritious, as well. But if you're being charged for the fresh and the frozen is substituted, you're being shortchanged. If a restaurant or caterer is taking a short cut here with pre-pre-

pared vegetables, this is a loud clue to alert you that they are probably relying on other pre-prepared items as well.

PRE-PREPARED PROCESSED FOODS

I had the feeling that the pre-prepared salads, vegetables, and poultry items were just the tip of the iceberg in the multimillion-dollar prepared food business. I've always thought of restaurants as places where food was prepared, cooked, and could be bought and eaten. Obviously, a common misconception. The latest edition of Webster's defines a restaurant by leaving out the preparation-cooking aspect altogether: ". . . a place where meals can be bought and eaten." Obviously Webster's has caught on to the processed food business. If restaurants legally had to display prominent signs saying "No Cooking Done on These Premises," I wonder if the trend toward processed food would continue so unabated.

Dr. Livingston told me that the practice of separating food *service* from food *preparation* is becoming commonplace. He predicts (I hope incorrectly) that in the very near future, in all but a very few luxury restaurants, total food preparation from raw ingredients will be unknown.

I was telling a friend about the new era in the restaurant business where restaurants have become reheating and dispatching depots for frozen foods processed elsewhere. Her reaction was, "Does it make a difference?" It makes a difference to me, and it should to most consumers because it is a question of deception and potential loss in nutritional values.

People who would not think of eating a frozen TV dinner at home are eating them regularly and probably unknowingly in restaurants and paying a high rate. We've all tasted these precooked foods on airline flights where we are captive and the food is served undisguised in the expected plastic and aluminum trays. When I complained to Nancy Bishop, a travel agent, about airline food, she said, "What do you expect from twice-cooked food? It's cooked once in the processing kitchens and then reheated in the airline galley." As processed foods continue to saturate the restaurant market as well, Nancy's question—What do you expect from twice-cooked food?—is becoming equally valid in many restaurants across our country. It certainly is not the picky question of do these prepared foods *taste* good? Some of them, like the Sara Lee institutional products, do give good food value and most people would agree they taste good. And this is not to say that all processed foods are good or bad, but it does reveal the restaurant business as the shell business that it is becoming. The shell is the real estate space that the restaurateur fills with atmosphere and décor, maybe even some music, and then hauls in the pre-prepared foods.

The more restaurants rely on processed foods, the less the consumers have any control over the healthfulness of the food they are eating. You can't ask for no salt, for a polyunsaturated fat to be used in the cooking, or for any substitution, because the food is only being reheated where you are ordering; it is not in any way being "cooked to order."

Back at Josie's when it came to turkey products, the previous salesman told me that I'd never want to cook my own fresh turkey, "too much shrinkage." So I feigned interest in their turkey roll instead of breast of turkey because it offered a 30 per cent price savings. He told me, "Turkey roll is injected with water to make it appear moist. *That stuff is for selling, not eating.*" Another substitution that is popular with restaurants selling breakfasts is substituting turkey ham for regular ham. The price difference to the restaurant is substantial, but the salesman admitted that this is one of those times when you *do* have to 'fess up and tell the customer what he's getting. (But I wonder how often and how truthfully even this is done, especially when processors like the Plantation Company go to all the trouble of forming their product into a ham shape—"Natural Hickory Smoked Turkey Oval Ham.") In the case of turkey ham it is not a matter of getting less nutrition, for the engineered turkey ham product

is actually healthier: It has less fat than traditional pork ham, and if it has been made without the usual preservatives that go into ham, so much the better for you. The problem instead is one of misrepresentation.

Take 1 from Column A and 9,999 from Column B

After meeting with Redi-Spuds and having conversations with professional consultants, I felt street-wise enough to start meeting with big-time suppliers. I decided on International Food Service Company, one of the three biggest food distributors in the nation, with annual sales of $260 million. Their sales representative, whom I shall refer to as Mr. S., called on me promptly, just as if I was going to be his biggest account, but he didn't bring any samples. When I expressed my disappointment, telling him I hoped to have a taste of some of his company's offerings, he explained that his company had over *10,000* frozen entrees to choose from and it was impossible in advance for him to know what I might like to sample. (I was astonished at the numbers. Even the Department of Agriculture puts the number of convenience food items introduced in the last 5 years, from all firms together, at only 5,299.) To make his point, Mr. S. pulled out his firm's

Product Sales Book, which is 1″ thick with single-space typing on both sides of the pages. When I expressed my amazement at the breadth of the pre-prepared and frozen items that were available, from entrees like kosher beef pot roast dinners and Mexican cheese enchiladas and chili rellenos to Greek stuffed grape leaves and even a frozen avocado dip, Mr. S. said, "There's *nothing* you want for your restaurant that you can't buy frozen and prepared." Using these products I wouldn't have to hire a decent chef; I could hire cheap laborers who would follow directions on the package for microwaving. That appears to be the way many restaurants prepare their main items. But then wouldn't my restaurant be serving the same food as other restaurants down the street? "No," he said, "put your own touch on it—a sprig of parsley, a sauce—and call it by your own name."

I decided I had heard enough and was ready to taste some of these foods and we set up a meeting at his plant in Carson City, California. His departing message to me was: "Dealing with International Food Service is like dealing with the Bank of America, because we are owned by the Bank of America." I thought: I'm not dealing with food or good nutrition or establishing a restaurant anymore, I'm dealing with the Bank of America!

At his invitation, I went through the thick Product Sales Book he had left behind and selected thirty items I was interested in sampling, from ground turkey (restaurants can substitute this for ground veal and save money) to eggvantage (12″ long rolls of frozen hard-boiled eggs) to stuffed green peppers and frozen asparagus spears (which aren't available to the consumer processed in this way).

The Restaurant Business Isn't What People Think It Is

The International Food Service plant has such tight security it resembles a missile site. At every stopping point from parking attendant to upstairs receptionist, I was name-tagged, checked in, and buzzed up to the next station. The security seemed excessive to me. I wondered what sort of tricks they were up to that they needed such protective security? I met my salesman and the firm's public relations man and was handed a white lab coat to wear while touring their plant, which covered several acres.

They said they serviced over 1,000 restaurants in the San Fernando Valley alone, and restaurants all over the *world,* too. Not only do they service restaurants and hotels (Marriott and Hyatt, to name two), but hospitals, schools, nursing homes, caterers, airlines, steamships, railroads (Amtrak), amusement

parks (Knotts Berry Farms and Disneyland), stadiums, convention centers, and military facilities.

I was beginning to understand how the food items they make could have a major impact in establishing people's food preferences and taste patterns. With their thousands of commercial customers feeding millions of consumers, they have the power to improve the health of the country. By making just a few changes to start, like not adding salt to their foods, for instance, they could improve the health and possibly lessen hypertension in this country. I was also becoming aware that food processors, especially big ones like International Food Service, *must* begin to make a concerted effort to examine and modify their food processing procedures for the health of the public.

After walking through the frozen hamburger patty room (there were so many of them a snow shovel was being used to transfer them from one bin to another), I went on to the *pièce de résistance:* a sub-zero hurricane-fenced room with 30′ high stacks of frozen foods. My guides explained to me that this room represented the restaurant business *today*. This was their Fort Knox where they stored their 10,000 frozen prepared foods ranging from Macaroni Noodle Soufflés and 3 Star Salmon Nova trays to Mrs. K's 2.5″ Heat and Serve Potato Pancakes and Zippi Beef and Bean Unwrapped Burritos. I was assured that there were enough varieties of food frozen in this storeroom to run any kind of restaurant, *without hiring a chef.*

During the tour I asked if this huge business had anyone on its staff with a background in nutrition who could answer my questions relating to the nutritional quality of the food I might be selecting. "Oh yes!" my guides said. "There is a dietician available for nutritional advice to all the restaurants International Food Service handles." *One* person for thousands of restaurants. Either there aren't many questions asked, or there aren't many that are answered. I think it's the latter, since I tried reaching their nutritionist for days, left repeated messages, and none of my calls were returned.

We finally arrived at the Pub, where I met

"*My compliments to the Chef.*"

their "chef." Their chef was masquerading in kitchen whites complete with toque blanch, but he wasn't a chef in any old-fashioned sense of the word. He was a chef in the Orwellian *1984* sense: the lunch we sampled was not what he had *made* for us, but what he had "fixed" up, assembly-line style, from frozen pre-prepared items. The menu for our sample lunch[2] was:

Green Salad with Crab Legs
Chicken Cordon Bleu with Sauce
California Blend Vegetables
Scalloped Potatoes
Peach Compote

Commenting on the lunch, I said I thought my restaurant would use a salad dressing we made ourselves to avoid the questionable BHA and BHT found in commercially available dressings. They laughed. They said that I couldn't afford to make it myself, that it was too expensive to buy the ingredients, to wash all the pots afterward, and besides it might vary from time to time. I became aware that this company was selling Consistency, Standardization, and easy Inventory Control, but it had little to do with good taste, or consideration of nutritional quality.

They were proud of how *flexible* their vegetables were. The "chef" boasted he had cooked them that morning and they had been sitting around all day. That's *flexibility?* The scalloped potatoes were made from dehydrated flakes and tasted like chewing on dry paper. I sampled two Chicken Cordon Bleus: both were very salty and oily. (Although in a restaurant a consumer can't request the cook to "hold the salt" because processed items come presalted, in the rare instance where a restaurant has stocked a modified, salt-free item, that can be ordered instead.)

For dessert we had a frozen peach compote. Fruits don't freeze well, and this was served in August when fresh peaches were in abundant supply. When I asked why they

[2] I was told this menu represented $1.50 in food cost when prepared totally from frozen processed items. Quite a saving from restaurants doing it from scratch.

didn't recommend that I go with some fresh products when they were available, they said, "There would be no consistency. Today you'd have fresh peaches and canned asparagus. Tomorrow, canned peaches and fresh asparagus. And do you really want to peel peaches? There has to be a compromise somewhere!" (And you wonder why restaurant food from Omaha to San Diego often tastes the same? *It is the same food!*) Why go out for a meal that you'd never consider serving in your own home?

When I staged a timid protest and said that I thought at Josie's we would try to serve more fresh items, especially vegetables, they said, "You cannot serve mainly fresh-prepared food, because it isn't done. *The restaurant business isn't what people think it is.* From meat to vegetables, we clean, cut, and cook it for you. We can guarantee the price on frozen foods for 90 days. With fresh you have to swing with daily market fluctuations. We're the experts. You're not. You make it different with your garnish, your sauce, but everyone starts with the same." I cringed to think that at that moment over 1,000 restaurants in nearby San Fernando Valley were serving the exact same Chicken Cordon Bleu I had just tasted.

Perhaps it was my feigned naïveté that prompted Mr. S. to confess that *years* ago, way back in 1958, he had been a pretty "hot potato" himself, a European-trained chef. But, he said, "You don't see European chefs associated with the actual *preparation* of the foods anymore. Now the chefs are the food *directors* for the big chains and they prepare the menus and the Chicanos do the preparation." This European-trained chef also told me if he were starting a restaurant today, he wouldn't do any cooking of his own, except for meat. He would put in a

steamer and a microwave and that would be it.

When lunch was over, I asked if I couldn't sample a broader range of items. They told me that by buying their products, I was paying *them* to do the tasting for me. None of their other customers requested extensive samplings, and they didn't have the facilities to open up so many cases. Apparently restaurants across America were ordering this stuff *taste unseen.*

From their thousands of items, the "chef" brought out a few more. An item of particular interest was a 12" long frozen egg roll (and you thought an egg roll was a Chinese specialty?) which lasts 1–2 weeks once thawed and its advantage is that it makes perfect egg slices. The slices *looked* like an egg, but tasted like nothing. The company's fresh turkey breast had a strange wetness to it that had nothing to do with moisture. And a vanilla pudding was sickly sweet, with a taste that not even faintly resembled a vanilla bean.

Eating-out Survival Guide

Meeting with these industry representatives and talking with others, I realized the consumer needs a survival guide to know what he or she is getting when ordering food in a restaurant. Some states have recently passed Truth in Menus laws which make it a crime to deliver something other than what is described on the menu (see Trends, page 253). But even then, even if it appears to be fresh, you often don't know if the item has preservatives, if it was made on the premises, or if it was processed elsewhere.

To combat some of these questionable and camouflaged practices, I've compiled an Eating-out Survival Guide. It is a list of questions to ask when you're eating out—designed to raise your consciousness about what exactly it is you're going to be served before you even order it.

In restaurants, the average American is too nice, too understanding, too patient, too easily intimidated, and as a result often gets shortchanged. Don't feel you're out of bounds by asking questions. When you buy other consumer products, a sweater, for example, if the information about its fabric content and its wash and care is not plainly labeled, you always ask, right? The food you eat is much more important to your health than a sweater.

If the restaurant industry was more health and nutrition conscious, and if menus were written with less deception, and if one of the requirements for a restaurant to get a license was to have a staff person with a background in nutrition, then just maybe you wouldn't have to be asking these questions. Obviously you won't want to ask the Survival Guide questions every time you eat out, but at the very least, keep these questions in mind when you order from a menu because they signal problem areas.

Another point. You can't arm wrestle a waiter to make him swear to tell you the truth, but I've found waiters are often helpful in supplying useful information. If a waiter doesn't know an answer, have him check with the chef or the owner. If your questions aren't answered to your satisfaction, order something else and think about going to a different restaurant next time.

BASIC QUESTIONS TO ASK:

Salad

Is it prepared on the premises?
This is an important question because salads filled with preservatives are often hauled in for your eating enjoyment. If it's prepared on the premises, it's less likely to have preservatives.

When was it made?
If it's prepared on the premises, *when* was it made? Since the nutrients in salads oxidize over a period of time, if it's made reasonably close to serving time, you stand a better chance of getting a salad that still has some nutritional impact.

Madame, 1898 was a very good year for salad.

Is it possible to get a salad with some dark greens?

The standard premade restaurant salad is an assortment of almost lily-white greens. The darker the greens, the more likely it is made on their premises and it's likely to have more nutrients. If the restaurant is indeed making its own salads, when you place your salad order, ask yours to be made with darker leaves ("Heavy on the spinach, romaine, and watercress, please. Light on the head lettuce.")

Are the hard-boiled eggs made on the premises?

If you're ordering a chef's salad or a salad niçoise with hard-boiled eggs, you would do well to ask this question. If the restaurant is using a frozen egg roll, although it has the same nutrition, the freezing saps the egg of its taste. You're well within bounds to ask for a substitution. Perhaps some additional strips of cheese instead?

Vegetables

Are they fresh or frozen?

Although by the time most restaurants get finished they both have about the same nutrition, fresh still usually has the better texture, color, and taste. With potato products, just about the only time you get a fresh potato is with a baked potato. Stick with the baked, unless you want dehydrated flakes mashed or hashed into a familiar-looking shape. *If the vegetable is exotic-sounding or has some complicated process done to it, it's probably processed.* Processed breaded onion rings, zucchini rounds and sticks, breaded okra, and eggplant can all be quite delicious; their only disadvantage is the potential for nutrient loss.

Are they steamed or boiled?

From Chapter 1, Vegetables, you know that steaming is the preferred method, nutritionally. If the vegetables are coming from a steam table, ask if they have been cooked in advance. Vegetables put on a steam table lose their nutrients as the hours while away and the vegetables are, in effect, getting an unnecessary second cooking if indeed they were cooked before as is usually the case.

Main Course

Do I have a choice regarding the size of the portion?

Until recently, the only different size offered was a children's portion. Now restaurants are beginning to offer a variety of sizes to fit different appetites and caloric needs more appropriately. (See Trends, page 253.)

What kind of oil is used?

Because it is cheap and reusable, 15 per cent of restaurants use animal fat that is highly saturated. Some restaurants use an animal/vegetable combination. Ask if they have a pure vegetable oil they could use.

Is it prepared on the premises?

This question doesn't have so much to do with nutrition, but with getting the best value for your money and with avoiding misrepresentation. It would be easier if the main courses came with their freezer tags still attached, but since they don't, how can you *tell* if the foods you are being served are the processed items I've been discussing? Here are some giveaway clues:

*   If the menu goes on for pages, I guarantee the restaurant is using at least some frozen, prepared entrees. There is no way they could possibly keep on hand the ingredients to do such a multitude of dishes. (A restaurant consultant told me the only way to run a successful restaurant these days where the food is cooked on the premises is with a limited menu of not more than 12 items.)

*   The frozen prepared entrees have a certain form and finish. They are *too* perfect. If they are browned, they are browned too perfectly. Their shape is too uniform, as if they have been made out of a mold (they have).

*   They have a pervasive saltiness. Although most restaurant food seems too salty to me, these prepared foods are especially so.

*   If the food is served at the snap of a finger, or the press of a microwave button, be suspicious.

*   High price is no indication of anything other than the sheer gall restaurants have in order to pass off a 75¢ entree for $12.

* An exotic-sounding name is no guarantee that it's made on the premises. In fact, the more exotic the less likely it is that restaurants can still actually hire chefs who know how to cook such complicated food.

DO'S AND DON'TS FOR SUCCESSFUL RESTAURANT DINING

* DO search out small restaurants with limited menus where the preparation and cooking is still done on the premises.

* DO look for restaurants where it is possible to see the kitchen. A working stove is a good sign.

* DON'T go to the large touristy hotels and restaurants and expect much, except frozen, prepared food items.

* DON'T think because the restaurant is serving foreign or ethnic food, it necessarily is made on the premises. Frozen, prepared entrees come French, Polish, Mexican, kosher . . .

* DO ask the waiter to remove your plate the instant you have finished the amount you want to eat. In Italy, the land of *bella figura,* the waiters whisk dirty plates away the moment it appears an eater is *about* to be finished. God forbid you should sit with a soiled plate in front of you. This is a good trick, too, for weight watchers. If you feel satisfied, and there's no food in front of you to continue picking at, how can you overeat?

* DO ask for a person bag to take the leftovers home. Although in most states you can't take your wine home, you can and should take your leftover food home. This is also a good tip for people of the clean-plate syndrome. When you feel you've eaten enough, instead of watching your waistline go out the window, ask for your person bag and eat the rest at another meal.

* DO call the restaurant in advance. Outline your requests—no salt, only fresh vegetables, etc., and ask if they can comply. If they can't, decide then if you want to go ahead and make a reservation.

* DO bring your own soy sauce to Japanese restaurants. Since Japanese restaurants use soy sauce in such quantities, most buy the cheapest and the strongest (saltiest) stuff around. Bring your own mild soy sauce (with less salt) and you'll enjoy your dinner more.

 Trends

Restaurant concepts used to last a good 15 years, but according to Joan Black Bakos, editor of *Restaurant News* magazine, the business is changing so constantly that new trends are starting all the time. Often, these trends, like salad bars and soup kitchens, show up first on college campuses and then successfully filter their way to standard restaurant establishments. Some of the latest food trends, like frozen yoghurt, first enjoyed their popularity on the West Coast and then headed east.

I thought maybe I was witnessing a trend in the making one day at Richard Simmon's Anatomy Asylum in Beverly Hills, California. A very clever restaurateur, Richard has combined a beautifully laid out 30' long salad bar with an exercise room. His clients exercise first and don't feel guilty about having just a little more from the salad bar. (But watch out for the calorie count at salad bars in general. Letuce sprinkled with lemon can have as few as 25 calories, but a plate laden with cottage cheese, potato

salad, lettuce, carrots, chives, bacon bits, croutons, and slathered in dressing can exceed 700 calories.)

Joan Black Bakos also revealed some schizoid behavior among today's restaurant-goers. "Although more attention is being paid to health food and the healthful preparation of foods, our reports show that dessert sales have never been higher!" Some of the trends in the making are:

* *Fish.* Seafood restaurant sales have increased 123 per cent in the 2 years between 1975 and 1977. More fish is eaten now in restaurants than at home.

* *Take out.* Always popular with Chinese restaurants and pizza joints, now better restaurants are starting to offer take out as well. This has a special appeal to the increasing numbers of working women.

* *Sedentary and active lifestyle menus.* This idea is being tossed about in restaurant circles and is a further refinement on the idea of offering a low calorie meal. It has been suggested that since dietary needs differ so greatly with lifestyle, whether you're using up a lot of calories as a lumberjack, or very few as an accountant, restaurant menus should reflect this varying need and make it easy for people to select a meal that is more appropriate to their caloric needs.

* *Diet restaurants.* In the Los Angeles area, there are many restaurants with names like "The Thinnery," which are trying to appeal to dieters who want to order more than a green salad when they eat out. In my casual survey of these diet restaurants, I found these establishments to be relying on food items that were highly preserved (and they didn't taste good either).

* *The cafeteria returns.* As more people are eating out and demanding freshly prepared, reasonably priced meals, the comeback of the old-fashioned cafeteria, with cooking done on the premises, is predicted.

Three trends I feel warrant a more in-depth examination are: truth in menus, portion variation, and nutritional labeling of restaurant foods.

TRUTH IN MENUS

As a result of the consumer movement truth in menus (that's the term used in Washington, D.C.), or accuracy in menus (that's New York City's term), has come to the forefront. Consumers were not satisfied to go into a restaurant and feel they were sometimes being hoodwinked. The emphasis is on the truthfulness of *menus* because in restaurants, the menu is all the consumer has to go on. In a department store or supermarket, you can *see* the merchandise before you buy it; in a restaurant, all you've got is a description on the menu, so that description should accurately reflect what is being served.

Truthfulness in menus is important because it's an economic issue for consumers. The misrepresentation that goes on in menus gives food items labels and names that refer to a higher quality, or greater desirability, than may actually be served in the restaurant. Because the restaurant purports to be serving better food, of course, it charges the consumer more.

Los Angeles

So far, the most active truthfulness in menus campaign has been waged in Los Angeles. The Los Angeles Community Health Services established an Office of the Food Detective and he had the law of California on his side. In California, the Sherman Food, Drug, and Cosmetic Law prohibits menu misrepresentation with criminal penalties for violations.

I followed the Los Angeles Food Detective, Dale Reeves, on his rounds one day. It was fascinating as we walked unannounced into back storage rooms, crawled into cellars, poked into pantries, and looked at restaurants in a way the average consumer can't (and probably wouldn't even *want* to). When the detective couldn't readily identify a suspected infraction (skate being substituted for scallop, for example), the item was taken back for laboratory analysis.

Dale Reeves told me that the three most common areas of infractions are: misrepresenting the quality of meat, the origin of the food, and unannounced substitutions. The geographic misrepresentation of the food's origins is a common merchandising gimmick that makes a restaurant look like it is doing something extra the competition isn't. To entice you, a restaurant might write that their fish is "flown in daily," or that it's "from Chesapeake Bay." If that fish never flew, or never slept in Chesapeake Bay, that restaurant is in trouble. Here are some examples of creative menu writing that may reflect geographic misrepresentation. Watch out for them when you next dine out.

* Colorado trout
* Maine lobster
* European ham
* Hawaiian mahimahi
* Wisconsin cheese
* Louisiana River trout
* Imported Swiss cheese
* Homemade apple pie

Beware also of the following merchandising terms used on a menu that refer to quality, quantity, or method of preparation:

* Best blend
* Our own special sauce
* Finest quality
* Roasted, sautéed, fried, boiled, baked, smoked, etc.

* Picture—three pieces of fish shown and consumer is served two.
* Fresh daily

In California, unannounced substitutions or offering food of lesser quality or value than indicated on the menu constitutes false advertising. Some typical substitutions to look for:

* Substituting frozen food items for fresh.
* Substituting a species of fish or meat other than described.
* Substituting nondairy products for dairy products.
* Substituting a type/cut of meat other than advertised.
* Substituting domestic products for imported products.
* Substituting a brand name other than advertised.

Evidence of this deception is everywhere. A friend and researcher, Joyce Baron, shared two stories with me. She and her husband stopped at a roadside café. Before ordering the soup, she asked if it was homemade. The waitress' baffling answer: "We get it already made and then we make it at home here." At Fisherman's Wharf in San Francisco, Joyce noticed a deliveryman carrying gallon containers of Bumble Bee canned crab meat underneath a restaurant's large sign proclaiming "Fresh Crab Daily."

Although Mr. Reeves has been working toward voluntary compliance, and has tried to emphasize education and co-operation, it is his experience that restaurants don't take corrective steps until they are caught.

Getting caught (and restaurants regularly are, in Los Angeles) has meant being fined as much as $5,000 or more, accompanied by a lot of negative publicity. The law provides for the fines and with repeated offenses prosecution and jail, but Mr. Reeves says, "We don't have repeaters."

Playing the devil's advocate for a moment, I asked Dale Reeves, since consumers go out to restaurants to enjoy themselves, if the consumer feels satisfied after his meal, do these

misrepresentations really matter? Let's say
Joe Francis eating breakfast couldn't tell that
Sam's Diner substituted turkey ham for Virginia baked ham, and the promised "fresh
grade AA eggs" were really scrambled
artificial egg product. Does it matter, if he
was satisfied and didn't know the difference?
Dale Reeves was adamant and livid. "It matters because the consumer is promised something that isn't delivered. The restaurants
knowingly perpetrate economic fraud on the
public and pocket the difference in profits."

If your town doesn't have a truth in menus
plan, contact Los Angeles for help in es-
tablishing one. Write: Food Detective,
County of Los Angeles, Department of
Health Services, 313 North Figueroa Street,
Los Angeles, California 90012.

Washington, D.C., and New York City

In Washington, D.C., the Department of Environmental Services has trained agents to go
into restaurants to check for violations. Their
system is different from Los Angeles': they
don't fine the restaurants, but work on a system of demerits and post a violation notice in
a prominent place in the restaurant. If the
restaurant gets too many demerits, supposedly, it is closed. I have not heard how well
their system is working.

A *Menu Dictionary,* which is a food language guide for Washington, D.C., diners, is
available free from the Environmental
Health Administration, District of Columbia,
Department of Environmental Services,
Room 300, Washington, D.C., 20004. It is
hoped that consumers will find the dictionary
useful in their efforts to make intelligent decisions when ordering meals.

In comparison, the New York City Accuracy in Menus (AIM) program seems more
like a case of Madison Avenue hype than a
program of real substance. AIM has little
enforcement punch behind it and it appears
to be the local Restaurant Association's attempt at self-regulation so that a government
body won't come in and do it. In New York,
consumers in a restaurant are still pretty
much on their own.

SIZE OF PORTIONS

There is a trend toward changing the *size* of
portions served in restaurants. It's about
time. When I walk into a restaurant, I am
served the same portion as my 200-pound
husband. Uniformly large portions create
needless waste for the restaurant and needless
temptation for the customer. Out of respect
for our food supply and because of a concern
for our national problem with obesity, restaurants should be offering a variety of portion
sizes, with corresponding price differences.
But this demands a new consciousness on
the part of restaurant diners: it isn't necessary to gorge themselves to feel they got
their money's worth.

I talked with two restaurant owners in
Manhattan's Greenwich Village about portion variation. I was eating at their restaurant, Chez Stadium, and was presented with
a stuffed fish that was big enough for all
three of us. The problem of portion size, they
told me, puts them in a double bind. As
restaurant owners, they would like to serve
more appropriate portions, but their customers like to see a heaping plate, even
if they can only eat half of it. I think the
solution lies one step further. If the customer were told in advance he or she had a
choice and that the choice also meant a
price saving, the customer might not feel
cheated with less of a heaping plate.

The Sheraton Hotels in Washington, D.C.,
have a pilot program to test "choice of portion." For example, a customer can order:

Escargots by the piece, 3 or 6
Oysters by the piece, 3 or 6
Steak, small or large
Chops—lamb or pork chops—1, 2, or 3
     chops
Prime ribs, 2 different sizes
Fish portions, by the piece
Shrimp cocktail, by the piece

According to Peter Karpaty, Executive
Vice-president, in charge of food, the Sheraton experiment has had a very positive reaction from the customers, and the program is
being expanded to the Midwest.

Size of portions

Although experimentation with portion sizes goes back a long way, and Sheraton has had some recent success with it, Joan Black Bakos, editor of *Restaurant News*, says that portion variation is difficult for restaurants. She does suggest, however, that customers ask specifically for small and large meat portions, which are often available upon request, even if the information isn't printed on the menu.

The trend to offering varying portions should be accelerated, but this will only come about if consumers make their preferences loudly heard. You could begin by calling your local Restaurant Association, or by making it your personal mission to request an appropriate portion when you go out. It can be accomplished when ordering simply by saying, "I can't eat *that* much. Can't I have a half portion?"

NUTRITIONAL LABELING

By now, the average grocery store shopper has gotten accustomed to the nutritional labeling on food items from cans of tomatoes to boxes of breakfast cereals. Very soon, if not already, that turkey sandwich you were served for lunch, or the steak you ordered at dinner, could be accompanied by nutritional labeling as well. Since 1977, the Food and Drug Administration has permitted restaurants to make advertising or labeling claims about the total nutritional value of a combination of foods (e.g., veal scallopini, pasta, and green salad), providing that complete nutrition information is available at both the point of ordering and the point of consumption. Restaurants can accomplish this by using placards, wall posters, printed napkins, and in some cases, printed bags for customers who carry food out. The people who want this information can refer to it; the people who don't, can ignore it.

Too often nutritional labeling can be a gimmick restaurants use to cloak the food they were going to serve anyway in more respectable terms. This means the consumer should read between the lines. For example, take the Mr. Steak restaurant chain. Some of their restaurants feature menus with "three nutritionally balanced meals based on sound nutritional principles." On closer inspection the menus are questionably "balanced" and the foods contain artificial ingredients. But in some instances (e.g., the Pizza Hut chain), the posted nutritional information can be used to make better food choices. For example, from a Pizza Hut menu you can quickly see that MSG is an ingredient in some of the pizzas, and you have the choice of whether you want it or not.

Fast Foods

In comparison with restaurant food just discussed, fast foods are *quick* order foods served in *quick* service restaurants. They include places like Denny's, Bagel Nosh, Taco Bell, and Pizza Hut.

How *fast* they are depends on the establishments. In a fast-food outlet, a wait of even a few minutes can seem interminable since we're conditioned to fast food being instant food. A food technologist who was about to retire from his consulting business, told me that we haven't seen anything on the fast-food scene yet. He says he has invented a 20-second pizza and a 20-second macaroni and cheese dish and that he's ready to go into business. Now that's *fast*.

In the restaurant expansion bingo game, the fast-food establishments are collecting the biggest winnings with $16 billion yearly sales. According to the Department of Agriculture, the fast-food establishments now account for 25 per cent of the food eaten away from home and this figure represents a 16 per cent growth in the decade between 1965 and 1975. The Commerce Department reported that as of the end of 1979, the number of franchised outlets had almost doubled to 66,000 from 36,600 in 1973.

In the inflation-ridden 1980s it's predicted by CREST (Consumer Reports on Eating Share Trends) that this growth is coming to an abrupt halt. Diners have less money to spend now and are cutting back on unnecessary driving because of high gas prices. But even if the fast-food chains don't continue to grow as quickly as they have in the past, there's no denying their popularity. Marketing experts offer a variety of reasons for their success. Take your pick:

* We're becoming a single nation, and singles eat out more because they get lonely in their apartments.

* Fast food fills the bill for increased numbers of working wives.

* The emphasis is on festivity. Ordering and eating, from fribbles to fishamejigs, can be fun.

* It's a modestly priced way to take the whole family out to dinner.

Fast-food chains suffer from an image problem of being classified as "junk food." (Who knows how phenomenal their growth rate would be if people thought a Big Mac was *good* for them?) A survey conducted by Yankelovich, a Manhattan market research firm, revealed 66 per cent of the people surveyed felt that fast foods were "worse" than what they would eat at home, and 69 per cent felt that fast foods were less nutritious than what they would consume at home.

As people are eating more fast foods, it is imperative that we know if this food is indeed "junk food," or if it really makes a significant nutritional contribution to our diets. Sound nutritional information has not been available until recently and the information is still too skimpy for an industry that is now doing $16 billion a year in business.

Fast Foods

NUTRITIVE VALUE

To the die-hard fast-food freaks who cling to their fast foods precisely because of their junk food appeal, it may seem like a contradiction in terms to speak of nutritive *value* in fast foods. Fast foods are, according to Dr. Howard Appledorf, not junk food, but "technological innovations." He's found fast foods are just like any other foods. "If you eat the right ones, you get a balanced meal." (Could it be that the junk label has more to do with *taste* than nutrition?)

Dr. Appledorf, an M.I.T.-trained biochemist, is an Associate Professor of Nutrition at the University of Florida. His students wanted to know, for example, if a Big Mac had more going for it than a Whopper; and is fast food really "junk"?

Dr. Appledorf couldn't answer their ques-

tions because in all the years he'd spent studying food chemistry and nutrition he had not come across information on fast foods. He began investigating (we should all have such professors), and has since taught the nutritional *benefits* that can be derived from fast foods. By examining what Dr. Appledorf says is right about fast foods, we can also learn where their weaknesses and problems lie. With this information in hand you'll know better what to order and what to avoid.

His investigative techniques began with buying a typical fast-food meal. Back at the laboratory, the edible portions were ground up individually and samples were freeze-dried and analyzed. One of the first studies Dr. Appledorf did was to compare the offerings of three franchise outlets to see if there were any substantial *differences*.

Comparison of Nutrient Values
of typical fast-food meals with recommended dietary allowances
fifteen- to eighteen-year-old males

| | | % RDA | | | | | | | | | | | |
| | | Hamburger French fries Vanilla shake | | | Cheeseburger French fries Vanilla shake | | | Specialty French fries Vanilla shake | | | 2 Hamburgers French fries Vanilla shake | | |
Nutrient	RDA	McDonald's	Burger King	Burger Chef	McDonald's	Burger King	Burger Chef	McDonald's	Burger King	Burger Chef	McDonald's	Burger King	Burger Chef
Energy (kcal)	3,000	27	27	25	29	29	27	37	39	40	34	35	33
Protein (gm)	54	49	46	54	58	55	63	71	81	82	72	66	77
Calcium (mg)	1,200	35	36	42	41	44	50	42	46	47	38	40	46
Phosphorus (mg)	1,200	36	50	44	41	62	56	45	63	54	42	59	52
Iron (mg)	18	8	11	10	9	14	15	14	24	26	13	17	16
Magnesium (mg)	40	16	23	20	17	24	21	19	30	26	19	28	24
Zinc (mg)	15	15	25	23	20	30	29	27	49	48	24	38	35
Copper (mg)*	2–3	13	34	42	13	35	47	18	42	50	16	40	50

SOURCE: Compiled by Howard Appledorf, National Academy of Sciences-National Research Council.

*Although an RDA for copper does not exist, a level of adequacy is recommended (NAS/NRC, 1980).

He drew the following conclusions:

* There is a remarkable similarity in composition among the three franchises as well as outstanding portion control.

* The major difference is in the size of the specialty item. The burger from Burger Chef was the largest specialty item, but it also had the highest fat content.

* People on sodium-restricted diets should be concerned about the relatively high sodium content of the specialty items.

For the sake of comparison, Dr. Appledorf also looked at that most beloved of American meals: steak, potato, and salad. As you will see, many of the fast-food meals compare more favorably than the traditional steak meal, and, over-all, some, like the pizza, hold up well on their own. The main fault of most of the fast-food meals is their relatively high percentage of calories from fat.

Another way of looking at the nutritional value of fast-food meals is to look at the carbohydrate, fat, and protein breakdown. The ideal breakdown suggested by the Senate Select Committee on Nutrition's Dietary Goals is:

% Calories from carbohydrate   55–61
% Calories from fat   27–33
% Calories from protein   10–14

Keeping this breakdown in mind, let's look at the following chart and see what Dr. Appledorf has discovered about some favorite fast-food items.

Carbohydrate, Fat, and Protein Breakdown

	10" Cheese Pizza (Pizza Hut)	Big Mac, French Fries, Shake (McDonald's)	Fried Chicken*	N.Y. Strip Steak, Baked Potato, Salad
% Calories from Carbohydrate	68	49	26	38
% Calories from Fat	12	37	51	40
% Calories from Protein	20	14	23	22
	Taco	Burrito	Enchirito†	Frijole‡
% Calories from Carbohydrate	24	52	36	48
% Calories from Fat	47	28	39	28
% Calories from Protein	26	20	24	24

*Establishment name not revealed.
†An enchirito consists of ground beef, cheese, black olives, and mild red sauce served in a soft flour tortilla.
‡Frijoles are whipped pinto beans topped with shredded mild Cheddar cheese and covered with red sauce.

SOURCE: Compiled by Howard Appledorf, National Academy of Sciences—National Research Council.

Next, Dr. Appledorf did what I think is one of the most interesting parts of his study. He compared the nutrient values of four typical fast-food meals with the Recommended Daily Allowances. Since teen-age boys have one of the highest nutritional requirements, and they wolf down these fast-food meals with regularity, I chose to look at that group.

Assuming an intake of the standard three meals a day, fast foods should provide 33 per cent of the RDA to be considered nutritionally adequate.

As you can see from the previous chart, the consumption of a Burger King Whopper, french fries, and a vanilla shake for a growing sixteen-year-old boy supplies:

Adequate	*Per cent*
Calories	39
Protein	81
Calcium	46
Phosphorus	63
Zinc	49
Copper	42
Inadequate	
Iron	24
Magnesium	30

If a soft drink was substituted instead of the milkshake, this would considerably lessen the nutritional value of the meal.

PIZZAS, SUBMARINE SANDWICHES, AND MEXICAN FOODS

Pizzas are certainly a popular fast-food item and Dr. Appledorf found that if a fourteen-year-old boy ate a whole 10″ cheese and tomato pizza (I'm not sure how likely this is), he would get:

87% of his protein
70% of his calcium
60% of his phosphorus
17% of his iron
26% of his magnesium
48% of his zinc
50% of his copper

When you start putting special toppings on this pizza, of course the count goes up even more. The main drawback of the pizza? It contains more sodium than anyone on a sodium-restricted diet should have at one meal, and most pizzas fail to meet one third the RDA for vitamin C.

PROBLEMS WITH FAST FOODS

Okay, you say, fast foods have virtues: they contain variable amounts of protein and calories and therefore are probably mislabeled as "junk food," which connotes that they supply only empty calories. However, what about the problems—quality control, the high fat levels, high calories, excess sodium?

As far as quality control, a friend told me about a burger stand that received bad publicity because it was mixing pink styrofoam in with their hamburger meat. That seems to be an isolated example and is *not* representative of the sort of major problem facing the fast-food outlets today; everyone in the food field I spoke with marvels at the quality

control at places like McDonald's. However, in the future, one of the problems may be that chains have to turn to *synthetic* ingredients—cheese and meat substitutes—to keep costs down. But for now, the major problems aren't pink styrofoam and synthetic ingredients, but calories, fat, sodium levels, the oils used, and *how* the foods are cooked.

Sodium Levels

Sodium levels in fast foods are too high for anyone on a sodium-restricted diet and probably too high for most of the rest of us as well. The specialty items are almost always presalted as are the french fries. There seems to be no escape. If the item itself is not presalted, then salt is added to the batter in which it is cooked, not to mention the salt in the oil in which it is fried.

Consumer Reports looked at eight fast-food meals (Burger Chef, McDonald's, Burger King, Pizza Hut, Kentucky Fried Chicken, Hardee's, Arby's, and Arthur Treacher's), and found the Pizza Hut meal had the highest sodium content of all—4 gm. The other six meat meals each contained 1 teaspoonful of salt. They found only negligible amounts of sodium in Arthur Treacher's fish meal.

In speaking with the management at Pizza Hut, they told me they were re-evaluating their products in terms of the sodium level. Since companies do periodic product reviews, a customer's comments regarding the sodium level, for example, may actually be heard and sometimes even have an impact.

Suggestions for improvements:

* Food processors should not presalt fast foods.

* If foods are presalted, which most are, consumers should refrain from resalting.

Fat Content

A big problem with fast foods is their reputation as being fatty, oily, and greasy. Some of them *look* greasier and fattier than home

prepared, so I set out to find if they just *looked* it, or if they really were.

The Senate Select Committee on Nutrition in its Dietary Goals made a recommendation that Americans reduce their daily proportion of calories from fat from 40 to about 30 per cent. Fast foods have generally been condemned as being high in fat. Upon examination, Dr. Appledorf found all the pizzas, burritos, and frijoles provide less than 30 per cent of their calories in the form of fat. The tacos, enchiritos, and tuna submarine sandwiches do not meet these lower requirements and can be considered high fat foods. The typical fast-food combination meal (burger, fries, shake) has been shown to have as little as 28 per cent of its calories in the form of fat, while on the other hand, a fried chicken dinner has 51 per cent of its calories in the form of fat. Perhaps blanket indictments of fast foods as being notoriously high in fat are out of place, and only those foods that truly are—tacos, some submarine sandwiches, fried chicken—should be indicted.

But the fat question as we saw earlier in Chapter 6, Protein, is always a two-sided one, of not only how *much*, but what *kind*? It is generally recommended that our diets consist of more polyunsaturated fats and less highly saturated animal fats. In the restaurant business today, the question of the *kind* of fat used is considered a red hot issue. There are indications that major fast-food chains are increasing their use of tallow, one of the most highly saturated fats, as the preferred frying medium, especially for french-fried potatoes (this partially has to do with its nongreasy look). The choice of the oil used for frying is important because virtually all fast foods, from breaded shrimp and fish sticks to poultry and potatoes, are fried. Although only one out of three meals is consumed away from home, the per capita consumption of visible fats is 1.15 per cent greater in restaurants than consumption at home. The P/S[3] of visible fats and oils consumed in restaurants is 0.44 vs. 1.98 at home.

[3] For an interpretation of P/S values, see Chapter 6, Protein, page 145.

(The restaurant figure of 0.44 represents saturated fats like lard and chicken fat. While the at-home figure of 1.98 could still be improved and thus be higher—safflower oil has a P/S value of 7.1—this figure of 1.98 does represent the trend toward using more vegetable oils.) Dr. Livingston told me that the use of saturated fats by fast-food operators is continuing and even increasing because "they are not aware of the nutritional consequences of what they are doing."

In talking with the various fast-food chains regarding the oils they used, this is what they revealed.

Company	Kind of Oil Used for Frying
Kentucky Fried Chicken	Vegetable oil
Burger Chef	90 per cent animal, 10 per cent vegetable
McDonald's	Mixture of beef tallow and vegetable oil; won't release exact proportion
Arthur Treacher's	Peanut oil—P/S= 6.25
Nathan's Famous	Corn oil

McDonald's' Dennis Detzel said they use primarily animal oil because, "there is a world of difference in taste between vegetable and animal oil." But, Procter and Gamble, one of the major suppliers of vegetable oils to restaurants, has done consumer studies that reveal no perceived difference in taste between the animal and the vegetable oils. They say operators who use beef tallow do so for one of three reasons:

1. Many fast-food establishments started with tallow fat as part of their fried food formula and the operators don't like to tamper with success.

2. The initial cost of tallow is less, although vegetable oils have longer reusability.

3. Cholesterol and saturated fat levels are not a consideration in restaurants, since customers aren't aware of what frying fat an establishment is using.

Suggestions for improvements:

* Consumers should ask what *type* of fat or oil is being used and then they won't have the fat pulled over their eyes so easily.

* Fast-food operators should be encouraged by consumer demand to substitute shortenings higher in polyunsaturates than those currently in use.

* Fast-food operators should be required to place nutritional signs in their restaurants with information including the type of frying oils they use, so this will no longer be one of their industry "secrets."

* Types of cooking methods should be developed so dependence on deep-fat frying is minimized.

Vitamins A and C

Most of the fast-food meals are lacking in vitamin A, and some in vitamin C, as well. This is because fast-food outlets sell virtually no vegetables and fruits. McDonald's has introduced tomato, orange, and grapefruit juices, but according to Dennis Detzel, these haven't been big sellers. (McDonald's was also involved in a lawsuit in Los Angeles over their orange juice, which they advertised as "fresh" when, in fact, it was a frozen concentrate. They paid a $10,000 fine.)

Suggestions for improvement:

* If you eat at fast-food establishments often, make sure your other meals include fresh fruits and vegetables.

* Order your burger with tomato and lettuce.

* Fast-food operators should offer salads, like coleslaw. If they do, order it.

* Their menus should also include unadulterated fresh fruits. An orange or apple for dessert, for example.

How *It Is Cooked*

People have long been concerned from a health point of view that fast food means fried food, but there's been another reason for alarm about the way fast food is cooked. Researchers at Washington University in St. Louis have reported that when hamburgers are cooked too long on a hot metal surface, chemical substances are formed that might conceivably cause cancer in humans. The substances affected the genes of bacteria in a laboratory screening test, which means they might cause cancer if they were tested in laboratory animals.

The risk is of unknown magnitude, but billions of patties are cooked every year on metal surfaces in fast-food restaurants as well as at home. (This risk does not apply to broiled burgers.) Most people will probably wait until more results are in before giving up their fried burgers. If additional testing does reveal this to be a serious problem, in the near future we'll see more fast-food chains cooking food in a larger variety of ways.

Calories

Nearly all fast-food meals are too heavy on calories; most of them provide at least half the calories a person needs for the day, which means if people eat two other regular meals, they will be gaining weight. If you are eating one fast-food meal, you should omit one other meal to maintain your weight.

HOMEMADE VS. FAST FOODS

Many consumers think they are being cheated by the quality of the food restaurants serve to them; they think if they made it at

Homemade vs. fast food.

home they'd be getting better nutrition and better food. The *Family Economics Review* did a comparison study between fast foods and similar foods prepared at home. They questioned the mass-produced assembly-line production techniques of fast foods and wondered if the same food prepared at home would not produce a more nutritious end result. Their findings are very interesting. Their comparisons show that fast foods from McDonald's,[4] are similar nutritionally to foods made at home, but cost twice as much.

Nutrition

The foods prepared at home duplicated as closely as possible the ingredients used by McDonald's, so this wasn't a case of substituting more nutritious home ingredients for the ones McDonald's was using. The nutritive values of the seven meals from McDonald's compared with corresponding meals prepared at home were quite similar. Of the seven fast-food-type meals, five provided one fifth or more of the U. S. Recommended Daily Allowance for protein, thiamin, riboflavin, and ascorbic acid. None of the meals provided much vitamin A. Only the meal with the milk shake exceeded one fifth the RDA for calcium.

Fat

The calories provided by fat in the Big Mac and fillet of fish sandwich substantially exceeded their home-prepared counterparts. One explanation offered was that McDonald's uses more spread on each sandwich. The fast-food apple pie also had much more fat.

The McDonald's french fries had more fat than the homemade possibly because they had more surface area; weightwise, three homemade french fries equaled ten of McDonald's: the more surface area, the more

[4] Since fast foods are nutritionally quite similar from franchise to franchise (see Appledorf's previous charts, pages 259, 260), these comparisons for McDonald's would hold true for other fast-food outlets as well.

fat can be absorbed. If you have a choice, get bigger size fries, rather than little skinny ones. The skinny ones have little potato, and act primarily as blotters for grease. The french fries made at home had a little more vitamin C, but this is probably inconsequential because there is such a variation in vitamin C due to storage and method of preparation.

McDonald's shakes made with a nonfat dry milk provided more calcium and less fat (and less vitamin A) than the shake made at home from whole milk and ice cream.

Cost

Consumers think fast food is bargain eating; that fast foods are cheaper than they could make comparable food at home. Because of this belief, supermarkets were experiencing a loss in business during 1978 and took out aggressive ads like this one:

> Homemade chicken at down home prices. . . . Did you know that if you've been buying chicken at one of the fast-food places, the regular price for a large bucket of ready-cooked chicken is about $7.00? Compare that with the fact that this week at Lucky [grocery store] you can cook up the same chicken on your barbecue (without the grease) for only ½ the price!

The *Family Economics Review* survey found the information in the ad to be true: fast-food meals eaten out average to be about *twice* the price of making them at home.[5]

One of the hamburger meals cost 1.8 times as much as the home-prepared meal, while the Big Mac cost 2.2 times as much. The best

buys were the hamburger and cheeseburger, costing only one quarter to one third more than the home-prepared ones. But fast-food apple pie cost a whopping 3½ times more than the homemade.

According to Betty Hoyt, a research associate at the National Restaurant Association, these price comparisons between eating at home and eating out can only be expected to get worse. Between 1970 and 1979 grocery store prices rose at an annual rate of 7.4 per cent while menu prices were up 7.3 per cent. But in 1979 the Bureau of Labor Statistics revealed that food-at-home prices rose 9.5 per cent while food-away-from-home rose 11.4 per cent. With this variation in price, consumers increased their food-at-home purchases in 1980.

You have some choices. You can go to a fast-food establishment on occasion and spend roughly twice the money you would at home and get nutritionally about the same thing. What's better, I think, is, when you're preparing these foods at home, don't slavishly duplicate the methods and foods used by the fast-food chains, but use this opportunity to improve on the nutrition. Suggested improvements on fast food at home:

* Use lots of dark green leaves on the burger, perhaps spinach, and serve your burger with a dark green salad.

* Broil the burger instead of frying it.

* Use a portion of soy protein mixture in the hamburger meat to yield an equal amount of protein with less fat.

* When making milk shakes, use only low fat, or nonfat ingredients.

* Have a piece of fresh fruit for dessert.

* Use whole wheat buns.

* Use no salt and rely more on spices— onions, garlic, and pepper.

* If you must have french fries, use thick steak fries—less surface area than matchstick-thin fries, less fat absorbed.

[5] Although the specific prices may have changed by now, the comparisons are still valid. The cost of meals prepared at home does not take into account the cost of fuel used in cooking, or the value of time spent shopping for food, preparing the meal, and cleaning up afterward. Expenses traveling to and from McDonald's were also not considered.

THE CARE AND FEEDING OF MOTHERS AND INFANTS

As more women are having careers and postponing motherhood until their late twenties or thirties, having babies is no longer taken for granted. But just as the decision of *when* to have a baby is now more under a woman's control, so are the decisions of how to best prepare for her baby, how to best nourish herself and the baby, and how to avoid taking unnecessary risks.

Infant mortality in this country is shockingly high. In fact, we rank seventeenth in the world. That means babies stand a better chance of surviving in sixteen countries other than ours. Food—what the mother eats or does not eat—plays a role in infant mortality. Pregnancy gives new meaning to food because the nutrients a pregnant woman eats are actually the building materials from which a whole new life is being created and, unfortunately, malnutrition can happen to a baby even before it is born. This chapter includes the most up-to-date information to guide the pregnant woman and new mother in making responsible dietary choices for herself and her baby.

Common Myths About Pregnancy and Food

Let's look at some of the most pervasive myths:

Myth: Weight restriction makes delivery easier during pregnancy since small babies come through the birth canal more easily.

Fact: It is found that weight restriction is more likely to cause the uterus to malfunction during labor and labor is often more difficult.

Myth: A pregnant woman who is dieting does not harm the fetus since it is a parasite and takes what it needs from the mother. If baby is small, it is merely "perfection in miniature."

Fact: Weight loss causes babies of low birth weight, which subjects the babies to additional difficulties.

Myth: Weight restriction does not harm the baby because the baby's weight is determined by heredity.

Fact: The baby's weight is determined by the mother's diet and food intake.

Myth: Eating of nonfood substances gives an extra nutritional boost to the baby, and can make delivery smoother.

Fact: The eating of dirt, clay, laundry starch, refrigerator ice or frost, plaster, or cornstarch is prevalent in some groups of women, usually from the South, where folklore suggests these nonfood substances do everything from contributing to the proper positioning of the fetus to prevention of nausea. A nutritionist friend who has worked in a home for pregnant teen-agers said one of her worst problems was to get them to stop eating laundry starch or sending home for red clay. Apparently, this practice is more widespread than I imagined. Dr. Roy Parker, Professor and Chairman of Obstetrics and Gynecology at Duke University, estimates 25 per cent of his obstetrical patients eat clay. But this questionable practice is not relegated just to the South. A study at Cook County General Hospital in Illinois showed that 65 per cent of the pregnant women ate starch.

Aside from their horrible taste, serious complications arise from the eating of these substances. Anemia and excessive weight gain accompany the starch eating. The diets of clay eaters are low in calcium, vitamin C, vitamin A, and thiamin since clay absorbs these nutrients and makes them unavailable to the body. Dirt has substances which bind calcium and iron and make them unavailable for absorption and may make the person deficient in these nutrients.

Myth: Abnormal cravings for ordinary food can be safely satisfied.

Fact: A pickle here and there and an occasional 2 A.M. hot fudge sundae are the perks of pregnancy, but ordinary food in great excess should be avoided and can produce bizarre results. One report tells of a pregnant woman who drank 3 quarts of milk and the

Myths

juice of six oranges daily to prevent damage to her teeth. In the process, she gained *110 pounds!*

Myth: A pregnant woman needs to eat for two.

Fact: There are certain nutritional requirements that *do* change with pregnancy, but usually not to the degree that a mother is eating for two. Increased nutrients are needed for nourishing the fetus as well as nourishing and maintaining the mother; if a mother-to-be does not increase her intake of nutrients, she could become malnourished. The effect of malnourishment during pregnancy depends on the duration of the inadequacy and the time during the pregnancy when it occurs.

*   If malnutrition occurs in the first months when organs are differentiating in the fetus, the baby's organs may be affected in size and function and malformations are possible.

*   If malnutrition occurs after the fetus' organs are formed but when cells are dividing or enlarging, size of organs may be affected, including brain cell number and brain size.

*   If malnutrition occurs in the last 2 months when the fetus is fully formed but weight is added, the birth weight of the baby will be affected and chances of a premature delivery are more likely.

The specific requirements are shown on the Recommended Daily Dietary Allowances chart.

 Nutritional Guidelines for the Pregnant Woman

HOW MANY CALORIES ARE NEEDED?

The increased caloric requirement is probably one of the most misunderstood. Unfortunately for those who view pregnancy as a

chance for a nonstop eating binge, all that is actually needed is an increase of 300 calories a day, or the equivalent of 4 thin slices of cheese. It is not a question of eating a *lot* more, but of selecting nutritionally dense foods, rather than foods with empty calories that supply no nutrients along with the calories. These additional calories are primarily needed because the extra demands of the fetus make it harder for the heart muscle to pump the nutrients to all the tissues.

It is very important that the pregnant woman consumes sufficient calories because if she doesn't, the protein in her diet will be used for energy and the fetus may not get the protein it needs.

HOW MUCH WEIGHT SHOULD BE GAINED?

It is now generally accepted that a total weight gain of about 24–30 pounds is ideal; even obese women should gain this amount. The accompanying drawing shows where this weight goes.

Weight gain, either too much, or too little, has a profound effect on the successful outcome of the pregnancy. Restricted diets with little weight gain affect the birth weights of the babies and future growth. The California Department of Health reports a not untypical case history in which a fashionable woman did not want to "ruin" her figure with her pregnancy. She skipped breakfast, her favorite lunch was a fruit salad, and nearly half her calories at dinner were consumed in alcohol. Her diet was inadequate in calories and almost all nutrients.

Studies have shown that if the mother's diet is restricted, the placenta weighs less and is less able to provide the necessary nutrients and oxygen to nourish the fetus.

The weight gain should be spread out as follows:

First 3 months — 2–4 pounds in all
Last 6 months — 1 pound each week

Even if the 24-pound weight gain is reached early in the pregnancy, a gain should continue since the baby's weight gain is most rapid right before birth.

The weight-gain curve should look like this; and if you tip the book to the right side, you'll recognize a familiar shape.

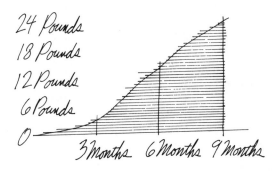

WHAT ABOUT PROTEIN?

The protein requirements increase by 65 per cent for a total of 74–76 gm each day and

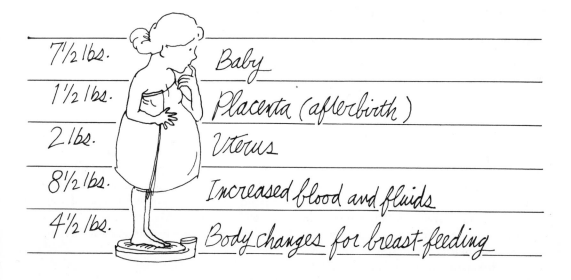

7½ lbs. — Baby

1½ lbs. — Placenta (afterbirth)

2 lbs. — Uterus

8½ lbs. — Increased blood and fluids

4½ lbs. — Body changes for breast-feeding

*Recommended Daily Dietary Allowances**

| | AGE | WEIGHT | | HEIGHT | | PROTEIN | FAT-SOLUBLE VITAMINS | | | WATER- | |
| | | | | | | | | | | Vita-min C | Thia-min |
	(years)	(kg)	(lb)	(cm)	(in)	(gm)	Vit A (IU)	Vit D (IU)	Vit E (IU)	(mg)	(mg)
Infants	0.0-0.5	6	13	60	24	kg x 2.2	1400	400	4	35	0.3
	0.5-1.0	9	20	71	28	kg x 2.0	2000	400	5	35	0.5
Children	1-3	13	29	90	35	23	2000	400	7	45	0.7
	4-6	20	44	112	44	30	2500	400	9	45	0.9
	7-10	28	62	132	52	34	3300	400	10	45	1.2
Males	11-14	45	99	157	62	45	5000	400	12	50	1.4
	15-18	66	145	176	69	56	5000	400	15	60	1.4
	19-22	70	154	176	70	56	5000	300	15	60	1.5
	23-50	70	154	178	70	56	5000	200	15	60	1.4
	51+	70	154	178	70	56	5000	200	15	60	1.2
Females	11-14	46	101	157	62	46	4000	400	12	50	1.1
	15-18	55	120	163	64	46	4000	400	12	60	1.1
	19-22	55	120	163	64	44	4000	300	12	60	1.1
	23-50	55	120	163	64	44	4000	200	12	60	1.0
	51+	55	120	163	64	46	4000	200	12	60	1.0
Pregnant						+30	+1000	400	+3	+20	+0.4
Lactating						+20	+2000	400	+4	+40	+0.5

*The allowances are intended to provide for individual variations among most normal persons as they live in the United States under usual environmental stresses. Diets should be based on a variety of common foods in order to provide other nutrients for which human requirements have been less well defined.

[a]1 NE (niacin equivalent) is equal to 1 mg or 60 mg of dietary tryptophan.

[b](μg) equals microgram, one millionth of a gram.

SOURCE: Food and Nutrition Board, National Academy of Sciences—National Research Council, Revised 1980.

this need is greatest in the last trimester. This requirement should be met by at least two 3-ounce servings of high quality protein —meat, milk products, eggs. Studies have shown a definite correlation between protein intake of the mother during pregnancy and the reflexes, coloring, and size of the new-born. Additionally, adequate protein intake helps to prevent miscarriages. In a study of 105 pregnant women, no spontaneous abortions took place during the first 3 months in women consuming over 85 gm of protein daily; while almost 90 per cent aborted who were consuming less than 55 gm a day.

| SOLUBLE VITAMINS | | | | | MINERALS | | | | | |
Ribo-flavin (mg)	Niacin (mg NE)[a]	Vita-min B-6 (mg)	Fola-cin (µg)[b]	Vitamin B-12 (µg)	Cal-cium (mg)	Phos-phorus (mg)	Mag-nesium (mg)	Iron (mg)	Zinc (mg)	Iodine (µg)
0.4	6	0.3	30	0.5[c]	360	240	50	10	3	40
0.6	8	0.6	45	1.5	540	360	70	15	5	50
0.8	9	0.9	100	2.0	800	800	150	15	10	70
1.0	11	1.3	200	2.5	800	800	200	10	10	90
1.4	16	1.6	300	3.0	800	800	250	10	10	120
1.6	18	1.8	400	3.0	1200	1200	350	18	15	150
1.7	18	2.0	400	3.0	1200	1200	400	18	15	150
1.7	19	2.2	400	3.0	800	800	350	10	15	150
1.6	18	2.2	400	3.0	800	800	350	10	15	150
1.4	16	2.2	400	3.0	800	800	350	10	15	150
1.3	15	1.8	400	3.0	1200	1200	300	18	15	150
1.3	14	2.0	400	3.0	1200	1200	300	18	15	150
1.3	14	2.0	400	3.0	800	800	300	18	15	150
1.2	13	2.0	400	3.0	800	800	300	18	15	150
1.2	13	2.0	400	3.0	800	800	300	10	15	150
+0.3	+2	+0.6	+400	+1.0	+400	+400	+150	d	+5	+25
+0.5	+5	+0.5	+100	+1.0	+400	+400	+150	d	+10	+50

[c]The recommended dietary allowance for vitamin B-12 in infants is based on average concentration of the vitamin in human milk. The allowances after weaning are based on energy intake (as recommended by the American Academy of Pediatrics), and consideration of other factors, such as intestinal absorption.

[d]The increased requirement during pregnancy cannot be met by the iron content of habitual American diets nor by the existing iron stores of many women; therefore, the use of 30-60 mg of supplemental iron is recommended. Iron needs during lactation are not substantially different from those of nonpregnant women, but continued supplementation of the mother for 2-3 months after parturition is advisable in order to replenish stores stores depleted by pregnancy.

WHAT ABOUT CALCIUM?

Calcium requirements increase by 50 per cent during pregnancy, from 800 to 1,200 mg daily. If the normal calcium requirement is being met, this increase requires only an additional 8-ounce glass of milk plus leafy greens; however, the Department of Agriculture's 1980 Food Consumption Survey revealed that the diets of both teen-age girls and women did not meet even the basic recommendations for calcium. So, this is an important requirement to pay attention to, especially because many experts now believe that the basic amount currently recommended for adults—800 mg a day—is about 50 per cent lower than it should be to maintain strong, healthy bones and teeth throughout life.

The fetus takes what it needs for bone development and the effect on the mother with an inadequate diet during pregnancy may not show up until later in life when she may develop osteoporosis. The correlation between lack of calcium during pregnancy and increased likelihood of osteoporosis in old age is an interesting point that has not yet been adequately researched. (For more information on osteoporosis, see Chapter 11, Youthful Aging.)

IS IT NECESSARY TO RESTRICT SALT INTAKE?

In the past, physicians have routinely advised their pregnant patients to restrict their salt intake and have frequently prescribed diuretics to reduce fluid retention. There has been a turn about in the thinking in this area. It is now known that a slight degree of fluid retention is normal during pregnancy and it is currently thought that moderate salt intake is associated with fewer complications during pregnancy.

Iodine deficiency in pregnancy can cause mental retardation in the baby. In Switzerland, the number of mentally retarded babies born was decreased when iodine was added to salt. The use of iodized salt is recommended. (Processed foods do not contain iodized salt.) Recommendations: No sodium restrictions, iodized salt, and no diuretics.

WHAT ABOUT FOLACIN AND IRON?

The requirement for both these minerals is substantially increased during pregnancy and cannot be met by dietary means alone. For example, the folacin (folic acid) requirement is doubled; to meet this increased need, it is probably necessary to take folate supplements. Malformations are five times more frequent in the newborn when mothers' diets are deficient in folacin acid. Low levels in pregnancy are often due to:

* Diets that are lacking in fruits or vegetables.

* Increase in blood volume that occurs with pregnancy and causes a decrease in folacin concentration.

The increased iron needed in pregnancy is from 30–60 mg/day and it is recommended that this be given in daily tablets.

WHAT ABOUT VITAMINS A AND C?

The vitamin A requirement increases by 25 per cent to 5,000 I.U. and can be satisfied by 1 extra serving a day of a food rich in vitamin A. Examples of a serving of vitamin A vegetable or fruit are:

  ½ cup greens
  ½ cup broccoli
  ¼ cantaloupe
  1 peach
  1 apricot
  1 carrot
  ½ cup spinach
  1 tomato
  ½ cup squash
  1 sweet potato

The vitamin C requirement increases by 30 per cent from 60 mg to 80 mg; it is needed for the formation of protein matrix in the bones, in addition to keeping teeth and connective tissue healthy and increasing the absorption of iron. (For detailed food sources, see Chapter 1, Vegetables, and Chapter 3, Fruits.)

The temptation to take megadoses, as recommended by Dr. Linus Pauling, should be avoided during pregnancy. Studies of pregnant animals given megadoses of vitamin C have shown this causes them to abort. Another possible side effect is that large doses taken by pregnant women may result in a very high vitamin C requirement by the infant, and cause "rebound scurvy."

WHAT ABOUT THE B COMPLEX—THIAMIN, RIBOFLAVIN, NIACIN, B_6, AND B_{12}?

Riboflavin requirements increase by 25 per cent from 1.2 to 1.5 mg/day. The best food sources are milk and milk products, liver, and leafy green vegetables.

Niacin requirements increase by 15 per cent, from 13 mg to 15 mg a day. The food sources of niacin are proteins, whole grains, and enriched grains and cereals.

Thiamin requirements increase by more than 30 per cent during pregnancy, from 1 mg to 1.4 mg. Pork, beef, whole or enriched grains and cereals, and legumes are good sources.

A B_{12} deficiency in animals causes destruction of the fetus. Vegetarians are at special risk and should take supplements. The need for B_6 increases from 2 mg daily to 2.6 mg during pregnancy.

Double Jeopardy: Alcohol, Smoking, and Drugs

Every woman wants to have a healthy baby. In the early seventies the March of Dimes had a program aimed at protecting the environment—that is, the baby's first environment, the mother's womb. When that environment is polluted, death or damage can result. Although most babies are born healthy, there are certain dietary measures the pregnant woman can take that will help ensure a healthy baby. Keeping in mind that almost everything a woman eats or drinks during her pregnancy gets to the fetus through the placenta, there are certain items of such high risk magnitude that they should be avoided, or taken only with extreme caution and with doctor's advice. Alcohol, caffeine, cigarettes, and drugs fall into this high-risk category. All are now known to be capable of jeopardizing a baby's future before it even begins, and pose a danger to the nursing infant as well. This section discusses the necessary precautions and some of the new evidence, indicating why, for example, even one drink of wine before dinner is no longer thought to be advisable for a pregnant woman.

When I was speaking about some of these risks to a young woman who was contemplating pregnancy, her attitude was, "Egad. All this just to have a baby?" My answer to her was, yes, because you don't want just a baby, you want a healthy baby.

I am what you eat.

ALCOHOL

I was at a party recently where a mother-to-be's entrance created a sensation. Dressed in white pants and white shirt, she had flamboyantly draped a bold iridescent blue scarf around her belly. She announced to the party-goers what was obvious: she was due any moment. Then she joined some people at the bar and ordered two strong drinks, one for herself and one for baby. She explained they were to get her through till the baby was born. I wondered for how long this pregnant woman had been drinking this much. After the birth, I doubt that she would mix a jigger of scotch in with the baby's formula, but, in effect, by drinking while pregnant, she was already sending a shot down to the baby.

It is now known that alcohol consumption during pregnancy poses a serious risk to the vulnerable fetus. If the mother is drunk, so is the baby. But it's an additional problem for the fetus since the liver is the key organ for removing alcohol from the blood and in the fetus the liver is not yet fully developed. This concern about alcohol and pregnancy is not new, but in the last 10 years it's been given a name: the Fetal Alcohol Syndrome. The characteristics of the syndrome that may appear in newborn babies include: small birth size, small head, mental retardation, and facial irregularities.

How *much* can one drink without these dire consequences? A safe guideline used to be 1 ounce of alcohol[1] a day. In other words:

2 mixed drinks	(each have 1 ounce 50-proof whiskey, which equals 1 ounce alcohol)

or

| 2 (5-ounce) glasses of wine | equals 1 ounce alcohol |
| 2 (12-ounce) glasses of beer | equals 1 ounce alcohol |

Dr. Ernest B. Noble, Director of the National Institute of Alcohol Abuse, warns that this "safe" figure may now be too high. Although full Fetal Alcohol Syndrome appears to start at 3 ounces a day, Dr. Noble cautions that the Institute is now not certain that parts of the syndrome will not show up with consumption as low as 1 ounce a day or less.

Is there a critical period for drinking during pregnancy when the fetus is the most vulnerable, or is the danger the same for the duration of the pregnancy? The first month,

when differentiation and organ development are occurring, is the most crucial period for the deleterious effects of alcohol. Unfortunately, this is usually before a woman knows she's pregnant. It is now also known that a single drinking binge during this critical period may have as damaging effect as regular daily consumption during the entire pregnancy. A study reported in *Nutrition and the M.D.* revealed that drinking 2–4 ounces of 100-proof liquor daily during the month preceding recognition of pregnancy produces clinical signs of altered growth in about 10 per cent of the infants; when pregnant women drank *more* than 4 ounces of 100 proof, 19 per cent had abnormal infants. Elsewhere in other studies, I've seen this figure stated to be as high as 40 per cent.

Not a bottle for babies.

What is also surfacing is the fact that alcohol consumption may be more significant than realized in the development of more subtle and frequent abnormalities of attention, behavior, and learning called Minimal Brain Dysfunction. The National Institute of Alcohol Abuse estimates that 5–7 million youngsters of school age are considered to have MBD. Strong indications

[1] To determine the alcohol content of distilled spirits, divide the "proof" in half. For example, 100-proof alcohol is about 50 per cent whiskey, so 2 ounces of whiskey contains 1 ounce of alcohol.

are that a significant number of these cases of MBD are due to consumption of alcohol by the mother during pregnancy.

The answers are not all in regarding how much, or how little, is the wisest amount for the pregnant woman to drink. But it is crystal clear that reduction in alcohol consumption benefits the baby. The best answer obviously is to err on the side of caution and avoid alcohol completely, or at the least, to drink no more than 1 ounce a day. If one is trying to get pregnant, this decrease in alcohol consumption should coincide with the time of ovulation.

A provocative side note is the current consideration by the FDA that alcoholic beverages and certain drugs and food containing alcohol should be labeled "Caution—consumption of alcoholic beverages may be hazardous to your health, may be habit-forming, and may cause serious birth defects when consumed during pregnancy." The alcoholic beverage industry naturally is strongly opposed to any such labeling, so for the time being, it's up to pregnant mothers to do their own mental labeling of alcoholic beverages.

SMOKING

It is now an accepted fact that both the active smoker and the passive smoker (the nonsmoker who is in the same room with a smoker) run a risk when they smoke. This risk is magnified for the pregnant smoker, who tends to have lower birth-weight babies (less than 5½ pounds) who are more likely to develop problems. Contrary to the ingestion of alcohol, which is most harmful at the very beginning of pregnancy, smoking is most harmful during the second half of pregnancy.

In a study of more than 2,000 pregnant women, C. S. Russel, in a report to the Surgeon General, showed that women who smoked had a significantly higher percentage of unsuccessful pregnancies (abortions, stillbirths, neonatal deaths), than women who did not smoke. The exact mechanism by which fetal growth is retarded is not definitely known, but elevated carbon monoxide levels have been found in the maternal and fetal blood of women smokers. According to the National Foundation for the March of Dimes, many doctors suspect nicotine is directly responsible for stunting fetal growth. The suspicion is that since smoking constricts blood circulation in varying degrees, this may deprive the fetus of adequate nutrients through the placenta.

The only responsible answer seems to be give up smoking when pregnant. I have observed that this seems to happen naturally. Several cigarette-smoking friends have told me they "lost the taste" for cigarettes when they were pregnant. Good for them.

DRUGS

Today, virtually all scientific sources agree that a placental barrier to drugs does *not* exist. By and large every drug that enters the mother's circulation also enters the fetus'. (There are a few exceptions: tyramine, serotonin, angionin, and histamine.) The thalidomide and the DES tragedies are tragic reminders of the potentially devastating effect of drugs on the fetus. Several important factors affect whether a drug causes fetal malformations; these include the time during the pregnancy when the drug was taken and the physical and chemical nature of the drug.

Most birth defects are caused in the first 12 weeks of pregnancy when organs like the body, arms, and legs are forming. The wrong drug taken at this time can drastically interfere with the fetus' development. For example, thalidomide is known to have teratogenetic effects (malformations) if taken from the twenty-eighth to the forty-second day of pregnancy, but has no effect if taken near term.

During pregnancy, drugs should be used only when the need far outweighs their known risks. It is significant that the U. S. Department of Health, Education, and Welfare calculates the average number of medications taken by a pregnant woman (exclusive of vitamin preparations and iron, folic acid, and calcium tablets) averages a high of four drugs per woman.

To Have or Not to Have[2]

BAKING SODA AND OTHER STOMACH REMEDIES

These contain sodium, which may cause fluid retention and swelling of hands and feet. If there is no problem with fluid retention, one dose of bicarbonate or antacid won't hurt the baby, but frequent doses may cause trouble.

ASPIRIN

In the early part of pregnancy, aspirin should not be harmful if taken with plenty of fluid. Toward the end of pregnancy, frequent use can lead to interference with baby's blood-clotting mechanism, which causes thinning of blood. There is also some evidence that heavy use of aspirin may delay normal onset of labor.

ANTIBIOTICS

These cross the placenta easily and are sometimes used to treat the unborn baby, but if used carelessly can damage it. Tetracycline, a common antibiotic, can affect bone growth and cause discoloration of the baby's teeth.

VITAMINS

This is not the time to be on a self-prescribed vitamin diet unless it is with the precise knowledge and close supervision of your physician. With a few exceptions (folic acid tablets, iron supplements) eating a good variety of food is the best way to get the vitamins you need. If a deficiency indicates a need, a physician can prescribe the kind and quantity. Megavitamins (vitamins in large doses) can harm the unborn baby.

SLEEPING PILLS AND TRANQUILIZERS

Use of some tranquilizers have been shown to increase the risk of babies born with cleft palate. Occasional use may do no harm, but no drug is absolutely safe, even for people who aren't pregnant.

LAXATIVES

Avoid mineral oil, which causes loss of fat-soluble vitamins. Avoid all over-the-counter remedies. It is best to alleviate constipation by drinking more fluids, getting more exercise, and using more fiber foods, such as bran, whole grain cereals, fruits, and vegetables. (For a complete list of high fiber foods, see Index.)

NARCOTICS, HALLUCINOGENS, AND AMPHETAMINES

These should be avoided, as should all drugs.

CAFFEINE

Caffeine is a stimulant found in coffee, tea, colas, and in many common drugs (see Index). Of the great variety of substances that can affect the fetus adversely, caffeine is perhaps the one used most widely.

Caffeine readily crosses the placenta and enters the fetal circulation. In a study conducted at the University of Illinois, a daily consumption of 600 mg[3] of caffeine or more resulted in *more pregnancies* that ended in spontaneous abortion in the first trimester or *more stillbirths* or premature births later on in the pregnancy than among pregnant women who were not heavy coffee drinkers. A Belgian study of 175 women confirmed the Illinois findings and showed that 23.4 per cent of the mothers who gave birth to abnormal babies drank 8 or more cups of coffee a day, compared to 12.9 per cent of the mothers of normal babies.

Both the Illinois and Belgium studies establish a relationship between high caffeine consumption and a predisposition to reproductive difficulty. Previously, the attention focused on high caffeine consumption should not have alarmed moderate coffee drinkers

---

[2] Compiled by the U. S. Department of Health, Education, and Welfare and the March of Dimes.

[3] The 600 mg was arrived at figuring 75 mg for a serving of coffee, 30 mg for a serving of tea, 45 mg for a serving of cola.

since only 3 per cent of the U.S. population drinks these excessive amounts of coffee. However, a study published by the National Coffee Association in the summer of 1978 reveals the equivalent of only *4* cups of coffee daily causes birth defects in rats. The answer with caffeine: moderation or, better yet, abstinence.

 # *Teen-age Pregnancies*

I was startled to discover the extent of teen-age pregnancies: in 1975, *20 per cent* of babies were born to girls under nineteen years old, and one tenth of those were to girls under sixteen years old. Nationally, this adds up to 600,000 babies a year. California now considers adolescent pregnancies to be a number one health problem. I leave it up to the sociologists to explain why this phenomenon of early motherhood is reaching epidemic proportions; what I'm concerned about are the nutritional implications of adolescent pregnancies and why as an entire class, teen-age mothers are categorized as a high-risk group.

From a medical point of view, if a teenager becomes pregnant during the 4 years after menstruation begins, she is considered still to be physiologically immature and is at greater biological risk than a mature woman. Pregnant adolescents face twice the risk of premature births, more early infant deaths (1 month after birth), more prolonged labor, and more congenital abnormalities. Infant mortality is two to three times higher among babies born to teen-agers. Some of the problems and difficulties with teen-age pregnancies can be avoided by combining proper nutritional care with obstetrical guidance.

Poor Eating Habits

The serious nutritional concerns are often magnified by the poor eating habits of teen-agers, coupled with their lack of knowledge about how to "cook" more than a Coke and chips.

Having two teen-age stepdaughters I have some familiarity with faddish adolescent eating habits; however, my first experience with teen-age mothers came recently when I approached a young girl at a fast-food restaurant to ask permission to film her. The girl, who was no more than thirteen or fourteen, was cradling a baby in her arms. I thought she was the baby-sitter, but no, she was the mother and she was eating a classic teen-age lunch of fries, Coke, and a burger. Since I was doing a fast-food story at the time, I interviewed her and found out that not only did this young mother eat lunch there every day, she sometimes ate breakfast there, too!

One fifth of all teen-age girls skip breakfast, and of those who do eat breakfast, 50 per cent eat a poor breakfast. Skipping meals seems to be a general habit of teen-agers, and

Send down a cheese sandwich

snacking a way of life. Since 25 per cent of their daily food consumption comes from snacking, if the snacks are good quality there is no problem; however, if the snacks are the usual teen-ager fare, poorly selected and of questionable value, then it is a case of double jeopardy: the girl's diet will be jeopardized, and she and the yet unborn child may pay the price.

The solution is for pregnant girls to choose a healthy diet embracing a wide variety of foods. Pregnant girls from eleven to twenty-two years old, who need approximately 2,300 calories, should compare what they eat against the suggestions outlined below.

Item	Number of Servings Daily
8-ounce glass milk	5
Egg	1
3 ounces meat, poultry, fish	2
1 slice whole grain bread	5
Cereal	½ cup
Pasta, rice	½ cup
Dark green leafy vegetables	½ cup
Other vegetables	2 cups
Citrus or vitamin C rich food	1 cup

Special Nutritional Demands

The nutritional demands of pregnant girls are greatly increased since the physical growth and development of pregnancy are superimposed upon those of adolescence. Although there is little specific information on the special needs of pregnant adolescents, there are nutritional estimates for teen mothers based on requirements for teen-age growth, plus the basic requirements for pregnancy. In light of their eating habits, I am emphasizing the following three areas of particular concern to pregnant teen-agers: calories, protein, and calcium. For other food requirements, see discussion of Nutritional Guidelines for the Pregnant Woman (page 270).

CALORIES

Many pregnant teens still want a slim figure, like their girl friends, and attempt to limit their calories. In so doing, they are limiting the amount of essential nutrients they receive, and the ultimate height and skeletal development of their babies may be compromised. The caloric requirements for pregnant teen-agers are an extra 300 calories a day.

PROTEIN

Although studies have shown that the protein intake for most teen-age girls exceeds the RDA, in those instances where the calories are restricted, protein is used for energy and is not available for synthesis of protein, this may retard physical growth. Inadequate protein intake affects the birth weight of the baby.

CALCIUM

There is an increased need for calcium in adolescent girls and in pregnancy. Adolescent girls from eleven to eighteen require 1,200 mg of calcium and to meet the demands of a growing fetus an additional 400 mg is recommended. What this boils down to is a requirement of four glasses of milk for the average adolescent—five for the pregnant adolescent.

For pregnant teen-agers I recommend *Munch;* this twelve-page booklet may help them make wise food choices in a variety of school and social situations, and also encourages them to continue with their usual school and social routine throughout the pregnancy. *Munch* is available from Martha Kjentvet, Public Health Nutrition Program, Division of Health, P. O. Box 309, Madison, Wisconsin 53701.

WHERE TO GO FOR NUTRITIONAL HELP OF A SPECIAL KIND

In October 1975, the United States Department of Agriculture authorized a special supplemental food program for women, infants, and children. It provides specified nutritious food supplements to pregnant and nursing women and infants and children up to five years of age who are determined by nurses, physicians, nutritionists, or other public health officials to be at "nutritional risk" because of inadequate nutrition or inadequate income. The food supplements are iron-fortified formula, cereal, eggs, cheese, juice, and milk. To find the WIC program nearest you, call your local county Department of Health Services.

 # *The Baby's Nutritional Requirements**

The nutrients that make an infant grow strong and healthy are the same as for the rest of the family, only, obviously, in baby-size quantities. If the baby is breast-fed and the mother is healthy, these nutritional concerns will usually take care of themselves. Because one of the aims of infant nutrition is to contribute to proper growth, some simple growth guidelines to keep in mind are:

* infants double their birth weight by 4–6 months

* by 12 months, infants triple their birth weight

* by 12 months, birth length increases by 50 per cent

WATER

In infancy, babies' bodies have a high percentage of water. Water is supplied sufficiently in breast milk or in formula. Additional supplemental bottles of water are not needed except when fluid losses are abnormal as in vomiting or diarrhea.

CALORIES

From birth to 6 months, the Recommended Daily Dietary Allowance for the breast-fed baby is 53 calories per pound and for the formula-fed baby, about 24–26 ounces of formula based on the average birth weight of 7½ pounds. This requirement decreases to 49 calories per pound from 6 months to 1 year. By six months, the calories may be coming from some solid foods as well as breast milk or formula. From 1–3 years the daily caloric requirement increases to 1,300.

PROTEIN

The Recommended Daily Dietary Allowance of protein is based on the amount in breast milk. A 7½-pound infant needs from 7–10 gm of protein a day, or 2.2 gm of protein per 2.2 pounds of body weight. This translates to 3 cups of breast milk or formula. This requirement decreases slightly for the 6 month to 1-year-old infant to 2 gm of protein per 2.2 pounds body weight. For 1 to 3-year-olds, the requirement stabilizes at 23 gm a day,

* In terms of tending to an infant's nutritional needs, for simplicity in style, I consistently refer to the baby's caretaker as "mother." Because of my personal views, I would appreciate it if readers would read "mother/father" when they see "mother," except in the specific area of nursing, since these areas involving infant nutrition can and should be shared by both parents to enhance the emotional closeness of all three.

and comes from traditional sources of cow's milk, eggs, and cereal.

FAT

Fat provides a concentrated form of energy in the diet, which is important since it is difficult for an infant to consume the volume of food necessary to meet caloric requirements. There has been some discussion that changing the kinds and amounts of fats eaten by infants might prevent premature heart disease when they are older (e.g., substituting skim milk for whole milk). The Committee on Nutrition of the American Academy of Pediatrics feels, on the basis of present data, there is no justification for infants or children to alter their diets radically.

CARBOHYDRATES

Carbohydrates should provide at least 40–50 per cent of calories, but if solid foods take the place of much of the formula or breast milk, the carbohydrate content of the diet can go as high as 80 per cent. When carbohydrate content increases to 80 per cent (often from refined carbohydrates found in baby noodle dinners, prepared cereals, teething biscuits), protein and nutrients may be inadequate.

VITAMINS

Vitamin A — While on breast milk or commercial formulas, infants do not need vitamin A supplements. Because excess vitamin A may lead to toxicity, the Committee on Nutrition of the American Academy of Pediatrics advises mothers not to use vitamin A preparations which provide more than 1,000 I.U. per dose.

Vitamin D — Vitamin D supplements of 400 I.U. are recommended for infants who are breast-fed. If infants are on formula or receiving fortified whole milk, no supplement is necessary.

MINERALS

Calcium — There is no concern about meeting the calcium requirement since breast milk, formula, and cow's milk all fulfill the infant's needs.

Iron — The infant is born with iron stores that last through the first 3–6 months. It is recommended that once solid foods are begun, iron supplements should be given and all infants not breast-fed should receive iron-fortified formulas from birth. If not receiving iron-fortified formula, give liquid iron drops.

 *Breast-feeding*

What looks more natural than a mother feeding her baby at her breast? And yet in current times, this is an area fraught, probably unnecessarily, with controversy and confusion. About 30 years ago, at the time canned and frozen food processors were selling processed foods to my mother's generation as big labor-saving devices, the formula makers were also selling the bottle as the answer to feeding baby. The formula makers' pitch to the new mother was much the same as the food processors' pitch to the overworked housewife: freedom. Just as she no longer had to be tied down to buying fresh foods daily, the new mother no longer had to be tied to her baby; she could rely on the manufacturers' judgment of what a good formula should be.

The advantages of breast-feeding

The formula makers in the United States were quite successful. I was not breast-fed and neither were a large percentage of other children born in the forties and fifties. The formula makers were encouraged by the medical profession because prescribing a formula was a time-saving device for doctors; they did not have to be involved in lengthy discussions and questions about breast-feeding.

In the last decade, we've seen a strong counter trend. The nutritional, economic, and psychological advantages of breast-feeding are being heard, and the trend toward using formula is slowly reversing. The following discussion includes eight strong advantages in favor of breast-feeding. But since the nutritional composition of breast milk is not yet fully known and new information is constantly being uncovered, in all likelihood, there are probably many more as yet unearthed points in its favor. It is now known that a newborn actually searches out its mother's breast attracted by highly potent hormones produced by glands on the breast. When nature provided this built-in attraction, she could not know that society would try to program mothers not to deliver.

ADVANTAGES

Protection Against Infection

Breast milk has been found to protect infants against illnesses, including both intestinal and respiratory disease. This protection is especially evident during the early months and increases in proportion to the duration of breast-feeding. The number of viruses present in breast-fed babies is much less than in those bottle-fed. During their first year of life, 253 babies were monitored at the Pediatric Outpatient Clinic of the Ray Imogene Bassett Hospital in Cooperstown, New York. Dr. Alan Cunningham found that significant respiratory and gastrointestinal illnesses occurred two to three times as frequently in bottle-fed babies. The advantage of breast-feeding was especially striking with respect to bronchitis and pneumonia. These health advantages were most evident in babies breast-fed more than 4–5 months. (It is recommended to breast-feed through the first year.)

Although this advantage against infection is important in industrialized societies like ours, it becomes paramount in developing countries where general sanitary facilities are lacking and environmental contamination increases the risk of infection from bottle-feeding (e.g., no hot water to sterilize bottles, no sterile water to add to formula, etc.).

Colostrum

A thick yellowish secretion produced in the first days of lactation, colostrum not only provides extra nutrition, but is further protection against infection. According to U.C.L.A. Drs. Roslyn Alfin-Slater and Derrick Jelliffe, colostrum represents "a bonus

The advantages of breast-feeding

dose of several nutrients and a protective umbrella against various infections to which the newborn is susceptible." In some parts of the world, low birth-weight babies are fed colostrum in hospitals as a biological protection against disease.

Nutritional Benefits

It used to be thought that the formula companies could make a better milk than mother could (a bit of sexism?), but it has now been shown that mother's milk has nutritional properties in certain proportions (cholesterol, protein, vitamins A and B_6) that cow's milk-based formula is not able to copy. *Consumer Reports* (March 1977) pointed out that milks are tailored to the particular needs of each species. Whale milk, for example, is higher than most milk in fat and calories, important elements for living in cold water. Rabbit milk is particularly rich in protein, which is needed for the very rapid early growth of young rabbits. And the difference in cow's milk and human milk also reflects the different needs of these two species. Since calves double their birth weight in one third the time human infants do, it's appropriate that cow's milk contains three times more protein than human milk. It is becoming clear that there's no reason to suppose that a cow's milk-based formula should be similar to human milk any more than baboon's milk ought to be appropriate to feed elephants.

Scientists are just beginning to understand how a mother's milk is *precisely* attuned to the nutritional needs of her baby. In a fascinating study it was reported that nursing mothers in Yugoslavia expressed better quality milk in terms of volume and protein content when they knew it was going for their own babies rather than to a milk pool.

Antiallergic Effects

The most common food allergy in infants is to the protein in cow's milk. Up to 7 per cent of all infants may be sensitive to cow's milk-based formulas with reactions that range from wheezing and rashes to diarrhea. It has

The advantages of breast-feeding

been found that the best protection against allergies in babies is breast-feeding coupled with avoidance of introduction of semisolids until 4–6 months.

Economics

Cost-comparison studies have shown bottle-feeding to cost two to three times as much as breast-feeding. On a world-wide basis, breast milk can be an international asset of economic importance. In 1976, Dr. Michael C. Latham of Cornell University estimated there were over 60 million infants alive in the world with mothers possessing over 120 million breasts. Latham deduced these mothers could produce over 10 billion liters of milk yearly that would provide 7,500 billion calories and 130 billion gm of protein. Using U.S. supermarket prices for whole fluid milk (even though cow's milk provides less calories than human milk), Latham estimated the value of this breast milk at about 5 billion dollars. He also pointed out that in third world countries like Tanzania, where to feed an infant with formula sometimes takes half the minimum wage for a family, it makes clear-cut economic sense not to spend half the family's income on food for their youngest member.

Convenience

This is an advantage that is not often noted in medical and scientific journals, but one that nursing mothers are certainly aware of. How convenient not to have to charge off to the store to purchase more formula. How practical instead always to have your baby's food with you, always heated to the perfect temperature. The other conveniences are obvious: there are no bottles to wash, no formula to measure, and nothing to heat up.

Psychological

The psychological bonding that is formed between mother and infant during the process of breast-feeding plays an important positive role in their relationship. One of the best advantages of breast-feeding is simply that infants and mothers *like* it; the entire psychology of the warm contact and the sucking is a pleasurable experience.

The advantages of breast-feeding

DISADVANTAGES

Social

Even though breast-feeding has some overwhelming advantages, it's not without its problems. A woman may suddenly leak milk in the middle of a business meeting or when she's out shopping, and as ludicrous as it sounds, some people are still offended by the sight of a woman breast-feeding in public. But if the woman has a network of support from her husband, family, friends, and her doctor, she should be able to cope with the problems that can accompany breast-feeding.

Hazards

There are some clear-cut hazardous situations in which mothers should *not* breast-feed. These are situations in which the mother is in danger of passing on harmful substances to her infant, or in which she may malnourish the infant because of her own insufficient diet.

The women who should *not* breast-feed are:

* Women who are on drugs or medication.

* Women who are malnourished.

* Women with debilitating diseases.

* Women who use alcohol or marijuana should ask their physicians about breast-feeding.

There are other situations where the hazard is less clear cut and the advice has been contradictory and confusing. About 2 years ago, the discovery of PCB in the milk of certain groups of breast-feeding mothers created a panic among nursing mothers and professionals alike. High levels of PCB's (polychlorinated biphenyls—potentially toxic industrial compounds) were found in the breast milk of mothers who lived in particular parts of the country. Some mothers were advised to stop breast-feeding and others stopped because of general concern. The professional thinking at first was that these mothers were doing more harm than good by passing on potentially toxic substances in their breast milk. When the scare settled down, some advice emerged that can apply to similar situations of environmental hazards.

Advice #1:   Make Dietary Changes

* Since most people are subjected to chemicals through their diets, modify your diet so you will be subjected to fewer chemicals.

* Since pesticides and chemicals concentrate in the fats of animals, avoid fatty foods (e.g., certain red meats and fatty fish and dairy products).

* Only eat meat that is well cooked. The better cooked the meat is, the lower its fat content, the less likely one is to eat pesticides.

* Eat more low fat dairy products and avoid butter, cream, and ice cream.

Advice #2:   Be Cautious About Your Environment

* A study of vegetarian women was done at the request of the Environmental Defense Fund. This study showed that the levels of pesticides in the breast milk of 50 vegetarian women were very close to those women on conventional diets. This result indicates that chemicals may be absorbed from the air, or in household products, rather than primarily through the diet. Avoid household and industrial chemicals or pesticides as much as possible.

The bottom line is: With the presence of environmental hazards, whether PCB's or pesticides, should a woman breast-feed or not? Dr. Robert W. Miller of the American Academy of Pediatrics' Committee on Environmental Hazards feels that unless a woman has a history of exposure,[4] she should be encouraged to breast-feed as usual. At the time when the PCB controversy erupted, I spoke with Dr. Jelliffe and he agreed that the benefits of breast-feeding vastly outweigh any risks, which are theoretical at this stage.

ADDITIONAL SOURCES OF HELP

For more specific help and information, contact the La Leche League in your town. The La Leche League is an international organization dedicated to the idea that breast milk produces healthier kids and happier mothers. They have materials available from local offices or their headquarters at 9616 Minneapolis Avenue, Franklin Park, Illinois 60131. Membership in the League is $8.00 a year.

The La Leche League publishes a manual, *The Womanly Art of Breast Feeding*, a complete guide to nursing. It is available from their offices.

If you want to buy only one book on breast-feeding, probably the one you're looking for is *The Complete Book of Breast Feeding*, by Marvin S. Eigler, M.D., and Sally Wendkes Olds, published by Bantam Books, New York, $1.75. This terrific book with black-and-white photographs and diagrams should answer all questions you may have about breast-feeding techniques.

Another highly recommended book on breast-feeding is *Please Breast Feed Your Baby*, by Alice Gerard, published by Signet Books, New York, $1.25. This is filled with the why and how of breast-feeding, written by a mother of three breast-fed babies, and is well worth the small cost. *Nursing Your Baby*, by Karen Pryer, published by Pocket Books, New York, $1.95, is longer than the others and hits on the social and psychological aspects of breast-feeding. It has great photos and is recommended by the La Leche League.

---

[4] If someone has a history of exposure to PCB, possibly in a work-related situation, tests can be done to determine the level of PCB that is present in the breast milk. But Dr. Jelliffe and others cautioned me that at best these tests are misleading. One test reveals nothing because an entire series must be done to establish the norm for an individual. And the validity of the test results is influenced by a variety of complications that the professionals are not yet able to interpret.

Formulas

The formula companies have softened their advertising campaigns in recent years. Now they downplay the superiority of formula over breast milk and instead suggest formula "should be first *after* breast milk." For mothers who decide not to breast-feed or who cannot, formulas specifically engineered for babies should be used, not cow's milk. The formula should be used for the same amount of time suggested for breast-feeding (through the first year); *then* cow's milk can be introduced.

It is expected that by 1981 there will be new federal laws that will make infant formulas even safer and that will more strictly regulate formulas to avoid any repeat of the disastrous 1979 Syntex recall incident. (After prolonged feeding with Syntex, which was later shown to lack sufficient chloride, some infants had severe developmental difficulties.) In the fall of 1980 the U. S. Senate unanimously approved legislation to review current federal requirements for labeling and endorsed a study to determine the effect of proper labeling on infant nutrition and the proper use of infant formula.

Formulas

WHICH FORMULA TO CHOOSE

How is a mother able to choose the best formula for her baby? Is it like choosing chicken soup? You read the label and see which ingredients you want and which you do not want, and then decide to go home and make your own chicken soup instead? Not exactly. There are essentially three milk-based formulas: Enfamil, Similac, and SMA. Enfamil and Similac are formulated to be *improvements* on mother's milk and they are so similar that they are listed together in nutritional guides. SMA is "humanized," which means it is formulated to be most *like* mother's milk.

Nutritional Considerations

Although all three products are nutritionally very similar, let's see how they stack up in terms of protein, iron, minerals, vitamins, and fat.

Protein: The amount of protein in formulas has been reduced to one half the amount of cow's milk, which is still more than in breast milk. In Enfamil and Similac, the amount and kind of protein are the same. SMA uses a demineralized whey protein which predominates in breast milk and is more digestible for infants.

Iron: Since iron deficiency is a problem for some young children, it is suggested that formula-fed infants start building iron stores by being fed iron-fortified formula. Enfamil and Similac have less than one third the iron content of breast milk and one tenth the iron of SMA. Enfamil or Similac products should only be used with iron fortification since their unfortified product does not have the recommended RDA for iron. (An interesting note is that SMA and SMA Iron Fortified both have exactly the same amount of iron.)

Minerals: Cow's milk is very high in minerals such as calcium, phosphorus, sodium, and potassium. These large quantities put a strain on the infant's immature kidneys. SMA reduces the content of these minerals more than Enfamil or Similac and, except for calcium and phosphorus, which are higher, the other minerals in SMA are in the same range as human milk.

Vitamins: The vitamin content of all three formulas meet the RDA and in all instances exceed what is known to be present in mother's milk.

Carbohydrate: The carbohydrate in all three is lactose and is present in human milk in comparable quantities.

Fat: The fat content is similar in all three formulas.

Cost, Convenience

Since the three milk-based formulas are so similar nutritionally, the real choices a mother faces are the *form* the formula is sold in, the cost, and whether it is iron-fortified or not.

I've put together a Cost Comparison chart which shows the price differences between four forms: concentrate, powder, ready to feed, and nursettes (in bottles where all you supply is a nipple). Although specific prices may change, the levels should remain comparable. The conclusion is that on a cost

Cost Comparison

Brand/Size	Manufacturer	Form	Cost ¢/Oz.
Enfamil, 13 oz.	M/J*	Concentrate	2.46¢
SMA, 13 oz.	Wyeth	Concentrate	2.50
Similac, 13 oz.	Ross	Concentrate	2.46
With Iron:			
Enfamil, 1# 3.7 qts.	M/J	Powder	2.14
Similac, 1# 3.7 qts.	Ross	Powder	2.15
Enfamil, 32 oz.	M/J	Ready to feed	3.22
Similac, 32 oz.	Ross	Ready to feed	3.09
Enfamil, 6 oz.	M/J	Nursette	7.79
Similac, 8 oz.	Ross	Nursette	6.81
SMA	Wyeth	Ready to feed	4.89
Similac, 8 oz.	Ross	Ready to feed	4.56
No Iron:			
Enfamil, 6 oz.	M/J	Nursette	7.79
Enfamil, 8 oz.	M/J	Nursette	7.63
Similac, 6 oz.	Ross	Nursette	10.38
Similac, 8 oz.	Ross	Nursette	6.81
Enfamil, 8 oz.	M/J	Ready to feed	4.65
Similac, 8 oz.	Ross	Ready to feed	4.56

NOTE: If you buy formula in a supermarket or grocery store rather than in a drugstore, expect to save 10 per cent. There also appears to be no difference in cost with or without iron.

*Mead/Johnson

basis, the cheapest form is powder, the most expensive, the nursettes. However, this conclusion is only from a cost perspective and it is recommended that busy or preoccupied mothers would be better off using the ready to feed form since there is no chance of error in mixing.

These cost differences seem like pennies when figured on a per serving basis, yet over the first year, they add up. How much can a family plan on spending for baby's formula, plus food, the first year?

The following two situations show the comparable differences of a total convenience baby food feeding pattern and a breast-feeding situation.

Food Cost of Two Feeding Patterns in First Year

TOTAL CONVENIENCE:

Ready to feed formula w/iron consumed through 1 year	$273.37
Commercial baby food started at 3 months and fed through 12 months	281.19
	$554.56

BREAST-FEEDING:

Breast feeding for first 6 months	$ 84.68
Convenience formula with iron for remaining 6 months	110.93
Homemade baby food 6–12 months	157.88
	$353.49

NOTE: These costs are 1977 costs and although specific prices may go higher, the comparison remains relatively the same. The costs are extrapolated from a study published in Pediatric Clinics of North America, February 1977.

How Much Do You Give?

New mothers often wonder how *much* formula to feed their baby. The breast-fed baby is at an advantage since the breast-fed baby stops when he or she is filled. It has been found that mothers of formula-fed babies are more likely to overrule the baby's built-in appetite control and give extra bottles. The chart shows suggested guidelines according to weight and age.

Suggested Amounts of Formulas for Average Infants

Baby's Age	Baby's Weight (lbs.)	Number of Feedings Daily	Amount Each Feeding (fl. oz.)	Total Calories Daily
1st week	7	6	2½	280
2nd week	7	6	3	324
3–4 weeks	8	6	3½	398
1–2 months	9	6	4	472
2–3 months	11	5	5	560
3–4 months	13	5	6	708
4–6 months	15	4	8	692*
After 6 months	16	3	8	572

SOURCE: University of New Mexico, Department of Pediatrics.

*Additional calories and protein are provided by solid foods, which are generally started by this age.

MILK ALLERGIES

So far, I have been discussing milk-based formulas, but some babies, especially in the black population, have an intolerance to milk. They may either be allergic to cow's milk, which occurs in no more than 1 per cent of infants, or they may have a deficiency in the enzyme lactase. The lactase deficiency works this way: lactose is the sugar in milk. You need the corresponding enzyme in the body—lactase—to break down the lactose into glucose in the body. If the lactose is not broken down, it will cause abdominal symptoms like diarrhea, constipation, and colicky pains. The solution for infants who cannot tolerate milk is usually the soy-based formulas.

NURSING BOTTLE SYNDROME

A few years back the "nursing bottle syndrome" received wide publicity. And justifiably so. It was found that prolonged sucking caused young children's teeth to rot.

The nursing bottle syndrome is a condition where the sucking habit persists beyond the usual weaning period. In toddlers, it has been linked with frequent nocturnal feedings maintained beyond the first year; in Germany and England it has been seen in children who suck a pacifier dipped in honey, and it has even been seen in children who breast-feed for prolonged periods.

Here's what happens. During the sucking, the liquid bathes the top teeth and is held there with suction. If the liquid contains a carbohydrate, bacteria in the mouth interact with it to produce acids which dissolve the teeth. The decreased salivary flow during sleep further encourages damage to the teeth. Usually the decay begins as a dull white band under the gum line of the top four teeth and often goes undetected by parents. In advanced cases, all four teeth may be destroyed, leaving only decayed root stumps.

Recommendations

*   Do not add sweeteners to the nursing bottle or dip pacifier in sweeteners.

*   Try weaning the one-year-old from the bottle at bedtime.

*   After feeding is complete, if a child wants a bottle for security, use water.

*   Avoid fruit juices in the bottle at bedtime. Especially avoid apple juice, which is acidic and can erode the teeth.

 # When to Introduce Solids

It has become common practice to introduce solid foods very early, in some instances, as soon as the baby gets home from the hospital. But for the first 6 months the only food most babies need is milk. In the 1920s and before, solid foods weren't introduced until after the first year. If the baby doesn't *need* solid food before 6 months, why should a mother want to introduce solid foods in the first week or two of her baby's life? From nutritionists and mothers I've spoken with, I've learned that too often many mothers view their infant's early eating as a milestone. Their baby is winning the race to adulthood. "Look, he's already eating a Danish at 4 weeks!"

They assume they are helping their baby to "get ahead" and nothing drastic seems to happen. Nothing, that is, except it's a waste of time, a waste of food, and the baby may end up obese. It's a frustrating waste of time

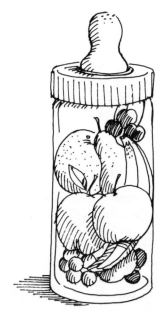

(and food) because the mother is trying to push food in at a time when the baby's natural reflex is to push it out. For the first 3 months, the sucking reflex causes the baby to purse his lips, raise his tongue, and vigorously push *against* any object entering his mouth.

It has also been suggested that baby food companies have a stake in persuading mothers to feed their babies early.

Leah Margulies, who has been active in the movement for more natural baby foods, feels that young mothers are being encouraged to give their infants solid foods at an earlier age. She says, "Six months used to be the age recommended for the beginning of solid food. Then it was three. Several years ago, six weeks was the age in vogue. Now, many new mothers leaving the hospital are told that they should start almost immediately. The emphasis is on variety. What? Baby is three months old and hasn't tried baby spinach, turkey, weiners, lasagna, raspberry cobbler?" Margulies' point is clearly that early introduction of solids is a marketing question, not a nutritional one.

Be aware that some nurses and doctors say it is okay to feed solids after the first month. They are not basing this information on nutritional need, but are simply telling the mother what she wants to hear and what many mothers end up doing anyway. It seems it is too hard for many health professionals to buck the tide, so they go along with it.

Part of the problem is that the effects of feeding solid foods too early are not clearly visible, but there are some clear-cut disadvantages:

* The digestive system may not be ready to accept solid foods.

* Some foods may cause allergic reactions if introduced too early.

* Solids unnecessarily raise the excretion load for immature kidneys.

* Solids raise the cost of feeding unnecessarily.

* Solids, too many, too soon, may make for a fat baby.

* Solids increase the time necessary to feed.

* Solids dilute the quality of the protein the infant is receiving. For example, the quality of protein in cereal versus the quality in milk.

WHAT IS A RECOMMENDED FEEDING SCHEDULE?

If the early introduction of solid foods is not recommended, then what is? What is generally recommended is represented in the following guidelines which are endorsed by the Committee on Nutrition of the American Academy of Pediatrics.

First 6 Months, or at Least First 4 Months: The 6-month guideline is recommended, but for the reasons previously discussed, it is the hardest for some mothers to adhere to. Be forewarned that you will read books on child care based on old research which suggest earlier feeding. (Recently, I thumbed through a variety of popularly available books on how to feed babies and every book suggested feeding earlier than 6 months. One book even had the baby on an entire varied menu plan by 6 months.) But feeding solids depends not just on the baby's *age,* but on his or her *weight* as well. A friend's baby weighed 9½ pounds at birth; by 4 months, he was like most 6-month-old babies and he was started on cereals.

6–7 Months: The introduction of cereals. Begin with rice, oat, and barley cereals fortified with iron. Reserve wheat, corn, or mixed cereals for later use because of possible allergies. Quick Cream of Wheat or the ready-to-eat baby cereals are preferable because they are fortified with extra iron. Add milk to cereals to increase the protein quality. Add breast milk if nursing, formula if bottle-feeding. Start with 1 teaspoon or less, gradually increase. In a few months, the baby may take 4 prepared tablespoons once or twice a day.

7–9 Months: The introduction of puréed vegetables or fruit. Some authorities, like Jane Lewis, Professor of Nutrition at California State, Los Angeles, advise that it is best to introduce vegetables first so that babies do not get conditioned to a sweet taste. This seems arbitrary, since the preference for sweets may be inborn. With vegetables, start with bland flavors—carrots, spinach, sweet potatoes, deep yellow squash. Cook and strain your own vegetables if you can (see Making Your Own, page 297). Start with 1 teaspoon or less, gradually increasing to 4–7 tablespoons a day.

With fruits, strain fruit that is used for the rest of the family. If the family uses sweetened canned fruit, pour off juice and rinse before giving to the baby. Start with 1 teaspoon and increase to 4–7 tablespoons.

Fruit juices can be started at the same time as fruits are started. Dilute to half strength with water at first. Start with 1 teaspoon a day.

9–10 Months: The introduction of puréed meats. Can be canned or strained from your table beef, lamb, veal, pork, liver, poultry, fish. Start with 1 teaspoon and gradually increase to 2–4 tablespoons per day. (Note that jars of meat/vegetable combinations are considerably lower in protein and are not a substitute for meat.)

10–12 Months: The introduction of finger foods for hand-to-mouth reflex—baby toast, zwieback, arrowroot cookies.

What interested me about feeding schedules in general is that they instruct you to introduce applesauce first, then other specific fruits and vegetables are suggested in an equally precise order. What happens if the order is reversed, is not followed at all, or if, horrors, melons are given instead of pears? How rigid are these recommendations? How closely is it necessary to follow this advice?

This feeding schedule is *not* rigid or fixed. In fact, this schedule should be used as a flexible guide, based on common sense. For example, introducing a rice cereal as baby's first solid makes sense for several reasons. If the baby is going to spit out half of his first solid food, which is typical, at least cereal is cheap in comparison to the cost of meat.

Rice is also generally nonallergenic. It is suggested that only one food at a time be introduced and to wait 5–7 days before introducing new foods as a way of avoiding allergies and ferreting out any allergies that may show up. The specific recommendations for fruits and vegetables once again should be viewed as flexible guidelines. The suggested fruits and vegetables, applesauce and squash for example, have been found to be the least irritating and the easiest to digest. Remember, babies do survive, but taking a common sense approach may help you interpret more wisely guidelines found in other books as well.

TIPS ON INFANT FEEDING SITUATIONS

* Avoid overfeeding by interpreting an infant's acceptance of food as an indicator of appetite. Babies may accept food, especially from a bottle, but may not be hungry.

* Avoid choosing food patterns for your baby that are based on opinion. Seek sound medical advice on feeding recommendations.

* Don't assume your doctor knows the entire nutritional scene. If he or she seems unwilling to discuss your nutritional concerns in detail, ask to be referred to a nurse, trained nutritionist, or a dietician.

* Avoid use of pacifier foods to quiet an upset infant who may seem to be hungry, but is not.

* Avoid rigid feeding patterns.

* Avoid "rushing" with solids and gradually introduce one at a time. Remember, the baby has an entire lifetime to get around to zucchini and macaroni and cheese.

* Avoid introducing solids to help an infant sleep through the night. Solids are not a sleeping pill.

EATING BEHAVIORS

Whether drinking milk or eating solids, there are many variations well within the bounda- ries of normal infant eating behavior. New mothers should be aware of both the normal behavior and the variations. Knowing both can make for a calmer mother.

The Usual Behavior	*Normal Variations in Behavior*
Is born knowing when hungry and cries to indicate hunger.	Does not know when hungry, does not de- mand food. Mother must set schedule for presenting food.
Knows how to suck from nipple at birth but may need help finding nipple.	Needs help in finding nipple and learning to suck.
Likes to eat.	Does not like to eat, poor appetite, vomits, needs smaller more frequent feedings than usual infant. Vomits if food is forced. Usually a slim, wiry, healthy infant. Mother should accept smaller eating capac- ity.
At 16–18 weeks has great fluctuations in milk intake.	Poor feeder, has consistent milk intake but drinks less than usual infant. Mother should accept the small milk intake.
Gives obvious signs of satiety as clamping lips, turning head away, or dozing off.	Gives no obvious sign of satiety. May eat too much and vomit or gain too much weight. Mother must set measured food intake.
Will not eat when full.	Gives up easily, can be persuaded to eat more food than wanted.
Has a built-in biological time clock, will spontaneously set a pattern for sleeping, eat- ing, etc.	Irregular baby, will never set a schedule. Needs a consistent schedule (no more than ½-hour flexibility). May adapt easily to set schedule or may fuss and cry on both sched- ule or self-demand. Mother needs encourage- ment to persist in setting schedule.
Has easy approach to new situations such as new foods or new textures. Or may object at first to changes but adapts easily.	Objects loudly and strenuously to *all* new changes. Mother must patiently and per- sistently offer changes (such as new foods) until infant accepts some changes. Mother should not attempt more than one new change at a time.
Not easily distractible, will eat or drink no matter what is going on. Will fuss when hungry until fed.	Will eat only if mother is only person in room. Can be distracted from hunger by being talked to, picked up, etc. Mother should feed infant in quiet surroundings.
Easy adaptability to change in routine such as eating and sleeping schedule.	Objects to change in routine, has great dif- ficulty in making changes. Mother may have to adapt some routines to the infant.

The Usual Behavior	*Normal Variations in Behavior*
Not particularly discriminating about food, will eat disliked food when added to liked food.	Will shudder at smell of disliked food. This infant often dislikes many foods. When mother consistently and persistently offers but does not force the food, infant will eventually accept some new foods.
Can gradually be weaned from 9–15 months.	Insists on weaning self at earlier age. Or refuses to give up bottle until 2–3 years.
When weaned, will drink milk from cup instead of bottle.	Refuses milk completely when weaned. May learn to accept milk without the bottle if served in brightly colored cup or if served with a straw. May also eat custards and other foods made with milk and may eat cheese in place of milk.
Changes fairly easily from puréed to mashed to chopped foods.	Slow to accept puréed or mashed foods in the first place, then will refuse chopped foods. Poor chewer, chokes on chopped food. May have small throat opening and gag easily. Insists on puréed or mashed foods but will eat crisp bacon or melba toast. May refuse chopped foods until 3–5 years old. Some experience away from home, such as a birthday party, may give courage to eat same kinds of foods as contemporaries.
Demands to help feed self. If mother objects, will refuse to eat.	Demands to help feed self. If Mother objects, will give up. Mother then will have to feed child until 3–5 years old. or Refuses to feed self, poor hand to mouth co-ordination. Mother should continue to feed child or help child feed self and encourage self-feeding. or Refuses to feed self and dislikes spilled foods. Mother should continue to feed child or help child feed self and encourage self-feeding. Child may delay attempts at self-feeding until 5–6 years old. May be encouraged in self-feeding by feeding mother or younger sibling.

SOURCE: Compiled by the East Los Angeles Child and Youth Clinic.

The Fat Baby

A fat baby used to be considered a healthy baby. Relatives and friends would peer into the baby carriage and positively marvel at a baby's chubby cheeks and pudgy arms and legs. Rubens and Michelangelo painted their babies this way, but if they were around today, they might change their style.

Weigh your options

THE FAT CELL THEORY

Since the mid-1970s, a theory has been postulated that fat babies turn into fat adults. Although fat babies may look cute, fat adults are something else. As proposed by Dr. Jules Hirsch of Rockefeller University, the fat cell theory hypothesizes that most fat cells are laid down in the first two years and that overnutrition (being fat) at a critical young age predetermines the eventual size and number of the fat cells. His work implies that obesity[5] manifested in early life is harder to treat in adulthood: in other words,

according to Hirsch, the fat infant grows into a fat adult because as a young child too many fat cells were accumulated as part of his or her natural make-up. And they don't go away.

Although the fat cell theory received wide coverage in the popular press, most researchers and scientists feel there are too many unknowns to make this simple relationship (fat baby equals fat adult) valid. The situation is further complicated by the fact that obesity is inextricably associated with other behavioral, psychological, and social factors. Before any hard and fast conclusions can be drawn more information is needed about the *normal* growth and development of fat tissue. Once normal growth patterns of fat cells are clearly established, it may indeed be possible through an investigation of fat cells in early life to identify individuals who may become obese later.

Part of the problem is that the effects of childhood eating patterns or rapid changes in weight during childhood on the subsequent development of obesity are unknown. The National Research Council, looking into fetal and infant susceptibility to obesity, felt that now it is only a *presumption* that individuals who are obese as infants or children become obese adults.

Even if the fat cell theory does not hold up, learned eating habits which continue through life can help make a fat baby into a fat adult. Following are some accepted causes of obesity in infants and children:

Overfeeding due to:
  Clean bottle syndrome.
  Use of food for security or to demonstrate love.
  Overprotective parents.
  Commercials and advertising.
  Peer or family pressure or advice.
  Too early introduction of solid foods.
  Use of sugar-sweetened baby foods, or heavy use of sweets.

---

[5] Obesity refers to someone at least 20–25 per cent over the ideal body weight. Overweight is 10–20 per cent over the ideal body weight.

Lack of physical exercise:

It has been shown that fat babies often do not *eat* more than lean babies, but they exercise less. It is uncertain which is the cause and which the effect.

Tradition and lingering cultural beliefs that a fat baby is a healthy baby:

Fat adults tend to raise fat children; this could be genetics, or simply learned food habits. If neither parent is obese, there's a 7 per cent chance of the child being obese; if one parent is obese, child has 40 per cent chance; if both parents are obese, child has 80 per cent chance.

PRACTICAL CONSIDERATIONS TO COMBAT INFANTILE OBESITY

* Encourage physical activity and exercise. An infant won't be able to move freely if kept restricted or confined, so do not keep a baby in a play pen or other devices that limit movement.

* Breast-feed as long as possible, at least 4–6 months. Early formula feeding seems to encourage overfeeding.

* If bottle-feeding, be sure to mix formula correctly. Do not overmix it, making it extra-rich. Do not force baby to empty bottle each time.

* Do not encourage foods, particularly sweet foods, for rewards or emotional satisfaction.

* Avoid commercially prepared baby foods that are overly sweet.

* Monitor your infant's weight gain with a physician's help.

* If infant is obese, remember the aim is not to lose weight, but to slow the rate of weight gain to that which is appropriate to his linear growth.

 Baby Foods

COMMERCIAL

When babies are ready to start on solid food, it's essential the food they eat be healthful food. In the last few years consumers have become aware that commercial baby food is often rich in water, unnecessary sugar, starches, salt, and occasionally even contains insect parts, rodent hairs, and paint chips. The solution for some mothers has been to make their own baby food. In an attempt to lure these mothers back into the fold, the baby food companies have changed their advertising substantially. But I wondered if they had changed their *food* as well. Beechnut, for example, in print ads, says in bold type that they took out the salt and sugar. In the same ad, in smaller print, they say *"most* with no sugar." However, when you look at the actual jar of baby food, say custard pudding, fruit dessert, or even cottage cheese, the sugar, honey, and corn syrup are right there.

With Gerber, the story is pretty much the same; some of their products still have up to 9 per cent sugar. When I asked a spokeswoman for Gerber why babies need sweet desserts, like cobblers and puddings, she couldn't answer me. The salt, which was originally added to appeal to mother's taste buds, does seem to be gone.

Aside from the addition of sugar or salt, commercial baby food often leaves much to be desired in other nutritional ways. The

Commercial baby food.

meat combination dinners have so much filler, starch, water, and broth, and so little protein, that nutritionists at Cornell University have advised that these meat combination dinners be served to babies as a *vegetable*. If you are using commercial baby food and want a more nourishing main dish, they suggest you combine ingredients from separate jars. For example, combine a jar of strained carrots with a jar of strained chicken. Prepared this way, baby ends up with three times more protein, over twice as much iron, and eight times more vitamin A than present in a jar of already combined chicken dinner.

Price

I compared the cost of homemade baby food with the commercial and found there are savings to be made by preparing it yourself. Although the specific prices will vary as inflation continues, the levels should remain comparable.

Item (4.5 oz.)	My Cost Homemade (serving)	Commercial Price (serving)
Carrots	9¢	21¢
Banana Purée	17¢	32¢
Squash	16¢	21¢
Applesauce	9¢	21¢
Meat	37¢	44¢
Combination Dinner* of Meat, Carrots, and Potatoes	27¢	26¢

* My combination dinner had meat, carrots, and potatoes. The commercial dinner had additional filler other than the vegetables and meat.

From my price comparison, I concluded that in most instances, I can make baby food far cheaper than it can be purchased. By making it, I also have control over its quality and the ingredients that are included.

MAKING YOUR OWN

How do you make your own baby food to assure that you're getting the best food and also saving money? It's easy. All you need are a few items: an ice cube tray, a blender, a steamer, and a baby food grinder.

The Grinder

The easiest way to feed baby is to use the same food you feed the rest of the family; a baby food grinder makes this possible. Available from places like Sears, they sell for about $4.00 and are miniature grinders that will grind up an appropriate amount of food for one baby-size meal. Let's say you're making stew for the family. When the meat and vegetables are cooked, before adding any spices or seasonings, grind up the amounts of vegetables and meat you need for your baby. What could be easier than putting a few freshly cooked carrots in the grinder and having carrot purée? Or doing the same with meat, chicken, or fish? It solves the problem of not having to fix extra food for the baby.

Freezing Ice Cube Trays

Part of the allure of the commercial baby food products is their convenience; they are ready in advance, in the right size, and in some instances need only to be warmed up by you. You can have these same advantages by preparing baby foods in bulk in advance. Here is what I recommend, using a bunch of broccoli as an example:

1. Cut broccoli into manageable pieces and steam for 5 minutes or until tender.
2. Put the broccoli pieces into a blender or food processor and purée. Use the water from the steamer as the thinning agent. (It

is important to make baby's every bite count.)

3. Now you have broccoli purée, but obviously too much for 1 serving. For individual servings as they are needed, fill a compartmentalized ice cube tray with the extra broccoli. Later, remove the frozen broccoli cubes and store in freezer bags; use within 1 month.

4. About 30 minutes before the next feeding, you can easily thaw an individual cube. This is certainly as easy as reaching for a jar of commercially prepared baby food.

The beauty of this steaming puréeing method is that it is so quick, and it can be used equally well with almost any fruit, vegetable, meat, poultry, or seafood that your doctor recommends for your baby.

Some basic points to keep in mind when preparing baby food:

* Do not refreeze foods that have been frozen. Refreezing increases the chance of contamination.

* Once prepared, purées should be used as soon as possible. Although fruit purées may last frozen for 1 year, vegetable purées are less stable and should be used within a month. Meat and combination dishes should be used within a month, also. Proper labeling is a must.

* To avoid contaminating baby food, scrub your hands, all equipment, and utensils with hot water and soap.

The following recipes and food ideas will help you get started in preparing baby food. The recipes can be reduced to single servings and the food served immediately after it is prepared; or it may be prepared in advance and used with the ice cube tray technique. The success of preparing your own infant food is dependent on its simplicity and ease of preparation. It must draw from food that the rest of the family regularly eats. It is the experience of dieticians that mothers who prepare "special" baby foods other than what the rest of the family is eating soon abandon making baby foods altogether because it's too much trouble.

Recipes

VEGETABLES

If puréed vegetables are too thick, add cooking liquid, milk, formula, or fruit juice. If they are too thin, a little cooked cereal, wheat germ, flour, or nonfat dry milk can be added. Freeze immediately any vegetable that is not to be used for that day's meals.

Asparagus: Discard lower end of stalk. Clean well and steam until tender. Strain or blend. *1 pound yields 1½ cups cooked or 8 food cubes*

Broccoli,[6] Cauliflower: Wash well, remove dirt spots, trim off lower, tough end of stalk. Cut into chunks. Steam 5 minutes. Purée in blender, add ¼ cup vegetable liquid during blending. *1 pound yields 1½ cups purée or 8 food cubes*

[6] Mix strong-flavored foods like broccoli with milder or naturally sweet foods, like applesauce or bananas. Don't add spices or salt: your baby will accept the taste of foods without flavor intensifiers.

Cabbage or Brussels Sprouts: Clean cabbage, cut into quarters (brussels sprouts can be cooked whole), and steam until tender. Purée in blender with cooking liquid. *1 pound yields 2 cups purée or 10 food cubes*

Collards or Greens: Wash leaves thoroughly, break off and throw away any tough stems. Steam in covered pan for 5 minutes. Purée or strain. *1 pound yields 1¾ cups cooked or 9 food cubes*

Green Beans: Wash thoroughly. Cut off stem end, remove any tough strings. Cook whole in steamer. Purée in blender. *1 pound yields 1½ cups cooked or 8 food cubes*

Peas: Just before cooking, shell peas. Steam 3 minutes. Purée in blender. Add liquid while blending. *1 pound yields ¾ cup purée or 4 food cubes*

Potato: Prepare same as mashed potato for family. Thin with cooking liquid or milk. *1 large potato yields 2 cups mashed or 10 food cubes*

Summer Squash (soft skin): Wash well. Cut zucchini or other summer squash in half lengthwise and remove seeds; it is not necessary to peel. Steam 5–8 minutes. Purée until smooth; if too thin, use cooked cereal or wheat germ as thickener. *1 pound yields 1½ cups purée or 8 food cubes*

Sweet Potato or Yam: Scrub and wash, remove bad spots, and trim root. Do not peel. Steam or bake (400° F.) for 30–40 minutes or until soft. Scoop potato out and strain or mash. (It's not necessary to use blender.) *1 pound yields 1½ cups mashed or 8 food cubes*

Winter Squash (hard shell): The easiest way to cook a winter squash like acorn squash is with the shell on. Scrub the shell and cut squash into pieces with a serrated knife. Squash can be halved or quartered and baked in a covered dish at 350° F. for 40–45 minutes. When tender, scrape *meat* from shell and purée. *1 pound raw squash yields 1 cup cooked or 5 food cubes*

FRUITS

Select fully ripe, fresh fruits. Wash and prepare as suggested below.

APPLES

Ingredients:
  2 eating apples
  3 tablespoons water
  1 teaspoon lemon juice
    Yields ¾ cup purée or 3–4 food cubes

Wash, peel, and core apples. Cut into halves or quarters and put in small saucepan with the water. Cover and cook on low heat for 10 minutes. Remove fruit with slotted spoon and purée in blender with enough of the liquid to blend well. Add lemon juice.

APRICOTS

Ingredients:
  1 pound apricots
  ¼ cup water
  1 teaspoon lemon juice
    Yields 2 cups purée or 10 food cubes

Wash, dip in boiling water to loosen skin, peel, cut, and remove pits. Place fruit in pan with water and lemon juice. Cover and simmer for about 10 minutes. Purée with cooking liquid in blender.

PEACHES

Ingredients:
  2 peaches
  ½ cup water
  1 teaspoon lemon juice
    Yields ¾ cup purée or 3–4 food cubes

Peel and cut peaches, remove pits. Cover and cook in pan with water about 10 minutes. Test with fork. When flesh is soft, they are ready for the blender. Add lemon juice.

PEARS

Ingredients:

 1 pear

 1 tablespoon water

 1 teaspoon lemon juice

>   *Yields ½ cup purée or 2–3 food cubes*

Wash, peel, and core pear. Cut into pieces. Simmer in small pan with liquid for 5 minutes. Drain and purée in blender.

PRUNES

Ingredients:

 12 dry prunes

 Water

>   *Yields 3 cups purée or 15 food cubes*

Cover prunes with water. Bring to boil. Reduce heat and simmer for 25 minutes. Cool and drain, saving liquid. Remove pits and purée prunes in blender. If too thick, add some liquid.

Ask your doctor about using raw fruits for your baby. Peeled ripe but raw apples or peaches or apricots can be puréed in blender. Raw banana or avocado can be puréed or mashed.

PROTEIN FOODS

Use a blender for meats and poultry. Watch carefully for small pieces or fragments of bone.

MEAT

Ingredients:

 ½ cup cooked meat or hamburger (remove fat and gristle)

 1 tablespoon milk, formula, or cooking liquid from meat

>   *Yields ½ cup purée or 2–3 food cubes*

Place ingredients in blender and mix at high speed until very smooth. To test for smoothness, put a small amount on the palm of your hand. Rub with finger. If any large particles can be felt, blend again.

POULTRY

Ingredients:

 ½ cup cooked chicken or turkey (discard skin and cut chicken in pieces)

 1 tablespoon liquid, chicken broth, milk

>   *Yields ½ cup purée or 2–3 food cubes*

Place ingredients in blender. Blend at high speed. Add more liquid if necessary. Test for smoothness with your fingers to be sure food is free from lumps.

LIVER

Ingredients:

 ½ pound liver (any kind)

 ¼ cup liquid

>   *Yields ¾ cup purée or 4 food cubes*

Rinse liver under water. Remove outer skin and large veins. Steam in covered pan or broil until liver is cooked (8–10 minutes). Purée, adding liquid to blend and thin. Chicken livers are tender enough to mash with a fork.

EGG YOLK

Boil eggs until hard, cool and remove white. Mash the yolk with a fork and add enough milk to thin to desired consistency.

Custards are also a good way to serve eggs. To make a custard, combine ¾ cup milk with 2 egg yolks. The mixture can be baked (set custard cups in pan of water and bake at 350° F. for about 40 minutes) or cooked in double boiler until smooth and thick. Do not expect this to taste like traditional adult custard, which is usually highly sweetened. Serve as soon as possible. Do not leave at room temperature because custard is subject to bacterial growth.

LEGUMES

Ingredients:

1 cup dried legumes (dried beans, peas, lentils, soybeans)

3 cups liquid

¾ cup milk, formula, or liquid

Yields 2½ cups purée or 12 food cubes

Wash and presoak beans, or bring to boil and allow to sit covered for 1½–2 hours. Simmer in 3 cups liquid for 2–2½ hours or until soft. Purée with blender, adding ¾ cup milk, formula, or liquid.

Books

If you would like more detailed information about baby foods, there are many how-to books on the market. Keep in mind that although many give good advice on how to prepare baby foods, and excellent practical tips—going to a recycling center and getting used baby food jars to sterilize yourself—in some instances, their specific information, for example, *when* to begin solids, may be in conflict with current thinking.

Castle, Sue. *The Complete Guide to Preparing Baby Foods at Home.* New York: Doubleday & Co., Inc., 1973. $6.95. The virtue of this book is its wide range of ideas encompassing everything from stewed pineapples to fish stew.

Kenda, Margaret Elizabeth, and William, Phyllis S. *The Natural Food Cookbook.* Avon Books. $1.50. Attacks commercial baby food for, among other things, its long shelf life. Includes many recipes. Good sections on allergies, finicky eaters, and teething.

Morris, Melinda. *The First Baby Food Cookbook.* New York: Ace Books. $1.50. A book of recipes and ideas for adapting adult foods to baby.

Turner, Mary and James. *Making Your Own Baby Food.* New York: Bantam Books, 1976. $1.25. Includes an information section on prenatal nutrition and pointers on supplies and equipment.

Teething Treats

Most babies get twenty teeth in their first 3 years, and discomfort and crankiness are common symptoms. To make baby happier and to keep mother happier, too, here are some tips for teething treats:

* *Frozen bagel.* Wrap a bagel in plastic and freeze whole or in halves.

* *Frozen fruits.* Wash and peel bananas, peaches, nectarines, melons, and pears, and cut into bite-size pieces. Wrap in plastic and freeze individually so they don't clump together.

* *Frozen melon ices.* Take the seeds out of a melon; peel melon and mash in a blender. Place in ice cube tray with individual compartments to freeze. Store in plastic freezer bags.

CHILDREN:
Good Food Is Child's Play

Because kids are naturally curious, food can be a great adventure for them. They like to cook it; they like to eat it; they like to buy it, all of which involves new experiences to be explored and sensations to be savored. It's my experience that until they are censured by an adult, kids will try a wide variety of foods and like most of them. In experimental nutrition educational classes, I've observed preschoolers from oriental families, who have never seen a brussels sprout or an artichoke before, eat and enjoy both. I've seen ghetto kids from Brooklyn enjoy a plate of fresh raw vegetables that was foreign to their own diets.

Children, even very young preschoolers, are receptive to information that emphasizes good, healthful foods. Nutritional educators at California State University Child Development Center in Los Angeles are carrying out a 3-year project in the day care center to see how beneficial nutritional education is at the preschool level. After 2 years, the results are not all in, but it looks very promising. The teachers say the preschoolers are *selecting*

and *asking* for a wide variety of foods that they weren't even eating before the program started. An expected side benefit is that the children are asking their parents to purchase foods that are now known to the child, but that may be foreign to the parent.

One example of how impressionable children are when it comes to their favorite foods, is Sesame Street's Cookie Monster. Since children are so imitative, it was almost inevitable that children would be munching handfuls of their favorite cookies while watching the show. How much better if the producers had used this opportunity to create, for example, a Carrot Cruncher, a muppet who crushed carrots in his bare teeth.

But the Cookie Monster isn't the only television creation at fault. Robert Choate, President of the Council on Children, Media, and Merchandising, calls children's commercial television "edible TV." Others call it an affront to nutrition education. According to Choate, a child watching weekend daytime TV in the first 9 months of 1975 could have seen 3,822 commercials for cereal (many of them highly sugared), 1,627 commercials for candy and chewing gum, and only 2 for meat and poultry and 1 each for vegetables and cheese. When I spoke with Choate in the summer of 1980 he told me that this bombardment of commercials has not changed much. "In fact," he said, "there may even be more commercials for more products because the manufacturers are using 30-second spots, instead of the 60-second spot of the past."

Exposure to good food can be done more easily in a less formal situation than a classroom, or on television. Your own kitchen is the perfect laboratory, and with a few resources, which you most likely have on hand, the kids can have a great time. This chapter is chock full of food-related activities that can be fun for you to share with your kids, or for the kids to do by themselves.

Although food can be fun for children, it

Baby's first word.

is often a cause of worry and concern for their parents. Are they getting enough of the important foods? What are their nutritional needs? What do you feed a sick child, or do you? How do you pack a nutritious brown bag lunch? If your child's school lunch program is a bad one, how is it possible to improve it? Are snacks helpful to children, or are three meals a day preferred? This chapter provides the answers.

 # Are Our Children Malnourished?

I remember a press conference in which the hosts were trying to drum up interest in stories about hunger by dramatically referring to starving children in America. One of the writers offered to do a story on starving kids in America, but she wanted to meet some of them and take their pictures. She wanted the group to produce in concrete form what their rhetoric was saying existed. I'm sure they never did because for the most part, with the high availability of medical services and food programs, there isn't dramatic, widespread starvation here.

There is something quieter and less dramatic but just as disturbing for a country as rich as our own: malnutrition. Even malnutrition in this country doesn't show up in its most dramatic forms. Most American children don't have scurvy (vitamin C deficiency) or beriberi (thiamin deficiency). What is of more importance are the areas of practical nutritional concern. The chart shows the five nutrients that tend to be low in children and lists their dietary sources. The point of this chart is not to alarm, but to reassure. If you look at the five areas of concern, you'll see how easy it is, if you're serving wholesome foods, for your kids to get more than enough of these basic essentials naturally.

AREAS OF CONCERN IN CHILD NUTRITION

The nutrients that tend to be low are:

Iron, which carries oxygen in the blood and prevents anemia, and can be found in red meats, legumes and whole grains;

Vitamin C, which is important for bone formation, healthy blood vessels, and healthy gums, and can be found in fresh fruits such as citrus, strawberries, nectarines, and in fresh vegetables such as peppers, tomatoes, potatoes, and broccoli;

Thiamin (B_1), which is vital for healthy nerves, aids the body in the use of foods, and can be found in meats, eggs, legumes, whole grains, and enriched grain and cereals;

Vitamin A, which improves night vision and skin, is important for normal growth patterns, and can be found in milk, eggs (yolk), margarine, butter, dark leafy green and yellow-orange vegetables;

Calcium, which is essential in bone, muscle, and tooth formation and growth, as well as blood clotting, muscle contraction, and heart beat, and may be found in milk, cheese, ice cream, pudding, cream soups, greens and small fish with bones.

IRON deficiency, which results in anemia can be due to lack of dietary intake, intestinal parasites, or malabsorption problems. You could recognize this in your child if the child is lethargic, easily fatigued, and extremely susceptible to infection. According to "Recommended Dietary Allowances," 1980, iron intake is frequently inadequate during periods of rapid growth in childhood. Compare your child's intake with the list below and see how he or she is doing.

Servings	Iron/mg
1 egg	1.1
1 (3-ounce) hamburger	3.0
3 cups chili con carne	4.2
3 cups whole milk	0.3
½ cup peanuts	1.5
½ cup canned green beans	1.45
½ cup fresh green beans	1.45
1 cup orange juice	0.5
2 slices whole wheat bread	0.8
1 banana	0.8
TOTAL	15.1 mg

Child 3–10 years needs 10 mg of iron daily.

Vitamin C is needed for proper wound healing, for dentin formation; during development of teeth a vitamin C deficiency may result in weakened tooth enamel. You can recognize the symptoms of low vitamin C in your child if he has delayed wound healing, if bruises are slow to heal, or if gums bleed. Anemia is another symptom of inadequate vitamin C intake because the body needs adequate vitamin C in order to use iron.

Some suggested sources of vitamin C are:

Serving	Vitamin C/mg
½ cup orange juice	60
1 orange	66
½ grapefruit	44
1 (3-ounce) tomato	21
1 cup tomatoes	88
1 baked potato	20
1 cup cooked mustard greens	68
1 cup cooked broccoli	140

Child 3–10 years needs 40 mg of vitamin C daily. NOTE: The *leaves* of broccoli are especially high in vitamin C.

Thiamin deficiency is found in this country among pregnant alcoholic women, who may give birth to thiamin-deficient babies.

Thiamin deficiency, called beriberi, occurs most frequently in areas where the diet consists mainly of unenriched white rice and white flour.

Serving	Thiamin/mg
1 (3.5-ounce) pork chop	0.63
½ cup green peas	0.22
1 slice whole wheat bread	0.09
TOTAL	.94 mg

Children 3–10 years need 0.7 to 1.2 mg of thiamin daily.

Vitamin A is a fat soluble vitamin. One of the early symptoms of vitamin A deficiency is impaired night vision.

Serving	Vitamin A (I.U.)
1 raw 7″ long carrot	7,930
1 cup cooked collards	14,820
1 cup mustard greens	8,120
1 stalk cooked broccoli	4,500
3 apricots	2,890

Children 3–10 years need 2,000 to 3,000 International Units of vitamin A daily.

Calcium. In order for the body to make use of calcium, vitamin D is needed in adequate supply as well. A dietary deficiency of calcium can cause bones to weaken later in life.

Serving	Calcium/mg
3 cups whole milk	864
1 egg	27
1 ounce Cheddar cheese	213
½ cup cooked spinach	83

Children 3–10 years need 800 mg of calcium daily.

The three most common nutritional problems of childhood are *anemia, obesity,* and *dental cavities.* Anemia was discussed in connection with iron deficiency. The early onset of *obesity* in infancy is believed to lead to adult obesity and difficult weight loss in adult years. (For more on this, see Chapter 9 on the Fat Baby, page 295.) The problems with obesity are psychological in addition to physiological; the obese child is more likely to have a poor self-image, learning and behavior problems. Over 20 per cent of children are overweight and from a health point of view, the child's health is endangered by increased susceptibility to diabetes, heart disease, and adult obesity.

The third area of concern is *dental car-ies.* Cavities in the teeth are formed when teeth are exposed to high acid-forming foods, usually sugar and sticky carbohydrates. The exposure time of acid-forming foods to tooth enamel should be kept to a minimum by brushing often, avoiding sweet snacks, particularly items like cough drops and candies, which remain in the mouth a long time, and eating "detergent" foods such as raw fruits and vegetables that clean your teeth as you chew.

 Questions Parents Ask

At one time or another, most parents find themselves encountering new situations involving their children, often with no answers. Thus was born Dr. Spock. In the food and nutrition area, the same need exists. The parent wants to do the right thing in nourishing the growing child, but is often faced with special problems (a finicky eater, a fast-foods-only eater, etc.), and the average parent often is not knowledgeable enough about nutritional science to know exactly how to proceed.

With the help of a group of teachers who work in nutrition education in California public schools, I've put together some of the most often asked questions, with their answers.

* *My child does not like milk, what can I substitute?*

There's a difference between not *liking* milk and not being *able* to drink it. Some children, most often non-Caucasians, have difficulty digesting lactose, the main carbohydrate in milk. Now that it's been discovered that some children do have this problem, a substitute is being looked for, but it's difficult to find. Milk is inexpensive and provides 75 per cent of our total calcium, 40–50 per

cent of riboflavin (B_2), 25 per cent of protein, and 12 per cent of calories; fortified milk is also a main source of vitamin D.

Some children who are lactose intolerant may still be able to drink a normal amount of milk without adverse effects. Drs. Jean Mayer and Johanna Dwyer have reported that in India children and adults who had a high rate of lactose intolerance were tested. All the children were able to drink about ⅘ cup of milk with no difficulty. A study was done at MIT by Dr. C. Garza and Dr. N. S. Scrinshaw and it was found that although over half of the 69 black children were lactose intolerant, they still had no trouble drinking a cup of milk.

In a study done at Cornell by Dr. M. C. Latham, the vast majority of the children studied said they *liked* milk. If your child does not like it, and doesn't have any of the symptoms associated with lactose intolerance, such as stomach cramps, there are some things you can do:

MILK TIPS

* Drink a glass along with your child when you're expecting the child to drink milk. Adults gain nutritional value from milk and children are influenced by what they see their parents enjoying.

* Try the milk at a different temperature. Some children may prefer theirs room temperature, others might like it icy cold.

* Serve it with a meal, rather than by itself.

* Explain to your child the importance of milk and where it comes from. Take your child and some friends to visit a zoo or a dairy farm where cows are being milked. Arrange to have the kids actually milk a cow.

For the child who absolutely refuses to drink milk, the nutrients can be gained from other milk products like cheese, cottage cheese, yoghurt, cream soups, puddings, custards, and homemade ice cream.

* *Should I give my child vitamin pills?*

The vitamin pills created for children, in the colorful shapes of their favorite cartoon characters, are seductive. I became aware of them one Christmas when Bristol-Myers sent me a beautifully wrapped Christmas box of their products. And there sitting among the tinsel was a bottle containing Snoopy, Donald Duck, Yogi Bear, in easy-to-swallow vitamin form. But I wondered—are these vitamins for kids just another unnecessary hype or a practical form of preventive medicine?

The body needs over fifty nutrients in order to function in a healthy way. Vitamin pills rarely provide even half of these. A balanced well-selected diet can provide all the nutrients a growing child needs. If you feel more secure giving your child an additional source of vitamins, with your physician's knowledge you could give a children's multiple vitamin. Avoid the flavored multiple vitamins that establish the dangerous idea that

pills are candy. Since vitamin pills are expensive, avoid costly "natural" vitamins since all forms of vitamins are used by the body in the same way.

* *My child doesn't like vegetables, what should I do?*

Probably you should pay more attention to *which* vegetables are served, and the way the vegetables are prepared. Children, like adults, don't like overcooked, strong-flavored, or mushy vegetables. One of my strongest memories from childhood is being served turnips and rutabagas. It was one of those classic situations: my parents, mostly my father, demanded that I eat them, or I couldn't leave the table. I developed an elaborate, time-taking process, but I eventually got excused from the table. I would chew on the vegetables, then hold them in my mouth and wait for the moment when both my parents were occupied. At that point I would spit them into a paper napkin and later I would drop the napkin surreptitiously under my chair. After dinner, I would return and collect the wadded-up napkins before they were discovered. In general, I wasn't a finicky eater, so how much better and simpler it would have been for all of us if my parents had served other vegetables that I liked.

For a wide variety of suggestions, look over the specialty vegetables list in Chapter 1, Vegetables. Some offbeat suggestions are sure to appeal to kids. Often children prefer the snap, crackle, and pop of vegetables in their raw form instead of cooked. This is certainly okay, since the raw form has more nutrients anyway. Try raw cauliflower, green bell pepper strips, carrots, spinach salads, sliced turnips. If you're cooking turnips for the family, and JoAnn doesn't like cooked turnips, try raw strips of turnips served with Zany Peanut Butter Dip (see Chapter 1, page 43).

As a last resort, serve fruit instead.

* My child wants cereal for breakfast, but I don't want to provide sugary cereals. What are the alternatives?*

The main alternative is to read the label. Even cereals that *appear* to be nutritious and wholesome often are not. A friend once told me proudly there would be no more junk cereals in her house. Instead of selecting boxes that were labeled Boo Berries or Froot Loops, she chose those that were advertised as nutritious "whole wheat," and "natural"; yet on closer inspection of all three she had chosen, sugar was the second most prominent ingredient by weight on the label.

So read the labels, and choose whole grain cereals, granolas, hot oatmeals, and hot cereals made from whole grains instead of the presweetened cereals; or make your own. Top with fresh fruits and dried fruits to provide the sweetness children like. Or at the worst, let the kids put a little sugar on these nonsweetened cereals; they will never use as much as the manufacturers.

YUMMY HOMEMADE GRANOLA

As an alternative for a child who wants the sugared cereals he or she sees on television, you might want to try having the youngster help in the fun of making yummy homemade granola. The main ingredient here is rolled oats, which, like all the other ingredients, can be purchased in bulk at a health food store. This makes a special, hearty breakfast cereal everyone will want to eat. A recipe isn't really necessary, but the following can be used as a guide.

Ingredients:

3 cups rolled oats
2 cups wheat bran
1 cup sesame seeds
1 cup chopped almonds (optional)
1 cup shredded, unsweetened coconut
½ cup wheat germ
½ cup soy flour

LIQUID MIXTURE

¼ cup safflower oil
¼ cup brown sugar
¼ cup hot water
1 cup raisins

Makes 11 cups

1. Preheat oven to 325° F.
2. In large bowl mix together first seven ingredients.
3. Make a mixture of oil, sugar, and water and dribble on top of dry mixture to moisten. Spread mixture on cookie sheet and toast in 325° F. oven for 15 minutes until crunchy. When done, add raisins. Store in a covered jar in the refrigerator, and for lovely fragrance, put a vanilla bean in the container.

* My children prefer white bread, but I'm not convinced it's nutritious.*

Children I know call white bread squish bread because they can squish their hand in it and leave their fingerprints behind. That may be one of its best virtues. During the milling process, when wheat is made into white flour, the B vitamins are lost. The federal government now requires that white flour be enriched with these vitamins. So white bread does have nutrients, but the problem is that other nutrients may be lost in the milling process and not put back into the flour.

Encourage children to eat whole grain breads. But don't expect to make this change-over from squish bread to whole wheat breads too quickly. Maybe you might try making whole grain breads at home with the kids. Children love working with dough, so this should be fun. I've found kids like things their size, so instead of making adult-size loaves of bread, try individual rolls.

* When kids want a cold drink, what can I give them instead of sodas or Kool-Aid type beverages?

Part of the appeal of these beverages is their bright color and sparkling effect, but try using fruit juices instead, and add carbonated water for the fizzy part. True, fruit juices aren't cheap, but they provide many nutrients and not just calories and quesitonable additives. Try grapefruit and apple juice, or the apricot, peach, and strawberry nectar that are sold in individual-sized servings. (When buying fruit *juices,* be sure you are buying the unadulterated, un-sweetened, uncolored, natural fruit juice. Read the label and avoid anything labeled fruit *drink.*) Another cool idea is to freeze fruit juices into popsicles. (Tupperware has popsicle molds, or make your own with small paper cups and popsicle sticks.) Or try Rubbersicles.

The real thing

RUBBERSICLES

My stepdaughters, Snoogy and Melina, introduced me to rubbersicles. They are like pop-sicles, but better: they don't drip, they don't

melt[1], they bend on their sticks from side to side, which is fun, and they are nutritious. What more could you ask?

Ingredients:

   2 envelopes Knox unflavored gelatin

   ¼ cup water

   2 cups orange juice made from frozen
     orange juice concentrate

Makes 8 rubbersicles

1. Sprinkle gelatin over cold water to sof-ten. Heat over low heat to dissolve gelatin.

2. Add orange juice and pour into popsi-cle molds. Freeze for several hours.

3. When frozen, don't eat immediately after they are taken out of freezer. At room temperature, let them soften for 5–10 min-utes; they get rubbery and are more fun to eat.

ENDLESS VARIATIONS: Instead of using fro-zen concentrate for the 2 cups orange juice, use fresh oranges and their natural juice, or fresh pineapples, mangoes, nectarines, ba-nanas, strawberries, plums, papayas, or kiwis. (I would think some of these would appeal to adults as much as the kids.)

* I know that candy is not nutritious, but what about occasional treats?

Food provides more than just nutrients. It satisfies many social, emotional, and psycho-logical needs. And certain foods are cus-tomary for certain occasions due to either religion, tradition, or commercialism. Candy should be considered as an occasional treat (what's Easter without a chocolate bunny?), but not as a reward or used for daily per-suasion.

   This also answers the question of what to do with the grandparent who puts out candy when it's not regularly allowed at home. My sister-in-law Libby issued an edict to my mother: no more candy when the grand-children come to visit. The next time the kids came to visit, they went to the candy

[1] The gelatin acts as glue, keeping the juice together and keeping it from dripping popsicle-style. So this is an especially good treat for young kids who usually make a drippy mess out of a popsicle before they are finished.

bowls as usual and were shocked to find their candy wasn't there. Tony, who was five, asked what was going on. My mother had to explain that his mother had asked her not to give them sweet treats anymore. Tony implored, "But it's all right, you're my *grandmother*," implying that grandmothers have special license, and I suppose they do.

Healthful candies can be made at home from scratch without the extra additives found in store-bought candies. Try making fudge or peanut brittle and let the kids help.

* *My child doesn't like to eat much breakfast. Does it matter?*

Children need the energy as well as the nutrients provided by a morning meal. Studies show that children who do not eat prior to school have more trouble learning. One reason for not eating breakfast may be that the child may not yet be hungry if he is awakened and rushed to get ready for school. Some nutritionists recommend giving the child plenty of time in the morning and possibly some task or duty that will boost the morning appetite.

I think an even greater problem is that breakfast in most homes means *breakfast foods*: eggs, cereals, and toast. If your child prefers nontraditional, yet nutritious foods for breakfast, that's great. Pizza, toasted cheese, peanut butter and banana sandwiches, leftover spaghetti, casseroles, all provide good nutrients that the child needs to start the day.

But if it's a traditional breakfast, try to make it a little different.

* Instead of syrup or jellies on top of pancakes or waffles, try fresh applesauce.

* Instead of regular French toast, after dipping the bread in egg batter, coat it with a layer of a crisp cereal like Kellogg's Special K. It makes for an extra-crunchy French toast.

* Instead of a glass of orange juice, make fruit whips. Purée a banana or strawberries with cold milk in a blender. Mix in crushed ice and a raw egg.

* *My kid's hooked on fast foods and processed foods. Isn't it better than nothing?*

Generally, fast foods are high in fat and lacking in fruits and vegetables. With education and supplementation, fast foods can be part of a healthful diet. When choosing fast foods, choose milk, orange juice, or even milk shakes instead of nonnutritious soft drinks. Cheese on hamburgers gives extra protein and calcium. Choose hamburgers and sandwiches with lettuce and tomatoes. (See Chapter 8, Eating Out, page 258.)

The main rule is to get 4 servings of fruits and/or vegetables, 2 servings of meats, 4 servings of bread, and 2 servings of milk each day. Fast foods have a place in a diet but cannot be the *only* source of nutrition.

Or, let your children make fast foods at home. Improve on the recipes by including fresh fruits and vegetables and less fat. Children enjoy cooking and being creative and will probably come up with their own healthful variations of fast foods.

Below are my healthful alternatives to fast foods, and kids' favorite processed foods:

Favorite Foods: Healthful Alternatives

Hamburgers: Lean meat, sesame or whole grain buns, fresh lettuce or spinach, tomatoes.

Pizza: Great! Avoid greasy meat toppings. Rely more on cheese and vegetable toppings, or make your own. (See recipe, page 327.)

Carbonated Beverages: Juices, milk, hot cocoa.

Hot Dogs: Turkey dogs, chicken franks (both of these are half the price of beef dogs). In general, avoid products with nitrites.

Sweets for Snacks: Raw fruits, vegetables, whole grain cookies, fruit breads like pumpkin bread, applesauce, zucchini, and date nut breads, nuts and seeds.

Peanut Butter: Buy the old-fashioned kind with no preservatives that you have to stir and store in the refrigerator.

Candies: Nuts, seeds, sugarless gum.

Spaghetti: Great! Not the canned kind, but regular spaghetti that's rich in B vitamins, enriched with iron, served with tomato sauce that's high in vitamins A and C. Make your own. (See recipe, page 123.)

Popcorn: Good, no butter, no salt.

Sno Cones or Popsicles: Make at home with crushed ice and fruit juices instead of sugar syrups.

Candied Apples: Fresh apples.

Peanuts: Avoid salted kind.

Ice Cream: Lots of additives. Eat in moderation or make your own.

* *I'm a vegetarian, but my husband's concerned about this diet for our daughter. Will she get all the nutrients she needs for growth?*

In Boston, 119 vegetarian parents volunteered their preschool children for a study done by the Frances Stern Nutrition Center at the New England Medical Center Hospital. Some conclusions about growth were made: more vegetarian children were below the fiftieth percentile for height and weight than children on regular diets. An association between smallness and leanness was found among the vegetarian children. These characteristics were more pronounced among the non-breast-fed children on macrobiotic diets with a limited variety of animal protein. The larger the variety of protein, the better the growth. The children did best on lacto-ovo vegetarian diets, which included eggs, milk, and milk products. Children especially need protein and calcium for growth so the lacto-ovo approach is the recommended vegetarian diet. The other indicated areas of concern are lack of adequate iron and vitamin B_{12}.

* *What do you do when a child gets sick? Is what's right for adults, right for children?*

Children are different from adults in that they are smaller and some conditions become more acute and potentially more dangerous faster in a small person.

Fever: When a child has a fever, the fluid intake is very important because the small child can become dehydrated quickly. Give fruit juices, broth, and skim milk.

Diarrhea: Of course, if the diarrhea is persistent, you would want to seek medical treatment. Refrain from giving food and milk for the first 12 hours or until diarrhea lessens. Give water or weak tea until food can be started. When starting back with food:

1st: Skim milk
2nd: Gelatin, hot cereal, toast
3rd: Other foods

Vomiting: Avoid liquids for 2 hours after vomiting. Then give carbonated beverages, dry toast, crackers, and skim milk.

* *Does my child need fluoride? Does he get it in the water supply or should he get fluoride supplements?*

Although fluoride is often found naturally in some water sources, it is often added to public water supplies and to toothpaste because the ingestion of fluoridated water by young children who are forming their teeth is believed to be beneficial to the teeth. The American Medical Association feels that "fluoridation decreases caries in childhood and up to 44 years." Although there has been some opposition to fluoride from established scientific groups, it does have benefits and if you live in an area that either does not have natural fluoride in the water, or where fluoride has not been added to the water, you may want to consult with your physician about fluoride supplements for your child.

* *My son is hyperactive. I've heard this has been treated by diet, but now I hear these diets have been disproved. What's the story— can hyperactivity be treated by diet?*

I personally know parents who have children who have been diagnosed as being hyperactive. The children's symptoms are short attention spans, learning difficulties, and a demand for immediate gratification. In short, they are problem children. Their parents would do almost anything to help their children to settle down. So, a doctor suggests all they have to do is to feed the child (and the entire family) different food. It seems like a cinch. Wouldn't you change your child's diet if a doctor said it would keep the youngster from crawling the walls? Here's the story.

Benjamin F. Feingold, M.D. (after whom the Feingold diet is named), claims a significant percentage of hyperactive children show a dramatic improvement when placed on a diet eliminating foods containing artificial food flavors and colors. The diet also excludes fruits such as apples, oranges, and tomatoes as well as many green leafy vegetables, cucumbers, root crops, beets, butter, yellow vegetables, and meat. With the change in diet Dr. Feingold dictates a change in lifestyle. He requires that the *entire family,* not just the child, be placed on his diet and that the parents develop a close rapport with their child by spending more time with him. Since hyperactive behavior is often associated with disrupted family life and lack of attention, the critics point out that improvement in the child's hyperactive state may be related to this increased attention.

An in-depth study sponsored by the Food Research Institute at the University of Wisconsin reached the conclusion that a diet free of artificial colors and flavorings does not reduce the symptoms of hyperactivity in children. The Wisconsin group in releasing their findings stressed the preliminary nature of their conclusions. They also stated that there were sufficient subjects who showed improvement to warrant additional further study.

More recent studies described in the March 28, 1980, issue of *Science* support Feingold's hypothesis. Two studies were conducted at the University of Toronto and the University of Maryland and a third was sponsored by the FDA. Bernard Weiss, a University of Rochester researcher involved in the FDA study, said that the findings definitely showed that food dyes sometimes act like toxic drugs in children. James M. Swanson, a Toronto researcher, said the findings suggested that a subgroup of hyperactive children react to food dyes as if to toxic drugs. Although the FDA has downplayed the results, researchers have said their

findings strengthen the accumulating evidence that we're consuming agents with the potential to produce behavioral changes.

The subject still warrants further investigation. In the meantime, all of us would do well to eat more foods in their natural state.

Cooking for Hyperactive and Allergic Children, a 250-page recipe and reference book for children sensitive to food ingredients, is available for $5.95 in spiral paperback ($9.95 hardbound) from Cedar Creek Publishers, Fort Wayne, Indiana 46825.

Snack time!

* My child likes to snack. But isn't it better to eat three meals a day?

We're a snacking nation. Last year, Americans spent over $13.5 billion on snack food; $1 billion went for potato chips *alone* and almost $8 billion for soft drinks. These snacks contribute very little except fat and sugar.

Whether or not to snack is really a question of whether or not the snack is nutritious and is contributing to the day's nutrient intake. Many young children cannot get all the nutrients and calories they need in three meals a day, thus snacks, when they are properly selected, can help to fulfill important nutritional needs.

Charlotte Young and researchers at Cornell University found that the body did better physiologically when six snack-size meals were consumed each day instead of the three-meal-a-day pattern. They also found the incidence of obesity was reduced.

If your children's snacks are the fast-food, eat-on-the-run type, then you're right, they'd be better off with their three meals a day. If you compose nutritious snacks, the kids will benefit and you will, too.

Think up snacks that are nutritious, yet also interesting to a child. Try string cheese —it comes in 7″ long rolls and to eat it, you pull it apart and shred the strands with your fingers. Since kids like to play with their food anyway, this is a natural. Or, have them make Fruit Shakes or Easy Meat Turnovers, and keep them on hand for their snacks. Here are some ideas:

Dairy Foods:
   Fruit shakes[2]
   Hot cocoa[2]
   Chocolate milk
   Homemade ice cream
   Pudding
   Custard
   String cheese
   Cottage cheese
   Yoghurt with fresh fruit slices
   Orange Julio[2]

Fruits and Vegetables:
   Any and all fruits and vegetables cut into
      finger-size pieces
   Fruit or vegetable kebabs
   Stuffed celery—with cottage cheese, pea-
      nut butter
   Fruit juices (avoid ones with added sugar)
   Dried fruits—raisins, apricots, prunes
   Zucchini Chips[2]
   Applesauce

Meat/Protein Foods:
   Pizza[2]
   Eggs, hard-boiled
   Cubed meats
   Easy Meat Turnovers[2]
   Miniature Meatballs[2]
   Small beef patty
   Peanut butter
   Refried beans, bean dip

Grains and Cereals:
   Whole grain breads, rolls, biscuits, muffins
   Hot or cold cereals—Yummy Homemade
      Granola,[2] oatmeal, other whole grains
   Cookies made with whole grains[2]
   Pita bread
   Tortillas
   Bread sticks
   Whole grain or enriched crackers

Many crackers look good on the package, but they actually contain more additives, sugar, and salt than whole grain. The following list should be a helpful guide when buying crackers that contain a large amount of whole grain for snacks.

   Burry's: The Original Euphrates Bread
      Wafers, plus Sesame Seeds
   American   Sanger: Ak-Mak   Sesame
      Crackers; Armenian Cracker Bread;
      Whole Wheat Flour
   Old London: Rye Melba Toast
   FFV (Famous Foods of Virginia):
      Stoned Wheat Wafers; Roman Meal
      Wafers; Sesame Crisps
   Nabisco: Triscuits; 100% Whole Wheat
      Wafers
   Nabisco: Wheat Thins
   Ralston Purina: Seasoned RyKrisp; Nat-
      ural RyKrisp

✻ *My kid is a finicky eater. I seem to spend too much time yelling at him. He's still not eating, but what can I do?*

What follows are suggestions that should help in feeding children. These suggestions emphasize paying attention to simple elements ranging from color, texture, room temperature, and serving size to attitude and atmosphere at meals. Perhaps a change in only one of these areas will result in your child's eating you out of house and home.

FEEDING TIPS FOR CHILDREN

✻ Make food easy for children to eat: remove the strings from fresh celery, cut meats into small pieces (children can choke on tough meats).

[2] Recipe included in this chapter.

* Young children prefer bite-size pieces—"finger foods."

* Children prefer soft textures and crunchy textures. They dislike foods that are stringy, slimy, or too hard.

* Lukewarm temperatures are usually preferred to ice cold or steaming hot.

* Children often don't like strong-tasting vegetables such as cabbage, onions, and brussels sprouts—tame them down with cream or cheese sauce, or serve others they like better.

* Start with small servings that are not overwhelming. Let the child ask for more.

* Let children serve themselves and pour their own milk from small pitchers or plastic measuring cups.

* The child should have a chair that supports his or her feet so that they don't dangle at mealtime.

* Use of utensils that are easy to handle to make mealtime easier: small spoons, forks, cups (for the young child) with weighted bottoms that won't tip.

* Introduce fruits and vegetables in their raw form.

* Children mimic adults—watch your reaction to new foods; your child will be watching.

* Introduce one new food at a time.

* Be casual about encouraging your child to try new foods; avoid bribery, coercion, scolding.

* When your child says that he doesn't like a certain food, ask what food he does like—emphasize the positive.

* Encourage sanitary practices of washing hands before eating or cooking.

* Don't rush children through meals.

* Overtired children have poor appetites.

* Have children help in the preparation of the food.

* Have children accompany you to the store to help in the purchase of their food.

 ## School Lunch

For school-age children, one meal out of three is eaten in school. If parents are concerned about what their children are eating, they naturally should be concerned about what they are eating in school as well. That's why I've included school feeding programs in this chapter on children. The nation's $4 billion a year federally funded school lunch program is an area of great concern among food activists. Thirty years ago, the School Lunch Act was passed on the lofty principle of safeguarding our nation's health, and perhaps the less lofty principle of promoting the consumption of agricultural commodities by forcing school lunchrooms to use excess commodities from the Department of Agriculture.

What has evolved in most instances are unappetizing, overpriced lunches that often fail to meet minimum nutritional standards set by the Department of Agriculture. To

School lunch.

qualify for federal and state subsidies, the schools must serve a Type A lunch (for the curious, there's no such thing as a Type B or C lunch).[3]

Type A Lunch Requirement

* *2 ounces of meat or meat alternative*—this is often skimped on.

* *¾ cup of two or more vegetables or fruits*—these are rarely, if ever, fresh.

* *1 slice enriched bread*—it's almost always the white, squishy kind.

* *½ pint milk*—there's rarely, if ever, a choice between whole and skim milk.

* *1 pat of butter*—most children don't need this extra fat.

The importance of the school lunch is that by design, it is supposed to supply one third the nutrition a child needs for the day. For some children from impoverished families this may be their only food for the day. School lunch is also important because inept and bad as it is in most instances, it has become the model for other school feeding programs. In the beginning, there was only school lunch, now many districts have school *breakfast* programs, and as one member of the New York City Board of Education said to me, "Can school *dinner* be far behind?"

In New York City, I did a five-part investigative series on the school lunch situation and became a crusader against the bad practices of the school lunch program. (As a result of that series, I was asked to be a consultant to the Bureau of School Lunches, and help them improve their situation. Unfortunately, because of conflict of interest, my News Director wouldn't let me accept it, but it would have been a fascinating challenge.) I would like parents to use this section as a guide; use it to judge if your school is doing as well as it could. If it isn't, I discuss the

options and give names of people to contact who have gone before and paved the way. Or, if you decide to boycott the school lunch and have your child brown-bag it instead, there are ideas on how to do that more effectively, also.

WHAT'S BAD IN BRIEF

VISIT A LUNCHROOM

How many of you reading this who have kids in school have ever been inside their cafeteria, or eaten a lunch with them at school? Do it. It might be a real eye-opener. I'm not talking about minor annoying situations, like soggy sandwiches one day or a sour batch of milk. I'm talking about . witnessing major abuses in a food policy that should be striving to serve good, healthful food. From what I've observed, school lunch epitomizes the worst in our nation's food habits: it is usually too sweet, too fatty, too salty, and too overprocessed. Some school lunch directors responsible for serving this dismal food (sweet doughnuts, fatty hot dogs, greasy and salty french fries) defend their actions by saying that this is the only kind of food kids will eat.

HIGH WASTE

If this is true, then why is the food waste so incredibly high? The Department of Agriculture estimates that school lunchrooms throw out over $600 million worth of food every year. I saw this problem, which is referred to in the industry as "plate waste," firsthand in almost every school I visited. I also witnessed a pathetic by-product of it. The older people in the surrounding neighborhoods know a school's reputation for throwing out still usable food. The senior citizens often go through the garbage cans and pull out the

---

[3] This rigid Type A lunch pattern is in the process of being revised to allow for more flexibility of appetites (i.e., a six-year-old doesn't need the same portions as a high school student).

perfectly good food and bring it home for themselves. In New York City, I witnessed a woman in Chinatown making a haul of over 100 perfectly good breaded fish sticks that the kids had thrown out, untouched. In another incident, on Manhattan's upper West Side, I saw an elderly man collect from school cafeteria garbage cans a supply of fresh milk in unopened containers and an armload of apples.

TREND TO PROCESSED FOODS

The answers to why kids aren't eating and why a lot of their food is thrown out instead are complicated, but some school districts have further compounded their problems by ripping out conventional cooking facilities and installing microwave facilities that are capable of only heating up frozen TV dinners. These school districts say they can't cook food on the premises anymore, it's too costly, too time-consuming, takes too much skilled labor. So they resort to processed food, which means in some places, like New York City, having prepackaged lunches shipped in from as far away as Illinois.

LACK OF EDUCATION

From an educational point of view, what's also bad is that the lunchroom is a perfect living laboratory where food and good manners could be incorporated as a total part of the educational experience. But the general feeling is that many educators don't know a classroom when they see it. The school is looked upon as an educational experience *until* it comes to the lunchroom. Lunchrooms are loud, boisterous places, not conducive to eating or learning. And most teachers wouldn't be caught dead having to eat with their students.

COMPETITION WITH JUNK FOODS

Another suspicious area of the school lunch program is the junk foods that are sold on the school premises with the seal of approval from the school. In my visits to school lunchrooms, I repeatedly saw kids spend their lunch money on a bag of chips and a candy bar. This was observed in New York City public schools, where supposedly the sale of junk foods on school premises is prohibited—but since the money raised by these sales goes to support extracurricular activities (the sports program, the music activities), the school administrators are often loath to cut them off.

Different schools are handling the junk food problem in a variety of ways: In Fresno, California, the school trustees voted to ban junk food in the lower grades, but grades 10 through 12 will still have junk foods available on campus. In Los Angeles, the Board of Education resolved the conflict by throwing it back to each individual school to make its own decision. And in Montreal, the School Council for the past 4 years has adopted a food policy of no junk food in the vending machines or sold in the cafeterias. Their extracurricular activities are budgeted and not dependent on junk food sales. Another rendition I just heard about allows junk foods to be sold, but only *after* lunch. Who's going to monitor *that* plan?

WHAT'S GOOD

Some school systems have conquered these lunchroom problems and come out smelling like roses. I have eaten in their lunchrooms and I have seen their lack of plate waste, so I know it can work. The ingredients that combine to make these successful systems work are full student, teacher, and parent involvement.

The impetus for change and improvement comes from one of three places: from disgruntled school administrators who are fed up with losing money on their school lunch programs, from furious parents who are angry about the quality of food that is bought and served with taxpayers' subsidies, or from the school lunch staff, who grow weary buying and preparing food in large quantities that isn't eaten.

For the outsider, the motivation and desire to change what one sees may exist, but some of the biggest obstacles are the practical questions of where to start? How to do it? Following is a list of people and organizations that have either run successful school lunch programs or have actively worked from the outside to improve them. With one exception, I know these people and groups personally and have found them to be dedicated, willing and eager to share their insights and information with others. These are can-do people, who, if you ask, can supply you with everything from encouragement to practical recipes.

RESOURCE LIST FOR IMPROVING SCHOOL LUNCH

Thomas Farley in Milwaukee One of the best systems in the country is run by Thomas Farley in Milwaukee. Everyone told me I had to see his operation and I wasn't disappointed. They make all the food on their own premises from homemade bread and lasagna to sloppy Joes. The day I was visiting the plate waste was minimal. In fact, many students went back for a second lunch and some even for a third. One of the secrets of his program is that Farley works with the Student Council in preparing the menus and, to simplify ordering and preparation, all 150 schools in the district serve the same lunch on the same day. His personal enthusiasm and energy is what turned his school lunch program around, from the inside.

> Thomas Farley, Director
> Food Services Division
> Milwaukee Public Schools
> P. O. Drawer 10–K
> Milwaukee, Wisconsin 53201

Carrie Lipsig in New York City One of the school lunch systems with the most loving touch is the program run by Carrie Lipsig for the Board of Jewish Education. They pride themselves on making all their own food on their premises. One day I ate a delicious lunch of baked chicken, mashed potatoes, cranberry sauce, green beans, and peach cobbler. Carrie's attitude is one that many school districts that are turning to modernization or processed foods could learn from. She says, "The other school districts say they need to use convenience foods. What could possibly be more *convenient* than cooking a little chicken, putting a few seasonings on it, and baking it? Then you have something the children love." In her school, the teachers also eat along with the students and use the lunch period as another possibility for an educational experience, not just for children roughhousing.

> Carrie Lipsig, Director
> School Lunch Service
> Board of Jewish Education
> 426 West 58th Street
> New York, New York 10019

Clara Davis in Nesconset, New York Clara Davis is located in a suburban, once farm area, on Long Island, New York. A unique feature of her program is that all the students get a chance at having their say about what they'd like to eat. Each week, one class, ranging from elementary school students to high school students, chooses among thirty available selections and plans that week's menu. The Student Council meets with Ms. Davis once a month to discuss actively what changes they'd like. Clara Davis calls her program applied nutrition in the best sense. "We've found students who choose something themselves are more likely to eat it than if they're just handed a prepared lunch plate." Another interesting feature of her program is that she has the older kids working in the kitchen, actually preparing most of the food. The day I was there, the kids were chopping cabbage for salad, mixing the sauce in the macaroni, and making peanut butter cookies.

> Clara Davis, Director
> Smithtown Central School District
> School Lunch Office
> Southern Boulevard
> Nesconset, New York 11767

Margaret Stockert in Greenlawn, New York Margaret Stockert describes herself and her lunch program as being ahead of its time. Since 1959 she's been preparing natural lunches, with everything prepared on the premises, and she doesn't see why this can't be done in all and any school districts across the nation. She makes her own bread products, uses only fresh vegetables and fruits, and has found, contrary to what some people would think, that costs aren't any higher for fresh produce. From the beginning, she has had the help of parents and with their backing they were able to eliminate junk foods from the school's vending machines.

> Margaret Stockert, Director
> Harborfield School District
> 18 West Sanders Street
> Greenlawn, New York 11740

Consumer Action Now Consumer Action Now is a group of concerned parents who have been involved in a variety of consumer-related issues from solar heating to trying to improve school lunch programs in New York's private and public schools. They have done some pilot projects on improving lunch programs by substituting more wholesome food for the foods that are usually served. These pilot projects have been accompanied by instruction in nutrition, with classroom samplings of bean sprouts and whole wheat buns. Although their expertise is not in the area of nutrition, they are knowledgeable about organizing parent groups to improve school feeding situations.

> Consumer Action Now
> 49 East 53rd Street
> New York, New York 10022

American School Food Service Association The American School Food Service Association is a national, nonprofit group with over 67,000 members who work in school food service. With its extensive membership scattered throughout the United States, the association can be an invaluable resource if you live, for example, in Kansas and want to know quickly what the best school lunch programs are in Topeka. This is the only group I have not had personal con-

tact with, and I would think that because it has to mollify a large and diverse membership, the association's views might be on the conservative side, but so far it has come out on the right side of some of the controversial questions. For information, write to:

> Executive Director
> American School Food Service Association
> 4101 E. Iliff Avenue
> Denver, Colorado 80222

The Las Vegas Plan The Las Vegas Plan represents the most controversial approach to improving the school lunch situation and is being heralded by some as the savior of the school lunch system. Created by Len Fredrick, Director of the Clark County, Nevada School District Food Service program, the Las Vegas plan concentrates on giving kids the kinds of fast foods they've been eating on the outside and bringing that revenue into the school lunchroom. Fredrick has created his own versions of McDonald's Big Mac, Arby's Roast Beef Sandwich, and Super Shakes. Although his plan is a real kid pleaser and he says his food is nutritious (he adds vitamin C to the french fries and he says his milk shakes exceed the government milk nutritional requirement by 40 per cent), his detractors, and there are many, say his program is not an educational one. His opponents feel children eat too many of these fast foods anyway to the exclusion of more nutritious food choices and that he's copping out.

Although you might not be in agreement about the fast foods he's chosen to serve, I think most schools could learn from his creative merchandising techniques, which have stimulated a renewed interest in the school lunchroom. His jazzy, aggressive approach could be used just as effectively by school districts serving more wholesome, nutritious foods.

> Len Fredrick, Director
> Food Service, Clark County School
> 4499 South Arville Street
> Las Vegas, Nevada 89103

Greenburgh Central School District In Westchester County, a suburban area outside New York City, a group of parents banded together to protest the lunches their kids were receiving and to ask specifically that junk foods ranging from soda pops to Oreos be removed from the school lunch menu. With authority granted by the school board, they have reduced the amount of sugar in the school's food and eliminated every item that contained artificial coloring, flavoring, or preservatives. Their success encouraged them to put together a how-to guide for other schools.

Greenburgh Central School District No. 7
Citizens' School Lunch Committee
475 West Hartsdale Avenue
Hartsdale, New York 10530

The Food Research and Action Center has a handbook available for $1.00 that is useful for people organizing or monitoring school lunch programs. Called *FRAC's Guide to School Lunch and Breakfast Programs,* it is available from:

FRAC
2011 I Street, N.W.
Washington, D.C. 20006

The Center for Science in the Public Interest in conjunction with The Children's Foundation has published a 32-page booklet called *Eating Better At School. An Organizer's Guide.* It is available for $2.00 from:

The Children's Foundation
1420 New York Avenue, N.W.
Suite 800
Washington, D.C. 20005
or
Center for Science in the Public Interest
1755 S Street N.W.
Washington, D.C. 20009

 ## Brown-bagging It

In public schools, over 50 per cent of the children brown-bag it; in private schools, it's as high as 75 per cent. On my lunchroom trips, what I've seen in those brown bags was sometimes as much a wasteland as those hot school lunches of which I've been so critical. It wasn't unusual to see brown bags containing an assortment of cellophaned prepackaged chips, cakes, cookies, and soda. Sandwich meats like bologna that are rich in fat, artificial flavorings, and colorings were the standard fare. I saw lots of orange drink, which has nothing to do with oranges.

Since lunch can provide one third of the day's food intake, it needs to be nutritious. If the lunches your kid trots off to school with resemble those described above, you may mean well, but you're spending money on empty calories, fats, and sugar and perhaps even more importantly, you're establishing bad eating habits that might lead to learning difficulties now and health problems such as obesity and heart disease later.

Bagging it.

I think the best idea for improving brown-bag lunches is for parents to get together and share ideas to improve the lunches brought from home. No kid wants to be singled out as different, with a "different" lunch. If everybody's bringing more wholesome lunches, it gets the important "O.K." of the peer group. Maybe you could use a PTA meeting as a forum for a discussion. Ask a home economist to come in and share ideas. Call your local university and have them suggest a speaker. For example, in New York City, Cornell University's Cooperative Extension group has a Consumer Education Program that sends people out into the community to share their knowledge of nutrition and other consumer-related issues. You could also rely on the mothers to lead the discussion. After all, they pack lunches every day and probably have practical, creative, clever ideas to share.

What follows are some suggestions for spicing up brown-bag lunches with better nutrition, not artificial colors and flavors. These ideas for children could be adapted for adults who carry lunch to work and also for campers, backpackers, and picnickers.

And remember, this lunch business needn't be deadly serious. Nobody dictated that the bags must be brown or the lunch wrapped in white waxed paper only. Why should it just be the Cracker-Jack people who put a surprise in every package? Drop a little something extra in the lunch now and then. Make it fun for the kids to see what they've got today. Put in a crazy straw (those straws that twist and swirl while you drink). A game of jacks. A love note. A funny eraser to use when lunch is over. Buy small novelty items in bulk; it needn't be a big chore.

SUPPLIES

Basics

1. Paper lunch bags: If you're using a brown bag, have the child write her name on it, or decorate it. Make it her *special* bag.

For something different, try the bright neon orange, green, yellow, red, or blue bags that stationery stores sell to wrap presents in.

2. Lunch box: A lunch box offers the advantage of being easy to clean and reusable. When I was in school, Zorro lunch boxes were the rage. Let your child pick out his favorite. If a child has a lunch box he likes, he is less apt to "lose" it.

3. Sandwich bags.

4. Plastic wrap.

5. Napkins, paper towels . . . make these colorful, maybe with cartoon characters.

Additional

6. Thermal containers, vacuum bottles.

7. Plastic containers with lids.

8. Plastic forks, spoons, knives.

9. Straws.

10. Colored tissue paper to overwrap the sandwiches or wrap a special treat.

WHAT TO PUT IN THOSE LUNCH BAGS?

Sandwich Bread

Start with whole grain bread, raisin bread, pocket bread (pita), whole wheat English muffins. If your child has a weight problem, put the sandwich on the thinnest slices of pumpernickel.

Fillers

Use something that's not an artificially red and prepackaged luncheon meat. If you opt for prepackaged cold cuts, read the label and select those with the least additives.

TRY

Tuna fish, chicken salad, ham salad, sliced chicken, sliced turkey, cheese, meatloaf, roast beef, corned beef, egg salad, natural peanut butter topped with apples, cottage cheese and chopped peanuts.

Add to Sandwiches

Sliced tomatoes, bean sprouts, dark lettuce leaves, spinach, shredded cabbage, sliced carrots, pickles, zucchini slices, slivered nuts.

Fresh Fruits and Vegetables

This is limited only by seasons and availability. Apples, bananas, apricots, peaches, pears, grapefruit, orange slices, tangerines, nectarines, melon balls (in freezer bags), grapes, berries, raisins, plums, prunes.

Other dried fruit, fruit leathers, strips of green pepper, carrot, celery, or turnips.

Cooked corn on the cob.

Raw cauliflowerets, raw peas in the pod.

Celery stuffed with peanut butter or cheese.

Instead of Potato Chips

Nuts in shells.
Pumpkin seeds.
Sunflower seeds.
Granola.
Bread sticks.
Bag of unsweetened cereal.
Bagels.
Small shredded wheat biscuits mixed with nuts.
Whole wheat crackers.
RyKrisp crackers.
Olives, dried fruit.

ALSO TRY
Cheese kisses
Hard-boiled eggs

Soups and Hot Foods

Using a wide-mouthed thermal container, you can send last night's chili, tonight's stew, or baked beans, chowder, chop suey, stuffed cabbage roll, spaghetti, and a wide variety of soups.

To Drink

Something real—not artificial. Individual 6-ounce cans with easy open tops are available with apple, vegetable, tomato, and grapefruit juice, and peach and apricot nectar.

Milk, chocolate milk, lemonade.

Desserts

Avoid high sugar, low nutrient foods for desserts. Use fruits for that sweet taste, or try oatmeal, oatmeal-raisin, peanut butter, oatmeal-peanut, or applesauce cookies.

Pumpkin, zucchini, cranberry, date-nut, banana breads.

Blueberry, corn, bran, or whole wheat muffins.

Small containers of applesauce, stewed apricots or stewed apples.

Individual size yoghurt. Put it in the freezer the night before and just before the child is ready to leave for school, put it in the lunchbox.

PACKING THEM SAFELY

When you pack a lunch for school (or the office) it's out of refrigeration for 4–5 hours before it is eaten. Harmful bacteria grow easily in sandwich fillings made with protein foods like meat, especially when the sandwich remains in a warm room for several hours before it's eaten. You might consider packing *frozen* sandwiches from a convenience as well as safety measure. If the sandwich is frozen when it leaves home, it will remain cold through most of the holding period before lunch and bacteria will have little chance to grow. Having a selection of frozen sandwiches in your freezer also cuts down on the time it takes to pack a lunch.

Here are some tips to keep in mind when making sandwiches for the freezer, assembly-line style:

* Make a production line out of this and do as many at one time as you need for a week or two.

* Spread each slice of bread with a thin layer of butter or margarine. This layer acts as an insulator so that when the sandwich

is thawing the filling doesn't make the bread soggy.

* Spread with a suitable filling for freezing that includes meat, poultry, cheese spreads, egg yolk mixtures, and nut pastes. Mayonnaise and sour cream don't freeze well by themselves, but as dressings in combination with other ingredients as a sandwich filler, they do just fine. Do not use raw vegetables, hard-cooked egg whites, or fruit jellies; these don't hold up well when the sandwiches thaw.

* Wrap and seal the sandwich and date it. Freezer sandwiches should keep well for 1–2 months at temperatures of 0° F. or lower, but are best if used in a few weeks.

* When you're ready to put the sandwich into the lunch box, slip in tomato slices and lettuce leaves.

 # Fun Food Activities

COOKING

Kids are natural bakers; they love to throw dough around. They are born pizza makers and eaters. They love to paint and decorate, so birthday cupcakes are their realm. Whether these activities are successful or not often depends on the way the parent handles them. Give the child some independence. All people, especially children, need the freedom to be messy when they cook. In fact, I think this must be one of the great appeals of cooking to kids—they get to do things like smashing, mashing, and squishing food, which are usually off limits. I have a friend whose husband vacuums up after her while she's still cooking! That's not an attitude that's likely to make little kids (or my friend for that matter) feel very comfortable.

Thoughtful gestures make it more fun for the kids. You wear an apron when you cook, right? Buy one for the kids. Give them their own cupboard at their level where they can keep their cooking equipment. For starters, give them a set of their own plastic mixing bowls, some measuring spoons, and a hand beater.

When planning food activities for and with children, here are some tips to keep in mind:

Activities

Keep the activity relatively short.

There's less chance of losing their interest.

Keep it limited to just a few steps and be well organized.

If the kids have to wait interminably while you find the baking soda, forget it. You'll end up making those special goodies by yourself.

Make foods that are their favorites—

Spaghetti, pizza, and ice cream. (You can point out how these are being made with the best ingredients and that their fast-food equivalents usually aren't.)

Whenever possible, when dealing with kids, eliminate complicated steps.

For example, in making a pizza, it may be enough of an adventure for most kids that they made the dough. Instead of extending this activity and risking losing their interest by suggesting they make their own tomato sauce, too, either furnish them with some you've previously made, or, for simplicity's sake, let them spoon on a store-bought sauce.

The following activities are designed around healthful concepts in food and nutrition, so the child learns that spaghetti, for example, doesn't grow in cardboard boxes on grocery shelves, but is made from wheat and eggs. He can even make it himself. Depending on the age of the child, some will need supervision from the parents. I've had a lot of chuckles and many good times doing these activities with youngsters.

PASTA-MAKING

Since spaghetti is one of their favorite foods, kids love to make this. Once when Julie Levine was five years old and going through her bridal stage, she came to my apartment to make pasta. She wore a white bridal dress and a flowing, ankle-length veil. I'll never forget the curious transformation of "bride" into pasta maker. Once in the kitchen she abruptly threw off her veil, rolled up her

sleeves, climbed on a chair, and settled down to work. After we finished, Julie put on her veil, straightened her dress, and the little bride went home with pasta in hand. It was such fun, she often asks me when we're going to make pasta again.

But don't think the kids have to be as old as five to enjoy this. I've done it with three- and four-year-olds as well and I've also done it with adults. You should enjoy it as much as the kids.

Traditionists say the best way to make pasta is to roll the dough by hand and cut each noodle separately with a knife. Since this is an activity I enjoy sharing with kids, I prefer using a pasta machine. The machine simplifies the process to such an extent that children can actively participate. The machines vary in price from $25 to $200, depending on the size and whether they are manual or electric, but I figure they are well worth the investment as an ongoing form of family entertainment. I started out with a manual machine and was happy until one Christmas when my husband was gifted with the electric model. An electric machine is so quick and easy that you can make pasta every day.

Before you start, arrange for a drying area —this could either be a dining room table covered with paper towels, or better yet, a portable clothesline for draping the pasta. The drying area can be as simple as a heavy string hung between two cupboards.

PASTA

Ingredients:

3 cups flour[4]

4 eggs

Water (about ¼ cup)

Makes enough for 8 servings

---

[4] There's a controversy about the flour. Some Italians insist on semolina flour made from durum wheat, which has more vitamins and protein than the all-purpose flour. Many people don't have access to it in their communities, so you can use an all-purpose flour (make sure it's not bleached) with equally good results.

1. Using a large counter space, or table, so the kids have plenty of room to work, pour the flour into a big bowl. Make a well. Have the kids break the eggs and beat slightly. Add eggs to flour and mix together in a ball; moisten any dry bits of flour with water and add to ball.

2. Start to knead. You can do this with your adult hands for a moment to get it ready, and then, have the kids feed it into the machine and let the machine do the kneading. Continue rolling out the dough with the machine until it's soft and shiny and the flat strips are as thin as you want your noodles to be. Strips are most easy to handle when they are 4″ wide and no longer than 15″.

3. The next process is actually *cutting* the strips into noodles. How you proceed next depends on whether you have an electric machine or a manual.

With the *manual,* you don't have to wait for the strips to dry, but can immediately begin feeding them into the machine to be cut, and this has its advantages because kids tend to get impatient and there's no waiting around.

With the *electric machine,* wait for the strips of dough to dry slightly before putting them into the machine. This drying should take no longer than 5–10 minutes. If you feed wet strips of dough into an electric machine, you'll end up with gummy strips that clog the machine. Cut the dough into noodles and hang them or lay them flat to dry.

The kids can be useful at all these stages: in guiding the dough through the machine to be cut; in catching it after it comes out; and in hanging or laying it to dry.

4. Cooking the pasta is fun, too, because it takes *no* time. Get a big pot of water boiling, add a little oil, and throw in the pasta. When the water returns to a rolling boil, which is a matter of seconds, the pasta is cooked. It cooks instantly because it is so fresh and there are no preservatives.

5. Serve with any sauce you like. Prepare sauce in advance and pour over steaming hot pasta. (Any extra pasta could be frozen—before it is sauced—but that's adult stuff and the kids will want to eat it all now.)

COLORFUL PASTA

Once the kids get the hang of basic pasta, they might like to try it in different colors. How about green (spinach or broccoli), or orange (carrot), or red (tomato or beet)?

To make colorful pasta, cook and purée 1 cup of cut-up vegetables of your choice. Add beaten eggs to the puréed vegetables, then add this mixture to the flour. Because of the water content of the vegetables, you will need to add less water, perhaps none. Proceed as in the above recipe.

EASY MEAT TURNOVERS

Little kids like things in small packages and this is a favorite they love to make. Even preschoolers can do this with very little help.

Ingredients:
   1 package refrigerated crescent rolls
   1 (3½-ounce) can chicken or tuna
   2 tablespoons minced onions
   2 cloves garlic, pressed
   Parsley, torn into small pieces
   Sweet pickles, cut into pieces
   ¼ cup grated Monterey Jack cheese,
      or 1 slice for each turnover

1. Using crescent rolls that are premade and refrigerated in the can (select brand with least additives), lay them out flat.

2. Make mixture of chicken, or tuna, and onions. (Cutting the onions is reserved for older kids.) Press the garlic and add it along with parsley and sweet pickles, to chicken mixture.

3. Put mixture into center of crescent roll. Top each roll with a little grated cheese. Be careful not to let ingredients spill over sides, roll up cresent rolls into sweet little

packages. Bake in oven according to directions on can, or about 10–12 minutes.

MINIATURE MEATBALLS

These are essentially the ingredients for a meatloaf, but kids like it better in little balls.

Ingredients:

1 pound lean ground beef

2 cloves garlic, pressed

½ onion, chopped

1 egg

¼ cup rolled oats or Quaker Oatmeal or soy cereal

½ cup tomato sauce

Makes about 12 balls

1. In a big bowl, mix all ingredients together. Roll into 1″ diameter balls.

2. Bake on cookie sheet in 350° F. oven until brown.

PIZZA

There's probably nothing kids like better than pizza. So for lunch or dinner with their friends, why not help them make their own? I got this idea from Dan Tamkus, a friend who has been making pizza with his two

daughters for years. Depending on the age of the kids, they'll need more or less help. If their attention span is short, this can be done in two parts with the children, or you can do the first part by yourself (preparing the dough), and the children can participate in the second part only (making the dough into pizza). I think the latter is the best plan.

Ingredients:

DOUGH

1 envelope yeast

1 cup lukewarm water

4 cups (at least) unbleached flour

1 tablespoon olive oil

SAUCE

1 (29-ounce) can tomato purée

Oregano, tarragon, basil

Garlic

2 cups (2 handfuls) grated mozzarella cheese

1 cup (1 handful) grated Romano cheese

GARNISH

Roasted green pepper slices

Sliced mushrooms

Olives

Makes 2 (12-inch) pizzas

1. Preheat oven to 350° F. Have kids grease two pizza pans.

2. Dissolve yeast in water and add to flour in large bowl. Add enough flour to create proper consistency to knead. The amount will change depending on the humidity of the day. Knead until smooth and let rise 1½ hours in warm place.

3. After the dough has risen, divide it in half and, using a rolling pin and your hands, do a combination of rolling out and pushing out the dough to fit the pan. When the dough is in place on each pan, prick it with a fork in several places.

4. Place in 350° F. oven and bake for 10 minutes. This first baking makes a crunchy

crust, and keeps the sauce from sinking in and making it soggy.

5. Spread the sauce over the crust. The kids can use a premixed pizza sauce or, using tomato purée as a base, you can help them add traditional Italian herbs—either fresh or dried oregano, tarragon, basil, and garlic. After spreading the sauce, add 2 cups of mozzarella (2 handfuls) to the top of each pizza and top that with 1 cup of Romano (1 handful). Add whatever other ingredients the kids might like: roasted green pepper slices, sliced mushrooms, olives, but avoid fatty toppings like salami and pepperoni.

6. Bake again until golden and cheese is melted. About 10 minutes.

ZUCCHINI CHIPS

Ingredients:

Zucchini—enough to make as many
   slices as you want

Cut unpeeled zucchini into thin slices, and place on a cookie sheet in a low oven, 150° F., for about 2 hours or until dry. Or, on a sunny day, place zucchini slices out in the sun. You will have to turn them once. You can use dried zucchini chips with a dip for a snack, and they are good enough to eat by themselves.

OLD-FASHIONED DOUBLE-BOILED HOT COCOA

Ingredients:

2 cups water

½ cup cocoa powder

3 teaspoons sugar

6 cups milk, scalded

¼ teaspoon vanilla

1 tablespoon cinnamon

Serves 8 cold kids

1. Using top part of double boiler, heat water, cocoa powder, and sugar for 2 minutes over direct flame.

2. Add 6 cups scalded milk and place over boiling water in double boiler. Heat thoroughly.

3. Add vanilla and cinnamon (they cut down the necessity for the usual amount of sugar). Before serving, stir with a whisk to make frothy.

FRUIT SHAKES

Ingredients:

1 cup cold milk

1 cup mashed fresh fruits or fruit juices
   or fruit nectars

Cinnamon or vanilla (optional)

Serves 1 kid and a friend

Using a blender or shaker, add milk to mashed fruits. Fruit can be cherries, berries, peaches, bananas, etc. Mix well. For more flavoring, add cinnamon or vanilla. Serve with wide straws.

MEG'S FANCY

This delightful thick drink falls somewhere between a shake and a soda.

Ingredients:

Strawberry ice cream

Raspberry ice cream

Milk

1. In a blender, mix equal parts of both ice creams. If you can't find raspberry ice cream, use vanilla and add some frozen raspberries.

2. Add enough milk to make it barely liquid. Drink with a smile. It makes you feel delicious.

ORANGE JULIO

For a pause that refreshes, try this as an after-school snack instead of a soda.

Ingredients:

4 cups cold orange juice

1 cup crushed ice

1 egg

Serves a gang of 4

1. Using a blender or food processor, crush the ice and add all ingredients.

2. Blend until fluffy and well whipped.

MAKE YOUR OWN FRUIT JUICES

Using a simple hand juicer, or an electric one, if available, extract the juice from lemons, oranges, grapefruit, limes, tangerines. Make whatever combinations you like best. With a melon ball cutter, cut some melon balls and float on top. Add crushed ice.

DOG BISCUITS

Kids love their pets, so encourage them to make their favorite puppy some special food. This recipe for dog biscuits can be eaten by the kids, too.

Ingredients:

  1 cup all-purpose flour

  1 cup wheat flour

  ½ cup wheat germ

  ½ cup powdered dry milk

  1 egg

  6 tablespoons lard or shortening

1. Combine dry ingredients and stir in egg. Add lard and as much water as necessary to make a dough that can be kneaded. Knead until smooth. Roll out to a thickness about ½″.

2. With a cookie cutter, cut into shapes you think your dog might like: a cat? a bird? Bake at 325° F. until lightly browned, about 10 minutes.

GROWING FOOD

Some of the best activities for kids involve growing food and its by-products. It's fun for kids to see that something they did caused a sweet potato to grow a lovely lush vine, grapefruit seeds to turn into a tree, or beans to sprout. These are all easy to do.

Growing food

Sweet Potato Vine

All you need is a sweet potato, a container to put the potato in with water, and a sunny location. The water is the plant's food and the light is necessary for its growth. The vines that sprout can be left to trail, or can be trained to climb. Although the vine isn't edible, this can lead to a discussion of potatoes, and why not accompany this with a potato tasting of sweet potatoes, white potatoes, red potatoes, and yams?

Citrus Trees

Orange, grapefruit, and lemon seeds will grow into glossy green plants, but they take an eternity (2–3 *years*), so this should be viewed as a long-term project.

To make your own citrus tree, before the citrus seeds dry out, pot them in small containers with soil 3″ below and above. Give the seeds a warm, sunny place to grow and water thoroughly. In a few *years,* you will have a nice plant—but don't count on oranges.

Bean Sprouts

Kids like instant results (so do I) and that's one of the virtues of sprouting your own beans. They're the closest thing to *instant* food. You can practically see them grow in front of you. And kids like the way they taste, although if this is a new food for your children, you might want to try the tactic I once witnessed. Introducing sprouts to her class, a teacher said each child could only have three sprouts. It worked; she had that class clamoring for handfuls. The Chinese call bean sprouts nature's most convenient vegetables because they can be grown in a few days, any time of the year. And they are perfect for apartment farmers in the middle of winter.

Increasingly, bean sprouts already sprouted are showing up in supermarkets. But there are additional reasons for sprouting your own. They have more nutrients because you can eat them immediately after they are sprouted and you're not going to take the husks off (the husks are the storehouse of the B vitamins) the way the commercial sprouters often do.

Here are the basics for sprouting:

1. Start with ⅓ cup dried beans. Buy soybeans, garbanzos, lentils, or mung beans from your grocery store; it is not necessary to make a trip to a health food store. Experiment and see which make the most tasty sprouts. Soak the beans overnight in lukewarm water. This soaking will double or triple them in size, and that's already fun. The kids will be able to see this difference immediately.

2. Rinse the beans and drain. Place beans in a colander or sprouter. If you're using a simple kitchen colander, cover it with a dampened cheesecloth. You could also use a glass jar with a cheesecloth over the top. I've experimented with both these techniques and I've found the hardest and most cumbersome is the glass jar route: the beans clump together in one area. The easiest is the Kitchen Garden sprouter, which has four levels that make it easy to grow, and keep separate, four different kinds of sprouts. The Kitchen Garden is available in health food stores or from the Kitchen Garden Company in Salt Lake City, Utah. Place any kind of sprouter and beans in refrigerator.

3. Rinse beans a couple of times a day

with cold water. These frequent rinsings ensure they don't develop a strong, bitter flavor. Continue this rinsing until they reach their optimum length, about 1½–2½ inches for mung beans, a little shorter for the others. This should take about 3–5 days in all. On the last day, put them in the sun to give them a little greening. You'll notice that some didn't sprout. Throw those away. Any you don't use immediately can be stored in their sprouter in the refrigerator.

Encourage kids to try sprouts in ways they usually use lettuce. What will probably happen is the kids themselves will come up with their own special uses—ones you never could have imagined.

THE LEMONADE STAND

A good food activity for kids is putting together a lemonade stand. Having a stand is one of the traditional rites of childhood. Even Amy Carter had one in Plains, Georgia, when her father ran for President the first time. If parents get involved behind the scenes, this can also be a fun way for children to learn about good nutrition in their own front yard.

At five years old, I had my first stand and I remember it well. It was a hot summer day for Seattle, Washington, which is much better known for its rainy days, so I thought business would be good. And since we lived on the boulevard which people passed on the way to the beach, I knew I'd have customers. For some reason, probably the heat, I decided not to wear a halter or top. I had the first topless lemonade stand on my block.

Today's lemonade stands serve an assortment of drinks ranging from Kool-Aid and Hawaiian Punch to iced tea. You might say, "What does it matter what's served. That's kids' stuff." It matters because this can be a learning lesson for the children. They're *asking* people to buy their product so what they're selling, even for pennies, should be something that does good rather than harm. Something they can be proud of.

What are the choices in terms of convenience, cost, and nutrition?

Kool-Aid is the old stand-by. It's certainly colorful and cheap. Even though the manufacturers now let you decide how much sugar you want to add, to get that Kool-Aid taste it takes a *lot* of sugar. The manufacturers boast that their Kool-Aid is fortified with vitamin C. But the label clearly shows there's more artificial color than vitamin C.

Fruit Drinks   What about fruit drinks? Hawaiian Punch is promoted in bold-face type on its container as having "7 real fruit juices, vitamin C," and being "low in sugar." They have a banner that stretches across the can proclaiming "⅔ less sugar." Well, this is another case of reading the label before believing the advertising. When you read the label, you'll see it still has more sugar than fruit juice.

Iced Tea   If you think the lemonade stand will cater to some adult customers, what about iced tea? Unfortunately, if it's tea you're after, all the iced tea mixes I've seen have sugar as the first ingredient and sometimes tea is listed way down as the fourth ingredient.

Lemonade   What about lemonade for a lemonade stand? If it's lemonade punch or frozen concentrate, it still has sugar as the most prominent ingredient. And with the price of lemons, you're not going to run out to buy fresh lemons for the kids to squeeze to

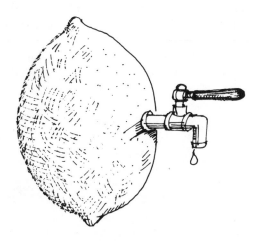

make the old-fashioned stuff. Unless, of course, you have a prolific lemon tree. So what are some more healthful alternatives?

Water   One of the healthiest is the original thirst quencher: water. Make it a special glass of mineral water. Have your kids keep the container right out in full view to show their customers they are getting the real thing. And for eye appeal, float a thin slice of fruit on top.

Fruit Juices   Since not everyone would be satisfied with just water, probably the best alternatives are real fruit juices, like orange juice and apple juice. Usually for orange juice, the frozen concentrate is cheapest. In New York City they have fruit juice stands on the street corners with vendors squeezing the oranges right in front of you. Although this might be too industrious and too expensive for young kids, the idea is a sound one.

POPCORN MAKING AND EATING

When I was a child, sitting down to watch Sunday night television movies at home involved an elaborate popcorn eating ritual. I alternated a mouthful of popcorn with one mouthful of Frederick and Nelson's Frango Chocolate Candies, followed by a swig of lemonade. This was repeated until the popcorn, candy, and lemonade had disappeared. Until a few years ago, it was hardly possible for me to look at popcorn and not think of chocolate candies. Gradually, I've weaned myself away from the accompanying chocolates and from the salt and butter, too. From my early excessive indulgences, I have now become a purist; I eat the popped corn and nothing else with it or on top of it. It's probably better to start your kids off this way, too.

Plain popped corn makes a good snack because it provides a natural food, some fiber and bulk, and 1 cup (plain) has 23 calories (which may or may not be important to children). And it's a safe, fun activity for kids.

It is sold in many different forms; which is

the *best* way to buy it? When you buy the kind that comes in a self-pop aluminum pan, you're paying two thirds the price for that aluminum container. This kind also comes with or without butter and artificial butter flavors; but you have no choice about the salt —it's always added. Also, be aware that using one of these aluminum containers takes much longer than using a regular pan, or a popcorn machine, because you have to use such a low heat to avoid burning the aluminum. (This time factor might be a disadvantage with impatient kids.)

You can also find kernels sold in containers premixed with oil. Artificial butter flavor has usually been added to the oil. When popped this is a tough popcorn, which makes sense since the recommended way to store kernels of popcorn is at room temperature in an airtight container. If it's stored in a refrigerator, or without a lid, or in oil, as in this case, you'll get tough, chewy popcorn.

The best is just plain old do-it-yourself popcorn and the best way to buy it is in a reusable, airtight glass container. If you're in the market for a new popcorn popper, I'd recommend the new hot air machines that pop the corn without any oil. These are fun, easy, and safe for kids to use. The kids can be in charge of measuring out the kernels and holding the bowl in place while the machine churns out the popped corn.

GAMES

Since there aren't many food games manufactured, when I came across this one I was pleased. It's called Soup's On and it's a bingo game with a difference. The object of the game is to be the first to complete a balanced meal. Winning is achieved by filling in a horizontal row of six food categories. Instead of shouting "Bingo," the players shout "Soup's on" when their scorecard is filled correctly. It's a fast-moving game suitable for either a classroom situation or a group of kids who want to play a different game. It's available from National Health Systems, P. O. Box 1501, Ann Arbor, Michigan 48106.

 Holiday Foods

The holidays and the festivities surrounding them are a time for food activities and children should be encouraged to play a large part. In Jane Howard's book *Families,* she explores the important ways in which clans hold themselves together, emphasizing holiday traditions. "My own clan owes a good part of its strength to the reflexive way we dye and hide the eggs, wave the sparklers, bake the cakes, carve the pumpkins, stuff the turkeys, deck the halls, and ring out the old." Mine, too.

But just because it is the holidays doesn't mean that you have to let the principles of good, nutritious food go out the window. If it's a birthday party, it doesn't necessarily mean you *must* bring chocolate cake and ice cream. There are alternatives.

I'm not including all the holidays—just my favorite ones—starting in winter with Valen-

tine's Day and going through to Christmas. The following ideas are fun as well as healthful.

MENU FOR A VALENTINE'S DAY PARTY

Heart-shaped Pizzas
Homemade Strawberry-Banana Ice Cream
on top of Heart-shaped Biscuits
Strawberry-Banana Ice Cream Shake
or Fruit Punch

PIZZA

Follow the recipe on page 327, but press the dough into the shape of a heart! Small, individual hearts are nice.

QUICK AND EASY HOMEMADE STRAWBERRY-BANANA ICE CREAM

With the help of an electric ice cream machine, kids can do this by themselves. If you have only a hand crank, an adult will have to help.

Ingredients:
  8 cups half and half
  1½ cups sugar
  5 teaspoons vanilla
  1½ bananas
  2 baskets fresh strawberries

Makes 1½ quarts

1.   Combine half and half, sugar, and vanilla in blender. Use potato masher or fork to smash fruit until you have "mashed fruit," then add to milk mixture.

2.   Put mixture in ice cream freezer and wait until it thickens and becomes ice cream.

A note about the sugar: The sugar level depends on the sweetness of the fruit you're using. If it's summer and you're adding fresh strawberries and bananas, you can get away with less sugar because these ingredients are naturally sweet. If you're using frozen berries, you may have to use more sugar.

The variations are endless. Use other fresh seasonal fruits or frozen berries.

STRAWBERRY-BANANA ICE CREAM SHAKE

Scoop some of your ice cream into a plastic container with lid. Add enough milk to make it liquid. Shake it with lid on. Pour into glasses and drink through pink straws.

HEART-SHAPED BISCUITS

Buy a package of frozen biscuit mix. Following directions on package for thawing, roll the biscuit dough out, and using a heart-shaped cookie cutter, cut biscuit dough into heart shapes. Bake according to the directions on the package. When ready, serve biscuits with Homemade Strawberry-Banana Ice Cream on top. Sprinkle chopped nuts or granola on top of the ice cream for extra crunchiness.

FRUIT PUNCH

For red-colored fruit punch, use any fruit juice and add cranberry juice to give it that Valentine red coloring.

EASTER

Although there's truly no substitute for a chocolate Easter bunny, there are healthful food ideas that can go along with the candied bunnies.

Two good ideas come from my sister-in-law, Libby. This year at her son's school Easter party, one of the mothers dressed up as a bunny and handed out carrots. These were big carrots with the green tops still attached (bunnies don't cut the tops off). The kids loved it and were running after the bunny for her special carrots. Whether your

Easter celebration is complete with bunny or not, a few carrots placed in an Easter basket may be very well received. Libby's other idea is Mexican in origin. She makes miniature piñatas out of hollowed-out eggs.

Libby's Egg Piñatas

To make egg piñatas, you should start several weeks before Easter to make the hollowed-out eggs. Each morning at breakfast, or whenever you normally use eggs, have the kids help you cut off the top of an egg. With a small, sharp knife, make a hole big enough to let the egg run out and small enough so that when you stuff confetti inside, the confetti won't fall out.

Wash out the insides of the shells and turn them upside down to dry. When you have accumulated enough hollow shells and it's almost Easter, dye them as you would normally dye Easter eggs. Now you're ready to stuff them. The kids can either stuff them the way the Mexicans do, with the thinnest pieces of cut-up newspaper, or you can buy small bags of colored confetti and use that.

When the shells are stuffed, take a piece of tissue paper a little larger than the hole. Put glue on its edges and paste it over the hole. Leave these in an obvious place where the bunny will find them to hide on Easter morning.

On Easter morning, these piñata eggs make for a rowdy and fun-filled hunt. When they are found, the kids smash them against walls, the ground, or each other, and the confetti falls out. (It's best to do this outdoors.) It's a colorful Easter celebration.

Colored Hard-boiled Eggs

When it comes to making traditional Easter eggs, there are some points to keep in mind: no matter what commercial dye you choose, the colors will have been U.S. certified. So you aren't so crazy about how the Food and Drug Administration certifies its colors? This time, relax. Easter-egg dyeing comes about once a year and a little bit of coloring is not worth getting the jitters over.

I've seen suggestions for dyeing eggs natural colors using onion skins, but when I think of the shocking pink and deep turquoise eggs I'm used to, I can't get excited by the prospect of beige-brown eggs. One natural idea that is pretty, too, is to dye the eggs in beet juice. Use the juice from canned beets and let eggs steep in it for just a few minutes and you have gorgeous, naturally pink eggs.

When you're dyeing those eggs, it's fun to have the shells a glorious color, but when the egg itself—the part you're going to eat—also gets colored, as sometimes happens, is that harmful? It isn't harmful, but it can be avoided. The dye gets into the eggs when they are cracked in the cooking process. The solution? Cook the eggs more slowly.

HERE'S THE RECOMMENDED EGG-COOKING PROCESS:

* Put eggs in cold water in pan.

* Bring water to boil.

* Simmer eggs—don't *boil* them—for 6 minutes.

* Let eggs rest for 3 minutes in the hot water.

* Rinse in cold water. The cold-water rinse creates a separation between the white and the shell and makes shelling the eggs later on easier.

After the hunt, when you're shelling those eggs, have you ever noticed a gray-green ring? That's the sulfur that's always in the egg, but when the egg is overheated or cooked too quickly, it appears as a ring. The only harm is that the eggs might have a metallic taste. You can avoid it by using the Recommended Egg-cooking Process.

Square Eggs

Another idea for eggs on Easter, or any other time for that matter, is to try square eggs. From the Square Egg Company in Miami, Florida, or from Cost Plus Imports, 2552 Taylor Street, San Francisco, California, comes an amazing three-dollar gadget that turns regular hard-boiled eggs into square shapes. *Consumer Reports* magazine thought the gadget was unnecessary, but a nine-year-old wrote in and said the "Easter Bunny would like square eggs so he could hide Easter eggs in the corners of the house." Makes sense. Their biggest virtue is probably their power to amaze kids (and adults), who have never seen a square egg!

Pastry Bunnies and Rabbits

Another Easter idea is to decorate quiches and other pies with fanciful pastry cutouts. Using scraps from pie dough, roll into thin sheet. Cut into whimsical shapes appropriate to Easter: bunnies, ducks, little flowers. Place on baking sheet and brush lightly with egg. Bake at 450° F. until golden.

MOTHER'S OR FATHER'S DAY BREAKFAST

Ever since I was little, for special Sunday breakfasts my grandmother Josie made big German pancakes filled with fresh fruit. Although her biggest pancakes were probably no larger than 12″ (the size of her biggest frying pan), to a child, they seemed astonishingly gigantic. My brother and I would share one between the two of us.

This makes a delightful breakfast and certainly easy enough and special enough for kids to make—maybe with a little help from one of their parents the first time—to celebrate the other parent's special day.

BIG GERMAN PANCAKES

Ingredients:

2 cups unbleached flour

4 eggs

1 cup skim milk

1 cup water

4 tablespoons safflower oil

Margarine

Fresh fruit filling of your choice

Dash confectioners' sugar

Makes 7 (12″) round pancakes

1. Have children blend first five ingredients in blender or food processor. Use largest heavy skillet. (I usually use a 12″ pan, but I have used a large 14″ frying pan as well.) Place the pan over high heat; coat the bottom of the pan with margarine.

2. Just before smoke begins to form, let kids pour ½ cup of the liquid batter mixture into the pan. This should have a consistency slightly thicker than a crepe.

3. Now have kids shake the pan constantly as you would when making a crepe. They should enjoy this since it makes quite a racket. With a rubber spatula, they should loosen the edges to prevent sticking.

4. When the bottom is brown and crisp, the pancake is turned by putting two rubber spatulas under it, (one from each side), and flipping it. (This turning is easy to do because, although the pancake is big, it is thicker than a crepe and doesn't fall apart.)

5. Brown the other side and slip the pancake off onto a plate. Keep warm in oven.
NOTE: If the first one doesn't turn out marvelously, don't worry. It usually takes one practice run to get the heat of the pan, the amount of the oil, and the batter in the right proportion. The heat of the pan is very important. Keep it on high.

6. When the pancakes are done, the children can stuff them with your favorite jams or use fresh raspberries, strawberries, or blueberries, as I like to. If none of these are in season, I defrost their frozen counterparts. After pancakes are filled, roll them up into a fat roll, sprinkle top with confectioners' sugar, and serve while still warm.

HALLOWEEN— TRICK OR TREAT

Trick or treat is a problem. What do you give to kids who are geared to getting bags of candy? I remember from my childhood,

we would make such big hauls that sometimes I'd have to go home for a second or third shopping bag before the night was out. Then the neighbor children would get together and my parents would take our picture with the loot in front of us. We'd spend the next few days admiring and fondling our candy before we even *thought* about eating it.

I love Halloween. I hated the idea of growing up and not being able to concoct a costume and traipse from door to door. But, unfortunately, this is a holiday indelibly associated with sugar and sweets and all those things that kids should be eating less of. So, what do you do when you're faced with a porch full of kids with outstretched bags all ready to receive their bounty of candy, or they're up to tricks?

One year, I wrapped apples in orange-colored tissue paper tied with yarn bows. It made the apples look festive and at least the kids didn't seem so disappointed that first moment. That same year, I also made delicious popcorn balls and added less sugar than usually required.

But the last few years have seen a rise in crime associated with Halloween trick or treating, so many communities have outlawed homemade goodies that might some-

how furnish an opportunity for someone to conceal a razor blade. Here are some suggestions for candy substitutes:

* Small apples or oranges—wrap them in paper and tie with ribbons.

* Raisins—individual packages.

* Peanuts in the shell—make into bunches and wrap in paper, tied with ribbon.

* Individual packets of nuts, sunflower seeds, pretzels, and dried fruit.

* Granola bars—Buy the 1-ounce bars. They come in various flavors: honey 'n' oats, coconut, peanut, cinnamon, and a peanut butter with cinnamon and raisins.

* Pumpkin cookies—if you have the time —see recipe for Whole Wheat Pumpkin Cookies on page 337.

* Pumpkin seeds—toasted.

* Hard-boiled eggs—dyed orange.

* Cheese Kisses.

* Sugarless gum.

* Spooky Cupcakes—See recipe, below.

When I was speaking with some food people about this list and possible candidates, one woman suggested giving little disposable toothbrushes. The brushes are 2″ long, about the size of a small candy bar and the same price at about twenty cents. The disposable brushes can be ordered from Brushaway, Inc., 9510 Owensmouth Avenue, Chatsworth, California 91311. A mother I spoke with said her kids love their tiny brushes. Instead of disposing of them, they keep them in their pockets along with their yo-yos, snakes, and string.

SPOOKY CUPCAKES

Ingredients:

1 package carrot cake mix (use packaged cake with least amount of additives— read the label)

½ cup dried figs, steamed until soft

Soft white frosting mix (use as little sugar as possible)

Whole figs (1 per cupcake)

Makes about 1 dozen

1. Preheat oven to 375° F.
2. Make cake according to package instructions, folding in figs, which have been cut into small pieces.
3. Fill individual cupcake pans two thirds full. Bake 25 minutes at 375° F.
4. To make the spooks, turn cakes upside down. Place a dab of icing in the center and set whole fig upright with stem standing erect at the top. Let stand until firm, then cover with frosting. Let frosting flow around the base to resemble spook's sheet. Mark off slits for eyes. Weird-looking and good-tasting.

WHOLE WHEAT PUMPKIN COOKIES

This uses 1 cup whole wheat flour and 1½ cups flour; all whole wheat flour makes the cookies too heavy.

Ingredients:

⅓ cup shortening

1⅓ cups sugar

2 eggs, well beaten

1 cup canned pumpkin (it's easier when kids are involved)

1 teaspoon vanilla

1½ cups flour

1 cup whole wheat flour

¼ teaspoon ginger

1 teaspoon nutmeg

1 teaspoon cinnamon

½ teaspoon allspice

½ cup chopped nuts (optional)

¼ cup toasted pumpkin seeds (optional)

1 cup raisins (optional)

1. Preheat oven to 400° F.

2. Cream together shortening and sugar. Add eggs, pumpkin, vanilla, and all other ingredients.
3. Drop by small spoonfuls onto greased cookie sheet and bake for 15 minutes.

Pumpkin

The pumpkin can be used in many ways during Halloween: You can carve it into a jack-o'-lantern; or, save the seeds from inside and roast some of them, keeping others to plant and grow more pumpkins next year, and you can make cookies and cakes with the meat from the pumpkin.

Pumpkins to Carve The secret of making this easy for yourself is in the selection of the pumpkin. Buy one that feels hollow. Select the heavy-feeling ones with lots of meat only when you want to cook the pumpkin meat.

Expect a carved jack-o'-lantern to last about 4 days before it starts to collapse. I always get excited and carve mine too far in advance of Halloween and by the big night my pumpkins have collapsed into a soft, oozing pile. If you're equally as enthusiastic about carving pumpkins and you want to carve yours ahead, there is a way to retard the inevitable mold growth and extend its life: after carving, rinse the insides with a solution of 9 parts water and 1 part liquid bleach.

Roasted Pumpkin Seeds Take the seeds from the pumpkin and wash them well. After they are thoroughly dry, arrange seeds on slightly greased cookie sheet and bake in 350° F. oven until crunchy and crisp. About 20 minutes. Allow to cool before storing in an airtight jar.

Pumpkin Seed to Plant To hold pumpkin seeds over the winter simply dry them and keep the dry seeds in a cool place until the summer. The drying is the secret. It must be a thorough drying and this may take a week spread out on newspaper in the sun. It is better to err on the side of the seeds being too dry than possibly a little moist. Moist seeds will start sprouting and you won't have anything to plant.

When it is almost time to plant them in the ground, put the seeds in water to soften. Start them out in a milk carton that's been cut halfway down and half filled with dirt. When the seeds start turning into small green plants, transfer to the garden.

Pumpkins to Sculpt From a group of pumpkin growers and produce men on Long Island, I learned about pumpkin sculpting. Each year around Halloween, they have a friendly competition for the most original sculpted pumpkin.

To sculpt, take one pumpkin, and using whatever fresh vegetables and fruits you have on hand, attach the produce with toothpicks, or glue. Some suggestions: try a small carrot for a nose, sliced turnips for eyes, and black grapes for pupils. A row of cranberries can make a mouth; for straight hair, try leeks hanging down. The possibilities are endless and the result should be funny.

SARAH'S PUMPKIN FESTIVAL PIE

One of the most obvious things to do with a fresh pumpkin is to turn it into a pie.[5] A resounding advantage to cooking with the fresh is *taste*. Until you've tasted a pie made from fresh pumpkin, you've never really tasted pumpkin. Be prepared for a treat.

One fall day Sarah Pillsbury and I went to a Pumpkin Festival outside Los Angeles where the celebration of the pumpkin was taking place. Pumpkin pies, pumpkin breads, and just plain pumpkins in all sizes and shapes were being sold. Sarah made me a most extraordinary pie from the pumpkins we lugged home. (Yes, she is from the *same* Pillsbury family and yes, she does know a

---

[5] You don't gain or lose anything nutritionally by cooking your own fresh pumpkin. By the time the cooking is finished the thiamin and the vitamin A are about the same in the freshly cooked product as in the canned product. However, a distinct advantage of cooking your own is the avoidance of the preservatives and unnecessary sodium that are almost always added to canned goods.

thing or two about baking.) Making a pumpkin pie this way is a good way for kids to learn where pumpkin comes from: not the can, not the grocer's shelves, but the patch.

Ingredients:

2 cups cooked pumpkin
¾ cup brown sugar
1 teaspoon cinnamon
½ teaspoon ginger
½ teaspoon nutmeg
¼ teaspoon ground cloves
¼ teaspoon mace
4 eggs
1½ cups half and half
1 (9″) pie shell, unbaked

ADULT VERSION

2 tablespoons rum or brandy

Serves 8

1. Preheat oven to 450° F. Cut small, (6–8″), pumpkin in half and remove seeds. Cut into ½″ chunks. Place a steamer over small amount of water and steam the pulp until it is easily pierced with a fork, about 30 minutes. Let cool until you can handle, then scrape pulp from skin into bowl.

2. In a large bowl, combine pumpkin, sugar, and spices.

3. In another bowl, beat the eggs and half and half together. Add rum (or brandy) if making the adult version. Add to the pumpkin mixture and blend thoroughly.

4. Put in pie shell. Bake in 450° F. for 5 minutes, then lower heat to 350° F. and bake for 45 minutes or until knife inserted in center comes out clean.

BIRTHDAY PARTIES

In my family we like birthdays so much that we observe them for far longer than just a day; we celebrate until we get tired. So, it's not unusual that my nephew Chris, who obviously likes the candles and cakes and fuss as much as the rest of us, originated the idea of the Happy Unmarked Birthday. Accord-

Birthday fruitcake

ing to four-year-old Chris, the big advantage of an unmarked birthday is that you can celebrate it whenever you feel like it—you don't have to wait around for the real thing. So far, he's given unmarked birthday parties when his father has returned from work and when his older brother came back from a summer trip.

Whether your birthdays are marked or unmarked, a birthday party traditionally means cake and ice cream and I admit to being reluctant to vary much from that myself. But recently some school administrators have started outlawing sugary desserts, even the sacred birthday cake.

What you can do instead is to make fruit "cakes." I heard about this being done at a school in California. They put candles in watermelon, or fresh pineapple, and give the kids a slice with a candle. I thought this sounded too much like an idea adults thought up and I wasn't sure how successful this would be with the kids, but I was told it was a big hit. The kids got to select the watermelon themselves and helped arrange the candles on it. Other good snacks for birthday parties are homemade ice cream (see recipe for Valentine's Day, page 333), Rubbersicles, page 311, frozen yoghurt with whole fruit in it, and punches made from fruit juice.

FRUIT PUNCH

VARIATIONS

1. 1 part cranapple juice and
    1 part frozen orange juice and
    1 part frozen lemonade

2. 1 part frozen orange juice and
    1 part canned pineapple juice

Combine with sliced oranges floating on top.

3. 1 part canned strawberry nectar and
    1 part lemonade

Combine with sliced berries.

4. Mix and Match Fruit Juices
Apple, grape, or orange juice, limeade, with pineapple, apricot, peach. Make fruit juice into ice cubes with pieces of fresh fruit. Float a frozen fruit cube in each glass.

CHRISTMAS AND COOKIES

In my family, Christmas means homemade goodies. The day after Thanksgiving isn't too early for mother to begin her chess pies, snowball cookies, and banana and date-nut breads.

As kids, our responsibility was the sugar cookies. It was a grand production. With a flourish we made them; with much debate and squabbling we decorated them; with

Christmas and cookies

pride we served them throughout the holiday season, timing it perfectly so the last ones were served on New Year's Eve.

This is a tradition that my sister and I have continued into adulthood, collecting unusual shaped cookie cutters along the way. Each year as Christmas approaches I gather the children of friends and we make these cookies. Usually as much flour ends up on the kids as in the cookies, but it's great fun.

As an adult, my concessions are: to use less sugar; to use a whole grain, unbleached flour; and to be more aware of the decorations I use. For example, did you know that the silver beads that are sold for cake decoration (the kind that I once used to make the gingerbread man's buttons) have written in small print on their package: *To be used as decoration; this is not a confection and is not to be eaten.* But the warning is ludicrous because, of course, decorations of this kind are placed on pastries that are eaten.

GRANDMOTHER JOSIE'S ORIGINAL SUGAR COOKIES

Ingredients:

3 cups flour

1 tablespoon baking powder

½ cup sugar[6]

1 cup shortening

3 eggs

1 teaspoon vanilla

Makes 40 cookies

1. Preheat oven to 325° F.
2. Grease large cookie sheets.
3. In a large bowl, mix dry ingredients. Add shortening and mix with fork. Add unbeaten eggs and vanilla. Knead into a ball. (Or this can all be done by a machine with a dough hook attachment.)
4. Spread flour on a large working surface and with a rolling pin, roll dough very thin, ⅛" thick. Some people may prefer a fatter sugar cookie and a thicker dough. I like mine very thin and crunchy.
5. Dip the cutting edge of the cookie cutters in the flour and start cutting out the cookies.
6. Decorate with confectionary beads or other decorations. One of my favorite decorations is peppermint-stick candy, crushed, sprinkled on top of the cookies and baked. It gives the cookies a nice pink blush.
7. Bake for 10 minutes on greased cookie sheet or until crusty and golden.

[6] My grandmother's original recipe called for 1¼ cups sugar, but I've cut this to less than ½. I find that, with the sugary decorations on top, you can get away with less sugar in the cookie.

 Storybooks and Cookbooks

Good books about food are often difficult to find. The shelves are loaded with retreads of the princess that got away or the wicked stepmother, but what's also needed I think are interesting stories that will stimulate a child's interest, say, in growing his or her own vegetable garden, or in eating healthful foods, stories that share my delight and joy in good food. With the help of Linda Greenlee, a specialist in nutrition education for children, I've compiled a list of available books that cover food subjects ranging from pancakes and popcorn to eggs and jam. Some of the books can be read to young children, others children can read themselves. These are selected for the child up to age eight or nine, with the exception of the six books by Millicent Selsam, which are geared for the junior high age group.

ANNOTATED BIBLIOGRAPHY STORYBOOKS

Black, Irma Simonton. *Is This My Dinner?* Chicago: Albert Whitman and Company, 1972.
An easy story about a boy in search of his dinner. Deals with the diet of animals and humans. Color pictures.

Brustlein, Janice. *Little Bear Learns to Read the Cookbook.* New York: Lothrop, Lee and Shepard Co., 1969.
An illustrated story about a bear who's thrilled to learn how to read a cookbook and make a cake.

Carle, Eric. *Pancakes, Pancakes.* New York: Alfred A. Knopf, 1970.
Jack wanted pancakes for breakfast . . . he gathered all of the ingredients and helped to make them. Colorful pictures. Emphasizes where we get foods, such as eggs from chickens, etc.

———. *The Very Hungry Caterpillar.* New York: World Publishing, 1970.
An enchanting story about a caterpillar who eats a large variety of foods while on a journey to become a butterfly.

Cottrell, Edyth Young. *The Sugar Coated Teddy.* Santa Barbara, Calif.: Woodridge Press Publishing Company, 1975.

Oversize paperback. Interesting book to read to small children about the reasons why they should eat good food. The story is centered around a lovable Teddy bear and is illustrated with brown-and-white drawings. Simple recipes are included that children can prepare by themselves. The end of the book has a religious message, which some readers might find out of place.

dePaola, Tommy. *The Popcorn Book.* New York: Holiday House, 1978.
A book about the history, including Indian legends, of popcorn.

———. *Pancakes for Breakfast.* New York: Harcourt Brace Jovanovich, 1978.
Pictorial story about a woman who makes pancakes for breakfast. Good for a discussion of breakfast foods or as a stimulus for kids cooking their own pancakes.

Devlin, Wende and Harry. *Cranberry Thanksgiving.* New York: Parents' Magazine Press, 1971.
A story about Grandma's secret cranberry bread recipe and a plot to steal it. Book includes the recipe, which makes a good cooking activity.

———. *Old Black Witch.* New York: Parents' Magazine Press, 1966.
An illustrated story about a witch who helps to cook blueberry pancakes for a tearoom. Colorful.

Goffstein, M. B. *Fish for Supper.* New York: Dial Press, 1976.
Simple black-and-white sketches and narration about a lady who goes fishing. Perfect to read when you're cooking fish.

Greene, Carla. *I Want to Be a Storekeeper.* Chicago: Children's Press, 1958.
Short story with illustrations. The story follows a boy who learns about the duties of a storekeeper.

Gretz, Susanna. *The Bears Who Stayed In-doors.* Chicago: Follet Publishing Company, 1971.
A cartoon-style story about five bears who stayed indoors one day and had a picnic.

Hoban, Lillian and Russell. *Egg Thoughts and Other Frances Songs.* New York: Harper and Row Publishing, 1972.
Contains a poem about eggs as well as other poems of interest to young children.

Hoban, Russell. *Bread and Jam for Frances.* New York: Scholastic Book Services, 1964.
A lovable story about a raccoon named Frances and her extreme fondness for bread and jam. She learns that she needs a variety of foods and not just bread and jam.

Krauss, Ruth. *The Carrot Seed.* New York: Harper & Row, 1945.
Delightful short tale of a boy and his faith in a carrot seed. Very adaptable for dramatic play. I would be surprised if this didn't stimulate children to grow some carrots themselves.

LeSeig, Theo. *Ten Apples Up on Top.* New York: Random House, 1961.
A comical counting story involving apples.

Loof, Jan. *Who's Got the Apple?* New York: Random House, 1975.
Adventure of a man who buys an apple. Good for primary age children.

McCloskey, Robert. *Blueberries for Sale.* New York: Viking Press, 1976.
All about the adventures of Sal, her mother, and two bears at Blueberry Hill. Lends itself to a discussion on how fruits/berries grow.

Marshall, James. *Yummers.* Boston: Houghton Mifflin Co., 1973.
The adventures of Emily the pig and her "weight loss diet."

Merrill, Claire. *A Seed Is a Promise.* New York: Scholastic Book Services, 1973.
Colorful narrative about seeds. The book fits in well with summer gardening activities.

Paterson, Diane. *Eat!* New York: Dial Press, 1975.
Martha would not eat her food until she got a pet frog. Short and lively.

Poulet, Virginia. *Blue Bug's Vegetable Garden.* Chicago: Children's Press, 1973.
Great pictures of blue bug and all of the terrific vegetables in his garden.

Selsam, Millicent E. *The Apple and Other Fruits.* New York: William Morrow and Company, 1973.
Follows the style of the other Selsam books. Text is good for older children; pictures are good for young children.

――――. *How Puppies Grow.* New York: Four Winds Press, 1971.
Narration and lovely black-and-white photographs about puppies. Use with a discussion on growth and feeding.

――――. *Peanuts.* New York: William Morrow and Company, 1969.
An informative book about peanuts and how they grow. Pictures make the book adaptable to preschoolers.

――――. *Popcorn.* New York: William Morrow and Company, 1976.
Geared to junior high school age—excellent pictures about popcorn can be adapted for young children.

――――. *Seeds and More Seeds.* New York: Harper and Row, 1959.
Story and funny illustrations about seeds growing. May need to be shortened for young children.

――――. *Vegetables from Stems and Leaves.* New York: William Morrow and Company, 1972.

Good black-and-white pictures and narration about vegetables and gardens.

Sendak, Maurice. Chicken Soup with Rice. New York: Scholastic Book Services, 1962.
The months of the year are each illustrated with a little poem that ends with chicken soup and rice.

Seuss, Dr. *Scrambled Eggs Super!* New York: Random House, 1953.
About "scrambled eggs super-dee-dooper-dee-booper, special de luxe à la Peter T. Hooper." Have your children make scrambled eggs or omelets after reading this book.

Showers, Paul. *What Happens to a Hamburger?* New York: Thomas Y. Crowell Company, 1970.
This is geared toward older children but the ideas and pictures can be adapted for younger children for discussion of digestion and use of food by the body.

Steiner, Charlotte. *The Hungry Book.* New York: Alfred A. Knopf, 1972.
Jock, the dog, learns about the different foods that animals and people eat. Colorful.

Stevens, Carla. *The Magic Carrot Seeds.* New York: Scholastic Book Services, 1976.
Cute story about a rabbit who plants magic carrot seeds and the enormous, delicious result.

Tolstoy, Alexei. *The Great Big Enormous Turnip.* New York: Franklin Watts, 1969.
A community effort to harvest an extra-large turnip.

Wiersum, Gale. *The Runaway Squash: An American Folktale.* Racine, Wis.: Golden Press, 1976.
Imaginative short tale centering around a squash.

COOKBOOKS

If some of the previous storybooks about food interested your kids, next they will probably want to get in there and do it themselves. Of course, they can just wing it, but since many of the cookbooks for children are creative and educational, they can act as a springboard to introduce kids to healthful food activities. I've included comments to guide you to the books that will be the most appropriate. Most of them are written for children to use by themselves, but two are designed for adults to use with children.

Children's cookbooks and other activities

Ault, Roz. *Kids Are Natural Cooks.* Boston: Houghton Mifflin Co., 1974.
This thoughtful book features unusual recipes and food ideas ranging from making your own gelatin (from pigs' feet) to baking your teacher's wedding cake! It stresses natural processes and wholesome ingredients.

Cadwallader, Sharon. *Cooking Adventures for Kids.* Boston: Houghton Mifflin Co., 1974.
Full-page drawings of children and adults involved in food preparation process. Nutritious, easy-to-follow recipes.

Cauley, Lorinda Bryan. *Pease-Porridge Hot.*
New York: G. P. Putnam's Sons, 1977.
Nineteen mostly healthful recipes accompanied by delightful black-and-white illustrations. Some of the recipes are quite inspired. For example, Jack and the Bean-
stalk's green bean casserole, or the Big
Bad Wolf's little pigs in a blanket.

Cooper, Jane. *Love at First Bite.* New York:
Alfred A. Knopf, 1977.
A bright and witty cookbook for older
children that's filled with a sense of humor
and adventure. In many instances the
book is overillustrated; it would be hard
for children to read and follow some of
the recipes because of the drawings crowd-
ing them.

Cooper, Terry Touff, and Ratner, Marilyn.
Many Hands Cooking. New York:
Thomas Y. Crowell Company, 1974.
Recipes from around the world, illustrated
with wonderful, colorful drawings. How-
ever, it has too much emphasis on sweets.
The book is available from wherever
UNICEF (United Nations Children's
Fund) cards are sold.

Privately published, Creative Education
Craft Series. *How to Have Fun Making
Dinner.* P. O. Box 227, Mankato, Minn.
56001. 1974.
Easy-to-read narrative about dinner and a
menu for a dinner that kids can prepare.
Good for a child who likes to read and
would like to surprise Mom or Dad in the
kitchen.

Ellison, Virginia H. *The Pooh Cookbook.*
New York: Dell Publishing Co., Inc.,
1975.
Follows the Winnie-the-Pooh theme, so
needless to say there's lots of honey. Sugarless recipes include watercress sandwiches, pea-bean alphabet soup, and hay-
corn squash. Some of the recipes may be
new to the children, but maybe with the
help of Pooh, they'll try them.

Ferreira, Nancy J. *The Mother-Child Cook-*

book. Menlo Park, California: Pacific
Coast Publishers, 1975.
An especially loving book for mothers (or
fathers) who want to enrich their children's lives through food experiences.
Starts with the simplest tasks (tearing,
breaking, and snapping fresh vegetables)
and proceeds to full recipes including enchiladas and homemade noodles. Black-
and-white photographs.

Goodwin, Mary T., and Pollen, Gerry. *Creative Food Experiences for Children. Revised Edition.* Washington, D.C.: Center
for Science in the Public Interest, 1980.
Originally written for teachers, but certainly useful for parents, too. Lively, fun,
stimulating way to learn about foods and
try new foods. Expect great holiday ideas.
This book could be a life saver on a rainy
day when the kids are at a loss as to what
to do next. One of the best on the market.

Hall, Carolyn Vosburg. *I Love Popcorn.*
Garden City, N.Y.: Doubleday & Company, Inc., 1976.
Written in collaboration with the food editors of *Farm Journal,* this sixty-two-page
book is Everything You Always Wanted to
Know About Popcorn. It stresses popcorn
as a natural food and gives many ideas for
how to grow it, use it, and how to pop it
correctly.

Keene, Carolyn. *The Nancy Drew Cookbook
—Clues to Good Cooking.* New York:
Grosset and Dunlap, 1976.
Follows the spy theme—featuring simple
recipes with intriguing titles and Nancy's
added information on how to improve the
nutritional value of the recipe. Tasty section on cultural dishes. Geared toward the
older, reading child.

Kositsky, V., McFarlane, B., and Swenson,
M. *I Made It Myself Cookbook.* Berkeley,
Calif., 1973.
Single-serving recipes that include: zuc-
chini boats, quick fruit bread, and 1-hour
whole wheat bread.

McClenahan, Pat, and Jaqua, Ida. *Cool Cooking for Kids*. Belmont, Calif.: Fearon Publishers, Inc., 1976.
Great fun. Geared toward preschoolers. Originally written for classroom, but can be used equally well at home. Lots of nutritious recipes and cooking fun.

Martel, Jane G., ed. *Smashed Potatoes*. Boston: Houghton Mifflin Company, 1974.
This book is really more a comic book. It is a child's eye view of the kitchen and is written by elementary school kids. It includes such observations by the kids as: "You open eggs with mittens on" and "A stove is really dangerous—you shouldn't go near one till you get married." It includes their "recipes" for dishes ranging from Skabetti to Basketti. It is fun and makes for humorous reading, but I would think it's one of those books written by children that might appeal to adults more than kids.

Newman, Nanette. *The Fun Food Factory*. New York: Harmony Books, 1976.
A delightful oversize hardback book with step-by-step, easy-to-follow color illustrations. It emphasizes natural foods prepared simply. Since it was originally published in England, it has an English bent; with recipes for kippers and beefcake.

Newman, R. *Recipe Card Set: Applesauce, Biscochitos, Copper Pennies and Lots More*. Dallas: Dallas Association for Education of Young Children, 1974.
Colorful, easy-to-use, illustrated recipe cards.

Nitta, Sharon. *A Child's Cookbook*. Privately published at 656 Terra California Drive, #3, Walnut Creek, Calif. 94595.
A compilation of over 100 recipe cards that feature single-serving-size recipes a child can make. Simple and easy to follow; directions are also given in metric system.

Paul, Aileen. *Kid's Cooking Without a Stove*. Garden City, N.Y.: Doubleday & Company, Inc., 1975.
Printed in red and green, easy to read and follow pictures. Contains a few nutritious vegetable recipes, but on the whole there are too many sugary desserts. Kids don't need to learn how to prepare only desserts.

———. *The Kid's Fifty-state Cookbook*. Garden City, N.Y.: Doubleday & Company, Inc., 1975.
Provides several, easy-to-follow recipes from each state, plus a little history and illustration. Recipes include Kentucky Fried Chicken, Persimmon Pudding from Indiana, Lentil Loaf-Idaho, Grapefruit and Melon Salad-Arizona, Cornish Pasties-Michigan. Unfortunately, the cover portrays a happy child with sugary frosted cake. Black-and-white print with black-and-white illustrations.

Rabin, David. *The Now You're Cooking Cookbook: A Cookbook for Kids by a Kid*. New York: Pyramid Books, 1972.
A well-rounded selection of recipes paying special attention to safety and cooking terms. Written by a kid in kid's language.

Riggs, Em, and Darpian, Barbara. *I Am a Cook Book*. Los Angeles: J. P. Tarcher, Inc., 1977.
Although the authors concentrate on healthy, imaginative food ideas, this small book (8"×6") suffers from being overcrowded with illustrations. I wonder if kids can decipher the directions from the jumbled pages.

Shull, Elizabeth. *Turn Kids On to the Good Food*. Los Angeles: Wise Owl Publications, 1976.
Done in a large black-and-white format similar to a coloring book, this book emphasizes natural foods and easy ways for kids to prepare them nutritiously. Fun and easy to follow for kids who can read.

Stein, Sara Bonnett. *The Kids' Kitchen*

Takeover. New York: Workman Publishing Company, 1975.

This book features over 120 imaginative food ideas to cook, make, grow, and do in and out of the kitchen. I think this is one of the most outrageously creative and wonderfully fresh books I've seen for children. It should excite their curiosity on everything from sourdough bread to vegetable monsters, rubber eggs, and bendable bones. There are activities suitable for children of all ages.

Watson, Pauline. *Cricket's Cookery*. New York: Random House, 1977.

Traditional recipes for foods children like (Rainy Day Popcorn, Mighty Meatballs, Roly-poly Pancakes) accompanied by songs about each.

Weeks, Dorothy. *The Jar Garden*. Santa Barbara, Calif.: Woodbridge Press Publishing Co., 1976.

This how-to book gives detailed instructions on how to make sprouts and suggestions for what to do with them after they have sprouted.

YOUTHFUL **11** AGING

As a society we've become aware of our sexism, and very slowly we're becoming more aware of our ageism—discrimination against people because of their advancing age. This discrimination against the elderly carries into nutrition as well. Nutrition as it affects the elderly has been ignored for such a long time that there is little adequate research or basic information available. But as the numbers of the elderly increase (today there are over 25 million "over sixty-fivers"), their special concerns, including nutrition, can no longer be ignored.

The cost of health care for the elderly is astounding. In 1976 those over sixty-five made up only 10.5 per cent of the population, yet fifty-four cents of every health dollar was spent on their care. It is predicted that in another 50 years older people may make up as much as 20 per cent of the population. That means 1,400 people per day entering the ranks of the elderly.

And one more for good luck

How does nutrition fit in with soaring medical costs? The White House Conference on Food, Nutrition, and Health in 1970 left little doubt that a significant number of older persons in the United States were malnourished. Estimates from hospitals and nursing homes indicate that up to 10 per

cent and possibly more of the elderly may be malnourished. Dr. Robert Butler, Director of the National Institute on Aging, which was established in 1974, says that six of the leading chronic diseases of old age, cardiovascular disease, diabetes, hypertension, osteoporosis, cancer, and senility, are diet related.

Nutrition is the cornerstone of preventive medicine, yet today only four cents of every health dollar is spent on prevention and nutrition gets only a tiny part of that. Dr. Butler believes better knowledge of nutrition can result in lower health care costs not to mention a better, more satisfying life for the elderly themselves. In 1977, the Nutrition Research Program was funded with $1.3 million; by 1982 this amount will be quadrupled. Although this is still not enough, it does indicate a beginning in focusing attention and money on this important area.

As you'll see in this chapter, the nutritional requirements for older people are often more critical than for their grandchildren because, in the elderly, one nutritional deficiency can bring on another and another, creating a domino effect. For example, with younger people a lack of vitamin D is not as crucial as it is in an older person: in the elderly a vitamin D deficiency can lead to osteoporosis (weakening of the bones), which can lead to a fall, which leads to a broken bone that never heals, which leads to a person becoming bedridden, and undoubtedly shortens his or her useful life. Older people don't bounce back as quickly from ill health, so the nutritional consequences of their diet tend to be compounded in serious ways.

The day I began writing this chapter, my aunt Evelyn died following a long and exhaustive recuperation period after falling off a ladder years before. Evie always had a special place in my heart; when I was little, she made a miniature, 2′ high, set of bunk beds for my dolls, which I still cherish. Her death brought home to me the fact that for older people nutrition assumes a role of increased importance because they don't recover from ill health and regain their strength the way younger people do. Good nutrition can be one important ally they have on their side.

There are positive steps that can be taken to ensure later years that are as healthy as possible. Our society emphasizes starting out with the right nutrition; pregnant women and new mothers receive a lot of nutritional guidance. An equal amount of attention needs to be focused on the special nutritional considerations of the aging and the known potential for youthful aging. For best results, people should not wait until old age to start this preparation for a youthful old age; just as they put money aside for their financial security in advance, they should adopt a sound and healthful nutritional plan as well. Undoubtedly it's easier to cultivate better diet habits when you're young than to struggle at sixty-five to overturn a lifetime of poor eating patterns; however, if you're already older, it's still not too late to start.

While it's true that *chronological* age is invariable—if you're sixty years old, you're sixty—the good news is that your *physiological* age has a variable of thirty-five years.

According to Laurence Morehouse, founder of the U.C.L.A. Human Perform-ance Laboratory, if you're sixty you can have the outward appearance and the internal system of someone who is forty-five to seventy-five. In addition to nutrition, one of the most important variables is physical activity. You can help to keep your body young by always including some form of physical activity in your life. I know one woman in her fifties who is old beyond her years because she has literally stopping moving. She's confessed to me that her only physical exercise is to lie on her bed, raise her legs, and wiggle her toes. Physical activity need not mean leaving the house for a gym; it can be a simple on the spot activity done in the living room like running in place or using a stationary bicycle. But for a healthy second fifty years, nutrition *and* physical activity have to go together.

This chapter should not only be helpful to people who are getting older themselves, but also to sons and daughters of aging parents, or nieces and nephews with older aunts and uncles. With this information in mind, you can better understand what physiological processes are considered normal, in what areas the elderly have special dietary requirements, and what common drugs may interfere with proper nutrition.

 Physical Aspects

The physiological changes that occur with age vary widely with individuals and take place in some people much earlier, or later, than in others. Think of the people you know in their seventies, eighties, and nineties who are still vigorous and active physically. I never cease to be amazed by the range of activities of some of the older people I know. (Perhaps the fact that I am "amazed" that older people can still be so active is my "ageism" showing.) It's hard for me not to think of Rodney, an orchid grower, who is

104 And still flowering

104 and still raising seedlings which take at least 5 years to flower. He told me his only concession to age is finally to admit he's grown hard of hearing. Now that he's admitted it, people talk louder and he doesn't miss anything. Dr. McPherson and his wife, in their seventies, work out five times a week at an Olympic-size pool and compete in Senior Olympic swimming meets. Up until just a year ago, my grandmother Jane, in her eighties, went fishing in her own camper trailer. She stopped, not because of any illness associated with age, but because the campsites had become too crowded to suit her. In my New York apartment building, there's a sweet little woman who looks as though she might be happy doing nothing but being someone's grandmother, but she is still a practicing petrogeologist. These active people are all excellent examples of living on the youthful side of physiological aging. However, regardless of how healthy one feels or how active one is, there are some common physiological aspects of aging such as graying of the hair, diminished eyesight, and a slower gait that are hard to escape. There are also some physiological changes, less overtly noticeable perhaps, but no less real, that can affect one's nutritional well-being.

As yet it is not known what percentage of people are affected by these changes or to what degree, but when and if these changes do occur, they should be taken seriously and used as signposts signaling potential areas of nutritional distress.

TASTE

It's not unusual for older people to claim foods don't taste as good as they used to. It isn't that the food is actually less tasty, but as people get older, they have fewer taste buds on the tongue—we start out with about 9,000 and by our sixties there are only about 4,000 left. Those that are left lose some of their taste sensitivity. As a result, some older people may lose their ability to recognize basic tastes: sour, sweet, salty, bitter. Because they can't taste as well they may develop poor dietary habits, perhaps excessively salt-ing food in an effort to capture a salty taste, or not eating adequately because the food is less enjoyable.

People with dentures may also complain about losing their sense of taste. Just because people have dentures doesn't mean they lose their taste sensitivity, but the decreased tactile sensitivity due to the dentures may affect the way the food tastes. If you can't *feel* the food in your mouth the same way, it follows that you may not be able to taste it as well. According to Dr. Neil Solomon, if dentures are fitted too tightly to the palate, a person's ability to recognize bitter and sour tastes is often impaired.

DRY MOUTH

Have you tried eating with a dry mouth? Recently I experienced this uncomfortable sensation firsthand when my dentist put a drying agent in my mouth. It didn't feel pleasant to have the flow of saliva cut off, but in my case it was a temporary situation. With the elderly, it's not uncommon to have the flow of saliva chronically reduced, which creates a situation called dry mouth. When it is chronic, it affects the ability to chew and swallow certain types of foods. This can lead to a further problem: trying to digest food that isn't chewed enough. Dry mouth can also lead to loosening of dentures. Some drugs like antihistamines worsen this condition (see chart, page 354–57).

One suggestion for the elderly with this problem is to eat foods that need little chewing; another better idea is to place a drop of lemon juice or apple juice on the tongue to stimulate the flow of saliva.

SMELL

A large part of the enjoyment of food is the way it smells, its wonderful aroma as it permeates the air. Smelling freshly baked bread is almost as pleasurable as eating it. With age, the sense of smell often diminishes. The problem is that without smell to make food alluring, the food is less attractive and people may not be stimulated to eat enough to nourish themselves adequately.

DIGESTIVE

Older people have a decreased ability to digest fats and protein. Because of this they may not be able to tolerate high protein diets. They may require more time to digest a meal. Eating smaller, more frequent meals may be helpful. A decrease in frequency of bowel movements can also be expected.

KIDNEYS

The kidneys act as a filtering system for the body—filtering out waste products. The filtering rate of people eighty years old is 50 per cent lower than the rate of twenty-five-year-olds. As the blood flow through the kidneys decreases, substances that should be filtered are not and substances that are sometimes should not be. High protein diets may put an extra load on kidneys for elimination of waste products, and for protein metabolism that can tax an already low functioning kidney.

 Nutrition and Senility

Senility is a catch-all phrase that is applied to people over sixty who seem confused, forgetful, dazed, disoriented, or antisocial. In my family there were mysterious, but true, stories about a friend of my mother's who would use the fire escape to leave her nursing home at night, dressed only in a white nightgown, and aimlessly wander the streets. The reason given for her nocturnal escapes: senility. Older people with somewhat unusual behavior are customarily judged senile and society views this condition as untreatable.

Many people believe that if you live long enough you'll be senile—that this sort of decline is inevitable—but studies at Duke University have shown that only about 15 per cent of all old people ever become senile, and we know some kinds of senility can be treated.

One type of senility that is treatable is called Reversible Brain Syndrome. As many as 13 per cent of people judged senile may have Reversible Brain Syndrome. Reversible Brain Syndrome can result from a variety of causes ranging from malnutrition, anorexia, congestive heart failure, and infection to cerebrovascular accident, drugs and other toxic substances, heart trauma, and numerous other causes. However, if it is *caused* by malnutrition in the first place, there is reason to believe that proper nutrition can positively affect the therapy and also decrease the period of convalescence. Dr. Butler, at the National Institute on Aging, points out that if Reversible Brain Syndrome does result from malnutrition and is not treated, it can become a permanent disability requiring long-term care.

How is nutrition, or malnutrition, connected with Reversible Brain Syndrome and thus with senility? A study done at the Center for the Aging at the University of Southern California revealed that more than 10 per cent of the elderly have simultaneous deficiencies of at least three or four important vitamins: two B vitamins (thiamin and riboflavin), vitamin C, and vitamin A. The malnutrition which leads to these deficiencies may be due to poverty—which affects 35 per cent of older Americans—chronic illness, which affects 85 per cent of older Americans, or from poor eating habits, which often result from loneliness or grief.

Here again the critical problem is lack of information in the area of nutrition and the elderly. Doctors, medical researchers, and scientists until recently have not been interested enough to study the problem, so they don't as yet have answers to many questions. But they do know that certain nutrient deficiencies cause symptoms that look like senility in older people. Dr. Ruth Weg, Professor with the Gerontology Department of the University of Southern California, related a study to me in which college-age students were denied sufficient protein, vitamins, and minerals for a period of 30–60 days; they demonstrated many of the symptoms that have come to be associated with senility.

Since nutritional screening may be an important tool in diagnosing elderly patients who appear to be senile, and nutritional therapy in some instances may be the preferred method of treatment, it seems apparent we need doctors specializing in geriatrics who include nutritional screening and treatment as part of their practice. Although many doctors have publicly made positive statements about nutritional screening and therapy, in my research in Southern California I could not locate one doctor who currently includes this as part of his medical routine.

In the future when treating certain kinds of senility I believe doctors, nutritionists, and dieticians will start working more closely with each other so when an elderly person undergoes a medical examination, he or she not only gets the routine tests, but also receives a nutritional assessment which includes diet history and biochemical studies.

 # Drugs and Their Nutritional Consequences

Each year 24 per cent of the elderly are admitted to hospitals; they make an average of seven visits a year to doctors (middle-aged people make five), and 86 per cent of them suffer from at least one chronic disease (arthritis, diabetes, rheumatism, heart disease). Because the ailments of the elderly may be more difficult and time-consuming to diagnose and they respond less quickly to treatment than the young, there is sometimes a pessimism about treating the elderly. Some doctors, unfortunately even those *specializing* in geriatrics, have a tendency to dismiss the complaints of the elderly as inevitable concomitants of age. One of the biggest problems is that whatever the ailment, drugs are prescribed to combat it. Unfortunately, many doctors treating the elderly are like a specialist with a practice in geriatrics that I met in Los Angeles. His motto: every patient coming to see him goes out the door with something in his hand.

The problem with doctors methodically prescribing drugs is that this medical shorthand precludes a more in-depth analysis which might also reveal nutritional deficiencies and problems that could be better treated with diet. But diagnosing nutritional problems requires painstaking ferreting out —exploring food habits and preferences, rather than instantly zeroing in on a target and writing a prescription.

The chart on the next page lists some of the most common drugs (prescription and nonprescription), what conditions they are routinely prescribed for, the resulting effect, the side effects, and the drug's possible effect on nutritional status. As is often the case with older people suffering from chronic disease, they may be on several drugs at once, all of which could be contributing to jeopardizing their nutritional state by decreasing food intake, causing irritation and nausea.

Drugs That May Affect Food Intake, Digestion, or Nutritional Status of the Elderly

Drug	Prescribed For	Resulting Effect	Side Effects	Possible Effect on Food Intake, Digestion, or Nutritional Status
ANTIBIOTICS Erythromycin Tetracycline Penicillin	Infections	Inhibits or destroys bacterial growth.	Changes normal intestinal bacteria. Gas, loose stool, cramps, nausea, vomiting. Anorexia, diarrhea, heartburn. Poor absorption and synthesis of vitamins.	All antibiotics cause a change in the body's normal bacteria. This may cause an overgrowth of yeast or fungi in the body. Anorexia—decreased food intake. Diarrhea—loss of body fluid and some minerals. Poor absorption and synthesis of vitamins may precipitate vitamin deficiency.
ANTICONVULSANTS Dilantin	Epileptic seizures	Acts on the brain to reduce the severity and frequency of epileptic attacks.	Anorexia, loss of taste, sensation, nausea, vomiting, weight loss, swollen gums.	Decreased food intake. Difficulty in chewing food.
ANTIHISTAMINES Benadryl Chlor-Trimeton Teldrin Dimetane	Allergies, cold symptoms Sedation Motion sickness	Depresses action of histamine, which causes the allergic reactions.	Anorexia (loss of appetite). May cause drowsiness, lethargy, muscle weakness, disturbed co-ordination. Dries up nasal and salivary secretions. Diarrhea, occasional nausea, and vomiting.	Decreased food intake. Decreased food intake.
ATROPHINE-LIKE DRUGS Pro-Banthine Donnatal Robinul Lomotil	Ulcers, colitis, diarrhea	Decreases motility of the G.I. tract.	Dry mouth. Blurred vision. Excessive thirst.	Difficulty in eating (chewing or swallowing) food. May make eating more difficult. Large fluid intake.

Drug	Used for	Action	Side Effects	Effect on Food Intake
Artane (related drug)	Parkinson's syndrome	Antispasmodic.	Same as above.	Same as above.
CARDIAC DRUGS Quinidine Procainamide	Controlling irregular heartbeat	Depressant to heart muscle; depresses heart excitability conduction and contractility.	Anorexia, bitter taste in mouth, diarrhea, nausea, vomiting, abdominal pain.	Decreased food intake.
Digitalis	Efficient heart function	Increases force of heart contraction and improves heart efficiency.	Overdose quickly leads to anorexia, then nausea, vomiting, and occasional diarrhea.	Decreased food intake.
INSULIN Regular or long acting; Protamine zinc NPH Ultralente Lente	Diabetes	Replaces deficient supplies of body's natural insulin.	With prolonged use, decreases salt and sweet taste sensitivity.	May depress or stimulate appetite, affecting food intake.
LAXATIVES Colace Magnesium Citrate Milk of Magnesia Mineral Oil Cascara	Constipation	Aids in bowel regularity or stimulates elimination.	Interferes with absorption of vitamins.	May result in deficiency of vitamins. May result in loss of vitamins.
MINERALS *Iron Salts* Ferrous Sulfate Ferrous Gluconate	Iron deficiency anemia	Provides iron for synthesis of hemoglobin.	Stomach upset, stomach cramps, black stools.	Decreased food intake due to stomach upset.
Potassium Salts Potassium chloride	Replaces potassium lost from use of drugs which cause fluid loss, i.e., some blood pressure drugs or potassium loss from diarrhea or vomiting	Provides potassium.	Stomach irritation.	Decreased food intake due to stomach upset.

Drug	Prescribed For	Resulting Effect	Side Effects	Possible Effect on Food Intake, Digestion, or Nutritional Status
MINERALS (continued)				
Potassium iodide	Emphysema, asthma	Iodide helps break up mucus.	Stomach irritation.	Decreased food intake due to stomach upset.
PHENOTHIAZINE TRANQUILIZERS				
Thorazine Sparine Stelazine Mellaril	Agitated psychotic conditions Commonly used in nursing homes for persons in agitated states. Senile psychosis	Produces tranquilization without hypnosis or anesthesia. Antinauseant effect. Reduces excitability.	Anorexia; red beefy tongue and irritation of oral mucosa; constipation and dryness of mouth; occasional diarrhea. May cause jaundice (with abdominal pain). Convulsions.	Decreased food intake due to irritation in mouth and loosened dentures. Difficulty in eating dry foods.
SALICYLATES				
Aspirin	Pain, fever, arthritis	Analgesic (relieves pain). Antipyretic (lowers fever). Anti-inflammatory agent.	High doses can cause nausea and vomiting. Stomach irritant.	Decreased food intake due to stomach upset.
TRICYCLIC ANTIDEPRESSANTS				
Aventyl Sinequan Elavil Tofranil Pertofrane	Depression; alleviates depression caused by chemical changes in the brain.	Exact action is unknown.	Anorexia, constipation, nausea, drowsiness. May stimulate appetite. Dry mouth.	Decreased food intake. Increased food intake. Difficulty in eating foods; difficulty in swallowing.

		Decreased food intake due to stomach upset.
	Stomach irritation.	
	Aids passage of air to lungs to facilitate breathing.	
XANTHINES Theophylline Aminophylline Caffeine Theobromine	Asthma, bronchitis, chronic lung disease	

SOURCE: Compiled by F. Carole Fujita, Pharm. D., Los Angeles County Harbor/U.C.L.A. Medical Center, Torrance, California

If you're elderly or know someone who is, and they complain they are having difficulty eating, or that food doesn't have the same appeal to them anymore, find out what drugs they are taking and check the drugs against this chart for their nutritional consequences.

An additional thought to keep in mind when referring to the Drug Chart is that, unfortunately, pharmacologic guidelines for the aged follow the pattern of dietary guidelines and thus are generally extrapolations from young-adult data rather than based on information specific to the aged. For now, we have to make do with these extrapolations until more correctly age-based information becomes available.

Special Nutritional Requirements

The elderly have some special nutritional requirements that are important for maintaining productive and healthy lives and for encouraging youthful aging. I've been told by some older persons that when they see their very bodies shrinking (losing inches in height, a common occurrence with age), there's a tendency to feel their dietary needs are less, too. But actually, in most instances, this is not true; in fact, sometimes the elderly have an increased need due to the body's less efficient absorption.

Dr. Theodore Reiff of the University of North Dakota has described a tragic triangle that occurs with elderly people: apathy coupled with depression leads to malnutrition. He says this makes him believe that some of the principal causes of death among older people are reversible and treatable.

Elderly people whose feeling of importance or self-worth is at a low ebb may also feel that what they eat, or don't eat, is of no importance either. A dietician who treats the elderly in Los Angeles has visited many of their homes and has observed the tea and toast syndrome to be quite common. They don't want to go the trouble of fixing food for themselves, and they don't want to trouble anyone else to do it for them, so they put themselves in a compromised nutritional state. Elderly people who fall into the tea and toast syndrome are becoming part of the tragic triangle. (Older men and women who are on severely restricted diets for reasons of economic hardship, see alternate affordable food ideas in this chapter under Title VII programs, Meals on Wheels, and Food Stamps.)

If elderly people require surgery when they are in a poor nutritional state, they need extra days or weeks to build themselves up enough to withstand the stresses of an op-

Special nutritional requirements

eration; they require a longer recuperation period, and because of their malnourished state, are often readmitted to hospitals unable to withstand even simple colds or infections.

Some basic food requirements, such as the need for an adequate fluid intake or carbohydrate consumption, don't change much with age. No matter what your age, for example, it is still important to consume 1.3 quarts of fluid a day. This section focuses on the information available about food requirements that change with age.

CALORIES

The typical pattern of physical activity associated with aging has been one of people going from an active life in their youth and middle years to a more sedentary life in retirement. This decreased activity has meant a decrease in caloric needs. But increasingly we see healthy older people like my friend Dr. James McPherson, retired, who at seventy-three years has gone from the comparatively sedentary job of dentist to the physically active life of running a fourteen-acre farm and overseeing the development of a large commercial flower business. For him, caloric *reduction* is the last thing he needs to worry about. In fact, his meals resemble a lumberjack's in quantity: for breakfast an apple, a persimmon, a banana, cereal, and toast. But for his less active cronies, caloric reduction is a positive and recommended step to keep their weight in check.

Caloric requirements for the elderly have been set lower because of decreased activity, decrease in lean body mass (muscle tissue), and decreased metabolic rate. (The metabolic rate is the rate at which the body converts food to energy, synthesizes new tissues, for example, hormones and enzymes, etc., and breaks down food into usable forms.) Among the elderly, differences among individuals become greater, therefore caloric requirements should be tailored to a particular individual based on activity, weight, and state of health.

The caloric reductions that the Joint Food and Agriculture Organization of the World Health Organization Committee recommends are:

Caloric Reduction	Years
5%	40–49
another 5%	50–59
10%	60–69
another 10%	70 and above

By the time people reach their seventies, if they are not physically active, they should have reduced their calories 30 per cent from what they were consuming when they were in their thirties. Since most elderly people do consume less calories, it becomes very important that the foods they select are not of the empty calorie variety (candy, soda pop, chips) supplying few of the essential nutrients.

CALCIUM

Calcium, as most people have been told since they were small, is the mineral responsible for building strong bones and teeth. In the elderly, the most important role calcium, or the lack of it, plays is observed in senile osteoporosis—a condition of bone depletion resulting in mechanical instability and frequent fractures that appears to be associated with declining absorption of calcium and increased loss in the urine. Although this condition appears in both men and women from age sixty on, it is four to six times more frequent in women than men (one out of four women over sixty-five is affected).

There is no certain known cure or prevention for adult bone loss, but an increase in dietary calcium throughout life is recommended. Dr. Chris Gallagher, Associate Professor of Medicine, Creighton University School of Medicine, a specialist in calcium requirements, feels strongly the effects of osteoporosis can be halted by diet. One way to picture this is to view your bones as a calcium bank. If you consumed adequate calcuim when you were younger, the calcium bank you've laid away could delay and perhaps prevent osteoporosis later. However, even if you're older now, Dr. Gallagher feels it is still possible to be in correct calcium balance (not to be losing more than you are taking in), by consuming correct amounts of calcium.

The exact amounts are somewhat in question. Dr. Gallagher believes the current calcium requirement set at 800 mg/day is too low and should be increased to 1,300–1,500 mg/day for the entire adult population. At a symposium on the elderly in San Francisco, June 1977, "Changing Age—Changing Food," other medical people questioned Gallagher's suggested figure as being too high and cautioned against it because it might lead to kidney stones. Most experts recommended a more moderate increase to 1,000 mg/day as the optimum calcium intake. In general, the elderly should be encouraged to eat a diet high in calcium-rich foods like milk, cheese, yoghurt.

Calcium Sources	Mg of Calcium
1 cup skim milk	359
3½ ounces peanuts	66
3½ ounces sardines	303
1 cup cooked beans	80
1 cup macaroni and cheese	362
1 cup low fat cottage cheese	180

(NOTE: As you can see from the above list of calcium sources, unless you include dairy products in your diet, it is very hard to meet the suggested requirement of 1,000 mg/day.)

In the elderly, there are other factors at work that affect calcium absorption; inactivity and immobility promote bone loss and stressful emotions can increase calcium excretion. In women, estrogen is known to have a protective effect on calcium loss. Although osteoporosis in women has been treated with estrogen, there are problems with this method, and the preferred treatment is for menopausal women to get increased amounts of dietary calcium.

VITAMIN D

Adequate calcium intake is not the only nutritional requirement important to bone health. Calcium absorption requires vitamin D, which comes mainly from dairy products and the sun. Because of decreased milk consumption in the elderly (milk is fortified with vitamin D), and decreased exposure to the sun, elderly people frequently become mildly vitamin D deficient. This deficiency can be partly responsible for decreased absorption of calcium. A dietary intake of 200 I.U./day of vitamin D appears to be safe (an excess of vitamin D poses the threat of toxicity). Vitamin D is consumed mostly through dairy products and the daily requirement is not hard to meet:

1 cup whole milk	100 I.U. vitamin D
1 cup skim milk	Trace—unless fortified with vitamin D, and is so labeled

Butter, egg yolks, liver, salt water fish, fish liver oils	Small amounts

An activity as simple, pleasant, and easy to do as sunbathing, if done with care and proper skin protection, helps fulfill the vitamin D requirement. The sunlight converts precursors of vitamin D in the skin to their active forms. But when elderly people go out covered with clothing from head to toe, that's not doing them much good. In front of my building in New York, there are several older people who lie on their chaise longues on the sidewalk (such is life in the city) catching the sun for a few hours. But they lie there in their topcoats, hats, lap blanket, and gloves with their faces barely peeping out. Elderly people out to catch the sun would do better to expose more of their body area to the sun.

VITAMIN A

The American Journal of Clinical Nutrition reports that vitamin A deficiency is not uncommon in the elderly, especially those subsisting on diets of little more than tea and toast. Since there is little fat in the diet, absorption of this fat-soluble vitamin (along with D and E) is diminished. Absorption of vitamin A may also be impaired by the use of laxatives and antibiotics (see chart, page 354–55). Unfortunately there are not yet any reliable data on vitamin A requirements and how they specifically relate to the elderly, but we do know this is an area of concern. Carrots, broccoli, spinach, sweet potatoes, mangoes, cantaloupe, winter squash, and liver are all good sources of vitamin A. (For other sources see Chapter 1, Vegetables, and Chapter 3, Fruits.)

VITAMIN E

Vitamin E has been heralded as doing everything from ensuring youth to reducing heart problems and increasing sexual potency. None of these have been adequately substantiated and for now the Food and Nutrition Board of the National Research Council recommends the same amount for older adults as for young people.

> *Men* I.U. Vitamin E, 15
> *Women* I.U. Vitamin E, 12

Since vitamin E is plentiful in fruits, vegetables, and grains there is rarely a deficiency.

VITAMIN C

Although some scientists and researchers tout vitamin C as an elixir, so far there is no research indicating a need for increasing vitamin C requirements among the elderly. Some researchers believe that more is needed to overcome the stress of infection, but other studies dispute this. It is suggested that among the elderly, as with other age groups, perhaps the best way to proceed with vitamins is to take a one-a-day capsule. To take more vitamins unnecessarily—megavitamins, for example—eventually subjects the body to side effects similar to taking too many drugs.

B VITAMINS (THIAMIN, B₆, B₁₂, FOLIC ACID)

Thiamin

Although studies do not show increased need for thiamin with age, the common use of therapeutic drugs may increase the urinary excretion of thiamin, thus resulting in an increased requirement.

A thiamin deficiency is possible in elderly patients whose diets consist heavily of tea and toast, since tea is rich in tannic acid, which has been shown to possess antithiamin activity. Some of the signs of early thiamin deficiency appear to be irritability, anorexia, and insomnia. Breads, cereals and meat are good sources of thiamin. Pork is an excellent source.

B₆, B₁₂, and Folic Acid

It is surmised that the elderly may have an increased need for B₆, B₁₂, and folic acid due to less efficient absorption or reduced intestinal synthesis of the vitamins. A low iron intake may also result in decreased absorption of B₁₂ and folic acid. It is not difficult to get an adequate supply of B vitamins from dietary sources. Whole grains, meat, peanuts, and tomatoes are high in B₆; animal protein is rich in B₁₂; fresh fruits and vegetables are good sources of folic acid.

FAT

As mentioned, sufficient fat is needed in the diet for absorption of fat-soluble vitamins A, D, E, and K (K is not often mentioned, but it helps blood clotting). For most of us on the regular all-American diet, getting enough fat is hardly a problem; getting too much is the quandary. The difficulty exists for elderly people on less than adequate diets.

Obtaining 30 per cent of one's calories from fat appears to be a reasonable level— translated that means a 1,500-calorie diet allows for 500 calories from fat. Each teaspoon of fat has 45 calories. On a regular diet, this fat requirement is not hard to meet since 1 ounce of meat averages 1 teaspoon of fat or 45 calories. But it doesn't take an expensive diet to meet this fat requirement. For example, people on a modest food plan could do it simply by including peanut butter on their toast, a mayonnaise spread on their sandwich, and by eating the skin on a piece of chicken.

PROTEIN

Information regarding protein requirements for the elderly is still inadequate, since most requirements are based on data from healthy young adults. Vernon R. Young, a professor of Nutrition Biochemistry at M.I.T., is recommending as a result of his research that, with advancing age, protein intake be *increased* as a percentage in the total diet. He suggests 12–14 per cent of the elderly person's calories should be consumed as protein. That is, if the diet is 1,500 calories, about 225 of the calories should be protein or about 57 gm. This translates to:

2 servings of milk or milk equivalent (cottage cheese, cheese, yoghurt)

5 ounces of meat or substitute (beans, nuts, peanut butter, eggs)

3 servings of bread (crackers, cereals, rice, pasta)

Although his suggestion represents an increase over what was formerly recommended, he feels, in most instances, this increase already represents the normal pattern of consumption because people in this country tend to overeat protein.

One reason the need for protein may become larger with age is that the efficiency of the body's utilization of protein decreases with age. There is a decrease in muscle tissue in the elderly, which suggests a decreased requirement for protein; but there is also less body cell mass to maintain the efficiency of protein utilization. Psychological or emotional stress associated with aging can also promote protein loss.

It is likely that the less than adequate protein intake among the elderly can often be attributed to economic factors since protein foods have traditionally been the most expensive foodstuffs. (For less costly protein suggestions, see Protein Comparison Cost chart, page 175.)

IRON

Iron requirements for the elderly are less than what is recommended earlier in life. The Food and Nutrition Board recommends a daily dietary allowance of 10 mg of iron for men and women over the age of fifty, which represents an 8-mg reduction from that recommended for younger individuals. Adequate vitamin C increases the absorption of iron.

Iron-deficiency anemia is relatively common and widespread among the elderly.

There's a profile of a typical older person most likely to develop this type of anemia: lives alone, reduced income, little interest in cooking and nutritional requirements, living on a diet with little animal protein because of the cost, and few fresh fruits or vegetables.

Although iron can be given in medicinal forms, these tablets can cause gastric irritation and constipation and it's preferred to increase iron-rich foods in the diet (see list). Six and one-half selections from the list would make an adequate day's iron intake for an elderly man or woman.

Good Dietary Sources of Iron

(minimum of 1.5 mg iron per listed serving size)

FOOD	SERVING
Apricots, dried	5 halves
Beans, dried, cooked	½ cup
Beef, cooked	2 ounces
Beet Greens, cooked	½ cup
Brazil Nuts	8 medium
Cereals	1 ounce
Chard, cooked	½ cup
Chicken, cooked	3 ounces
Cider, sweet	10 ounces
Clams	1 ounce
Corn Syrup	2 tablespoons
Dandelion Greens, cooked	½ cup
Dates	⅓ cup
Dried Beef	2 ounces
Egg, whole	2
Ham, cooked	2 ounces
Heart, cooked	2 ounces
Instant Breakfast	1 serving
Kidney, cooked	1 ounce
Lamb, cooked	2 ounces
Liver, cooked	1 ounce
Liver Sausage	1 ounce
Maple Syrup	3 tablespoons
Molasses	2 tablespoons
Oysters	1 ounce
Peaches, dried	3 halves
Peas, dried, cooked	½ cup
Pork, cooked	2 ounces
Prunes, dried	4 medium

Raisins, dried	1 small box (1½ ounces)
Sardines	2 ounces
Scallops	2 ounces
Shrimp	2 ounces
Spinach, cooked	½ cup
Strawberries	1 cup
Sweet Potato	3½″ × 2¼″
Tomato Juice	¾ cup
Tuna	½ cup
Turkey, cooked	3 ounces
Veal, cooked	2 ounces
Watermelon	6″ diameter × 1½″ slice
Wheat Germ	2 tablespoons

NOTE: It's been found vitamin C aids in the absorption of iron. To increase the iron absorption from whole grains, cereals, vegetables, and eggs, from which iron is poorly absorbed, eat vitamin C-rich foods along with them (orange juice, melons, strawberries, or broccoli).

FIBER

Although the exact fiber intake which would maintain optimal health in the elderly is as yet unknown, it is known that high fiber diets can naturally help promote and maintain proper bowel function. Proper bowel movements can be a problem for the elderly since intestinal tone is diminished and this makes them prone to constipation. See list for examples of high fiber foods that should be included.

High Fiber Foods

Biscuits and Cakes Whole meal flour or rye, oatmeal or rolled oats, dried fruit and nuts.

Bran Weight for weight, bran has the highest fiber content of all the readily available footstuffs. Unprocessed bran is the cheapest available. Bran can be mixed with flour for homemade bread, cakes, biscuits, or muffins, and mixed in sauces, puddings, or stewed fruit.

Bread Whole wheat, raisin, cracked wheat, and whole rye breads, and any made from whole wheat or whole rye flour of 100 per cent extraction. Extra-high fiber bread can be made by adding additional bran.

Breakfast Cereals All-Bran, Puffed Wheat, 40% Bran Flakes, Bran Chex, Raisin Bran, Shredded Wheat, porridge oats.

Flour Whole meal, such as whole wheat or whole rye. Use only flour containing 100 per cent of the whole grain.

Fruits and Nuts All kinds in generous amounts. Raw and dried fruits, skins included, are preferable.

Rice Use brown or polished rice if available; otherwise, bran can be added to white rice.

Vegetables All kinds in generous amounts, including plenty of raw vegetables. Potatoes should be baked or boiled in their skins.

FROM: *Current Prescribing*, July 1978.

 Practical Tips

In researching this chapter, I talked with many older people of different income brackets and cultural backgrounds about how they coped. Their problems ranged from eating on limited incomes and adjusting to modified diets to becoming accustomed to cooking for one. What I gleaned were practical tips on how some savvy oldsters are buying and cooking as well as some interesting ideas about appropriate-sized cooking appliances.

JENNIE'S TV DINNERS

A good home cooked TV dinner

One of the best food ideas is from Jennie, a midwestern woman in her eighties who used to be a home economics teacher. With only herself to cook for she now makes her own television dinners. When she's feeling ambitious she makes up enough dinners for a month: one whole chicken divides into at least seven dinners, a turkey breast gets barbecued for another seven meals, a beef stew makes into another week's worth of meals, a macaroni and cheese dish rounds out the month. She divides the main entrees into suitable portions and fills the largest section of aluminum TV dinner trays her friends collect for her. The smaller tray sections are filled with appropriate garnishes: cranberry sauce with the turkey, extra gravy for the beef stew. She also divides up already frozen vegetables and puts them in the section left for them. (This way, she doesn't have to eat peas for 3 days running just to finish one box.) She wraps these securely and freezes. The advantages of her system?

* It's no more than half the price of similar kinds of prepackaged foods in the stores.

* Her food does not have any additives, preservatives, artificial flavorings or colorings.

* She can still cook in large quantities and get the best prices and flavor.

* She always has something delicious on hand in case a friend drops in.

If you have elderly relatives or friends who temporarily can't cook for themselves, I think this would be a wonderful, practical thing to do for them. With less than one day's cooking you could fix them up for a month. (If you don't have a supply of the commercial TV dinner trays, just use aluminum containers.)

LUCY'S OLDER HUSBAND

Perhaps one of the most interesting people I met was a middle-aged woman named Lucy, who is married to a man ninety-eight years old. She married him eleven years ago, when he was a young eighty-seven, and believes good nutrition is one of the reasons he is still alive and going strong. Her suggestions:

* She saves six–seven dollars a month clipping and using coupons.

* She says older people have more time on their hands and should spend more of this leisure time shopping and planning their meals carefully.

* She suggests buying meats, chicken, and fish in larger quantities and repackaging them yourself for the freezer.

* She still entertains at home, but cuts her expenses by serving nonalcoholic mixed drinks—fruit punches.

* When visiting people convalescing in hospitals, she brings fresh fruit, rather than flowers.

APPROPRIATE COOKING APPLIANCES

Older people alone often don't want to turn the oven on for just one tiny meal for themselves, so, in fact, they don't turn it on at all, and may lose interest in cooking altogether. There are appliances widely available now that are designed to solve this particular problem and they conserve energy as well.

These appliances were originally developed for the single crowd, meaning young singles living alone, but they serve older singles just as well.

* *The Toaster Oven.* Toaster ovens can be used by the elderly for much more than just toasting. They can heat up casseroles, bake small meatloaves, and cook three-course frozen TV dinners. The oven temperature has a range of 200°–500° F., and they are reasonably priced.

* *Burger Cookers.* Some of the major manufacturers (Presto, Oster, Hamilton Beach, Norelco) are now manufacturing mini-griddles. Presto's smallest griddle is about 6″ square and sells for half the price of the large size. Although these are sold primarily to cook burgers, their versatility does not end there. With the lid open, they can grill bacon, sausages, pancakes, French toast, a slice of ham or eggs; closed, they grill burgers and grilled cheese sandwiches.

* *Small Electric Fry Pan.* From Presto comes the Wee Fry Skillet. It has easy-to-follow instructions right on the appliance, an easy-to-read temperature dial, and is a practical investment for someone cooking in small amounts.

* *Small Cooking Pans.* Buy smaller-size pans in general. I know a woman who bakes individual meatloaves in minature doll-size bread loaf pans. It's the perfect size for her appetite; she uses her toaster oven to bake in.

APPROPRIATE FOOD SIZES

It is possible to buy 1-cup servings of most canned fruits and vegetables, as well as some simple items like corned beef hash or chili con carne that could make a main part of a meal. How much more do you pay for the convenience? Checking prices, I found the difference is roughly 25–40 per cent, but usually averages around 30 per cent. In some

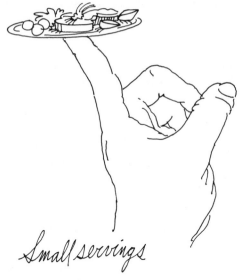

Small servings

instances, with half a carton of eggs, half a loaf of bread, half portions of margarine or butter, the price difference is negligible. Although with some items you do pay a higher price, there is usually no waste and it does allow a larger variety in your meals. Although I would not recommend them as a steady diet, already prepared frozen entrees and frozen TV dinners, which include such items as Salisbury steaks, chicken pies, and fillet of fish dinners, can offer variety and ease of preparation, with a slight increase in cost to cover the convenience. Read the package labels carefully to choose frozen selections with fewer additives and preservatives.

GERIATRIC FOODS—AN ALTERNATIVE

Over the years, it has been suggested that the food industry has been negligent in not formulating foods geared to the specific needs of the elderly. British scientist Arnold Bender questions why the food industry, which has successfully established a baby food market, has not yet seriously undertaken the marketing of geriatric foods. Alternative packaging could make shopping and cooking for one, or two, easier.

Geriatric foods could serve several purposes. For people living alone, they would make it easier to prepare well-balanced meals; for the elderly living with other family members, it could reduce the burden of preparing modified meals for one family member.

So far, the only company I know that is marketing geriatric meals is the Upjohn Drug Company. In Southern California, their line of modified dietary frozen entrees goes under the Jack Spratt label. I was concerned that their foods were essentially frozen TV dinners at three to four times the price. I sampled a few and compared them with the store-bought counterpart. In the summer of 1978, their exorbitant price, coupled with hideously low quality, made them a very questionable entry in the geriatric market.

There *is* a need for geriatric foods, but so far no companies have responsibly met this need. Although I looked at only one geriatric product (it's the only one I could find), you would probably do well to be equally suspicious of other new products entering the market until they prove themselves worthy of your trust. If a company comes into your area with a line of food aimed at the elderly, like Jack Spratt, protect yourself by ordering a sample meal first before signing up for a month's or a year's supply.

 Food Services

There's a wide variety of food services available to the elderly, ranging from totally free government-sponsored nutritional services to neighborhood- and church-sponsored feeding programs that usually have sliding fee scales based on the ability to pay. Grocery stores and restaurants often offer special discounts; there are luncheon clubs; and there are consulting dieticians who can be helpful with specific dietary concerns.

TITLE VII

Title VII is a bureaucratic name for the nutrition programs for the elderly sponsored by the federal government, which in most instances I've observed are refreshingly and lovingly unbureaucratic. The purpose behind Title VII (I'm sorry, the name sticks in my throat. Why couldn't it have been named the National Luncheon Club, or something else equally soft and pleasant?) is to promote better health among the elderly through improved nutrition and reduced isolation. These are communal dining programs designed to meet the nutritional needs of the elderly who, for practical or financial reasons, may no longer be cooking or eating at home, and also to provide the necessary companionship that makes eating worth while. It's been found, not surprisingly, that isolated, lonely people don't eat very well, so these centers provide a warm, sociable atmosphere that obviously represents more than just a hot meal. To the one out of four elderly who live alone, these centers can provide the necessary companionship that makes eating pleasurable once again.

Depending on the specific center, they offer at least one nutritionally sound meal a day in strategically located areas—schools, community centers, churches, senior citizens' centers. Some cater to particular ethnic groups—the Mexicans in Texas, the kosher Jews in New York—and many provide transportation as well.

In 1977, 100 million hot meals were served and 15 million more were carried to shut-ins. The Administration on Aging provides the major share of the meal costs, state and local governments share in the remaining costs. Volunteers, usually the elderly themselves, help serve the food and sometimes the elderly are also employed in preparing the food.

Anyone over age sixty can participate and, if they can pay, donations are accepted in the range of 25–75¢ per meal. Those who can't pay, don't. The actual food costs in 1977 averaged $1.73 per meal; with transportation the cost was $2.46. For reimbursement purposes, the various locations keep track of how many people they are feeding, but aside from that, I've never observed any formal keeping track of payees and non-payees.

I've been told that initially there was resistance from some of the elderly to attending these centers. At first, there was a feeling by retired people who had worked all their lives that these nutrition programs were a welfare or low-income activity. Eventually, as the centers opened, neighborhood people ventured in by ones and twos, and now most centers are being used to capacity.

I've had lunch and visited at several of these Title VII luncheon clubs. They have a personal touch about them that belies their government sponsorship. In the Bronx, on a blustery cold winter's day in January, I ate in a luncheon program that was located in a church basement. The streets were so icy and the day was so cold that one would think twice before venturing out, but every table was filled. The people told me this club was their family. Many of the elderly had arrived early in the morning for painting lessons, had their lunch, and then stayed part of the afternoon playing cards. During lunch, people entertained each other with violin recitals, piano playing, and even jazz singing, by a professional jazz singer now retired. It was a warm, loving place where delicious food in ample proportions was served.

In the Queens section of New York there's a luncheon club hosted by the Catholic Charities (with additional money from Title VII) that must be one of the best in the nation. In addition to the food, which is the initial drawing card, this center sponsors a large variety of constantly changing activities. On one day the people were square dancing with an official square dance caller; another day there was a lively discussion hosted among the men in the pool room about the merits, and demerits, of the Equal Rights Amendment, which was coming up for ratification in New York State.

In a Japanese center in Los Angeles, the activities center around Japanese calligraphy, flower arranging, and classical Japanese music.

There are probably many programs that are not as good as the ones I've singled out; however, when these Title VII programs work, they can be wonderful and, regardless of income, can truly enrich people's lives. When they don't work, it's usually because they are too rigid and regimented. Oh, the people still get fed all right, but the additional opportunity for a social happening is lost. (One hideous center I visited had the seniors filing in to eat, in lines, the way they did in kindergarden.)

I also observed that the food is good to very good. In the Japanese senior center in Los Angeles, the volunteers were concerned about the appearance of the food and took time to garnish each plate with parsley and seaweed. In the Bronx, at a center where the population is primarily Southern black, the tables had the proper condiments to go with fried turnip greens and corn bread.

To find a Title VII nutrition program near you, call your City Parks and Recreation Department, or your city councilman, and request the information.

MEALS ON WHEELS

For people who can't get out to a communal dining site because they are homebound, handicapped, or temporarily ill, the Meals on Wheels program delivers meals to their homes. This nonprofit program is privately run, usually by a community or church effort, and partially funded with government money (to cover office expenses and transportation) and supplemented with private contributions and meal fees when they can be collected. Eligibility varies depending on the community. Some programs restrict their deliveries only to the homebound and others make their service available to any senior citizen.

Meals to the Homebound, run by the San

Food mobilization program

Fernando Interfaith Council in San Fernando Valley, California, is typical of many of the programs. They deliver one hot and one cold meal Monday through Friday around noon each day, but only to the homebound. Meals have been approved by a dietician and they offer modified diet plans. Although only the cost of the food itself is passed on to the recipient, sometimes even this can be waived if a community group can pick it up. (Transportation fees are not added since volunteers deliver meals, and other fees for office space, part-time workers, and overhead are funded by the city.)

In Kalamazoo, Michigan, their program serves meals six days a week with a frozen meal sent along for the seventh day. Recipients may also receive a breakfast and cold lunch along with the hot meal.

How To Start a Meals on Wheels in Your Area

The Meals on Wheels network is now so vast that it serves even remote rural areas, as well as major metropolitan cities, but if there is no program already established in your area and you know elderly people who could benefit, start your own. Don't think you need

to serve hundreds to justify organizing a program; some local groups serve 20 or less.

To start your program, if you don't have access to kitchens, you need a source to provide the meals, a transportation system, and volunteers. Often the meal source can be a local hospital which is willing to contract out the number of meals you need. In other instances, private caterers have been used. The transportation system is provided by volunteers recruited from the community. The city itself is usually willing to fund additional overhead, such as office space, part-time office workers, as well as a project director if your program is large enough to need a full-time director. For more detailed information, encouragement, and advice on how to set up a program, the following three resources should be very helpful.

> Joseph Brown, Executive Director
> Meals on Wheels Rhode Island
> 175 Mathewson Street
> Providence, Rhode Island 02903

Although the whole state of Rhode Island delivers less than 200 meals, Joseph Brown has been associated with the Meals on Wheels program from its very beginning and has a wealth of information that he is willing to share.

> National Association of Meals on Wheels
> Lois N. McManus, President
> City Liaison to United Services for
>   Older Adults
> 101 H, North Park Drive
> Greensboro, North Carolina 27401

Although the national association is still in the throes of getting organized, it can be a valuable help in providing information.

> Meals on Wheels of Central
>   Maryland, Inc.
> 4904 York Road
> Baltimore, Maryland 21212

This group has published what is referred to as "The Bible" of the Meals on Wheels organizations. Called the *Organization Manual for Meals on Wheels,* it is a complete how-to book and gives all the information anyone needs to know to set up a local program. It is available from the above address.

FOOD STAMPS

Elderly people living on limited incomes may be eligible for additional help by participating in the food stamp program.

* *Who's eligible?* Households of 1 or more persons without incomes or with low incomes on Social Security or small pensions. Recipients must be able to prepare meals.

* *How to apply?* Applicants go to the local welfare office, such as the Department of Social Services or local food stamp office. Those applying must bring papers showing place of residence, number in household, total income, and expenses.

Food stamps can be used for grocery foods purchased ready to be prepared, and in some instances may also be used for restaurant eating as well. There are two publications that acquaint people with the food stamp program. They are both available free. (Note that the first publication describes special provisions for the elderly.)

> *The Food Stamp Program*
> Food and Nutrition Service, USDA
> Superintendent of Documents
> U. S. Government Printing Office
> Washington, D.C. 20402
> (Program Aid ✳1123)

TELLS: Who is eligible; where to get food stamps; how to apply for food stamps; how to use food stamps; special provisions for the elderly.

> *Shopping with Food Stamps*
> Food and Nutrition Service, USDA
> Superintendent of Documents
> U. S. Government Printing Office
> Washington, D.C. 20402
> (Program Aid ✳1109)

TELLS: Rules for using food stamps; reminders on how to shop for, store, and use foods; planning meals.

OTHER SERVICES FOR SENIOR CITIZENS

Phone Services

In Los Angeles, there is a Senior Line (213-483-1133) that seniors can call with questions; they will be directed to a specific agency, community group, or service.

Look in your local phone directory under Senior Citizen Affairs, Senior Citizens' Services, for a similar number in your area.

In Ventura, an area near Los Angeles, there is an Older American Special Information Service (OASIS) telephone service that is part of the Los Angeles County Public Library Service (805-948-5936). A caller can listen to 2- to 5-minute-long tapes on health and nutrition, as well as many other subjects of interest to the older American.

Senior Citizens' Clubs

Call your local Recreation and Parks Department and ask what activities and clubs are available through the senior citizen section.

Neighborhood Gardens

Community gardens, patterned after the World War II victory gardens and allotment plots, are cropping up on unused lots in every city around the country. They are a good way for seniors to do active physical work, to save money, and grow healthy food. Ask your senior citizens center for the ones nearest to you.

Food Co-operatives

Food-buying clubs can provide food at savings of 30–50 per cent and more. For more information, call your city's Senior Line phone number, or write to the address given for co-operatives in Chapter 4, page 119.

Senior Citizen Discounts

Restaurants Some restaurants give discounts to seniors, but they must ask for the discount to take advantage of it. The discount is usually about 10 per cent. Some restaurants issue a senior citizen discount card.

Supermarkets Most supermarkets now have days when they advertise discounts specifically for seniors.

Los Angeles has a Senior Citizen Discount Program co-ordinated by the Senior Citizens section of the city Recreation and Parks Department. Many merchants and businesses give discounts of 10–20 per cent on merchandise and services. In Los Angeles, for a list of participating businesses, theaters, and restaurants, call Senior Citizen Discount Plan, 213-485-4851. If your area does not have an organized discount plan for seniors, this group is a good source for information on how to get one organized. Write:

> Senior Citizen Discount Plan
> Department of Recreation and Parks
> City Hall East, Room 1350
> Los Angeles, California 90012

Television Programs

Check your local television directory for television programming geared to the senior citizen. "Over Easy" is one example of a daytime television program for and about older persons. Check your listing for other shows. If nutrition is ignored or downplayed, write to the producers and ask for stories relating to areas in nutrition that you would find useful.

Nutrition Classes

Although not frequently offered, some local colleges and universities on occasion give special courses in nutrition for the elderly. Check with your local schools. At Los An-geles City College, I attended one such class titled, "Your Second Fifty Years." I was surprised how well attended the class was (80 people), and how it was evenly divided between men and women. Part of the attraction was also a healthful picnic lunch that was provided as part of the class.

National Organizations

If you have difficulty finding local senior groups, write or call the national organizations, and they can direct you.

> American Association of Retired Persons
> 1909 K St., N.W.
> Washington, D.C. 20049
> 202-872-4700
> *Age fifty-five or older, retired or still employed.*

> Action for Independent Maturity (AIM)
> 1909 K St., N.W.
> Washington, D.C. 20049
> 202-872-4700

> National Association of Retired Federal Employees
> 1533 New Hampshire Ave., N.W.
> Washington, D.C. 20036
> 202-234-0832
> *Represents and lobbies for needs of retired civil servants.*

> The National Center on Black Aged
> 1730 M St., N.W., Suite 811
> Washington, D.C. 20036
> 202-785-8766
> *Provides comprehensive program of co-ordination, information, and consulting services to meet needs of black aged.*

> National Council of Senior Citizens
> 1511 K St., N.W.
> Washington, D.C. 20005
> 202-783-6850
> *Represents and lobbies for needs of the elderly. Membership at any age.*

> National Council on the Aging, Inc.
> 1828 L St., N.W.
> Washington, D.C. 20036
> 202-223-6250

Gray Panthers
3700 Chestnut St.
Philadelphia, Pennsylvania 19104
*Activist group of older people who resent
stereotyping.*

Publications

There are also publications geared specifically to the elderly that can be helpful. Although their emphasis is not solely on food and nutrition, this subject is usually covered. (The last publication mentioned is especially helpful for elderly people living alone because it can easily be adapted to cooking for one. It's also in large type and it might make a nice present for an elderly friend.

Aging
Superintendent of Documents
U. S. Government Printing Office
Washington, D.C. 20402
Subscription only.

Modern Maturity
Dupont Circle Building
Washington, D.C. 20036
*Subscription only. By the American
Association of Retired Persons.*

Senior Citizens Today
2530 J St., Suite 302
Sacramento, California 95816
*A State of California Senior Citizen
Newspaper. Keeps senior citizens
informed about special senior citizens'
days, events, etc. Provides list of
businesses, restaurants, theaters, etc.,
which give special privilege or discount
in California. Keeps senior citizens
informed on Social Security, property
taxes, housing, education, health, recreation, and Medicare programs.*

Cooking for Two (Large type)
Food and Nutrition Service, USDA
Superintendent of Documents
U. S. Government Printing Office
Washington, D.C. 20402
Program Aid ✕1043
*Helpful hints on planning and serving
meals, nutrition information, shopping
for food, storing food, recipes, menu
ideas.*

CONSULTING NUTRITIONISTS

Another relatively new service that is available to all age groups but might be especially helpful to the elderly are dieticians in private practice. These are registered dieticians accredited by the American Dietetic Association. There are now about 500 dieticians in private practice across the country and their numbers are increasing.

These dieticians are professionals who used to work solely for hospitals, or with the food industry, but who have now opted to work directly with the public in private practice, on an individual basis, much as a doctor does. From a consulting nutritionist, one can expect to receive nutritional counseling, guidance, and assessment of present eating habits, guidance for future diets, guidance in preventive nutritional care, and also help with specialized diets. Just like

An apple a day...

lawyers or accountants, some of these dieticians are better than others. There are certain things to look for or ask to make sure a particular dietician is qualified and reputable.

* They should be registered by both the American Dietetic Association and the state's local association.

* Ask specifically what services are offered and what is provided.

* If you have a specialized diet problem, ask what kind of concrete advice you will be given: printed menus, recipes?

* Over the phone, tell what you need or want and ask if they can help. (Example— my husband has renal failure and needs a special diet. Can you help me learn how to do this?)

* Ask what the nutritionist's academic training and background is.

* Ask how much it will cost and how many sessions are recommended.

To be referred to a consulting nutritionist in your area, you might start by writing the American Dietetic Association, 430 North Michigan Avenue, Chicago, Illinois 60611. Ask them to direct you to their Consultant Nutritionist Referral Service.

The snag with consulting dieticians is that so far the real and needed services they perform are not covered for reimbursement by insurance companies. In hospitals, nutritional counseling *is* paid for by insurance companies, but once this service is performed outside the hospital, there is no third-party reimbursement, as yet. In California this may be changing since many nutrition groups are actively lobbying. The irony is that many people with diabetes, hypertension, and heart disease could be helped by dietary counseling, but they aren't sick enough yet to be hospitalized, so they can't receive this service as part of their insurance plan.

Some of the services offered by consulting nutritionists are:

* Computer analysis of present diet

* Assessment of present nutritional status

* Family counseling on family eating habits

* Interpreters for Spanish speaking

* Individual as well as group counseling

* Menu planning and suggestions for food preparation

* If in the process of the nutritional assessment, medical problems are uncovered or detected, a physician will be consulted and special or modified diets can be approved.

 ## Long-term Care: Nursing Homes

When the elderly are no longer self-sufficient and can no longer live in their own homes, it becomes necessary to help them select appropriate long-term care. This is never an easy situation. When I was ten, my grandmother Josie, who lived with us, fell and, in a classic accident for her age, broke her hip. Three years later my family moved away from Seattle, but my grandmother wasn't well enough to move with us. None of the other family members were able to provide the necessary space, or the full-time supervision she needed, so she was placed in a nursing home.

This solution is becoming more commonplace. Since 1964, there's been a 47 per cent increase in the number of persons living in nursing homes; this population now easily exceeds 1 million. Although many aspects of a nursing home should be ques-

Home sweet nursing home.

tioned to ensure top-flight care, I'm concentrating on dietary concerns. It is an outrage if a patient loses ground because he or she is malnourished while in a nursing home, when food should be a pleasure—properly prepared and chosen with lifelong favorite selections in mind.

The following is a check list of questions that should be helpful in determining the quality of food service in a nursing home. If the nursing home responds negatively to too many of these questions, you would best look at a few more facilities before making your final selection.

* Is the kitchen clean and reasonably tidy? Ask to see the kitchen. Is waste properly disposed of?

* Ask to see the meal schedule. Are three meals served each day?

* Are meals served at normal hours, with plenty of time for leisurely eating?

* Are no more than 14 hours allowed between the evening meal and breakfast the next morning?

* Are nutritious between-meal and bedtime snacks available?

* Are patients given enough food?

* Ask to sample a meal. Is the food tasty and served at the proper temperature, hot food hot, cold food cold? Does the food look appetizing?

* Does the meal being served match the posted menu? Ask to see the menu. Are there any favorite dishes of the patient included in the menu?

* Are special requests for food likes and dislikes honored? Is there an extra charge for special food?

* If the individual is of an ethnic minority or a particular religious or social group, is the food acceptable?

* Are patients served in a dining room or in bed? Is the dining room attractive and comfortable, and does it provide a chance for socialization in pleasant surroundings?

* Do patients who need it get help in eating, whether in the dining room or in their own rooms?

* Are special meals prepared for patients on therapeutic diets?

* Is food prepared on the premises or catered?

* Are many convenience foods used or are conventional methods used?

* Is the patient weighed frequently? Patients should be weighed once a week in a skilled nursing facility.

* Is there an adequate supply of fresh fruits and vegetables in the diet?

* How many hours does the dietician spend per month in the facility?

* How frequently, if ever, does the dietician visit the patient?

To help out the nursing home, family or friends of the resident should provide, in writing, information on food habits and special needs. The kinds of information to be included should be:

—whether appetite is poor or needs encouragement

—if the patient needs plenty of time to finish a meal

—special diet or restrictions prescribed by doctor

—does the patient sneak foods if on restricted diet? i.e., salt or sweets on low salt or diabetic diet.

—any religious dietary restrictions. i.e., no meat, pork, shellfish, coffee, tea; kosher?

—the patient's likes and dislikes, "security foods."

—are there foods which cause distress? List them. Spicy, highly seasoned foods, gas-producing foods, fatty or fried foods?

—allergies to foods?

—usual meal times—is main meal generally lunch or dinner?

 Questions and Answers

As people get older, they have specific questions that relate to their age and to nutritional concerns. Here are some typical queries that have come my way over the past few years.

* *My mother-in-law is concerned about decreased frequency of bowel movements. Is she abnormal? Is there anything I can do to help?*

According to Harold Schnaper, M.D., Duke University Center for Aging, in old age it is normal to go 1, 2, or 3 days without a bowel movement. What counts is that she has one. With age there is a slowing of the functioning of the digestive system. The resulting decreased mobility of the intestines decreases the frequency of bowel movements.

This also varies with individuals based on their level of physical activity, their diet, and their physiological age. If they are still very physically active, if their diet includes plenty of fluids and high fiber foods, this combination of activity and bulky foods will stimulate the gastrointestinal tract and their bowel movements can be expected to be much more frequent.

There are certain foods which provide fiber in the diet and decrease the time necessary for the body to digest a meal. By eating high fiber foods, older people can expect bowel movements to be larger, heavier, and the mobility of the intestine to be stimulated.[1] High fiber foods are good for any age group, but have their special benefits for the elderly. (See list of high fiber foods, page 363.)

* *Many of the elderly people I know suffer from cataracts. I've heard that large doses of vitamin A prevent cataracts. Is this true?*

Cataracts occur in about 33 per cent of elderly people. According to the Institute of Food Technologists, so far there is no evidence that vitamin A in any amounts can prevent cataracts. But normal amounts of vitamin A are required for maintenance of good eye health and prevention of night blindness.

[1] It is now also thought that a high fiber diet leads to a lower incidence of colon cancer. It is postulated that with a low fiber diet, the food takes longer to pass through the intestines and the lingering bacteria produce carcinogens. A high fiber diet is associated with more rapid transit through the intestines.

*   *How should I control my craving for sweets?*

Many sweets are high in calories, but have little nutritive value. With many elderly people, if sweets are eaten in excess, or if *only* sweets are eaten, there is a danger that other important food groups will be ignored and the person could become malnourished and susceptible to diseases. You're right to be concerned. Your aim should be to select foods that can satisfy a sweet tooth, but at the same time provide a source of essential nutrients. Try fresh fruits, which are sweet and also provide bulk which the elderly need for regulation of the bowels. Also, custards, puddings, ice cream, and yoghurt (when made from natural products) can provide protein, calcium, riboflavin, and vitamin D while satisfying a sweet tooth. Except on special occasions, avoid foods which provide only empty calories—candies, cookies, pies, cakes, jellies, and jams.

*   *Does alcohol affect the elderly differently from the way it affects younger people?*

It doesn't affect the elderly worse, but if an older person is already in a mildly nutritional deficient state, alcohol may push him over the brink. Cirrhosis of the liver is more common among sixty-five to seventy-year-olds and is believed to be *geriatric alcoholism,* rather than the result of drinking over a lifetime.

This is a significant problem for both older men and women. The liver metabolizes alcohol preferentially before it metabolizes food. When diets are marginal nutritionally, the effect of alcohol on the body may be enough to precipitate a deficiency of essential nutrients, especially the B vitamins (thiamin, niacin, B_6, and folic acid).

Prolonged use of alcohol can also create a need for increased dosage of drugs. If the elderly are taking prescription drugs (i.e., anticonvulsants, antibiotics, oral diabetic agents), because of an accelerated rate of metabolism, increased dosage of the drugs may be required to give the same result.

*   *Can vitamin A cure or help arthritis?*

Unfortunately, no diet in itself will cure arthritis. Beware, especially, of health food mavens hawking "natural" food cures. Since there is no scientific evidence that any food or vitamin deficiency has anything to do with *causing* arthritis, there is no evidence that any food or vitamin is effective in *treating* or *curing* it.

People with osteoarthritis are frequently overweight and a reducing diet may be prescribed to avoid overburdening the joints. In rheumatoid arthritis, the patient is frequently underweight, appetite is diminished, and these people may need extra nourishment and higher calorie foods. In only one type of arthritis does diet play an understood part: gouty arthritis. For additional information or specific diets, write: Arthritis Foundation, 3400 Peachtree Road, N.E., Atlanta, Georgia 30326.

*   *My great uncle has gas and it causes him embarrassment. Isn't there a way he can handle this problem?*

A common problem for older people is flatulence, or the feeling of being bloated and gassy. Maybe he should avoid eating gas-forming foods (peppers, cabbage, onions, broccoli, cauliflower, brussels sprouts, cucumbers, turnips, radishes, beans, and peas). Gas formation is frequently a result of eating too fast, bolting food that has not been thoroughly chewed, or eating meals that are too large. The problem is also apparent with people who can't chew their food properly because of lack of saliva: the bulk of the food causes gas formation.

The problem can be reduced if smaller meals are eaten, if the food is eaten more slowly and chewed more thoroughly.

*   *I've heard coffee causes the heart to skip a beat. I've already had heart problems and I certainly don't need that.*

Excessive consumption of caffeine has been shown to cause palpitations or unduly rapid heart beat, which may give a person the feeling that his or her heart is "skipping a beat."

As you can see from the list below, coffee is not the only source of caffeine.

Item	Mg of Caffeine
Ground coffee (per cup)	85
Instant coffee	60
Decaffeinated coffee	3
Tea	30–50
Cocoa	6–42
Cola (per 8-ounce glass)	32
Dristan, Sinarest (per tablet)	30
Excedrin, Anacin	32
No-Doz, Vivarin	100–200

* *Does vitamin E have a favorable effect on heart and circulatory problems?*

According to an Experts Panel at the Institute of Food Technologists, the only medically proven benefits of vitamin E therapy are: treating hemolytic anemia in premature infants, treating poor absorption of fats and dietary fats and oils (usually in patients with cystic fibrosis), or in treating intermittent claudication (a condition that leads to calf pain).

Properties of vitamin E that prevent cell destruction (antioxidation) have been demonstrated in the laboratory, but despite the claims made for it, there is no proof that vitamin E is effective in curing or eliminating diseases or conditions like heart disease, arthritis, or ulcers.

At the Cardiovascular Research Department of Cornell Medical College investigators have monitored the effects of 300 mg of vitamin E administered daily for an average of 16 weeks on patients with chronic chest pain and arteriosclerosis and hypertensive heart disease (this is ten times the daily required dosage). They found there was no significant difference between the group getting vitamin E and another getting a placebo in either chest pain or capacity for work of the cardiac muscle.

* *Should I limit the number of eggs I eat per week?*

For most elderly persons, eggs provide an inexpensive excellent source of high quality protein, in addition to supplying essential vitamins and minerals. If an individual is not overweight, if there are not large quantities of meat or high fat dairy products consumed, and if the total amount of fat in the diet is not excessive, eggs in the diet would probably enhance the nutritional status, rather than contribute to increased cardiovascular risk.

The purpose of limiting the number of eggs is to reduce the amount of cholesterol in the diet, to prevent the increase in blood cholesterol levels which are associated with increased risk of cardiovascular disease.

* *My elderly mother appears to be becoming more obese as she grows older. I'm concerned this will shorten her life.*

After age sixty-five, about one third of women are considered obese and about 15 per cent of men. Obesity in the elderly is especially a problem in people with osteoporosis, since the extra weight makes movement painful.

Up until age sixty-five, obesity appears to decrease longevity because of the diseases associated with obesity, but in the elderly, it appears that *mild* weight gain (but not obesity) may actually have some *beneficial* side effects. Major nutritional problems occur in the elderly when they are ill. In acute illness, the older patient has less lean body mass (muscular tissue) and will deplete muscle protein proportionately to a greater degree than a younger person with normal lean body mass. Thus, a *slight* degree of overweight may provide a protective barrier against losses during illnesses and infection. Although this appears contrary to all thinking about getting and staying thin, research now being done at the National Institute on Aging has not found any increased risk of early death for people up to 30 per cent over their ideal weight.

In fact, in a follow-up study to the National Institutes of Health's eleven-year study of healthy men who were free of obesity and hypertension, Leslie S. Libow, M.D., Chief, Geriatric Medical Division, Mount Sinai City Hospital, uncovered some unexpected findings regarding weight as a predictor of survival and mortality. Contrary to expectations and to previous well-known findings, he found that those who had died by the five-year follow-up had had the lightest weight initially. Those who died between five and eleven years after the study was launched had an intermediate weight and those alive at the eleven-year follow-up had the *heaviest* weight at the beginning of the study.

FOR THE LIFE OF YOU:
Exercise

As a nation, we're jogging, cross-country skiing, playing tennis and soccer as if our life depended on it. And it does. I'd be remiss in writing about food and nutrition without including physical fitness and exercise. A healthy diet is only a step in the right direction toward health; to be totally effective, it must be combined with a lifetime of physical activity. According to Dr. Peter Wood, the slim and trim director of the Stanford Heart Disease Prevention Program, their extensive research shows that our national obesity problem is caused more by *inadequate exercise* than by overeating.

Some cities and towns lend themselves to fitness more than others. In Southern California, at a public beach near where I live, it is not unusual on a Saturday afternoon to bicycle by roller skaters, gymnasts working out on parallel bars, surfers, weight lifters, people jumping rope, and skateboarders. I see runners waiting for the light to change doing the same stretch exercises I used to do in my bedroom. In this kind of atmosphere, anyone who is *not* exercising feels out of place and out of shape.

Along with the interest in exercise has come a fondness for special foods and diets "guaranteed" to improve our game and turn us into super-athletes. Almost everyone who exercises and eats has a theory about what foods will help him or her run faster and longer and jump higher. In fact, a whole industry selling special foods and diet supplements has grown up around the fitness image. Most of these food theories are totally unsupported by fact and only serve to turn weekend athletes into hypochondriacs continually searching for the perfect nutritional formula to enhance their performance, or, better yet, to make up for those missed sessions at the gym. There is no such thing as the "perfect" formula. As long as you're eating a healthy diet with a wide variety of foods in quantities that don't cause you to gain weight, you're probably doing okay.

Food-related myths have sprouted which, in most instances, have nothing to do with furthering one's athletic ability, but instead have the effect of establishing unnecessary rules. Athletic activity should be fun and not filled with negative strictures; there should be less of: "You shouldn't go swimming until . . ." "You shouldn't drink liquids while . . ." and "You shouldn't eat X before . . ." Many of these myths filter down from professional athletes or world-class champions. In most instances, the intensity of competition of a world-class athlete virtually makes this advice worthless to the recreational athlete. Although when you're running around the neighborhood, you may *feel* like a world-class athlete, your nutritional needs are very different from someone trying to shave a fraction of a second off the 100-yard dash.

Since most of us fall into the category of the recreational athlete, it's for this group that I've written this chapter. Let's take a closer look at the connections between food and exercise. Begin the chapter with paper and pencil in hand and play "Foodball." If you get all the answers right, consider you've

Time to play foodball.

The Foodball Game

START

		True	False
1.	When you're sweating, you are losing a lot of salt and it needs to be replaced.	_____	_____
2.	Bringing a banana to the tennis court on a hot day is beneficial in restoring depleted potassium.	_____	_____
3.	Athletic potions (bee pollen, liver extract, wheat germ oil, gelatin, celery leaf powder, and rice polishings) can make an athlete run faster and jump higher.	_____	_____
4.	Since menstruating women are losing iron, this loss adversely affects their athletic performance.	_____	_____
5.	To avoid cramps, it is necessary to wait 1 hour after eating to go swimming.	_____	_____
6.	In order to build muscle, athletes need to eat more protein foods and take protein supplements.	_____	_____
7.	Sweating is a good indicator of dehydration.	_____	_____
8.	Thirst is a good indicator of dehydration.	_____	_____
9.	Never drink liquids while exercising.	_____	_____
10.	Gatorade and other specially prepared sport punches are the best drinks to use during exercise because they are absorbed faster than water.	_____	_____
11.	Eating an orange at half time while playing soccer makes sense.	_____	_____
12.	In terms of over-all athletic stamina and strength, vegetarian athletes rank low.	_____	_____
13.	Drinking milk before exercising should be avoided since it causes cotton mouth.	_____	_____
14.	One of the best pre-exercise snacks is canned peaches.	_____	_____
15.	Carbohydrates—pasta, bread, rice—should be avoided prior to exercising.	_____	_____
16.	Glycogen loading is an effective way to increase performance in endurance events like long-distance cycling and marathon running.	_____	_____
17.	Drinking a strong cup of coffee an hour before an endurance event can improve your performance.		
18.	A candy bar gives you quick energy before exercising.	_____	_____
19.	Athletes need extra amounts of vitamin C to compensate for the stress of athletic events and to promote quick healing of athletic injuries (e.g., pulled tendons, sore muscles, sprains, etc.).	_____	_____
20.	You shouldn't eat before exercising.	_____	_____
21.	It is necessary to avoid spicy and gas-causing foods before exercising.	_____	_____
22.	Recreational athletes should improve their diets when they start doing regular exercise.	_____	_____
23.	Different sports like cross-country skiing, racquetball, bicycle riding, and gymnastics have different nutritional requirements.	_____	_____
24.	If you bicycle 2 miles, you lose 1 pound.	_____	_____
25.	Fad diets to improve athletic performance have the same effect regardless of age.	_____	_____

FINISH

Score: # Correct   _____

\# Incorrect   _____

made a touchdown. If you get more than five incorrect, you've obviously fallen into the hands of the popular myth-makers and you're out. You can get back into the game by reading the chapter for the correct answers.

1. *When you're sweating, you are losing a lot of salt and it needs to be replaced.*

False.

This falls under the category of the great salt myth and deserves to be put to rest. When you're playing a hard game of squash and you're sweating, you're losing a lot of water and some small amounts of salt. The over-all effect is just the opposite of what many people think: the salt in the body is becoming *more* concentrated. During exercise accompanied by heavy sweating, the concentration of salt in the blood actually goes up, not down. As far as your body cells are concerned, you have too much salt. What you need is to drink water, not take in more salt. Manufacturers contribute to the confusion with the proliferation of aids like salt pills, salt tablets, and even salted chewing gum, all of which are routinely sold in sporting goods stores and promise to restore the "lost" salt. The salt in the body only begins to be depleted after long and copious sweating and then is readily replaced by eating normal foods which supply salt naturally.

2. *Bringing a banana to the tennis court on a hot day is beneficial in restoring depleted potassium.*

False.

I first heard about the banana and the tennis court when I was interviewing a chiropractor who practices sports medicine in Pasadena, California. He told me that when a person exercises strenuously on very hot days, the possibility of potassium depletion exists. To combat this depletion, he suggested athletes bring a banana, a fruit naturally high in potassium, along with them to the court.

Aside from the fact that it's highly questionable that the potassium in a banana could be absorbed by the body quickly at courtside, the misunderstanding of potassium

Running salt

has a lot in common with the salt myth. Potassium and salt act similarly: under conditions of extreme dehydration (e.g., possibly on the tennis court on a hot summer's day), the potassium becomes more concentrated, not less.

However, it is true that champion athletes at times of extremely strenuous activity may have an increased need for potassium. Their diet—in the form of tomato juice, orange juice, or that banana—normally provides enough to offset this need. Potassium depletion is not an area of nutritional concern for the recreational athlete.

3. *Athletic potions (bee pollen, liver extract, wheat germ oil, gelatin, celery leaf powder, and rice polishings) can make an athlete run faster and jump higher.*

True.

The reason these potions work, when they do, appears to be purely psychological; they do not fulfill any physiological need. In fact, these items, which are aimed at improving athletic performance, are called "psych pills" by the athletes who use them. The idea of course, is that if people eat something with the *belief* that it will help them, it probably will. To illustrate this, Dr. Laurence Morehouse, Director of the Human Performance Laboratory at U.C.L.A., told me a story about his work with swimmers. He had two tanks: one marked "Pure Oxygen" and one marked "Room Air." Before swimming, the athletes would take a few whiffs. Unbeknown to the athletes, Dr. Morehouse would change the content of the tanks at will. The athletes always performed better when they took their whiffs out of the tank marked "Pure Oxygen," even if, in fact, it was only "Room Air." The swimmers *believed* that the pure oxygen gave them more endurance and this belief affected their performance.

A "LOVE" potion

The potions might be as simple as oxygen or as expensive as bee pollen, which sells for 20 dollars a pound. In gyms across the country, trainers dump out the new samples and I've seen athletes gobble them up by the handful. But the weekend athlete is not left out. Sporting goods stores and health food stores are selling these potions to recreational athletes to the tune of hundreds of millions of dollars yearly. Let's take bee pollen as an example. It has been the rage with athletes, especially marathon runners. The publicity material claims it's a "treasure trove of nutrition and regenerative power." From the Bell Pollen of England people, I received a 3-month supply and was advised by the time I reached the last pill, I would "be broadcasting over NBC without the benefit of transmitter and flying from coast to coast

on my own powers." These outrageous claims are not too dissimilar from those made for athletes.

In fact, bee pollen is just a very expensive source of carbohydrates, proteins, and vitamins. Since a well-balanced diet provides this nutrition and at more reasonable prices, there is no physiological need for this outrageously priced product. But, if you *think* your performance will get an extra boost from bee pollen, mind over matter, it very well might. Other items sold as athletic potions to improve performance:

B complex vitamins It has been claimed that there is an increased need for B complex vitamins because of their role in making energy available for muscular work. There is no doubt of decreased athletic performance when B vitamins are deficient, but the value of B vitamins above required amounts is debatable.

Vitamin C Recent studies reported in the *Dairy Council Digest* have shown that vitamin C has a negligible effect when compared to a placebo in areas of endurance, performance, and severity and rate of healing of athletic injury. Although a vitamin C deficiency will decrease work performance, most researchers do not advocate additional vitamin C supplementation for athletes since excess water-soluble vitamins alter tissue saturation and are rapidly excreted in the urine.

Vitamin E This vitamin is supplied adequately in even the worst diets since it is found in sufficient quantities in traditional foods. It has been claimed that diets supplemented by vitamin E have improved the performance of athletes in a variety of track and field events, and that it makes higher endurance work possible (bicycle and treadmill); however, no benefits from vitamin E on athletic performance have ever been shown by a scientific body. Money spent on vitamin E is probably useless since it is found *not* to increase stamina, improve circulation, increase oxygen delivery to the muscles, or lower blood cholesterol.

Gelatin It is thought that glycine, an amino acid found in gelatin, might allay fatigue or increase endurance, but research does not support the claim.

Additional potions—sport punches, salted chewing gum, protein supplements—are discussed separately.

4. *Since menstruating women are losing iron, this loss adversely affects their athletic performance.*

False.

A lot of menstruating women are breaking records. According to Barbara Drinkwater, during the 1972 Tokyo Olympics a survey of 66 sportswomen revealed that only 17 per cent felt that their performances were adversely affected by their cycle. An interesting additional observation made at that time by the athletes who had had children prior to participating in the Olympics was that they "became stronger, had greater stamina, and were more balanced in every way after having a child."

Whether an Olympic champion or a weekend athlete, menstruating women can still perform and the iron loss should not be an inhibiting factor. Although it is true that menstruating women require more iron in their diets (18 gm of iron daily), iron is stored in the body and if there is an adequate amount of iron in the diet, there should be an adequate amount to draw on during menstruation when iron is lost in the blood. It appears that women athletes don't use more iron or need iron in greater quantities than nonathletic women. They just

need an adequate supply. Female teen-age athletes are the most vulnerable to the problems associated with iron deficiency because their generally poor diets do not furnish them with adequate iron stores from which to draw.

5. *To avoid cramps, it is necessary to wait 1 hour after eating to go swimming.*

False.

Remember all those times as a child you couldn't go swimming because there were still 10 minutes left on the clock? And yet as one sports director pointed out to me, there is no record in medical history of anyone ever drowning as a result of cramps after eating. In fact, the Red Cross took this advice out of their *Water Safety Manual* about 10 years ago.

Eating and swimming— food for thought.

The current Red Cross view is that any advice about eating and swimming should be viewed as *conditional:* it depends on how much you eat and how strenuously you are going to be swimming. For example, a mother needn't be concerned about the child who eats a light lunch and dawdles in the shallow end. However, if you eat a very large meal and plan on swimming strenuous laps, the large quantity of food *may* interfere with your diaphragm and affect your breathing.

Aside from the unpleasantness of an untidy pool, you can even eat *while* you're swimming. Marathon swimmers do, and they don't get cramps.

My private theory about "waiting an hour or you'll drown from cramps" is that it evolved during Victorian times when families were picnicking and mothers and fathers didn't want to leave the picnic to supervise their children. Offhandedly they would say, "Wait an hour, dear," and the admonition stuck.

6. *In order to build muscle, athletes need to eat more protein foods and take protein supplements.*

False.

This idea goes back to the Greeks, who believed that if you ate the meat of muscular animals you would become more muscular yourself. Myths like this one die hard and unfortunately the idea is still alive and well, especially among weight lifters pumping iron. I used to lift weights at Gold's Gym in Santa Monica where the Mr. Universes work out. I often overheard their conversations about increasing the size of their steak dinners, and how many protein supplements were just right. These modern-day Adonises feel pretty much the same way about protein the Greeks did; however, no scientific evidence supports their view.

True, the body needs adequate protein, but as was pointed out in Chapter 6, the normal American diet contains much more protein than is ever used in the body. In order to build muscle, you must *work* the muscle, not feed it unnecessary amounts of protein. Since the body can't store it, and it has a harder time converting it to energy, large amounts of protein are just plain wasteful.

What about protein supplements? When my 6′9″ brother played basketball back in high school, the first thing his coach gave him was a gallon-size can of protein supplements. Now, 18 years later, protein supplements are a multi-million-dollar business and coaches are still recommending them and athletes still use them, but there clearly seems to be no nutritional basis. Dr. Joan Ullyot, who works with the Institute of Health Research in San Francisco, has analyzed these protein supplements and found them to be mostly milk powder. She suggested athletes might just as well drink milk instead.

7. *Sweating is a good indicator of dehydration.*

True.

8. *Thirst is a good indicator of dehydration.*

False.

As long as you are sweating, you are dehydrating, but you can be dehydrating and still not be thirsty. It is suggested that the safest way to minimize dehydration during sports events—for example, during a game of tennis—is to drink small amounts of water, 3–4 ounces, every 15 minutes or so, before exercising, during exercising, and after exercising. This way, you are continually replenishing your supply, not waiting futilely for some thirst signal to go off.

9. *Never drink liquids while exercising.*

False.

The original basis for this approach was probably stern football coaches who wanted to toughen up their charges. They stressed the Spartan approach by endorsing exercising without water, figuring that eventually their athletes would be tough enough that they wouldn't need to be babied with water during the games. Unfortunately for those coaches and their athletes, when it comes to water, we're all softies. The human body cannot adapt to dehydration and there are high risks associated with the heat storage that develops. In general, the body functions less well when deprived of water, and this is even more true in athletic events where extraordinary demands are being made on the body. It is now generally recommended while exercising (as in questions #7 and #8) that small amounts of water be drunk continuously to replenish the water as it is lost.

10. *Gatorade and other specially prepared sport punches are the best drinks to use during exercise because they are absorbed faster than water.*

False.

The pitch for Gatorade is that it is absorbed faster than water. In truth, the only liquid absorbed faster than water is alcohol. (This may explain why athletes like Frank Shorter, gold medal winner, like their glass of beer.) The chemical drinks like Gatorade and ERG contain essentially a salt, potassium, water, and sugar mixture. In endurance events, one thing that may limit an athlete's ability to succeed is the supply of fuel. The primary sources of fuel are carbohydrates, starches, and simple sugars. But there appears to be an optimum sugar concentration for absorption—2 gm sugar/100 mm water—and Gatorade is about twice that strength. If you're hooked on it, dilute it by 50 per cent. The other sport punches, like ERG and Body Punch, are in the right ballpark.

You might wonder if drinks like Kool-Aid or soft drinks could be used instead of Gatorade. They don't work as well because the sugar is in the wrong proportion and the carbonation generates too much gas.

11. *Eating an orange at half time while playing soccer makes sense.*

True.

We've all seen champion football players

sucking on orange slices at half time. This can have benefits for the weekend athlete as

The Florida Citrus League

well. Juicy oranges are a good food item to bring along for quick sugar and fluid replacement as their sugar is absorbed quickly. In fact, diabetics beginning an episode eat half an orange and almost immediately begin to feel relief.

12. *In terms of over-all strength and stamina, vegetarian athletes rank low.*

False.

Although the protein sources are different (beans, nuts, legumes, grains), as long as protein, calories, and other nutrients are adequate, strength, stamina, and performance should not be affected. Most vegetarian professional athletes I've spoken to are not strict vegetarians; they almost always include at least eggs and drink milk and when they're on the road, their diets are determined more by what's available than any strict vegetarian code.

Vegetarianism is by no means the norm for athletes, professional or amateur. Maurice Lucas, vegetarian basketball star, told me that when he and Bill Walton walk down the street people yell at them, "vegetable head," or "string bean man." I asked Lucas if he felt he was as physically strong a player as the meat eaters he played against. He said that he played a very physical game and he was sure he was just as strong or stronger, at 6'9" and 218 pounds. I didn't doubt him for a minute.

13. *Drinking milk before exercising should be avoided since it causes cotton mouth.*

False.

Although athletic coaches say that in the lab they can't reproduce cotton mouth by feeding athletes milk, they concede that there are probably some athletes who get an extremely dry mouth reaction from milk and they should avoid it. Cotton mouth is due to the constriction of mucous membranes in the mouth and it appears to be a normal response of an athlete to nervousness regardless of whether or not he drinks milk. Mistakenly, some professional athletes avoid milk to try to prevent the condition. The result, to the recreational athlete's detriment, is that he may overhear that the pros avoid milk and unnecessarily he may avoid it as well.

14. *One of the best pre-exercise snacks is canned peaches.*

True.

U.C.L.A. athletes have seized upon canned peaches as the perfect pregame snack. They are sweet, easily digestible, and settle well in the stomach. The carbohydrates and other nutrients conveniently packaged in peaches, either fresh or canned, make them an equally valuable pre-exercise snack for the recreational athlete as well. This holds true for other soft, easily digestible fruits like pears and bananas. (I surmise the reason the U.C.L.A. champions take their fruits canned is because they can keep them in their lockers and before the big event they don't have to do last-minute grocery shopping for fresh produce.)

15. *Carbohydrates—pasta, bread, rice— should be avoided prior to exercising.*

False.

Carbohydrates are the best fuel for athletic performance. The body has less work to do getting energy from carbohydrates than from fats or protein. Before going out to play soccer, if you have a choice of a breakfast of toast, cereal, fruit, or one of bacon and eggs, you're better off opting for the first, which is loaded with carbohydrates. For lunch, opt

The spaghetti advantage.

for spaghetti and French bread instead of the luncheon steak.

In fact, serious athletes know the value of carbohydrates very well and with this knowledge have developed glycogen loading (see next question).

16. *Glycogen loading is an effective way to increase performance in endurance events like long-distance cycling and marathon running.*

True.

Anyone who reads *Sports Illustrated* even casually or who has ever run in a marathon is familiar with the term glycogen loading, or carbohydrate loading. Glycogen loading was developed in the early sixties in Scandinavia as a means of manipulating the diet to improve athletic performance in endurance events. It has been popularized in the United States since the 1970s. David Costill, Director of the Human Performance Laboratory at Ball State University, and one of the original practitioners in this country, says there's no doubt that it works and that it prevents premature exhaustion. He equates an athlete's entering a marathon without it to driving a long distance and having your car conk out halfway because it ran out of fuel.

What is glycogen and what's the point of loading up? Carbohydrates are the body's most accessible source of fuel. They are changed into glucose in the body and glycogen is the storage form of glucose. Since normally only a limited amount of glycogen is stored, the purpose of loading is to increase the amount stored and thus increase the amount of fuel available for endurance events.

The traditional method of glycogen storage is as follows:

Exercise to Exhaustion About 1 week before the event, the athlete performs a vigorous workout to the point of exhaustion. For example, for a cyclist, it is suggested to ride 20–60 miles. The aim of this strenuous workout is to deplete the stored glycogen.

High Fat-High Protein For the next 2–3 days, the athlete uses a combination of a high fat and high protein diet combined with very minimal carbohydrate intake. Athletic workouts should taper off during this low carbohydrate period.

High Carbohydrate About 2–3 days before the event, the athlete switches to a high carbohydrate diet with minimum protein and fat, accompanied by very light training.

This combination of exercising to exhaustion with decreased carbohydrate intake followed by high carbohydrate diet with little workout[1] enables the muscles of the trained athlete to store two to three times the glycogen. This obviously gives these athletes an edge over other athletes who might collapse earlier in endurance events because they have used up their glycogen stores.

How often do athletes load up this way? According to Dr. Costill, all the marathon runners he knows, including himself, are regularly on diets with a high percentage of carbohydrates and so are doing a partial aspect of this regime daily. He goes through the glycogen loading regime every few weeks, although not in any formalized way. He wouldn't think of starting one of the six marathons he runs every year without doing glycogen loading in advance.

Glycogen loading is also accompanied by an increase in water storage. For every gram

of carbohydrate stored, 2.6 grams of water are stored. Opponents of glycogen loading say this makes for waterlogged athletes and that the benefits of glycogen loading are far outweighed by the disadvantages of waterlogging. Dr. Costill sees the water storage aspect as a distinct advantage. Since the extra water taken on with the glycogen is released as the glycogen breaks down, he says this is a terrific built-in mechanism to prevent dehydration during endurance events.

However, everyone agrees that carbohydrate loading is useful only for the serious competitor in endurance events; for example, runners who cover 12–15 miles a day. For the recreational athlete, Costill suggests instead a balanced diet with extra helpings of foods high in carbohydrates—breads, cereals, and fruits.

17. *Drinking a strong cup of coffee an hour before an endurance event can improve your performance.*

True.

Although in large doses, caffeine, the stimulant found in coffee, has come under attack for its negative effects on the central nervous system, Dr. David Costill advises his fellow athletes to take a strong (double-strength) cup of caffeinated coffee an hour before an endurance event. He has found that after the coffee, athletes can exercise substantially

A good, strong cup of coffee.

[1] David Costill says many of the marathon runners have eliminated the high fat-high protein step because they personally didn't enjoy these foods and have had equally good results.

longer before becoming exhausted. In studies, his subjects had no idea what they were drinking, but in every case, the athletes found the exercise easier after the caffeine feeding. This coffee drinking can be accomplished as casually as Bill Rodgers, record holder for the Boston Marathon, does it. The morning of a big race, he has toast and coffee for breakfast.

The reason a cup of strong coffee (or 2 cups for a big person) works is that the caffeine in the coffee enchances fat metabolism. The only alternative for the body to burning glycogen is to burn fats. Caffeine has been found to stimulate the body to burn fats earlier, thus sparing the glycogen for later use and helping to avoid the threat of early exhaustion due to glycogen depletion. It is stressed that this use of coffee is only of value in athletic events lasting an hour or longer.

18. *A candy bar gives you quick energy before exercising.*

False.

The word sugar has become synonymous with energy, but the problem is the *amount* and *form* of the sugar; in such a concentrated form as in a candy bar, the sugar has exactly the opposite of the desired effect. Here's the story:

The brain and nervous system need certain amounts of sugar in the blood. When not enough is available, people are said to be *hypoglycemic* or to have low blood sugar; if they have too much, they are *hyperglycemic*. Having the proper level of glucose is so important that the body has a built-in control system that adjusts the amount in circulation. If you eat a chocolate bar before a swimming competition and it releases too much glucose into the blood, the body's control system responds by releasing insulin.

According to Dr. Richard Lewis, Professor of Exercise Physiology and Nutrition at the University of Arkansas, the insulin has a number of effects. It causes glucose to leave the blood and enter the liver and muscle cells to be stored as glycogen; it causes glu-cose to enter the fat cells where it is stored as fat; and it prevents the breakdown of fats into fatty acids. However, the immediate over-all result is a *reduction* in the amount of fuel available to muscle cells. And starting to exercise while insulin is being released (e.g., after eating a candy bar) triggers a further drop in the amount of fuel available.

So grabbing an Almond Joy on the way to the courts can actually cause an energy deficit, rather than the anticipated lift. The people who still claim to be getting a boost from candy are probably actually getting a caffeine kick from the chocolate.

19. *Athletes need extra amounts of vitamin C to compensate for the stress of athletic events and to promote quick healing of athletic injuries (e.g., pulled tendons, sore muscles, sprains, etc.).*

False.

It has been found that people under severe stress in life-threatening situations do have an increased vitamin C requirement; however, studies done on athletes have shown that athletic events do not constitute a comparable level of stress—necessitating additional vitamin C.

As far as vitamin C helping athletes heal faster, there is a lot of postulation, but there is no solid information corroborating this.

20. *You shouldn't eat before exercising.*

False.

21. *It is necessary to avoid spicy or gas-causing foods before exercising.*

False.

If you are a recreational athlete, unless you're eating a Thanksgiving feast, the amount and kind of food you eat right before exercising doesn't matter as long as it doesn't give you personal discomfort. How can you be exercising when you're still digesting food? Easy. The minute you start vigorous activity your digestion stops, the kidneys shut down, and you don't produce urine. (In contrast, for the serious competitive athlete, who will be exercising strenuously at full exertion, it is generally advised that his or her last food intake be 3 hours before the event.)

Advice about avoiding certain foods was put to test at the U.C.L.A. Human Performance Laboratory where their champions went through their paces and ate all the foods that through the sport ages have been labeled no-no. Some of the no-nos are foods like navy beans, green bell peppers, cooked cabbage, cucumbers, radishes, cantaloupe, and apples. It was found the athletes did equally well on these no-no foods, which had previously been avoided because they were labeled "gas-causing and potentially distressful."

22. *Recreational athletes should improve their diets when they start doing regular exercise.*

False.

23. *Different sports like cross-country skiing, racquetball, bicycle riding, and gymnastics have different nutritional requirements.*

False.

For you, the recreational athlete, if you're already eating an adequate diet that embraces a wide variety of foods, you don't need to change because you've started exercising. A change might be required if you are exercising enough to burn up substantial calories. Then, if you want to stay at the same weight, you would have to increase your calories. (NOTE: This advice is different for the endurance athlete—the marathon runner, swimmer, or cyclist—who needs to plan a diet more carefully and change to one markedly higher in carbohydrates.)

Different events do not have different and specific *nutrient* needs. As discussed above, the caloric needs may vary depending on how strenuous the event is, but the nutrient needs do not.

24. *If you bicycle 2 miles, you lose 1 pound.*

False.

This statement carries the idea that exercise and weight loss go hand-in-hand. Not necessarily. To lose 1 pound, you have to lose 3,500 calories. You can lose 1 pound by eating 3,500 calories less or by exercising in a way that burns off 3,500 calories more.

Dr. Laurence Morehouse devised the following schedule to show how many minutes of various activities it takes to consume 100 calories:

Minutes Activity — Consumes 100 calories

Minutes	Activity — Consumes 100 calories
7	Bicycle 2 miles (13 mph)
9	Swim 400 yards
10	Downhill skiing
14	Tennis
20	Golf
20	Gardening
20	Walking (1,500 yards)
22	Bowling
31	Washing, shaving, showering, etc.
80	Reclining in bed

Using these calculations, you have to bicycle *70 miles* (!) to burn up 3,500 calories and lose 1 pound.

Keep on biking

The recommended way to lose weight and keep it off is to increase one's activities substantially, while decreasing one's dietary intake *moderately*. This burns up more calories than are being consumed.

However, research at Stanford University Medical School has shown that if you're actively exercising (they focused on runners), you probably don't need to worry about losing weight. The Stanford study found that men and women runners on the average eat 600 calories a day *more* than their more sedentary peers and they stay at their ideal weight! So, the secret seems to be not to eat less, but to exercise more.

25. *Fad diets to improve athletic performance have the same effect regardless of age.*

False.

Poor nutrition at critical growth periods, especially during adolescence when most growth is taking place, can affect one's ultimate health and stature. This is especially apparent in high school sports like boxing and wrestling, where athletes prefer to weigh in at a lighter weight category to gain a competitive edge. A friend told me about her younger brother who participated in high school wrestling. The whole family would watch helplessly as he starved himself for days before an important match and then he would gorge himself (putting tremendous strain on his stomach) immediately after the meet. Not surprisingly, it has been found that growth during the wrestling season is frequently arrested and although catch-up growth does take place, both the athletic performance as well as general health can suffer.

Index